The Monetary Approach
to the
Balance of Payments

Edited by

JACOB A. FRENKEL

HARRY G. JOHNSON

UNIVERSITY OF TORONTO PRESS

Toronto and Buffalo

First published in Canada and the United States
1976 by
University of Toronto Press
Toronto and Buffalo

Reprinted in paperback 1977, 1980

© George Allen & Unwin Ltd 1976

ISBN 0–8020–2220–0 (cloth)
ISBN 0–8020–6316–0

Printed in Great Britain

Dedicated to the memory of
Elaine Goldstein

PREFACE

The purpose of this book is to collect for the convenience of the reader the 'basic documents' of a recently-developing new approach to the theory of the balance of payments and of balance-of-payments policy, the so-called 'monetary approach to the balance of payments', together with some avowedly highly tentative attempts to subject the new approach to empirical testing. The items included have been chosen from the work of economists associated with the Workshop in International Economics at the University of Chicago, where the new approach has been developed most persistently and systematically thus far. But, as will be documented in the Introductory Essay, the new approach is basically a return to the long historical tradition of international monetary theory, after some thirty years of departure from that tradition occasioned by the international monetary collapse of the 1930s, the 'Keynesian Revolution' in monetary theory, and the long period of war and post-war reconstruction in which the international monetary system was fragmented by exchange controls, currency inconvertibility, and controls over international trade and capital movements. It is also necessary to acknowledge that fundamentally the same approach has been developed contemporaneously by economists associated not at all with either the University of Chicago or its international monetary theorists, economists whose contributions will be mentioned in detail later in this preface as well as in the introductory essay. And, finally, it is a matter of pleasure that economists in other centres have begun serious large-scale work on the same general range of problems: we mention specifically the International Monetary Research Programme at the London School of Economics, the Programme on World Inflation at the University of Manchester, research of the Graduate Institute of International Studies of Geneva, and the recent research of the International Monetary Fund and of the Board of Governors of the Federal Reserve System.

This book presents the key articles and studies in the development of the monetary approach to the balance of payments as expressed in the work of economists associated with the Chicago Workshop. There is actually no intention to claim exclusivity for Chicago economists in the development of the new approach. A number of other important contributors to the early development of the theory are cited in the introductory essay. To these should be added as more recent contributors Victor Argy, until recently at the International Monetary Fund, Ryutaro Komiya of the University of Tokyo, Japan, and Pentti Kouri and Michael Porter, who have done important empirical work under the auspices of the International Monetary Fund. In addition mention should be made of Chicago Workshop members of the crucial period whose contributions are not included in the volume, notably Russell Boyer and Douglas Purvis among the recent graduate students and Arthur B. Laffer of the faculty of the University of Chicago Graduate School of Business.

The book is divided into two parts, theoretical and empirical. In the introductory essay, Frenkel and Johnson summarise the essential concepts and the historical origins of the monetary approach to the balance of payments. Following the introductory essay, the theoretical section is further subdivided into two sections. The first contains the basic article by Johnson, generalising the Meade and Alexander approaches into a basically monetary theory, although the generalisation is largely in terms of a framework within which the conventional post-Keynesian theory can be conveniently summarised; and an article by Mundell which introduces the connecting lines between classical international monetary economics and the theory of barter, and between classical and Keynesian concepts and methods of analysis. Mundell's thinking on the problem of the balance of payments evolved rapidly through a series of scattered articles, so that it is difficult if not impossible to select one, or a few places, as possessing the status of 'the classic article'. This paper does, however, seem the closest to a classic statement of the difference between the Keynesian approach and the monetary approach that can be found in the phase of Mundell's transition from one to the other approach.

The second subsection comprises theoretical contributions and extensions based firmly on the new approach. Mundell's contribution, only one of many in the literature, deals with the extension to a growing economy of an analysis that was in a sense central to the contribution made by Hume's price-specie-flow analysis—the international distribution of money. In this chapter Mundell provides a framework that links inflation, interest rates, money stocks, rates of credit expansion, and the balance of payments. Frenkel's chapter, one of his several contributions concerned with long-run changes in the structure of the balance of payments, integrates the monetary and the real sectors; it develops explicitly the dynamic behaviour of the secular evolution of the various balance-of-payments accounts, and thereby disposes of the criticism that the monetary approach ignores the capital account. Johnson's first chapter in this section describes at some length the development of Keynesian balance-of-payments theory and the defects in its formulation that led to the monetary approach, and presents the algebra required to apply the analysis of money and the balance of payments in a growing international economy to a small country in a large world system, a closed world system based on a fixed amount of international money, and a system in which, in addition to gold, reserves are provided by a reserve currency country.

Dornbusch's chapter emphasises the monetary aspects of devaluation using a model which includes non-traded as well as traded goods, thereby disposing conclusively of the criticism that the monetary approach is limited by its assumption that there is a world market price for all goods produced. The title of Mussa's chapter masks policy dynamite: tariffs, usually thought of as a means of improving the balance of payments as an alternative to devaluation, have nothing at all to do with the balance of payments, except to the extent that the price-raising effects of their imposition create an increase in the demand for money that is supplied by a transient balance-of-payments surplus.

Rodriguez's chapter scotches another casual criticism of the monetary approach, by applying it to an analysis of balance-of-payments adjustment in a Keynesian variable-employment model.

Swoboda's chapter presents a formal analysis that summarises and integrates a great deal of previous work by others touching on various aspects of the use of monetary policy under fixed rates, and makes original contributions in the analysis of the difference between the results of the monetary approach and the Keynesian approach to the range of problems first dealt with in Keynesian terms under the general rubric of the theory of fiscal-monetary policy mix. Johnson's second chapter seeks to reformulate Meade's classical analysis of the theory of balance-of-payments policy, itself an attempt to convert 'positive theory' into 'normative' guides for the formulation of international economic policy, into a monetary-theory-based as contrasted with a multiplier-model-based analysis of balance-of-payments policies.

In 1971, Mundell left the University of Chicago for the University of Waterloo, leaving behind him a group of graduate students working on the pure monetary theory of the balance of payments, whose supervision through the final stages fell to Johnson. Johnson was convinced, partly on the basis of encounters in policy debates with policy makers stubbornly committed to the elasticity approach to balance-of-payments policy prescription and analysis, that continued concentration on the refinement and elaboration of the pure theory would yield rapidly diminishing returns in terms of theoretical insight, and that to challenge the theories accepted in policy-making circles—mostly based on a crude elasticity analysis if not an even more unsophisticated purely arithmetical exercise—the theory would have to be backed up by solidly based empirical evidence. This emphasis fitted the 'Chicago' approach to economics, in general, and in particular attracted the interest of his colleagues Richard Zecher in monetary economics and Donald McCloskey in economic history, as well as students of an empirical rather than abstract theoretical turn of mind. Part Two of the book contains a selection of essays in empirical testing and verification. This part of the book is presented as a very tentative beginning on the problem. On the one hand, the theory of how to do econometrics has run far ahead of knowledge of how actually to do it in studying problems that are economically interesting and important. The man who attempts to apply econometrics he can understand, to a problem he thinks is economically interesting, is generally outnumbered by a factor of at least five by those who will gladly tell him what he has done wrong that makes his conclusions invalid, without feeling obliged to tell him how to do it right, let alone doing it right for him and showing that his method actually leads to wrong answers by comparison with the right method. In presenting this part, we have in mind the long history of attempts to give quantitative form to the Keynesian consumption function, and subsequently the debate over econometric studies of the domestic demand for money, and would stress that empirical studies based on the monetary approach to the balance of payments are at about the same stage as were empirical studies of the domestic demand for money some twenty years ago. We would also stress that confidence in the empirical usefulness of the monetary approach is not based only upon, or limited by, the studies presented here. Other studies, such as those by Kouri and Porter already mentioned, by the members of the Manchester programme of research on world inflation, by Peter Jonson on inflation in Australia, and preliminary results of the London School of Economics International Monetary Research Programme, are all favourable to the monetary approach.

Part Two presents five studies, of which four are studies of specific countries for which the 'small-country assumption' is eminently reasonable. Zecher's study tests and finds support for the hypothesis that Australian monetary policy largely influences the country's international reserves rather than the traditional credit market and money supply variables that central bankers usually assume that they control. Genberg's study of Sweden exposes and finds confirmation for the hypothesis, a preliminary requirement of the monetary approach, that Swedish prices and interest rates are connected to world prices and interest rates. After identifying and estimating the demand for money in Sweden, he draws some conclusions on the effects of Swedish monetary policy. Bean's study of Japan derives special interest from the popular, and mistaken, view that Japan is an inscrutable economic phenomenon. One of the interesting issues that are dealt with is the question of the appropriate price index for use in the empirical work. Guitian's study of Spain develops the theory to fit some special circumstances of the Spanish economy.

The final study by McCloskey and Zecher, of the gold standard 1880–1913, is the first fruit of a much larger study, currently in progress, which promises to radically change the understanding of how the gold standard worked in its heyday, prevalent among both economic historians and the contemporary monetary theorists. This study is significant both in demonstrating the possibility of extending the monetary approach from the single country to the system as a whole, and in applying the modern refined version of the pre-Keynesian monetary approach to the reinterpretation and deeper understanding of the international monetary system that prevailed while that approach dominated the international application of pre-Keynesian monetary theory.

The University of Chicago
May 1974

Jacob A. Frenkel
Harry G. Johnson

CONTENTS

CONTRIBUTORS

DONNA L. BEAN
International Financial Management Group, First National Bank of Chicago

RUDIGER DORNBUSCH
Associate Professor of Economics, Graduate School of Business, University of Chicago

JACOB A. FRENKEL
Associate Professor of Economics, Department of Economics, University of Chicago

A. HANS GENBERG
Assistant Professor of Economics, Graduate Institute of International Studies, Geneva, Switzerland

MANUEL GUITIAN
Economist, International Monetary Fund

HARRY G. JOHNSON
Charles F. Grey Distinguished Service Professor of Economics, Department of Economics, University of Chicago

DONALD N. McCLOSKEY
Associate Professor of Economics, Department of Economics, University of Chicago

ROBERT A. MUNDELL
Professor of Economics, Department of Economics, Columbia University

MICHAEL MUSSA
Associate Professor of Economics, Department of Economics, University of Rochester

CARLOS A. RODRIGUEZ
Associate Professor of Economics, Department of Economics, Columbia University

ALEXANDER K. SWOBODA
Professor of Economics, Graduate Institute of International Studies, Geneva, Switzerland

J. RICHARD ZECHER
Associate Professor of Economics, Department of Economics, Tulane University

PART ONE

Theoretical

I. INTRODUCTORY ESSAY

1

The Monetary Approach to the Balance of Payments

Essential Concepts and Historical Origins

JACOB A. FRENKEL AND HARRY G. JOHNSON

1 ESSENTIAL CONCEPTS

The main characteristic of the monetary approach to the balance of payments can be summarised in the proposition that the balance of payments is essentially a monetary phenomenon. The term 'the balance of payments' refers to items that are 'below the line' in the over-all balance of payments (which must balance exactly, by the principles of double-entry accounting); the items in question constitute the 'money account'. In general, the approach emphasises the budget constraint imposed on the country's international spending and views the various accounts of the balance of payments as the 'windows' to the outside world, through which the excesses of domestic flow demands over domestic flow supplies, and of excess domestic flow supplies over domestic flow demands, are cleared. Accordingly, surpluses in the trade account and the capital account respectively represent excess flow supplies of goods and of securities, and a surplus in the money account reflects an excess domestic flow demand for money. Consequently, in analysing the money account, or more familiarly the rate of increase or decrease in the country's international reserves, the monetary approach focuses on the determinants of the excess domestic flow demand for or supply of money.

Clearly, a consistent use of the budget constraint implies that the money account—the current rate of change of reserves—can be analysed in terms of the determinants of all the other accounts—at the simplest level of aggregation, the goods account and the capital account. The monetary approach, however, recommends an analysis in terms of the behavioural relationship directly relevant to the money account, rather than an analysis in terms of the behavioural relationships directly relevant to the other accounts and only indirectly to the money account via the budget constraint. Since the money account is determined by the excess flow demand for money, it is clear why the balance of payments is regarded as a monetary phenomenon and this approach is referred to as 'the monetary approach'. To repeat, the monetary approach should in principle give an answer no different from that provided by a correct analysis in terms of the other accounts. The main reason for preferring the monetary approach is that less direct alternative approaches have almost invariably attempted to explain the behaviour of the markets they concern themselves with, by analytical constructs in which the role of money in influencing behaviour, and the connection between these other markets and the money markets, are neglected as being 'of the second order of smalls', which may be a legitimate procedure for many economic problems, but cannot be so for an analysis which aims to explain or predict behaviour in the money market.

The surplus or deficit in the goods account (more generally the current account) measures the extent to which the economy's income is greater than consumption ('absorption') and the economy is therefore accumulating claims on future income (assets) from abroad or vice versa. By virtue of the budget constraint, the sum of the deficit on the capital account (net purchase of foreign securities) and the surplus on the money account equally represents the accumulation of foreign assets (decumulation if negative). The so-called 'absorption approach' to the balance of payments, associated with Sidney Alexander [1], emphasises the rate of accumulation or decumulation of foreign assets (securities plus money). In so doing, it constitutes an improvement over at least the cruder versions of the 'elasticity approach', which emphasises relative-price-induced substitution of domestic demand away from or towards imports and of foreign demand towards or away from exports, on the implicit assumption that such substitutions are matched by equal increases or decreases in absorption. The monetary approach selects for emphasis a subset of the spectrum of foreign assets whose accumulation or decumulation is emphasised by the absorption approach. The main reasons for this are, firstly, that the accumulation of foreign assets does not necessarily imply the accumulation of money through the balance of payments—it may mean the opposite, as for example when a monetary policy of lowering interest rates leads domestic asset-holders to move their funds from domestic to foreign securities. Secondly, the monetary authorities in their role as stabilisers of the exchange rate in a fixed rate system are concerned with what causes the stock of international reserves to change and how to prevent such changes. Thirdly, the monetary authority, as the ultimate source of domestic money, controls the rate of change of the domestic credit component of the monetary base—the other component being international reserves—and thereby the flow supply of money. It should be noted that control of the flow supply of money does not mean control of the stock supply of money, or of 'the quantity of money', since in an open economy the public can and does determine the total stock of money through its ability to convert domestic money into goods and securities in the international markets. The assumption that the residents of the country have a demand for money which depends on variables at least in part different from those that determine the quantity of domestic credit extended by the banking system, or alternatively that the rate of change of money demanded (the rate of hoarding) is independent of the rate of change of the domestic credit source component of the monetary base, implies that the money account of the balance of payments is influenced directly by monetary policy.

The accumulation or decumulation of assets depends on the aggregate relationship between domestic expenditure and income and does *not* depend on the composition of expenditure between exportables and importables, or between goods that, given the price structure, are classifiable into tradeable and non-tradeable goods. Consequently, though relative prices do influence the composition of expenditures, they play a secondary or negligible role in the monetary approach (as in the absorption approach). On the other hand the *general price level* does play a central role, since it determines the real value of nominal assets—money, and possibly fixed-interest debt traded internationally—and this role is emphasised along with the roles of other macro-economic aggregate magnitudes.

This brief account of the monetary approach to balance of payments theory, and comparison of it with the alternative elasticity and absorption approaches, implicitly disposes of various, and often ill-informed, criticisms that have tended to be made of it, and which amount essentially to red herrings across the trail of scientific study and understanding.

To begin with, the approach is described as 'monetary', and not 'monetarist', precisely to avoid confusion with recent domestic policy debates in which the term 'monetarist' has been used by the debaters to represent alternatively attaching 'appropriate' and 'too much' importance to money, and specifically to the use of monetary as contrasted with fiscal policy in economic stabilisation. The monetary approach to the balance of payments asserts neither that monetary mismanagement is the only cause, nor that monetary policy change is the only possible cure, for balance of payments problems; it does suggest, however, that monetary processes will bring about a cure of some kind—not necessarily very attractive— unless frustrated by deliberate monetary policy action, and that policies that neglect or aggravate the monetary implications of deficits and surpluses will not be successful in their declared objectives.

Secondly, the essential assumption of the monetary approach, like the restated quantity theory of money according to Friedman, is that there exists an aggregate demand function for money that is a function of a relatively small number of aggregate economic variables. In this respect it makes exactly the same assumptions as the Keynesian theory, except for the extreme versions of the latter theory, not to be found in the writings of Keynes himself, in which the demand for money as a function of interest rates is subject to a 'liquidity trap', or the supply of (domestic) money is made completely elastic by monetary policy itself; and these extreme cases cannot be made plausible for a single member of an international monetary system of fixed exchange rates. One need not even make the standard assumption of monetary theory, that the demand for money is homogeneous of degree one in all prices and nominal money assets (absence of money illusion), though this assumption is overwhelmingly supported by the empirical evidence and has the convenient result of ensuring the classical property of 'the neutrality of money'.

The monetary approach to the balance of payments, like the classical quantity theory of money, can be readily applied to conditions of price and wage rigidity and consequent response of quantities—employment, output, consumption—rather than money wages and prices to monetary changes. That the monetary approach largely assumes a fully employed economy is partly the result of the fact that in the context of a growing world economy in the long run the assumption of wage rigidity and variable employment becomes uninteresting; either employment expands into the full employment range and quantity adjustments yield to money price and wage adjustments, or it contracts and people either starve to death and go back to full employment numbers, or there is a revolution on Marxist lines, or more likely the public simply votes for the other political party than the one in power, since all of them promise to maintain full employment and the public expects them to do it. More fundamentally, the assumption of normally full employment reflects the passage of time and the accumulation of experience of reasonably full employment as the historical norm rather than the historical rarity that Keynes's theory and left-wing Keynesian mythology made it out to be.

The fact that the essential foundation of the monetary approach is the assumption that the demand for money is a stable function of a few macro-economic variables, incidentally, disposes of a criticism that has been brought against it, as it has been against the restated quantity theory of money before it, and also the old quantity theory of money, namely that it is not a theory but merely a tautology. Every theory starts from a tautology of some kind, and has to do so to define the variables it seeks to explain. Thus for example demand theory starts from the tautology that income must be spent on a particular commodity or something else, and Keynesian theory from the tautology that expenditure must be classed as either consumption or investment expenditure. What converts the first tautology into demand theory is the assumption that expenditure choices are rationally dependent on income and prices, the second, that consumption is rationally dependent on aggregate income received. What converts the quantity equation into the quantity theory is the assumption that velocity is some kind of stable function (primitively, an institutionally-determined constant); and what underlies the monetary approach is the same assumption that the demand for money is a stable function. In each case, the tautology–converted–into–theory is useful and interesting only if the arguments of the posited stable function can be treated aᶜ independently given prices by the market, factor prices, or technology and tastes, investment by rational entrepreneurial calculation, money supply by policy, or by fractional reserve banking based on an ultimate reserve.

Thirdly, a number of criticisms that appear to be cogent from the standpoint of the received alternative theory that suggests them turn out not to be so, either intrinsically or because they can be and have been easily incorporated in the monetary approach. To be specific, criticism has been directed against 'the small-country assumption', that is, the assumption that the country under analysis can be regarded as faced with a parametric set of world prices and interest rates. But there is in principle no theoretical difference, or increased theoretical difficulty, in regarding demand and supply functions dependent on prices, rather than the prices themselves, as parametric. More fundamentally, size becomes relevant to the analysis only if the process under analysis involves changes in relative size; and this problem will arise only if the analysis must compare a surplus-deficit situation in which one side absorbs more and the other less of a total of current production than it would in the case of international equilibrium with the equilibrium situation. Apart from the question of the meaning and relevance of such a comparison, the difference between the two situations will depend, as transfer theory has long understood, not on the relative sizes of the national units but on the marginal effects on demand for goods and assets of a shift in expenditure from one nation's control to the other's—and there is no presumption of correlation between national sizes on the one hand and direction of expenditure-shift and effects on the terms of trade (or, by extension, relative interest rate levels) between the two countries on the other hand. Where the small-country assumption does become relevant is on the monetary side of the analysis; concretely, a large country—the United States, and to a lesser extent other international financial centres—may be able to operate its domestic policies on the assumption that its national money is internationally acceptable so that, say, an expansion of its domestic credit through a 'cheap money' policy will lead to an accumulation of its money in the hands of foreign holders—and eventually to world inflation—rather than to a loss of international reserves.

By the same logic, the changes in the terms of trade—relative prices of import and export goods—that are the centre-piece of the elasticity approach, are by the monetary approach either a secondary consequence of the movement from payments disequilibrium (more accurately, balance-of-payments imbalance, since such an imbalance must always in some sense represent a temporarily chosen equilibrium position for the nation whose aggregate behaviour it represents) to equilibrium (balance) in the balance of payments— which, it should be repeated, may go either way, according to standard transfer theory—or else a transient feature of adjustment from an equilibrium prevailing before a disturbance to the same equilibrium after the disturbance.

The standard elasticity model, like standard 'real' trade theory, assumes that all goods are traded, or in other words can be divided into export and import goods. Criticism of this assumption in the pure theory of international trade, stressing the presence and role in 'real' adjustment to 'real' disturbance of non-traded goods and the fact that in their presence the relative price of imports in terms of exports cannot be simply related to the nature of the disturbance, has been accompanied by the development of elasticity models of monetary and exchange rate adjustment aggregating goods into traded (including both exportable and importable) goods, and non-traded goods, and focusing upon relative price-change—induced substitutions between tradeables and non-tradeables. This alternative to the standard 'elasticity' approach, with its presumption of a predictable direction of terms-of-trade changes in adjustment to a specified disturbance, instead emphasises predictable effects on the relative prices of non-traded as compared with traded goods, and has naturally led to criticism of the commonly used formulation of the monetary approach on the basis of the small-country assumption, taken to imply that all goods have common world-market prices. To this there are two conclusive counter-arguments. Firstly, even if goods cannot be traded, the factors used in producing them generally can be, in the sense that in the relevant run of time a barber has the alternative of being a machine tool operator producing machinery or consumers' durables for export, or instead of imports, and the price of haircuts must be such as to give the barber labour earnings comparable to the wages paid in exporting (and import competing) industries. Secondly, even where there are no comprehensive direct links between costs of production of tradeable and non-tradeable goods, the obvious case being that in which the non-tradeable good employs an internationally immobile specific factor such as climate or land of a specific quality—note that cases are harder to construct than might seem true at first sight, since though coal mines are specific, coal can move, though at a cost—the prices of non-traded goods will be linked to the prices of tradeables through tastes, supply conditions, and the over-all budget restraint, and fixed given the other factors and the relation between domestic expenditure and income. In other words, the influence of non-traded goods must either depend on a situation involving comparison of an imbalanced with a balanced balance of payments, or be merely a transient feature of the adjustment process. On this basis, the abstraction of the main core of the analysis—though not of all analyses based on this approach—from the existence of non-traded goods is a secondary matter. The existence of non-traded goods does, however, become relevant in the empirical application of the theory, in both the static case when price indexes may differ from the prediction of simple purchasing power parity theory owing to differences in the money prices and expenditure weights of such goods between countries, and the dynamic case of growth of productivity at different rates in the traded and non-traded goods sectors, which implies different price trends in the two sectors when factor mobility equalises factor prices between them.

A somewhat different species of red herring is the objection that the monetary approach puts all the emphasis on adjustment of the trade or current account and not on the capital account, which the critics—especially the 'practical-minded' central bankers—regard as the more important arena for international adjustments. This criticism is far more valid as applied to the pre-Keynesian version of the monetary approach, which developed well before the emergence into visibility of the institutional machinery of international capital movements, and the Keynesian approach, with its special concern with the effects of international adjustment on domestic employment, than as directed against the modern monetary approach (classical theorists such as Mill were, however, concerned with capital movements and adjustment in the capital account). For concentration on the balance of payments as mirroring the excess demand or supply of money leaves open the question of which of the other two markets bears the main burden of adjustment, whereas an approach centring on either of the other two markets inevitably tends to prejudge the issue.

A final red herring is the contention that the monetary approach is inapplicable to the current regime of generally floating exchange rates. This is a red herring in the empirical sense that the numerical majority of countries still maintains parities explicitly or in practice with one of a few major currencies, and in the historical sense that much of the development of the monetary approach has been occasioned by concern with the analysis of currency devaluation in a theoretical world of low trade barriers and high international mobility of capital. It is a redder herring, that is, a misunderstanding in a more fundamental sense, in terms of basic theory. In a fixed exchange rate world, a country controls neither its price level nor its quantity of domestic money in anything but the short term; its money supply is endogenous, and what it controls by credit policy is simply the international reserve portion of the monetary base. In a floating rate world, the theory commonly misapplied to a fixed rate world—that the monetary authority controls the money supply and the price level—again becomes valid; but for the monetary approach this merely shifts the focus of analysis from the determination of the balance of payments to the determination of the exchange rate. This is an easy switch of emphasis; it was certainly clear enough to Gustav Cassel [6], who saw purchasing power parity as determining either a nation's price level via its exchange rate under a fixed rate system, or its exchange rate via its domestic money supply under a floating rate system.

The Contemporary Revival of the Monetary Approach
As documented in the next section, the monetary approach to balance-of-payments theory has a long, solid, and academically overwhelmingly reputable history. The continuity of its development, however, was reversed and the approach suppressed in international economic theory for upwards of a quarter of a century by the events of the 1930s. These included the international monetary collapse of 1931 and after, which produced a situation in which tolerable price and wage level adjustments could not possibly have operated as rapidly to restore monetary equilibrium as classical monetary and balance-of-payments theory assumed, adjustments occurred through quantity changes (mass unemployment), and it was natural,

though fundamentally wrong, to regard monetary behaviour as irrelevant to real problems; and the 'Keynesian revolution' in monetary theory, which had the effect of making quantity rather than price adjustments the focus of theorising and money relevant, if at all, only as an influence through the effects on investment flows of interest rates, as influenced by the real quantity of money. (In fairness, however, it must be emphasised that Keynes did not deal with an open economy or a closed but international monetary system, and that his closed economy analysis incorporated demand for and supply of money and the necessity of equilibrium between them as part of his general equilibrium framework; also that the better trained and more perceptive of the economists who applied the multiplier analysis to an open economy were quite aware of what monetary influences and equilibrating forces they were excluding from consideration.)

The modern revival of the monetary approach may be said to have begun, in an important but indirect sense, with James Meade's *The Balance of Payments* [35]. The sense is in part an unintended one—Meade's taxonomic compulsion led him to close the monetary side of his general model with a formal analysis of the gold standard —and in part a Pickwickian one, since Meade, in contrast to many of his contemporaries, spelt out the formal structure of his model and ways in which it could be modified, at great length, and it was easy for successors schooled in Meade's analytical structure to extend the model to tackle new problems and in so doing to become aware of serious faults requiring repair or reconstruction of the model. This was particularly true of Johnson's work on the generalisation of the theory of the balance of payments, and of Mundell's concern with the theory of the policy mix on the assumption of international capital mobility, the first of which emphasised the fundamentally monetary nature of balance-of-payments disequilibria, and the second of which led gradually to the recognition that in a capital-mobile world the central bank controls not the money supply and employment, but domestic credit and the balance of payments. From the formal point of view, the main defect of Meade's work was the confusion of the marginal propensity to save with the marginal propensity to hoard, and the treatment of hoarding as a flow related to the income flow rather than as a transient stock-adjustment or portfolio-balancing phenomenon. Other writers of the same period, especially A. C. Harberger [14], had the insight to recognise that the concept involved was more properly described as a marginal propensity to hoard than as a marginal propensity to save; but this terminology if anything diverted attention from the inappropriateness of treating hoarding as a flow concept.

Significant, but at the time unappreciated, contributions to the revival and formal refinement of the monetary approach, were a short-lived burst of theoretical interest at the International Monetary Fund in the analytical foundations of the Fund's practices in prescribing for its balance-of-payments-crisis clients, typically small, inflation-ridden economies in Latin America—most notably a theoretical contribution by S. J. Prais [44]; an isolated treatment by F. H. Hahn [13] of the effects of devaluation in the framework of monetary general equilibrium analysis propagated by Don Patinkin's closed-economy analysis in *Money, Interest, and Prices* [42], which besides being starkly mathematical confined itself to the short-run impact effect of devaluation; an important contribution by I. F. Pearce [43] and a series of articles by Murray C. Kemp [21, 22] unfortunately rather aside from the main stream of international monetary theory, which worked the analysis through from the concept of a marginal propensity to hoard to a proper monetary analysis on contemporary lines. There were also some significant papers by R. I. McKinnon [33, 34], who emphasised the endogenity of the money supply and the role of public finance and capital mobility; some important contributions by R. Komiya [27, 28], and a useful analysis by A. Collery [7]. The core of the development of the monetary approach as commonly understood, and credited to the author, is to be found in the work of R. A. Mundell which, as already noted, began with a thoroughly Meade–Keynesian development of Meade's analysis to take account of two developments in the international monetary system that occurred subsequently to Meade's major work. One was the growing reluctance of countries to resort to either depreciation or appreciation of their currencies to correct balance-of-payments imbalances, together with the imposition of restraints on the ability of countries to use exchange controls and trade interventions—respectively through the restoration of European currency convertibility in 1958, and through successive GATT agreements on the lowering of tariff barriers and the elimination of quotas. This ruled out the practical application of the general structure of Meade's analysis, which assumed the use of two policy instruments—control over aggregate expenditure via fiscal or monetary policy, and control over the allocation of total expenditures between domestic and foreign goods, by exchange rate adjustment or variation of trade and exchange controls—to serve two policy objectives. On the other hand, currency convertibility and capital mobility introduced a differentiation between expansionary fiscal and expansionary monetary policy, the former improving the capital account by raising interest rates and the latter worsening the capital account by lowering interest rates. With two independent policy instruments again available, it was theoretically possible to serve the two policy objectives of full employment and balance-of-payments balance (internal and external balance) at fixed exchange rates by an appropriate 'mix' of fiscal and monetary policies.

The theory of fiscal-monetary mix, though important for policy theorising in the early 1960s, was essentially a by-product of Mundell's gradual realisation that with capital mobility the money supply ceased to be exogenously determined by the monetary authority, and monetary policy's prime role was to influence the international flow of reserves. This realisation was accompanied by a switch of analytical method from the Keynesian multiplier analysis to analysis in terms of the Walras' Law relation between excess demands and supplies in various markets, the need for equilibrium simultaneously in two out of three markets in a three-market system, and the dynamics of reaction of a system out of equilibrium, a method of analysis popularised by Patinkin, but going back to Hicks' *Value and Capital*. This development, embodied in a long series of scattered articles subsequently collected in Mundell's two books on *International Economics* [38] and *Monetary Theory* [39], and taught to his students in his courses at Chicago and in the International Trade Workshop, has been the main stimulus to the rapid development of theoretical and subsequently also of empirical work on the monetary approach.

2 SOME DOCTRINAL ASPECTS OF THE MONETARY APPROACH[1]

As was indicated earlier, the monetary approach to the balance of payments has a long tradition originating with the writings of the

[1] This section draws on Frenkel [8].

classical school in economics. It is for students of the history of economic thought to study in full scholarly detail the exact origins and evolution of the various ideas that are embodied in the monetary approach. In the present section we make no claim to provide such a comprehensive analysis. Rather, our purpose is to cite the writings of some of the eminent classical and neo-classical economists to document our assertion that throughout the last two centuries the monetary approach to the balance of payments has been the dominant intellectual approach to that collection of economic problems, even though, as always in intellectual history, progenitors for other approaches can be found.

A. The Integrated World

One of the major cornerstones of the classical and the neo-classical schools that is adopted by the monetary approach is the conception of a system of world markets. Profit maximisation implies that when there is free and frictionless trade in both securities and goods, rates of return on identical domestic and foreign securities must be equalised, as must the money prices of goods in terms of either currency. These equalities are brought about through international arbitrage. Consequently Mill's description of the determination of the terms of trade takes as axiomatic the fact that 'By the fall, however, of cloth in England, cloth will fall in Germany also. . . . By the rise of linen in Germany, linen must rise in England also.' (Mill, 1829, Essay I in [36].) This was later formulated, in 1856, by Whewell [51] as the 'principle of international prices', and was still later given a policy-oriented expression in Cassel's *Purchasing Power Parity* [6]. Of course, when goods are not identical and when transportation costs exist, the simple version of the purchasing power parity will not hold exactly; but for practical purposes the deviation from parity would be confined between very narrow limits and in any case would be logically secondary to the main proposition. These practical considerations led Wicksell to conclude that 'there could not possibly exist different prices of the same commodity on both sides of the frontier . . . , difference of prices in the two countries [w]ould be theoretically impossible and practically confined between very narrow limits'. (Wicksell, 1918 [52], p. 405.) Therefore, aside from the cost of carriage, arbitrage will assure that the 'law of one price' holds:

'[t]he action of the international markets, with telegraphic quotations from every part of the world precludes the supposition that gold prices would in general remain on a higher level in one country than another (cost of carriage apart) even for a brief time, because in order to gain the profit, merchants would seize the opportunity to send goods to the markets where prices are high.' (Laughlin, 1903 [30], p. 369.)

The relevant market in which prices are determined, is the *world* market: 'in truth, the value of gold is an affair of a world demand and a world supply' (Laughlin, 1903 [30], p. 370). Similarly Hawtrey, in his description of the organisation of the market, concludes that:

'[the] revolutionary changes in the means of communication . . . have unified markets to such a degree that . . . there is practically a single world market and a single world price. . . . It was fallacious to explain the adjustment wholly in terms of the price level. There was even at that time [Ricardo's time], an approximation to a world price.' (Hawtrey, 1932 [18], p. 144.)

The proposition that markets are unified due to arbitrage activities applies to a wide spectrum of transactions. This is the basis for Ricardo's *Reply to Mr. Bosanquet*, which contains a description of the mechanism of adjustment which assumes consistency of cross exchange rates:

'[T]heory takes for granted, that whenever enormous profits can be made in any particular trade, a sufficient number of capitalists will be induced to engage in it, who will, by their competition, reduce the profits to the general rate of mercantile gains. It assumes that in the trade of exchange does this principle more especially operates; it not being confined to English merchants alone, but being perfectly understood, and profitably followed, by the exchange and bullion merchants of Holland, France and Hamburgh; and competition in this trade being well known to be carried to its greatest height.' (Ricardo, 1811 [46], pp. 9–10.)

Similarly, the concept of a unified world capital market and an understanding of the role of capital mobility were an integral part of the analysis of the classical school. Such statements as 'capital is becoming more and more cosmopolitan' (Mill, 1893 [37], book III, ch. XVII), and 'A cosmopolitan loan fund exists which runs everywhere as it is wanted, and as the rate of interest tempts it' (Bagehot, 1880 [2]) were frequently made. In fact, securities are in a 'continual course of transition from places where the rate of interest is high to places where it is low'. (Fullerton, 1845 [9], p. 149.)

B. The Natural Distribution of Money Among Countries

The classical assumption that the various countries in the world comprise a well ordered *system* which is interdependent led to a concept of a natural equilibrium which is similar to the equilibrium concepts of the biological and physical sciences. One of the implications is the proposition that there is a 'natural distribution of specie' among the countries of the system.

The natural distribution of species hypothesis appeared in print more than 250 years ago in an impressive pamphlet by Isaac Gervaise: 'A Nation cannot retain more than its natural Proportion of what is in the world and the Balance of Trade must run against it.' (Gervaise, 1720 [10], p. 12.) The natural distribution theorem was regarded as almost a law of nature: 'All water, wherever it communicates, remains always at a level. Ask naturalists the reason; they tell you, that were it to be raised in any one place, the superior gravity of that part not balanced must depress it.' (Hume, 1752 [19], pp. 62–4.) The mechanism which assures this unique distribution is competition and arbitrage, as stated by Ricardo: 'Gold and Silver having been chosen for the general medium of circulation, they are, by the competition of commerce, distributed in such proportions amongst the different countries of the world as to accommodate themselves to the natural traffic.' (Ricardo, 1821 [47], p. 123.) What is the 'natural traffic' is left ambiguous—an ambiguity which is typical of many of the classical writings on the determinants of the demand for money. There are, however, quite a few classical economists who clarified understanding of the determinants of the demand for money, as documented by Patinkin in his historical appendix to *Money Interest and Prices*. With respect to the international distribution, Gervaise left very little ambiguity:

'Supposing two equal Nations, and that one hath a Power or Right

over the other; as, for example, one quarter of the yearly Produce of
its Labour be expended in the other: in that case the imperial
creditor Nation will support a Denominator one quarter above its
natural Proportion . . . , and the subjected debtor country will
support but three quarters of its natural Denominator.' (Gervaise,
1720 [10], pp. 23–4.)

Thus, the demand for cash balances depends on income (or assets),
rather than having merely a mechanical dependence on output. The
explicit recognition of an important corollary of the 'natural distribution' theorem, the neutrality of money from the world standpoint,
was provided by Mill: 'A newly acquired stock of money would
diffuse itself over all countries until money has diffused itself so
equally that prices had risen in the same ratio in all countries, so
that the alteration of price would be for all practical purposes in-
effective.' (Mill, 1893 [37], Book III, pp. 194–5.)

The important implication of the natural distribution hypothesis
for economic policy is that under a fixed exchange rate the supply of
money in any country is endogenous. The structural relationship
through which this endogeneity is effected is the balance of payments.
Consequently, the credit policy of the banking system is linked
directly to the balance of payments, and the adjustment mechanism
cannot be properly analysed without focusing on monetary policy
and the resultant excess flow demand or supply of money. In fact,
since the balance of payments reflects an excess flow demand for,
or supply of, money, it must—in the absence of continuous domestic
credit creation or economic growth—be a transitory phenomenon.
This was the major criticism that Hume advanced against mercan-
tilism: 'Suppose twenty million was brought into Scotland . . . , how
much would remain in the quarter of a century? Not a shilling more
than we have at present.' (Hume, 1752 [19], pp. 197–8.) Thus, the
gradual process of adjustment will continue as long as there is an
excess stock supply of money (which induces an excess flow supply).

This leads to one of the basic principles of the classics according
to which there can be no deficit unless there is an excess supply of
money: 'The temptation to export money in exchange for goods, or
what is termed an unfavourable balance of trade, never arises but
from a redundant currency.' (Ricardo, 1809 [45], p. 267.) Although
some of the classical economists used the term 'balance of trade'

instead of 'balance of payments', it is clear that some of them recognised the consequences of international mobility of capital, and incorporated these consequences into their analysis. According to Mill, a once-and-for-all rise in the money stock 'would create a sudden fall in the rate of interest, which would probably send a great part of the twenty millions of gold out of the country as capital. . . . All prices would rise greatly.' (Mill, 1893 [37], Book III, pp. 195–6.) How much of the adjustment will be reflected in the trade account and how much in the capital account was not analysed explicitly. As an empirical matter, however, Mill recognised that the role played by the capital account was larger than allowed for by previous writers: 'It is a fact now beginning to be recognised that the passage of the precious metals from country to country is determined much more than was formerly supposed, by the state of the loan market in different countries, and much less by the state of prices.' (Mill, 1893 [37], ch. VIII, p. 4.) Since the various behavioural relationships are interrelated by the budget constraints, an excess supply of money should be reflected in all of the other accounts of the balance of payments—a proposition which is clearly emphasised by Hawtrey and is an integral part of the monetary approach: 'An expansion of credit *causes* an unfavourable balance of payments . . . the change in the balance is no more than a symptom. And of course the balance that is in question is always the balance of *payments*, not the balance of trade in the narrower sense of the difference between exports and imports of material commodities.' (Hawtrey, 1927 [17], p. 75, italics in original.)

C. Absorption versus Relative Prices

As was argued in the previous section, the absorption and the monetary approaches to the balance of payments emphasise the fact that accumulation or decumulation of assets depends on the relationship between expenditures and income and does not depend on the composition of expenditures. Although the typical textbook version of the classical adjustment mechanism attaches much importance to variations in relative prices, there is much evidence that an adjustment theory which is based on the relationship between expenditures and income was widely accepted by the classic and, even more, the neo-classic writers.

One of the very first writers to emphasise the role of divergences between expenditures and income without mentioning relative prices is Gervaise (1720). A rise in the monetary stock raises expenditures and induces a deficit. The process continues until the excess stock is diffused, and simultaneously, once the stock is reduced to its equilibrium level, expenditures and income coincide:

'If a Nation adds to its Denominator . . . [t]he rich . . . consume more Labour [goods] than before, . . . so that there enters in that Nation, more Labour than goes out of it. . . . The deficit is paid in Gold and Silver until the Denominator be lessen'd, in proportion to other Nations; which also, and at the same time, proportions the number of the Poor [consumption] to that of Rich [production].' (Gervaise, 1720 [10], p. 7.)

If the balance of payments is viewed as a monetary phenomenon it is reasonable to apply the general principles of adjustment to monetary changes. This approach was adopted in the early 1730s by one of the originators of the theory of adjustment to monetary changes, Richard Cantillon: 'The increase in money will bring about an increase in expenditure . . . states which have acquired a considerable abundance of money ordinarily import many things from neighboring countries where money is scarce.' (Cantillon, 1735 [5], pp. 263–7.) Even Hume and Mill, who are usually quoted as the main proponents of the relative price theory, have made statements implicitly endorsing the contrary view of the adjustment mechanism. Hume in 'Of the Jealousy of Trade' (1758) writes: 'The inhabitants, having become opulent and skillful, desire to have every commodity in the utmost perception; . . . they make large importations from every foreign country.' (Hume [19], pp. 79–80.)

Mill's statement—on the basis of which, and other similar statements, he has been interpreted as supporting the relative price theory of adjustment—is as follows: 'The natural effect of a rise in the money stock would be a rise in prices. This would check exports and encourage imports.' (Mill, 1893 [37], Book III, p. 194.) Such statements were later criticised by Bastable who argued that people 'having larger money incomes will purchase more at the same prices and thus bring about the necessary excess of imports over exports'. (Bastable, 1889 [3].) However, it is quite possible that Mill's concepts of 'cheapness' and 'dearness' do not necessarily refer to actual price changes since he argues explicitly that: 'I say this being well aware that the article would be actually at the very same price . . . in England and in other countries. The cheapness however of the article is not measured solely by the money price, but by the price compared with money incomes of the consumers.' (Mill, 1893 [37], Book III, p. 187.) Similarly, 'the English public, having more money, will have a greater power of purchasing foreign commodities . . . there will be an increase of imports; and by this, and the check to exportation, the equilibrium of imports and exports will be restored'. (Mill, 1893 [37], ibid.)

We do not intend, however, to convey the impression that changes in relative prices did not play a role in the classical adjustment mechanism, but rather, that such changes were not treated as the essential factor in the process of adjustment.

In fact, the question of whether the adjustment process operates mainly through changes in relative prices, or through divergences between expenditures and income, was the subject of a series of debates that were mainly associated with the transfer problem. Among the key figures in these debates, Taussig, on the one hand, believed that changes in relative prices are an essential part of the process of adjustment: 'The Gold moves, not "automatically", but as a *result* of changes of prices, or (for short periods) of changed rates of discount.' (Taussig, 1918 [49], p. 411.) On the other hand, Wicksell argued forcefully that changes in relative prices are of secondary importance: 'The stimulus to these altered conditions of trade is not to be found in a difference of prices in the two countries . . . the increased *demand* for commodities in one country, the diminished demand in the other, would in the main be sufficient to call forth the change alluded to.' (Wicksell, 1918 [52], p. 405.)

A similar debate culminated in the discussion between Keynes [23], Ohlin [40] and Rueff [48] in a series of articles in the *Economic Journal* (1929), and the major issues were summarised by Haberler [12], Iversen [20], Kindleberger [26], Ohlin [41] and Machlup [32, pt. 5]. By the 1930s it had become generally accepted that divergences between expenditures and income are important in the process of adjustment, as reflected by Kindleberger's statement:

'Present-day writers generally agree that the price-specie-flow mechanism, with its emphasis on price levels, does not embrace the whole process of adjustment. Changes in demand schedules which have their origin in alterations in national income, which again can be related to changes in money or its velocity, perform a large part of the task of adjusting the balance of payments directly, without the necessity of price movements.' (Kindleberger, 1937 [26], p. 19.)

Although the analytical issues were clarified by that time, much was left to be done in assessing the empirical magnitudes of the alternative mechanisms. An early observation was provided by Bresciani-Turroni in his analysis of the German situation: 'I have the impression that the increase in imports was due much more to an increase in German demand (in the schedule sense) for foreign goods than to an expansion in demand provoked by a diminution of prices in lending countries.' (Bresciani-Turroni, 1932 [4], p. 93.)

D. Banking Policies

The central implication for economic policy of viewing the balance of payments as a monetary phenomenon is that as long as the exchange rate is fixed, monetary policy in the form of control over credit creation has a direct effect on the balance of payments. This strong link has been recognised throughout the development of balance of payments theory. Again Gervaise is among the first to emphasise this link: 'Increase in Credit will act on that Nation as if it had drawn an equal sum from a Gold or Silver Mine, and will preserve but its Proportion of that Increase.' (Gervaise, 1720 [10], p. 9.) Thus, the money supply is completely endogenous and credit policy is eventually reflected only in changes in the composition of the assets of the central bank. Similar statements can be found in Hume, 1752 [19], p. 70, and Mill, 1893 [37], Book III, pp. 195–6.

Since the balance of payments is a monetary phenomenon, the proper way to correct it is through an appropriate monetary policy:

'. . . a disturbance of the balance of payments from a change in the demand or supply of commodities, whether seasonal or other, is properly met by a suitable adjustment of credit. The transmission of gold is only necessary insofar as the adjustment of credit does not exactly keep pace with disturbance. The loss or gain of gold as the case may be tends to bring about the contraction or expansion of credit required. That, however, is pure mismanagement. It has no real connection with the Balance of Payments, and is merely a special case of monetary disturbance.' (Hawtrey, 1926 [16], p. 56.)

The policy implications are clear and in anticipation of Mundell's celebrated theory of the policy mix, Hawtrey concludes that 'It is a mistake to lay too much stress on the actual means of discharging the trade balance. An adverse trade balance may be *created* by a redundant currency and can be corrected by a contraction of the currency.' (Hawtrey, 1927 [17], p. 290.)

Since the world as a whole is a closed system, the balance of payments reflects monetary policies in the various countries. Consequently it is not determined solely by the domestic rate of credit creation but rather by the domestic rate relatively to that in the rest of the world: 'One lets credit expand a little faster than the others and loses gold; another lags behind and receives gold.' (Hawtrey, 1927 [17], p. 10.)

The basic truism that the world is a closed system that is composed of interdependent countries implies that an individual central bank in the world system has no more power than a single member bank of a national system. This simple fact and its policy implications were widely recognised and accepted. Keynes himself, in his pre-*General Theory* [25] writing, forcefully emphasised the mutual interdependence of the various central banks:

'One or two Central Banks acting alone would not, unless they were very preponderant in size, be able to change the weather or direct the storm—any more than a single member bank can control the behaviour of a national system. If a single Central Bank lags behind in a boom it will be overwhelmed by excess reserve-resources, and if it steps in in a depression it will have its reserve-resources quickly drawn from it. . . . each Bank is necessarily governed by the *average* policy of the Banks as a whole.' (Keynes, 1930 [24], pp. 281–6, italics in original.)

It is quite clear from these statements why the monetary approach to the balance of payments views the balance of payments as essentially a monetary phenomenon.

E. Commercial Policies

As was already emphasised, a theory of the balance of payments has very little to do with the composition of expenditures as between various aggregates of commodities, and therefore the effects of a devaluation on the terms of trade have little to do with their effects on the flow of reserves. Historically, however, much of the analysis of the effects of changes in the exchange rate was carried out by using the elasticity approach. Using this framework, the typical disaggregation of commodities has been between exportables and importables with much emphasis on the terms of trade. The popular version of that approach ignores considerations of general equilibrium and is marred by assuming that the behavioural equations depend on money prices rather than on relative prices and real income or 'expenditure' as well as by ignoring the consequences of the budget constraint. More sophisticated treatments have assumed that there are some things 'in the background' which assure consistency, though the nature of these is rarely, if ever, investigated in detail.

The monetary approach rejects this emphasis given to the role of relative prices in the analysis of devaluation. This rejection and the reasons for it are noted in the classical approach and are foreshadowed by analytical statements by some of the writers in that tradition. For example, Graham forcefully stated that 'so far as balance is concerned, elasticity is never of any relevance, either in the short run or the long run. . . . the whole discussion of elasticities in international trade has been of negligible or even negative value'. (Graham, 1949 [11], p. 249.)

The basic claim that is made by the proponents of the monetary approach is that the balance of payments effects of any policy measure cannot be properly analysed without specifying the monetary consequence of the policy itself. This principle implies that in contrast with the traditional textbook analysis of the effects of a tariff, which assumes without further discussion that a diversion of demand away from imports must improve the trade and payments balance, a proper analysis should investigate the effects of the tariff on the excess demand for money. Consequently, a tariff will improve the balance of payments only if it induces an excess demand for money. This rather simple condition is very different from the typical textbook analysis which emphasises the effect of the tariff on the relative price of goods.

Even this insight originates with the writings of earlier economists, such as Hawtrey: '. . . protective tariff does raise the price level . . . it accordingly requires an increased monetary circulation, and if the monetary system is such that that cannot be provided without the importation of gold, gold will be imported.' (Hawtrey, 1932 [18], p. 244.)

We conclude this section by repeating that there is plenty of evidence to support the claim that throughout the last two centuries the monetary approach to the balance of payments was widespread.[2]

REFERENCES

[1] Alexander, Sidney, 'The Effects of Devaluation: A Simplified Synthesis of Elasticities and Absorption Approaches', *American Economic Review*, xlix, no. 2 (March 1959), 22–42.

[2] Bagehot, W., *Economic Studies*, ed by R. H. Hutton (London, 1880).

[3] Bastable, S. F., 'On Some Applications of the Theory of International Trade', *Quarterly Journal of Economics*, iv (1889), 1–17.

[4] Bresciani-Turroni, C., *Inductive Verification of the Theory of International Payments* (Cairo, Noury and Son, 1932).

[5] Cantillon, Richard, 'Essai sur la nature du commerce en general (1755)' in Arthur E. Monroe (ed.), *Early Economic Thought* (Cambridge, Harvard University Press, 1927).

[6] Cassel, Gustav, *Post-War Monetary Stabilization* (New York, 1928).

[7] Collery, Arnold, 'International Adjustment, Open Economies, and the Quantity Theory of Money', Princeton Studies in International Finance, no. 28 (June 1971).

[8] Frenkel, Jacob A., 'Adjustment Mechanism and the Monetary Approach to the Balance of Payments: A Doctrinal Perspective', presented at the Third Paris-Dauphine Conference on Recent Issues in International Monetary Economics, March 1974; forthcoming in the Proceedings, edited by E. Claasen and P. Salin.

[9] Fullerton, John, *On the Regulation of Currencies*, 2nd edn, 1845.

[10] Gervaise, Isaac, 'The System or Theory of the Trade of the World, 1720'; reproduced as a reprint in *Economic Tracts* (Johns Hopkins University Press, 1956).

[11] Graham, Frank D., 'A Letter from Graham to R. Hinshaw', *Journal of International Economics*, i, no. 2 (May 1971), 249.

[12] Haberler, Gotfried, *The Theory of International Trade* (London, Hodge, 1936).

[13] Hahn, F. H., 'The Balance of Payments in a Monetary Economy', *Review of Economic Studies*, xxvi (2), no. 70 (February 1959), 110–25.

[14] Harberger, A. C., 'Currency Depreciation, Income and the Balance of Trade', *Journal of Political Economy*, lviii, no. 1 (February 1950), 47–60.

[15] Harrod, Roy F., *International Economics*, 1st edn, 1933, 2nd edn, 1939, 4th edn, 1957.

2 For further evidence see Frenkel [8].

44   JACOB A. FRENKEL AND HARRY G. JOHNSON

[16] Hawtrey, R. G., 'The Gold Standard and the Balance of Payments', *Economic Journal*, xxxvi (March 1936), 50–68.
[17] Hawtrey, R. G., *Currency and Credit* (London, Longmans, Green, 3rd edn, 1927).
[18] Hawtrey, R. G., *The Art of Central Banking* (London, Longmans, Green, 1932).
[19] Hume, David, 'Political Discourses, 1752' in E. Rotwein, *David Hume; Writings on Economics* (London, Nelson, 1955).
[20] Iversen, Carl, *Aspects of the Theory of International Capital Movements* (London, Oxford University Press, 1935).
[21] Kemp, Murray C., 'The Rate of Exchange, The Terms of Trade and the Balance of Payments in Fully Employed Economics', *International Economic Review*, iii, no. 3 (September 1962), 314–27.
[22] Kemp, Murray C., 'The Balance of Payments and the Terms of Trade in Relation to Financial Controls', *Review of Economic Studies*, xxxviii (January 1970), 25–31.
[23] Keynes, John M., 'The German Transfer Problem', *Economic Journal*, xxxix (1929), 1–7.
[24] Keynes, John M., *A Treatise on Money*, vol. ii (New York, Harcourt, Brace, 1930).
[25] Keynes, John M., *The General Theory of Employment Interest and Income* (London, Macmillan, 1936).
[26] Kindleberger, Charles P., *International Short-Term Capital Movements* (New York, Columbia University Press, 1937).
[27] Komiya, Ryutaro, 'Monetary Assumptions, Currency Depreciation and the Balance of Trade', *The Economic Studies Quarterly*, xvii, no. 2 (December 1966), 9–23.
[28] Komiya, Ryutaro, 'Economic Growth and the Balance of Payments: A Monetary Approach', *Journal of Political Economy*, 77, no. 1 (January/February 1969), 35–48.
[29] Kouri, P. J. K., and Porter, M. G., 'Portfolio Equilibrium and International Capital Flows', *Journal of Political Economy*, 82, no. 3 (May/June 1974), 443–68.
[30] Laughlin, J. Lawrence, *The Principles of Money* (New York, Scribner, 1903).
[31] Machlup, Fritz, *International Trade and the National Income Multiplier* (Philadelphia, Blakiston, 1943).
[32] Machlup, Fritz, *International Payments, Debts and Gold* (New York, Scribner, 1964).
[33] McKinnon, Ronald I., 'Portfolio Balance and International Payments Adjustment' in Mundell, R. A., and Swoboda, A. K. (eds), *Monetary Problems of the International Economy* (Chicago, University of Chicago Press, 1968), 199–234.
[34] McKinnon, Ronald I., and Oates, W. E., 'The Implications of International Economic Integration for Monetary, Fiscal and Exchange Rate Policy', *Princeton Studies in International Finance*, no. 16 (1966).
[35] Meade, James E., *The Balance of Payments* (London, Oxford University Press, 1951).
[36] Mill, John Stuart, *Essay on Some Unsettled Questions of Political Economy* (London, 2nd edn, 1874).
[37] Mill, John Stuart, *Principles of Political Economy* (New York, Appleton, 5th edn, 1893).
[38] Mundell, Robert A., *International Economics* (New York, Macmillan, 1968).

[39] Mundell, Robert A., *Monetary Theory* (Pacific Palisades, Goodyear, 1971).

[40] Öhlin, Bertil, 'The Reparation Problem: A Discussion', *Economic Journal*, xxix (June 1929), 172–8.

[41] Ohlin, Bertil, *Interregional and International Trade* (Cambridge, Mass., Harvard University Press, 1933).

[42] Patinkin, Don, *Money Interest and Prices*, 2nd edn (New York, Harper & Row, 1965).

[43] Pearce, I. F., 'The Problem of the Balance of Payments', *International Economic Review*, 11, no. 1 (January 1961), 1–28.

[44] Prais, S. J., 'Some Mathematical Notes on the Quantity Theory of Money in an Open Economy', *IMF Staff Papers*, viii, no. 2 (May 1961), 212–26.

[45] Ricardo, David, *The High Price of Bullion* (*1809*) (McCulloch edn, 1846).

[46] Ricardo, David, *Reply to Mr. Bosanquet's Practical Observations on the Report of the Bullion Committee* (London, 1811).

[47] Ricardo, David, *Principles of Political Economy and Taxation*, 3rd edn, 1821.

[48] Rueff, Jacques, 'Mr. Keynes' Views on the Transfer Problem: I. A Criticism', *Economic Journal*, xxxix, no. 155 (September 1929), 388–99.

[49] Taussig, F. W., 'International Freight and Prices', *Quarterly Journal of Economics*, xxxii (February 1918), 410–14.

[50] Viner, Jacob, *Studies in the Theory of International Trade* (New York, Harper, 1937).

[51] Whewell, W., 'Mathematical Exposition of Some Doctrines of Political Economy, Second Memoir', *Transactions of the Cambridge Philosophical Society*, ix, pt ɪ (1856).

[52] Wicksell, Knut, 'International Freights and Prices', *Quarterly Journal of Economics*, xxxii (February 1918), 404–10.

II. BASIC ARTICLES

2

Towards a General Theory of the Balance of Payments[1]

HARRY G. JOHNSON

The theory of the balance of payments is concerned with the economic determinants of the balance of payments, and specifically with
the analysis of policies for preserving balance-of-payments equilibrium. So defined, the theory of the balance of payments is essentially
a post-war development. Prior to the Keynesian revolution, problems of international disequilibrium were discussed within the
classical conceptual framework of 'the mechanism of adjustment'—
the way in which the balance of payments adjusts to equilibrium
under alternative systems of international monetary relations—the
actions of the monetary and other policy-making authorities being
subsumed in the system under consideration. While the Keynesian
revolution introduced the notion of chronic disequilibrium into the
analysis of international adjustment, early Keynesian writing on the
subject tended to remain within the classical framework of analysis
in terms of international monetary systems—the gold standard, the
inconvertible paper standard—and to be concerned with the role
and adequacy in the adjustment process of automatic variations in
income and employment through the foreign trade multiplier.
Moreover, the applicability of the analysis to policy problems was
severely restricted by its assumption of general under-employment,
which implied an elastic supply of aggregate output, and allowed

[1] Reprinted from H. G. Johnson, *International Trade and Economic Growth*
(London, George Allen & Unwin, 1958), 153–68.

the domestic-currency wage or price level to be treated as *given*, independently of the balance of payments and variations in it.

The pre-war approach to international monetary theory reflected the way in which balance-of-payments problems tended to appear at the time, namely as problems of international monetary adjustment. Since the war, for reasons which need not be elaborated here, the balance of payments has come to be a major problem for economic policy in many countries. Correspondingly, a new (though still Keynesian) theoretical approach to balance-of-payments theory has been emerging, an approach which is better adapted to post-war conditions than the 'foreign trade multiplier theory' and 'elasticity analysis' of the pre-war period in two major respects: it poses the problems of balance-of-payments adjustment in a way which highlights their policy implications, and it allows for conditions of full employment and inflation.

The essence of this approach, which has been termed 'the absorption approach', is to view the balance of payments as a relation between the aggregate receipts and expenditures of the economy, rather than as a relation between the country's credits and debits on international account. This approach has been implicit to an important extent in the thinking of practical policy-makers concerned with balance-of-payments problems in post-war conditions. Its main formal development is to be found in the works of Meade, Tinbergen, and Alexander, though many others have contributed.[2]

[2] See in particular J. E. Meade, *The Theory of International Economic Policy. Vol. I: The Balance of Payments* (London, 1951); J. Tinbergen, *On the Theory of Economic Policy* (Amsterdam, 1952); S. Alexander, 'The Effects of a Devaluation on a Trade Balance', *International Monetary Fund Staff Papers*, II, no. 2, April 1952, 263–78; also G. Stuvel, *The Exchange Stability Problem* (Oxford, 1951); A. C. Harberger, 'Currency Depreciation, Income, and the Balance of Trade', *Journal of Political Economy*, LVIII, no. 1, February 1950, 47–60; S. Laursen and L. A. Metzler, 'Flexible Exchange Rates and the Theory of Employment', *Review of Economics and Statistics*, XXXII, no. 4, November 1950, 281–99; R. F. Harrod, 'Currency Depreciation as an Anti-Inflationary Device: Comment', *Quarterly Journal of Economics*, LXVI, no. 1, February 1952, 102–16. The terminology of 'absorption' was initiated by Alexander; Machlup's criticisms of Alexander's argument (F. Machlup, 'The Analysis of Devaluation', *American Economic Review*, XLV, no. 3, June 1955, 255–78), though valid in detail, miss the main point of Alexander's contribution, a point obscured by Alexander's own emphasis on the contrast between the 'elasticity' and the 'absorption' approaches to devaluation and his attack on the former. The later argument of this paper attempts a reconciliation of the two approaches in a broader framework of analysis.

The purpose of this chapter is to synthesise and generalise the work of these writers, and to use their approach to clarify certain aspects of the balance-of-payments policy problem.

Let us first summarise the traditional approach to balance-of-payments theory. The balance of payments must necessarily balance when all international transactions are taken into account; for imbalance or disequilibrium to be possible, it is necessary to distinguish between 'autonomous' international transactions—those which are the result of the free and voluntary choices of individual transactors, within whatever restrictions are imposed by economic variables or policy on their behaviour—and 'induced' or 'accommodating' international transactions—those which are undertaken by the foreign exchange authorities to reconcile the free choices of the individual transactors—and to define the 'balance of payments' to include only autonomous transactions. To put the point another way, balance-of-payments problems presuppose the presence of an official foreign exchange authority which is prepared to operate in the foreign exchange market by the use of official reserves so as to influence the exchange rate; and 'disequilibrium' is defined by changes in the official reserves, associated with imbalance between the foreign receipts and foreign payments of residents of the country, where 'resident' is defined to include all economic units domiciled in the country *except* the foreign exchange authority.[3]

The 'balance of payments' appropriate to economic analysis may then be defined as

$$B = R_f - P_f$$

where R_f represents aggregate receipts by residents from foreigners, and P_f represents aggregate payments by residents to foreigners. The difference between the two constitutes a surplus (if positive) or a deficit (if negative); a surplus is accompanied by sales of foreign currency to the exchange authority by residents or foreigners in exchange for domestic currency, and conversely a deficit is financed by sales of domestic currency by residents or foreigners to the author-

[3] Where the central bank or other monetary authority also holds the foreign exchange reserves, it is necessary for the purposes of this paper to separate its functions conceptually into two parts, and to class its transactions as monetary authority (including those with itself as exchange authority) among transactions of residents.

ity in exchange for foreign currency. To remedy a deficit, some action must be taken to increase receipts from foreigners and reduce payments to foreigners, or increase receipts more than payments, or reduce payments more than receipts; and conversely with a surplus (though the rectification of a surplus is not generally regarded as a 'balance-of-payments problem').

The 'balance of payments' can, however, be defined in another way, by making use of the fact that all payments by residents to residents are simultaneously receipts by residents from residents; in symbols $R_r \equiv P_r$. Hence the balance of payments may be written

$$B = R_f + R_r - P_f - P_r = R - P.$$

That is, the balance of payments is the difference between aggregate receipts by residents and aggregate payments by residents. A deficit implies an excess of payments over receipts, and its rectification requires that receipts be increased and payments decreased, or that receipts increase more than payments, or that receipts decrease less than payments; and conversely with a surplus. In what follows, however, surpluses will be ignored, and the argument will be concerned only with deficits.

The formulation of a balance-of-payments deficit in terms of an excess of aggregate payments by residents over aggregate receipts by residents constitutes the starting point for the generalisation of the 'absorption approach' to balance-of-payments theory—what might be termed a 'payments approach'—which is the purpose of this chapter. It directs attention to two important aspects of a deficit —its monetary implications, and its relation with the aggregate activity of the economy—from which attention tends to be diverted by the traditional sectoral approach, and neglect of which can lead to fallacious analysis. These two aspects will be discussed in turn, beginning with the monetary implications of a deficit.

The excess of payments by residents over receipts by residents inherent in a balance-of-payments deficit necessarily implies one or the other of two alternatives. The first is that cash balances of residents are running down, as domestic money is transferred to the foreign exchange authority.[4] This can, obviously, only continue for a limited

[4] Where monetary authority and exchange authority are one and the same institution, domestic monetary liabilities may simply be extinguished by sales of foreign exchange.

period, as eventually cash balances would approach the minimum that the community wished to hold and in the process the disequilibrium would cure itself, through the mechanism of rising interest rates, tighter credit conditions, reduction of aggregate expenditure, and possibly an increase in aggregate receipts. In this case, where the deficit is financed by dishoarding, it would be self-correcting in time; but the economic policy authorities may well be unable to allow the self-correcting process to run its course, since the international reserves of the country may be such a small fraction of the domestic money supply that they would be exhausted well before the running down of money balances had any significant corrective effect. The authorities might therefore have to take action of some kind to reinforce and accelerate the effects of diminishing money balances.

This last consideration provides the chief valid argument for larger international reserves. The case for larger international reserves is usually argued on the ground that larger reserves provide more time for the economic policy authorities to make adjustments to correct a balance-of-payments disequilibrium. But, as Friedman has argued in criticism of Meade,[5] there is no presumption that adjustment spread over a longer period is to be preferred—the argument could indeed be inverted into the proposition that, the larger the reserves, the more power the authorities have to resist desirable adjustments. The acceptable argument would seem to be that, the larger the international reserves in relation to the domestic money supply, the less the probability that the profit- or utility-maximising decisions of individuals to move out of cash into commodities or securities will have to be frustrated by the monetary authorities for fear of a balance-of-payments crisis.

The second alternative is that the cash balances of residents are being replenished by open market purchases of securities by the monetary or foreign exchange authority, as would happen automatically if the monetary authority followed a policy of pegging interest rates or the exchange authority (as in the British case) automatically re-lent to residents any domestic currency it received from residents or foreigners in return for sales of foreign exchange. In this case, the money supply in domestic circulation is being

5 Milton Friedman, 'The Case for Flexible Exchange Rates', 157–203 in *Essays in Positive Economics* (Chicago, 1953), especially 186, n. 11.

maintained by credit creation, so that the excess of payments over receipts by residents could continue indefinitely without generating any corrective process—until dwindling reserves forced the economic policy authorities to change their policy in some respect.

To summarise the argument so far, a balance-of-payments deficit implies *either* dishoarding by residents, *or* credit creation by the monetary authorities—either an increase in V, or the maintenance of M. Further, since a deficit associated with increasing velocity of circulation will tend to be self-correcting (though the authorities may be unable to rely on this alone), a continuing balance-of-payments deficit of the type usually discussed in balance-of-payments theory ultimately requires credit creation to keep it going. This in turn implies that balance-of-payments deficits and difficulties are essentially monetary phenomena, traceable to either of two causes: too low a ratio of international reserves relative to the domestic money supply, so that the economic policy authorities can not rely on the natural self-correcting process; or the pursuit of governmental policies which oblige the authorities to feed the deficit by credit creation. In both cases, the problem is associated fundamentally with the power of national banking systems to create money which has no internationally acceptable backing.

To conclude that balance of payments problems are essentially monetary is not, of course, to assert that they are attributable to monetary mismanagement—they may be, or they may be the result of 'real' forces in the face of which the monetary authorities play a passive role. The conclusion does mean, however, that the distinctions which have sometimes been drawn between monetary and real disequilibria, for example by concepts of 'structural disequilibrium', are not logically valid—though such concepts, carefully used, may be helpful in isolating the initiating causes of disequilibrium or the most appropriate type of remedial policy to follow.

Formulation of the balance of payments as the difference between aggregate payments and aggregate receipts thus illuminates the monetary aspects of balance-of-payments disequilibrium, and emphasises its essentially monetary nature. More important and interesting is the light which this approach sheds on the policy problem of correcting a deficit, by relating the balance of payments to the over-all operation of the economy rather than treating it as one sector of the economy to be analysed by itself.

An excess of aggregate payments by residents over aggregate receipts by residents is the net outcome of economic decisions taken by all the individual economic units composing the economy. These decisions may usefully be analysed in terms of an 'aggregate decision' taken by the community of residents considered as a group (excluding, as always, the foreign exchange authority), though it must be recognised that this technique ignores many of the complications that would have to be investigated in a more detailed analysis.

Two sorts of aggregate decision leading to a balance-of-payments deficit may be distinguished in principle, corresponding to the distinction drawn in monetary theory between 'stock' decisions and 'flow' decisions: a (stock) decision to alter the composition of the community's assets by substituting other assets for domestic money,[6] and a (flow) decision to spend currently in excess of current receipts. Since both real goods and securities are alternative assets to domestic money, and current expenditure may consist in the purchase of either goods or securities, the balance-of-payments deficit resulting from either type of aggregate decision may show itself on either current or capital account. That is, a current account deficit may reflect either a community decision to shift out of cash balances into stocks of goods, or a decision to use goods in excess of the community's current rate of production, while a capital account deficit may reflect either a decision to shift out of domestic money into securities or a decision to lend in excess of the current rate of saving.

The distinction between 'stock' and 'flow' balance-of-payments deficits is important for both theory and practical policy, though refined theoretical analysis has generally been concerned with 'flow' deficits, without making the distinction explicit. The importance of the distinction stems from the fact that a 'stock' deficit is inherently temporary and implies no real worsening of the country's economic position, whereas a 'flow' deficit is not inherently temporary and may imply a worsening of the country's economic position.

Since a stock decision entails a once-for-all change in the composition of a given aggregate of capital assets, a 'stock' deficit must

---

[6] With the community defined to include the monetary authority, a substitution of securities for domestic money can only be effected by drawing securities from abroad in exchange for international reserves.

necessarily be a temporary affair;[7] and in itself it implies no deterioration (but rather the reverse) in the country's economic position and prospects.[8] Nevertheless, if the country's international reserves are small, the economic policy authorities may be obliged to check such a deficit by a change in economic policy. The policy methods available are familiar, but it may be useful to review them briefly in relation to the framework of analysis developed here.

To discourage the substitution of stocks of goods for domestic currency, the economic policy authorities may either raise the cost of stock-holding by credit restriction or reduce its attractiveness by currency depreciation.[9] Under both policies, the magnitude of the effect is uncertain—depreciation, by stimulating de-stabilising expectations, may even promote stock accumulation—while unavoidable repercussions on the flow equilibrium of the economy are set up. These considerations provide a strong argument for the use of the alternative method of direct controls on stock-holding, an indirect and partial form of which is quantitative import restriction.

To discourage the substitution of securities for domestic currency, the same broad alternatives are available: credit restriction, which amounts to the monetary authority substituting domestic currency for securities to offset substitution of securities for domestic currency by the rest of the community; devaluation, which affects the relative attractiveness of securities only through expectations and may work either way; and exchange controls restricting the acquisition of securities from abroad. Considerations similar to those of the

[7] A temporary deficit of this kind must be distinguished from a deficit which is 'temporary' in the sense that the causal factors behind it will reverse themselves, leading to a later compensating surplus: e.g. a deficit due to a bad harvest.

[8] The deficit involves the replacement of international reserves by stocks of exportable or importable goods and/or by holdings of internationally marketable securities, the change being motivated by private profit considerations. For this to constitute a deterioration from the national point of view, the alternatives facing private asset-holders must be assumed not to reflect true social alternative opportunities, or private asset-holders must be assumed to act less rationally than the economic policy authorities, or the national interest must be defined so as to exclude their welfare from counting. If any of these assumptions is valid, it indicates the need for a remedial policy, but not one conditional on the existence of a deficit or to be applied through the balance of payments. This point is argued more fully below, in connection with import restrictions.

[9] Stocks are built up by withholding goods from export or by increasing imports; depreciation makes both of these less attractive. A third policy might be increased taxation, either of stocks or of home-market sales of goods.

previous paragraph would seem to argue in favour of the use of controls on international capital movements as against the alternative methods available.

In both cases, evaluation of the policy alternatives suggests the use of control rather than price system methods. It should be recalled, though, that the problem is created by the assumed inadequacy of the country's international reserves. In the longer run, the choice for economic policy lies, not between the three alternatives discussed, but between the necessity of having to choose between them and the cost of investing in the accumulation of reserves large enough to finance potential 'stock' deficits. Also, nothing has been said about the practical difficulties of maintaining effective control over international transactions, especially capital movements.

In contrast to a 'stock' deficit, a 'flow' deficit is not inherently of limited duration. It will be so if the monetary authority is not prepared to create credit, but this is because its existence will then set up monetary repercussions which will eventually alter the collective decision responsible for it, not because the initial decision implied a temporary deficit. If the decision not to create credit is regarded as a specific act of policy equivalent to a decision to raise interest rates,[10] it follows that the termination of a 'flow' deficit requires a deliberate change of economic policy. Further, a 'flow' deficit may imply a worsening of the country's capital position, providing an economic as well as a monetary incentive to terminate the disequilibrium.[11]

In analysing the policy problems posed by 'flow' deficits, it is convenient to begin by abstracting altogether from international capital movements (other than reserve transactions between foreign exchange authorities) and considering the case of a current account deficit. In this case, if intermediate transactions are excluded, the

[10] This assumption, which is slightly inconsistent with the argument above concerning the monetary implications of a deficit, is made here to avoid the necessity of repeating the analysis for the case where limited reserves prevent the authorities from allowing a deficit to solve itself.

[11] Whether this is so depends on the use to which the finance provided by the deficit is put, which involves comparison with what would have happened in the absence of the deficit. If the deficit finances additional investment in productive domestic capital or income-yielding foreign assets the net effect on the capital position may be favourable; if it finances additional consumption it is likely to be unfavourable, though even additional consumption may sometimes increase productive capacity.

balance of payments becomes the difference between the value of the country's output (its national income) and its total expenditure, i.e.

$$B = Y - E.$$

To facilitate analysis by avoiding certain complications associated with the possibility of changes in the domestic price level, income and expenditure are conceived of as being valued in units of domestic output. A deficit then consists in an excess of real expenditure over real income, and the problem of correcting a deficit is to bring real national income (output) and real national expenditure into equality.

This formulation suggests that policies for correcting current-account deficits can be classified broadly into two types: those which aim at (or rely on) increasing output, and those which aim at reducing expenditure. The distinction must, of course, relate to the initial impact of the policy, since income and expenditure are interdependent: expenditure depends on and varies with income, and income depends on and varies with expenditure (because part of expenditure is devoted to home-produced goods). Consequently any change in either income or expenditure will initiate multiplier changes in both. It can, however, readily be shown that, so long as an increase in income induces a smaller change in aggregate expenditure, the multiplier repercussions will not be large enough to offset the impact effect of a change, so that an impact increase in output or decrease in expenditure will always improve the balance on current account.[12]

[12] Differentiating the equation in the text, we obtain $dB = (1 - e)dY + dE$, where e is the marginal propensity to spend out of income, dY is the total *increase* in output (including multiplier effects) and dE is the autonomous *decrease* in expenditure. If multiplier effects through foreign incomes are ignored,

$$dY = \frac{1}{1 - e(1 - m)} dA,$$

where dA is an autonomous change in demand for domestic output and m is the proportion of marginal expenditure leaking into imports. Splitting dA into two components, dO for output-increasing policies and $- hdE$ for expenditure-reducing policies (where h is the proportion of expenditure reduction falling on domestic output), gives the result

$$dB = \frac{1 - e}{1 - e + em} dO + \left(1 - \frac{(1 - e)h}{1 - e + em}\right) dE.$$

Hence either an output-increasing or an expenditure-reducing policy will improve

The distinction between output-increasing and expenditure-reducing policies may usefully be put in another way. Since output is governed by the demand for it, a change in output can only be brought about by a change in the demand for it; a policy of increasing domestic output can only be effected by operating on expenditure (either foreign or domestic) on that output. Given the level of expenditure, this in turn involves effecting a switch of expenditure (by residents and foreigners) from foreign output to domestic output. The distinction between output-increasing and expenditure-decreasing policies, which rests on the *effects* of the policies, may therefore be replaced by a distinction between expenditure-switching policies and expenditure-reducing policies, which rests on the *method* by which the effects are achieved.

A policy of expenditure-reduction may be applied through a variety of means—monetary restriction, budgetary policy, or even a sufficiently comprehensive battery of direct controls. Since any such policy will tend to reduce income and employment, it will have an additional attraction if the country is suffering from inflationary pressure as well as a balance-of-payments deficit, but a corresponding disadvantage if the country is suffering from unemployment. Moreover, since the impact reduction in expenditure and the total reduction in income and output required to correct a given deficit are larger the larger the proportion of the expenditure reduction falling on home-produced goods, and since different methods of expenditure-reduction may differ in this respect, the choice between alternative methods may depend on the inflationary-deflationary situation of the economy. Finally, since the accompanying reduction in income may lead to some reduction in the domestic price level, and/or a greater eagerness of domestic producers to compete with foreign producers both at home and abroad, expenditure-reducing policies may have incidental expenditure-switching effects.

Expenditure-switching policies may be divided into two types, according to whether the policy instrument employed is general or selective: devaluation (which may be taken to include the case of a deflation-induced reduction of the domestic price level under fixed

---

the balance, so long as e is less than unity. (Alexander has argued that since e includes induced investment it may well exceed unity; this possibility is ignored in the argument of the text.) Expenditure reduction will in fact improve the balance so long as multiplier stability is present.

exchange rates), and trade controls (including both tariffs and subsidies and quantitative restrictions). Devaluation aims at switching both domestic and foreign expenditure towards domestic output; controls are usually imposed on imports, and aim at (or have the effect of) switching domestic expenditure away from imports towards home goods, though sometimes they are used to stimulate exports and aim at switching foreigners' expenditure towards domestic output.

Both types of expenditure-switching policy may have direct impact-effects on residents' expenditure. Devaluation may result in increased expenditure from the initial income level, through the so-called 'terms-of-trade effect' of an adverse terms-of-trade movement in reducing real income and therefore the proportion of income saved. Trade controls will tend to have the same effect, via the reduction in real income resulting from constriction of freedom of choice.[13] In addition, trade controls must alter the real expenditure corresponding to the initial output level if they take the form of import duties or export subsidies uncompensated by other fiscal changes; this case should, however, be classed as a combined policy of expenditure-change (unfavourable in the case of the export subsidy) and expenditure-switch.

Whether general or selective in nature, an expenditure-switching policy seeks to correct a deficit by switching demand away from foreign towards domestic goods; and it depends for success not only on switching demand in the right direction, but also on the

[13] These arguments conflict with the assumption, more frequently made in connection with trade controls than with devaluation, that the public will consume less because it cannot obtain the goods it prefers as readily as before. That assumption may well be valid in the case of a policy expected to be applied for a short period only, after which goods will become as available as before, or in the analysis of the short run during which the economy is adjusting to the change in policy; but it is invalid in the present context of flow disequilibrium, since it overlooks the effect of the policy change in reducing the future value of savings and hence the incentive to save. An example of this type of faulty reasoning is the assertion sometimes made that quantitative import restriction is particularly effective in under-developed countries because their economic structure allows little possibility of substitution for imported goods in either production or consumption.

One qualification to the argument of the text, which also applies to the final sentence of the paragraph, is that if the goods towards which domestic expenditure is switched are more heavily taxed than those from which expenditure is diverted (a type of complication which is ignored in the general argument of the text), real expenditure may fall rather than rise.

capacity of the economy to make available the extra output required to satisfy the additional demand. Such policies therefore pose two problems for economic analysis: the conditions required for expenditure to be switched in the desired direction, and the source of the additional output required to meet the additional demand.

As to the first question, the possibilities of failure for both devaluation and controls have been investigated at length by international trade theorists, and require only summary treatment here.[14] Export promotion will divert foreign expenditure away from the country's output if the foreign demand is inelastic, while import restriction will divert domestic expenditure abroad if demand for imports is inelastic and the technique of restriction allows the foreigner the benefit of the increased value of imports to domestic consumers. Devaluation has the partial effect of diverting domestic expenditure abroad, via the increased cost of the initial volume of imports, and this adverse switch will not be offset by the favourable effect of substitution of domestic for foreign goods at home and abroad, if import demand elasticities average less than one half.

While the elasticity requirement for successful devaluation just cited is familiar, the approach developed in this paper throws additional light on what non-fulfilment of the requirement implies. From the equation

$$B = Y - E,$$

it is clear that, if direct effects on expenditure from the initial income level are neglected, devaluation can worsen the balance only if it reduces total world demand for the country's output. This implies that the country's output is in a sense a 'Giffen case' in world consumption; and that the market for at least one of the commodities it produces is in unstable equilibrium.[15] Neither of these ways of stating the conditions for exchange instability makes the possibility of instability as plausible *a priori* as their equivalent, reached through sectoral analysis, in terms of elasticities of import demand.

[14] Impact effects on the level of expenditure from a given income level of the type discussed in the next-but-one paragraph preceding this one are ignored in this paragraph.

[15] Cf. E. V. Morgan, 'The Theory of Flexible Exchange Rates', *American Economic Review*, xlv, no. 3, June 1955, 279–95. Morgan's statement (285) that instability requires 'very strong and perverse income effects' is fallacious—all that is strictly necessary is a preference in each country for home-produced goods.

The second, and more interesting, analytical problem relates to the source of the additional domestic output required to satisfy the demand for it created by the expenditure-switching policy. Here it is necessary to distinguish two cases, that in which the economy is under-employed and that in which it is fully employed, for both the relevant technique of analysis and the factors on which the outcome of the policy depend differ between the two.

If the economy has unemployed resources available, the additional output required to meet the additional demand can be provided by the re-absorption of these resources into employment: in this case the switch policy has the additional attraction of increasing employment and income. The increase in domestic output may tend to raise the domestic price level, through the operation of increasing marginal real costs of production, and conversely the foreign price level may tend to fall, thus partially counteracting the initial effects of the switch policy; but such repercussions can legitimately be analysed in terms of elasticity concepts, since under-employment implies that additional factors are available at the ruling price.

If the economy is already fully employed, however, the additional output required cannot be provided by increasing production; it can only be provided through a reduction in the previous level of real expenditure.[16] This reduction may be brought about either by a deliberate expenditure-reducing policy introduced along with the switch policy, or by the inflationary consequences of the switch policy itself in the assumed full-employment conditions.[17]

If the increased output is provided by a deliberate expenditure-reducing policy, the nature of this policy will obviously influence the effects of the expenditure-switching policy, since the composition of the output it releases may be more or less substitutable for foreign output in world demand. Thus, for example, an expenditure-reducing policy which reduces domestic demand for imports and

[16] Recognition of this point may be regarded as the fundamental contribution of the absorption approach, though none of the authors cited seems to have appreciated all its implications: Meade, for example, analyses the case on the assumption that an appropriate expenditure-reducing policy is in effect, without examining the interdependence between the two policies or the alternative of inflation, while Alexander does not recognise that the effects of inflation on absorption could be achieved by policy.

[17] For analytical simplicity, the possibility of both increased production through 'over-full employment' and of direct expenditure-reducing effects of a switch policy (discussed earlier in this chapter) are ignored here.

exportable goods will be more favourable to expenditure-switching than one which reduces domestic demand for non-traded goods. The analysis of the effects of an expenditure-switching policy supported by an expenditure-reducing policy must therefore comprise the effects of the latter in determining the composition of the productive capacity available to meet the increased demand created by the former, as well as the elasticity relations which govern the effects of the interaction of increased demand with increased production capacity on the prices and volumes of goods traded.

If the expenditure-switching policy is not accompanied by an expenditure-reducing policy, its effect will be to create an inflationary excess of aggregate demand over supply, leading to price increases tending to counteract the policy's expenditure-switching effects. Inflation, however, may work towards curing the deficit, through various effects tending to reduce the level of real expenditure from the full employment level of output. These effects, which are familiar and have been analysed in detail by Alexander, include the effect of high marginal tax rates in increasing the proportion of real income absorbed by taxation as wages and prices rise, the possibility of a swing to profits increasing the proportion of income saved, and the effect of rising prices in reducing the real purchasing power of cash and government bonds held by the public, so reducing their wealth and propensity to consume. All of these effects, it may be noted, depend on particular asymmetries in the reactions of the sectors affected to the redistributive effects of inflation on real income or wealth, which may not in fact be present. The important point, however, is that these factors, on which the success of an expenditure-switching policy depends in this case, are monetary factors, and that the analysis required employs monetary concepts rather than elasticity concepts. As in the previous case, the elasticity factors are subordinate to the factors governing the reduction in aggregate real expenditure, in determining the consequences of the expenditure-switching policy for the balance of payments.

The argument of the previous paragraph—that in full employment conditions the success of expenditure-switching policies depends mainly on the effectiveness of the consequent inflation in reducing real expenditure—helps to explain both the prevalence of scepticism about, and hostility towards, exchange rate adjustment as a means of curing balance-of-payments disequilibria, and the fact that historical experience can be adduced in support of the proposition that devaluation is a doubtful remedy. The argument does not, however, support the conclusion frequently drawn from the analysis of devaluation in these circumstances, that import restrictions are to be preferred; this is a *non sequitur*, since import restrictions are equally an expenditure-switching policy. Rather, the proper conclusion is that expenditure-switching policies are inappropriate to full employment conditions, except when used in conjunction with an expenditure-reducing policy as a means of correcting the employment-reducing effects of the latter.

But what of the choice between devaluation and selective trade controls, to which reference has just been made? So far, it has not been necessary to distinguish between them, since from the point of view of the balance of payments both can be treated as expenditure-switching policies. It is from the point of view of economic welfare that they differ; and the arguments on their relative merits have nothing to do with the state of the balance of payments, except that if controls are preferable a deficit may offer an opportunity for introducing them with less risk of foreign retaliation than if trade were balanced.

The welfare arguments for controls on a country's international trade may be divided into two groups, those centring on controls as a means of influencing the internal distribution of real income, by discouraging imports consumed by the rich and encouraging those consumed by the poor, and those centring on controls as a means of increasing the country's gains from trade through exploiting its monopoly/monopsony power in foreign markets. The former are of doubtful validity, both because the ethics of disguising a real income policy as a trade policy are suspect, and because both the efficiency and the effectiveness of trade controls as instruments for governing real income distribution are dubious. The latter are valid, to the extent that the country has powers to exploit the foreigner and can use them without provoking sufficient retaliation to nullify the gains.

This is the familiar optimum tariff argument. Its application to balance-of-payments policy depends on the level of trade restrictions already in force, as compared with the optimum level of restrictions.[18]

[18] See S. Alexander, 'Devaluation versus Import Restriction as an Instrument for Improving Foreign Trade Balance', *International Monetary Fund Staff Papers*, I, no. 3, April 1951, 379–96, for a lucid and pioneering exposition of this principle.

If an expenditure-switching policy is required to correct a deficit, and the level of trade restrictions is below the optimum, restriction[19] is preferable to devaluation until the optimum level is reached; in the opposite case, devaluation is preferable. But it is the relation of actual to optimum restrictions, and not the state of the trade balance, which determines whether restriction is desirable or not.

This concludes the analysis of alternative policies for correcting a 'flow' balance-of-payments deficit on current account. To complete the analysis of 'flow' disequilibria, it would be necessary to relax the assumption that international capital movements are confined to reserve movements between foreign exchange authorities, and to consider alternative policies for correcting a deficit on current and capital account combined. The central problem in this case is to determine the level of current account surplus or deficit, capital export or import, at which economic policy should aim. This raises two further problems too difficult to pursue here: the optimum rate of accumulation of capital for the community as a whole, and the degree to which it is desirable to discriminate in favour of investment at home and against investment abroad.

In conclusion, the argument of this chapter may be summarised as follows: formulation of the balance of payments as the difference between aggregate receipts and payments, rather than receipts and payments on international account only, has two major advantages. It brings out the essentially monetary nature of a deficit, which must be accompanied by dishoarding of domestic money or credit creation; and it relates the deficit to the operation of the economy as a whole. A deficit may reflect a 'stock' decision or a 'flow' decision by the community. The conditions which make a 'stock' deficit a policy problem indicate the use of direct control methods as against price system methods of correction. Policies for dealing with 'flow' deficits on current account may be divided into expenditure-reducing and expenditure-switching policies; in full employment conditions the latter must be supported by the former, or rely on inflation for

---

[19] Generally, optimum trade restriction entails restriction of both imports and exports; but if the country's currency is over-valued it may imply subsidisation of some or even all exports, and if the currency is under-valued it may imply subsidisation of some or even all imports. (These conclusions follow from the fact that a devaluation is equivalent to an all-round export subsidy and import duty.)

their effect, which in either case cannot be analysed adequately in terms of elasticities. When capital account transactions are introduced into the analysis, the choice between policy alternatives requires reference to growth considerations not readily susceptible to economic analysis.

3

Barter Theory and the Monetary
Mechanism of Adjustment[1]

ROBERT A. MUNDELL

The barter theory developed by Ricardo and his school evolved, in the hands of Mill, Marshall, Edgeworth, and modern writers, into a carefully tooled and sophisticated engine of analysis. Elaborations took many directions. Comparative cost doctrine was extended to the many-country many-commodity case by Edgeworth, Bastable, and Graham and was further refined by modern linear programming techniques. The theory of comparative costs was deepened by a model introduced by Heckscher that undertook to explain differences in productivity that the Ricardian school had merely postulated; the factor endowment model too was elaborated and refined in the hands of Ohlin, Iversen, Lerner, Stolper-Samuelson, and Samuelson in writings that have now become classics. The classical system was finally extended into the framework of general equilibrium theory in the hands of Yntema, Mosak, and Samuelson, while the earlier work of Edgeworth on the laws of contract under competition provided the starting point for the theory of the core of an economy.

There is a sense, however, in which the successful nature of the barter theory, in achieving constant refinement and extension, created a vacuum in international trade theory. There was no comparable development of the short-run monetary theory of the adjustment process. Whereas the barter theory of exchange exploited the powerful geometric and algebraic tools that had become prominent in value theory, permitting analytical developments surpassing the possible achievements of unaided intuition, international

[1] Reprinted from R. A. Mundell, *International Economics* (New York, Macmillan, 1968), ch. 8.

monetary economic analysis never received precise mathematical formulation. Restrained by limited techniques, international monetary analysis did not develop the rigorous base that was required for an orderly self-sustaining growth of scientific knowledge.

Even today we have a double standard. We demand rigorous logic from practitioners of the fine art of offer curve analysis, in striking contrast to much looser standards exacted in monetary economics as a whole. Attacking the real world from a lower level of abstraction, international monetary economics offers a greater appearance of realism than barter theory, but it is achieved at the sacrifice of precision and rigour. Monetary analysis appears to be a 'soft' area of research because it is harder to separate, on grounds of logic alone, the foolish from the fertile. Reaching further into the real world it has lost track of the 'axioms' along its trail by which its rigour can be established.

My purpose is not to belittle important developments in international monetary economics in the last two decades, but rather to emphasise that these developments have not succeeded in integrating classical monetary theory with classical barter theory. Innovations in the field since the 1930s have stressed the application of Keynesian economic concepts to the international sphere, rather than the integration of Keynesian international economics with classical barter theory or classical international monetary economics, creating a weakness in the area.

To a certain extent this weakness is the unavoidable product of two dominating forces. The 1930s witnessed simultaneously two important revolutions in the science: one was in macroeconomics, led by Hayek, Myrdal, and, above all, Keynes; and one was in technique, led by Frisch, Tinbergen, Leontief, and Samuelson. The younger people interested in trade theory at the time leaned toward Keynesianism and many also picked up the mathematical techniques that were becoming prominent in value theory and in business cycle theory. It was natural, therefore, that when mathematical techniques came to be extended to international trade theory the models chosen would be Keynesian.[2]

[2] Mosak's work was an exception, but he was working in a different milieu (Chicago) in the 1940s, where Keynes's ideas were not regarded as so novel; in any case his example is the exception that proves the rule because his treatise is itself an important landmark in international trade theory.

Good theory is good theory and there is no doubt that there was much in the *General Theory* that could be used to refresh and revise international monetary economics. But in practice the Keynesian revolution held back trade theory. Fundamental theoretical problems in macroeconomics had not been solved. The major weakness lay in the very place in which Keynes had hoped to make his major theoretical contribution, the integration of the monetary and real sectors of a closed economy. His attempt to integrate the two sectors was faulty. This turned out to be a weak spot in the *General Theory*, but it was one that could be concealed for a couple of decades in macroeconomic theory. Its weakness, however, could not be sustained for any length of time when one attempted to construct a model of the international economy incorporating monetary elements. As a result the Keynesian model applied to the international economy in the 1940s was the naïve one leading in the direction of matrix multiplier theory, a model of considerable mathematical interest, but of little use in resolving the problems of integrating a sophisticated theory of money into international monetary economics.

The purpose of the present enquiry is to make a fresh start at removing the weaknesses of international economics. But before defining the limits of the enquiry it is necessary to say something about the contributions of Meade to the subject.[3]

In his studies Meade attempted an integration of the work of Slutsky and Hicks and Mosak on the one hand, and Keynes on the other. In this he was only partially successful. The monetary and employment sectors were grafted on to the model rather than built into it. Writing as he was before the problems of valid and invalid dichotomisation of the monetary and real sectors of an economy had

---

[3] The two-volume work by Meade on *The Theory of International Economic Policy* is a landmark in the theory of international trade and economic theory in general, and it will be the source of fruitful insights into economic theory for years to come. There is no question in my mind that the reviews of this work published in the 1950s did not do justice to it or recognise its real significance as a major treatise on economics. This is only partly because of defects of its organisation and presentation. To be sure the dichotomy between lucid, but unexciting prose, forbidding notation in the first mathematical supplement, and the separate publication of an isolated companion volume of tough geometry were tactical mistakes in presentation; so was the author's reticence in drawing attention to the originality of his own work. But I should attribute its tepid reception rather to the state of confusion of the science in the early 1950s, and the lack of sensible criteria by which merit could be separated from chaff.

been brought out or resolved, it would have been extremely difficult to solve, at the time, the most subtle problems of the pure theory of money. That Meade's own model, buried in the mathematical supplement to *The Balance of Payments*, incomplete and unsatisfactory as it is, is still one of the best attempts at the integration of monetary and real analysis in the theory of international trade, is the most eloquent testimony to the importance of his contribution and at the same time the most devastating criticism of the current state of theoretical work in international monetary economics.

Bridges are necessary between the barter and the monetary models, on the one hand, and between the classical and Keynesian traditions in international economics, on the other. This need is, I think, obvious and needs no further elaboration. But, how should money be 'added' to barter models of trade, and how can classical analysis be united with Keynesian concepts?

The general purpose of this chapter is to make a start on this problem by creating connecting links between classical international monetary economics and the theory of barter, and between classical and Keynesian concepts and methods of analysis. The first bridge requires the development of an explicit theoretical model of the classical balance-of-payments adjustment process, a model that can be shown to be reducible in principle to a barter model, the second requires that the model can be expressed either in the classical language of the quantity theory of money, or in the Keynesian language of income-expenditure equalities.

I shall make two assumptions that in subsequent work can and should be generalised: One is that the country under consideration is a small economy looking outward on a large world, the other is that it lacks a credit market. These simplifications are not damaging to the logical structure of the model although they do limit the direct applicability of the conclusions to a small country that is under-developed in the sense that it lacks an important capital market.

Despite the simplicity of the model, I would maintain that it is of direct use in analysing simple open economies, and in that spirit I have discussed the effects of devaluation, income transfers, budget deficits, and reserve accumulation, and not made any attempt to conceal what I believe to be some practical implications for policy of the insights thus gained.

INCOME, EXPENDITURE, AND THE QUANTITY OF MONEY

The model I shall develop owes its origin to David Hume. Based on a very simple open economy, it assumes that wealth is held in the form of money and goods. The key assumptions that greatly simplify the analysis are that there is no market for securities and that the world price of imports is given by considerations outside the model.

Consider such a simple economy. The demand for money depends on money income or, assuming output is given, the price level, in accordance with the *quantity theory of money*. The supply of money is determined by the balance of payments, either because international reserves and domestic money are the same, as under a gold specie standard, or because domestic money is rigidly linked to the stock of international reserves through the banking system.

Three conditions must be met before the system can be said to be in equilibrium. Firstly, the supply of money must be equal to the demand for money; secondly, the balance of payments must be in equilibrium; and, thirdly, the demand for domestic output must equal the supply of domestic output. If the first condition were not met there would be a tendency for spending to exceed or fall short of income; if the second were not met the money supply would be increasing or decreasing; and if the third were not met the domestic price level would be rising or falling.

The significance of the equilibrium conditions can be seen diagrammatically. First let us represent the quantity theory of money by placing on one axis the quantity of money, M, and on the other axis the domestic price of home-produced goods, P. The line LL portrays the amount of money that would be demanded at each price level. Thus at a price level equal to OP_1, the demand for money is OM_1; and at a price level equal to OP_2, the demand for money is OM_2. Normally LL will have an elasticity exceeding unity on the assumption of the *homogeneity postulate* of economic theory, because a proportionate change in the price level implies a less than proportionate increase in the demand for money when the price of all imported goods remains constant.

Every point in Figure 3.1 corresponds to a particular combination of money and price level. For example, at the point G, the price level is OP_1 and the actual quantity of money is OM_2. G is not an equilibrium point, for it implies inequality between the demand for money

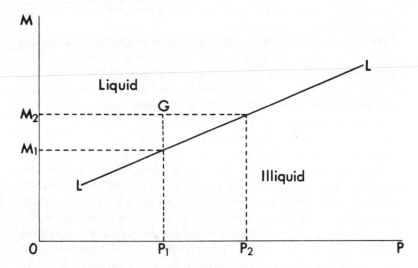

Figure 3.1.   The state of liquidity.

and the supply of money. At G there is an excess supply of money equal to M_1M_2. Only if the supply of money were reduced to OM_1 would the demand for money be equal to the supply of money at the price level OP_1, or only if the price level were at OP_2 would the demand for money be equal to the supply of money OM_2.

Only points on LL are equilibrium points. Above and to the left of LL the supply of money is greater than the demand for money, and below and to the right of LL the demand for money is greater than the supply of money. The area above and left of LL is an area of excess liquidity, and the area below and right of LL is a zone of liquidity scarcity. I shall refer to the first zone as 'liquid' and to the second zone as 'illiquid'.

From the characterisation of the two zones we may now ask what happens when there is an excess or deficient level of liquidity. This is a question in economic dynamics and can only be answered by reference to observable behaviour. The community holds money and goods, so that if they have an excess demand for money they must also have an excess supply of goods, just as an excess supply of money means that they have an excess demand for goods; this follows from Walras' Law that the sum of the values of excess demands for every economic object (including money) is zero for any individual economic agent.

We have not yet stated what happens in a position of excess or deficient liquidity, although we have found a clue. When there is an excess supply of money there is an excess demand for goods, and this will mean that, *unless increased supplies are forthcoming*, prices will rise. And similarly, when there is an excess demand for money there also is an excess supply of goods, so prices will tend to fall *if no additional demand is forthcoming*.

It is important to emphasise at this point, however, that it is not valid to assert in the context of an open economy, that the price level rises or falls according to whether there is excess or deficient liquidity. However valid this dynamic postulate may be in a closed economy, it is incorrect in an open economy. An excess supply of money implies an excess demand for goods *in general* and an excess of expenditure over income, but the *domestic* price level would only be pushed up in so far as the excess of expenditure reflected an excess demand for *domestic* goods. In so far as an excess demand for goods can be expended on imports, the price level will have no tendency to rise. Indeed, as the subsequent analysis will show, an excess of liquidity is entirely consistent with deflationary pressure in the market for home goods and services.[4]

Domestic expenditure—expenditure by domestic residents on both home and foreign-produced goods—is assumed to depend on income (defined as domestic output multiplied by its price) and liquidity. Specifically, we assume that expenditure equals income if the community is satisfied to hold the existing stock of money, and that any excess of planned expenditure[5] over expected income is proportionate to the excess supply of money. Thus an excess supply of money means that expenditure exceeds income, as the community tries to rid itself of excess cash holdings; and, similarly, an excess

---

[4] In what follows we assume that an excess demand for foreign goods (imports) is automatically satisfied to avoid complicating the analysis with the otherwise necessary distinction between the *ex ante* and *ex post* balance of payments; this assumption would be realistic enough if importers kept sufficient stocks on hand to satisfy any incipient excess demand, and were willing to accumulate stocks (and reduce orders correspondingly) in the event of any excess supply.

[5] Expenditure is defined in an *ex ante* sense of a schedule of plans rather than as an actual realised magnitude. An expenditure function of this sort was used by Prais and is a novelty that deserves wider application.

demand for money means that expenditure falls short of income, as the community tries to build up its cash holdings.

According to this assumption expenditure equals income only when the demand for money is equal to the supply of money, so we can describe the condition of balance between the two by the *LL* line in Figure 3.1, except that we now have an additional interpretation of it. Not only is *LL* the line along which the demand for money is equal to the supply of money, it is also the line along which planned money expenditure is equal to expected money income.

We next place in the diagram (Figure 3.2) a line *BB* expressing the locus of combinations of the price level and the money supply resulting in a zero balance of payments; assuming for now no capital imports, *BB* is also the line along which the trade balance is

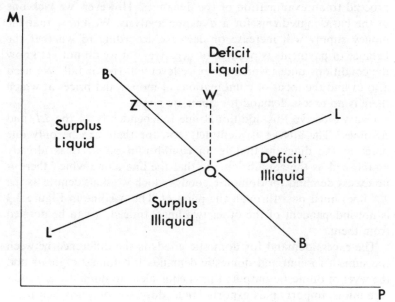

Figure 3.2.   The balance of trade and liquidity.

zero. We assume that the balance of trade depends both on domestic expenditure and on the price level. As we shall see, this means that the slope of *BB* will normally be negative.

To see why the slope is negative consider the point *Q*, where income equals expenditure (because Q is on LL) and where the balance of payments is in equilibrium (because Q is on BB); and suppose from Q the money supply is increased by QW. At W there is an excess supply of money so that expenditure rises in excess of income. Part of the increase in expenditure falls on imports, and part on export goods, increasing the former and decreasing the latter, creating, at W, a balance-of-payments deficit.

To correct the deficit the domestic price level can be lowered to shift both home and foreign demand away from foreign products on to domestic products. There must be some lower price level at which the balance of trade will again be in equilibrium if the system is stable. In the diagram this point is taken to be the point Z.

We now have two schedules that intersect at an equilibrium point, Q, at which the system will rest if it is stable. We could now proceed to an examination of the dynamics. However, we lack one of the basic ingredients for a dynamic analysis. We know that the money supply will increase or decrease according to whether the balance of payments is positive or negative, but we do not yet know the conditions under which the price level will rise or fall. We need also to find the locus of combinations of money and prices at which there is no excess demand for domestic goods.

Can we derive this additional line independently of the LL and BB lines? The answer is, definitely not, for there can be only one point in the diagram that is an equilibrium point. Q is already established as the equilibrium, so that the line along which there is no excess demand for domestic goods (which we shall denote as the XX line) must pass through the point Q. The XX line in Figure 3.3 is not independent of the other two lines. Indeed, it can be derived from them.

The excess demand for domestic goods is the difference between the sum of foreign and domestic demands for domestic goods and the level of domestic output; this is equivalent to domestic expenditure minus imports plus exports minus domestic output when these variables are all expressed in units of home goods. In other words, the excess demand for domestic goods is equal to the difference between the sum of planned domestic expenditure plus the balance of trade, and expected income. Thus by 'adding' the BB and LL curves we get the XX curve, the locus of money and price levels along which there is no excess demand for domestic goods.

It is easy to determine the position of XX in Figure 3.3. It must have a positive slope that is steeper than LL. To demonstrate this fact let E = expenditure, Y = income, and B = the balance of trade.

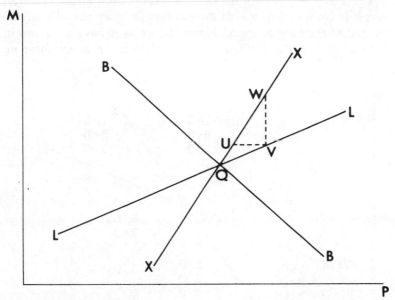

Figure 3.3. Liquidity, the balance of trade, and excess demand.

Then consider, in Figure 3.3, the point V on LL. At V, $E = Y$, so the excess demand for domestic goods ($X = E + B - Y$) is equal to the balance of trade surplus (B). But B is negative because V is in the deficit zone above and right of BB. Hence there is excess supply of domestic goods that can be corrected only by a decrease in the domestic price level or a liquidity-induced increase in expenditure. Thus, in Figure 3.3, an increase in the money supply of VW would eliminate the excess supply of domestic goods, as would a decrease in the price level by the amount UV.

THE ANATOMY OF DISEQUILIBRIUM AND DYNAMICS

Having established the new line XX, as derived from the BB and LL lines, we can note that we could have begun with any two of the lines to get the third line. Knowing *XX* and *BB* we can deduce *LL*, knowing *LL* and *XX* we can deduce *BB*, and knowing *BB* and *LL* we can deduce *XX* (as we did, in fact). No single one of the lines has any priority over the other.

The interdependence of the three curves does not mean, however, that it is not useful to use all three curves for purposes of analysis. Instead of the four zones of Figure 3.2 we now have six zones in Figure 3.3—repeated in Figure 3.4. The elaboration of the meaning

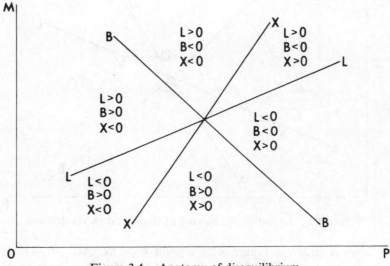

Figure 3.4.   Anatomy of disequilibrium.

of these zones can help us to determine exactly the nature of the disequilibrium. The six zones are characterised by the state of

EXCESS LIQUIDITY (L)
THE BALANCE OF PAYMENTS (B)
DEFLATIONARY PRESSURE (X)

which are denoted positive or negative by the inequality signs in Figure 3.4.

The separation of the zones is useful for policy purposes because it helps to determine the direction in which the money supply or price level should be adjusted to reach equilibrium. Thus, if we observe a situation in which $B < 0$ and $X < 0$, we know that the money supply must be reduced; if $B < 0$ and $X > 0$, the price level must be reduced; if $B > 0$ and $X > 0$, the money supply must be increased; and if $B > 0$ and $X < 0$, the price level must be increased. We can observe the disequilibrium situation, and, even though we are ignorant of the exact shapes of the curves, deduce the direction in which the money supply and the domestic price level have to move to restore equilibrium.[6]

The development of the XX line along with the anatomy of disequilibrium zones allow greater precision in formulating the dynamics of the system. It can be postulated that the money supply increases or decreases according to whether the balance of payments is in surplus or deficit, and that the price level rises or falls according to whether there is inflationary or deflationary pressure (excess demand or supply of domestic goods). In other words, the line demarcating price-level increases from price-level decreases over time is the XX line and that distinguishing increases from decreases in the money supply is the BB line. The dynamic forces are indicated by the arrows in Figure 3.5.

From a disequilibrium point like W, a point that could be reached as a result of an 'annihilation' of part of the money supply, following the famous experiment first considered by Hume, the reduction in the money supply would reduce expenditure and hence imports. This implies an improvement in the balance of payments, which would induce a replenishment of the money supply. (Unlike Hume's

---

[6] It is, perhaps, a harmless parody on the history of economic thought to refer to LL as the Say's Law line (because along LL the demand and supply of money are equal), to XX as the Keynes's Law line (because along XX the excess of investment over saving equals the excess of imports over exports) and to BB as the Hume's Law line (because along BB imports equal exports). In the conceptual language of the Keynesian model, supplemented now for completeness by including T, the rate of capital export, we can make the following identifications:

Along XX, SAVING − INVESTMENT = TRADE BALANCE
Along LL,   CAPITAL EXPORTS = SAVING − INVESTMENT
Along BB,   TRADE BALANCE = CAPITAL EXPORTS.

This illustrates the mutual interdependence of the schedules at Q, an equilibrium that could be characterised as 'Mill's Intersection' in view of Mill's correct statement of what has become known as Walras' Law.

In the following dynamic argument a partial dynamical approach is taken. More refined dynamical analysis would take account, in the formulation of dynamic hypotheses, of all markets in the system.

analysis, the present model shows that money can have a direct effect on the balance of payments through its immediate impact on expenditure, part of which inevitably falls on imported goods.)[7] From *W* deflationary pressure forces the price level down and the

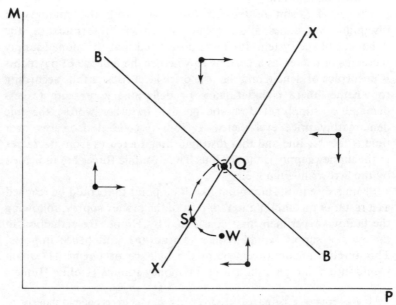

Figure 3.5.   The dynamics of disequilibrium.

balance of payments surplus stimulates a monetary expansion, both forces moving the path of money and prices to a point like *S* on the *XX* line. After *S* the system travels to the equilibrium *Q* either directly or in a spiral, as indicated in Figure 3.5.[8]

[7] I consider the immediate effect of a reduction in the money supply on the balance of payments as of the utmost importance in the adjustment mechanism, quite separate from ultimate effects on income. It accounts for a far more prompt adjustment under fixed exchange rates than has hitherto been realised.

[8] Strictly speaking, *Q* would no longer be the equilibrium if (1) the initial disturbance implied a change in the real wealth position of the country (as it would if foreign exchange reserves were 'annihilated' with no quid pro quo), (2) the process of restoring equilibrium itself influenced capital formation and real wealth ('hysteresis' effects), or (3) the domestic disequilibrium caused a

THE CLASSICAL CASE AND DEVALUATION

In developing the model we began with the money line LL, but in the dynamic computation it was shunted into the background. To be sure, it is implicit in the XX and BB schedules, because these curves depend on expenditure, which in turn depends on the excess demand or supply of money. But does it not deserve more explicit prominence? Does LL not have direct relevance?

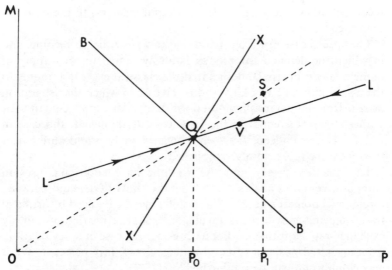

Figure 3.6. The classical approach and the quantity theory.

Its importance asserts itself in another form than in stability analysis. Its importance lies in the solution of those comparative statics questions that involve shifts of demand between domestic and foreign goods without any alteration in the demand for money, and it preserves its importance even for dynamic analysis in the special case where the community maintains equality of expenditure

permanent change in foreign wealth positions. In this chapter, which is a first attempt at an exact account of the mechanism, we emphasise first-order effects alone, and it seems legitimate to abstract from these considerations. Subsequent analysis, however, would, it is hoped, take them into account.

and income, a case that can be identified closely with classical analysis.

To investigate this interesting dynamic phenomenon first, consider Figure 3.6, where it is assumed that spending is always equal to income. Equality of E and Y automatically implies that the excess demand for domestic goods (the degree of inflationary pressure) equals the balance-of-payments deficit. The dynamic path therefore always remains on the LL line and adjustment consists solely of moving up or down the LL line. Under these conditions we should observe a strict conformity of money and the price level (or money income if allowance were made for output changes) to the quantity theory equation.

The special case in which spending is always equal to income, and in which the demand for money is always equal to the supply of money, may properly be designated the classical case: it amounts to the assumption of Say's Law and is the case in which the separation of real from monetary phenomena is exact. An excess demand for domestic goods is equal to the balance-of-trade deficit, the case in which a correspondence between monetary analysis and pure barter theory can be most closely established.

The quantity theory and the LL line have additional uses in comparative-statics analysis involving the shifts of demand between foreign and domestic goods. These shifts may be induced by artificial trade impediments such as tariffs or exchange restrictions, or by exchange-rate adjustments. Let us consider the case of a devaluation, from an initial position of equilibrium of, say, fifty per cent. What new equilibrium will be established?

We may find the new equilibrium by conducting a hypothetical experiment: what would happen if the domestic price level were doubled, the money supply were doubled, and the exchange rate (the price of domestic currency in terms of foreign currency) were halved. Clearly there would be no change in any real variable because market participants would have the same real money balances and incomes as before, and there would have been no change in relative prices. This is the case in which the purchasing power parity theory of the exchanges, which is the international counterpart of the quantity theory of money, is most relevant.

Devaluation from a position of equilibrium will in fact *induce* a proportionate increase in the price level and the money supply.

Again the relation between money and prices will be unaltered, as predicted by the quantity theory. For example, a devaluation, in Figure 3.6, in the proportion of P_0P_1/OP_0 would induce a rise in the price level and the money supply to the level indicated by S, a point along OQ-extended, above LL.

It is hardly necessary to point out, of course, that no country would need to devalue if it were already in equilibrium (unless it needed to accumulate exchange reserves). The usefulness of the analysis is rather in showing the type of *disequilibria* that can be corrected by changes in the exchange rate. We may reverse the procedure and suppose that *equilibrium* levels of money and prices are at Q, but that the price level and the money supply are *actually* at levels indicated by S. Obviously a deflationary process would reduce the price level and the money supply to Q under the atuomatic fixed-exchange-rate adjustment process. But the deflation involved may be a painful process, and would involve unemployment if factor prices were rigid. The adjustment can be avoided by a devaluation of the proportion of P_0P_1/OP_0 (without any accompanying change in the money supply or the price level).

BUDGETARY POLICY

Still another reason why the LL line is of great importance is in the analysis of *disequilibrium policies*. Suppose the government runs a budget deficit annually, which it finances by money creation. What new 'equilibrium' will be established?

To analyse this question we have to go back to the basic equilibrium conditions implicit in the system and introduce government spending, supposing this to be financed solely by money creation,[9] and a central bank equation determining the money supply. First we have the condition of equilibrium in the home goods market:

$$Y = E + B + G \tag{1}$$

where E (domestic expenditure) is defined exclusive of G (government

---

[9] It could be assumed that government spending is partially financed by taxes, but there is no need to introduce even this minor complication to establish the theoretical conclusion.

expenditure). Next we have a definition of the relation between exchange reserves and the balance of trade:

$$B = \frac{dR}{dt} \tag{2}$$

where R represents international reserves. And, finally, we have the banking condition stating that the increase in banking assets is equal to the increase in banking liabilities (the money supply), noting that in this system of no lending the banking authorities, merged with the government, can only hold goods or foreign reserves. Thus

$$G + \frac{dR}{dt} = \frac{dM}{dt} \tag{3}$$

remembering that G represents both the value of government spending and the budget deficit. Now if the domestic goods market is in balance [that is, if equation (1) is satisfied] and total expenditure equals income, it follows that

$$B + G = \frac{dM}{dt} = 0 \tag{4}$$

is a condition of equilibrium. This equality between the balance of payments deficit and the deficit in the government budget represents a condition of 'quasi equilibrium'.

Consider point V in Figure 3.6. This shows the nature of the quasi equilibrium that would result from a budget deficit financed by credit creation. The money supply is constant, but this is because the increase in domestic assets of the banking and government sector is exactly matched by a decrease in the foreign assets of that sector. The government, which may initially try to finance its deficit by creating more money, finds that its deficit is really being financed out of foreign exchange reserves; in every other respect the system is in equilibrium. Of course, the process cannot go on for ever, because exchange reserves are not inexhaustible; it is in that sense that position V is a quasi equilibrium.

By a similar analysis it can be shown that, by means of a budget surplus, a country can attract reserves at a rate equal to a budget surplus of the government, after equilibrium has been re-established in all other markets and sectors.

THE TRANSFER PROBLEM

We may consider next how analysis of the transfer problem fits into the model. When there are international transfers, the equations of equilibrium have to be supplemented. Before we used three equations:

$$Y - E = B$$

establishing equilibrium in the market for goods and services.

$$Y - E = 0 \quad \text{or} \quad M - L = 0$$

establishing equality of expenditure and income or equality of demand for money (L) and supply of money (M), and

$$B = 0$$

specifying balance of payments equilibrium. To take account of international transfers we have instead

$$Y - E = B \tag{5}$$

as before, for the market for domestic goods and services, but then

$$Y - E = T \tag{6}$$

for equality of income and expenditure plus transfers abroad (Y being defined as before exclusive of transfers), where T represents net outward transfers, and

$$B - T = 0 \tag{7}$$

establishing balance-of-payments equilibrium, that is, equality of the balance of trade surplus and outward transfers (or net capital exports).

To illustrate the transfer process let us consider the effect of an inward transfer so that T is negative; the country receives foreign aid or borrows. Following the traditional transfer analysis, expenditure in the rest of the world falls, and expenditure at home rises, by the full amount of the transfer, directly affecting the balance of trade. Part of the decrease in expenditure abroad reduces exports, and part of the increased expenditure at home increases imports. The financial transfer gets at least partially effected in real terms by the direct impact of the expenditure changes before any effects have been felt on the balance of payments.

Whether the financial transfer is over-effected or under-effected depends on the size of the marginal propensities to spend on imports, as compared to home goods, out of domestic expenditure inclusive of the transfer. If the marginal propensity to consume domestic goods in the receiving country exceeds the foreign marginal propensity to import, the result of the transfer will be an excess demand for domestic goods and a surplus in the balance of payments, which will induce an increase in the domestic price level as money flows in. In other words, a position on the LL line up and to the right of Q will be the new equilibrium.

If, on the other hand, the marginal propensity to consume domestic goods in the receiving country is less than the foreign marginal propensity to import, the primary effect of the transfer is to shift demand away from domestic goods, worsen the balance of payments, and induce a fall in domestic prices as the money supply declines.

In the intermediate case where the domestic marginal propensity to consume domestic goods is equal to the foreign marginal propensity to import, there is no change in the price level or the terms of trade. The expenditure changes caused by the direct effects of the transfer are the same as the final effects; the receiving country buys, as a result of the transfer, just those goods which the rest of the world gives up.

Thus, even in the case where monetary elements are explicitly introduced into the transfer analysis, the effect of the transfer on the terms of trade is ambiguous. Nothing *a priori* can be asserted. There is no reason to suppose, unless aid is 'tied' or without specific empirical information, that the receiving country gains by more or by less than the normal amount of the transfer.[10]

[10] This conclusion would have to be altered if it were assumed that the demand for the stock of money in each country were itself dependent, not only on the

GROWTH AND LIQUIDITY

In an economy that is growing over time the money supply will be rising over time and with it the willingness of the monetary authorities to acquire reserves. In this case we can relate the budget deficit or surplus to the rate of growth.

First note that if the non-government sector of the community wants to accumulate money, it must spend less than it earns, so that

$$Y - E = \frac{dL}{dt} \tag{8}$$

where dL/dt is the desire to accumulate money over time.

Next recall that a balance of trade surplus results in an increase in reserves, so that

$$B = \frac{dR}{dt}. \tag{9}$$

Finally, note the condition that increases in official foreign and domestic assets (net public spending) equal increases in monetary liabilities (the money supply), so that, as before,

$$\frac{dR}{dt} + G = \frac{dM}{dt}. \tag{10}$$

Then it follows that when $dM/dt = dL/dt$, that is, when the community's desires for additional money are satiated at existing prices, there is also equilibrium in the market for goods and services, as

$$B + G = \frac{dM}{dt} = \frac{dL}{dt} = Y - E. \tag{11}$$

---

value of domestic production, but on national income, inclusive of the transfer from abroad. This is an unsolved problem in monetary theory that is of considerable potential significance. In practice willingness to hold money will depend on the past nature of the transfer, and in particular whether working balances arising from the use to which the capital import is put are held in foreign currency or in domestic currency.

Now let the desire to accumulate money be proportionate to the growth of money income so that

$$\frac{dL}{dt} = k\frac{dY}{dt}. \tag{12}$$

We also have from (9) and (10) that

$$\frac{dM}{dt} = B + G \tag{13}$$

so that growth equilibrium requires

$$B + G = k\frac{dY}{dt} = k\left(\frac{1}{Y}\frac{dY}{dt}\right)Y = k\lambda Y \tag{14}$$

where λ is the rate of growth of output. If the rate of growth is positive, the budget deficit will no longer equal the balance of trade deficit. The sum $B + G$ must equal the resources sacrificed by the private sector to build up its cash balances over time.

Now assume that the authorities want to keep a fixed proportion of reserves to back domestic money creation, so that

$$R = \alpha M \tag{15}$$

where α is a fraction. Then, if this holds over time we have

$$\frac{dR}{dt} = \alpha\frac{dM}{dt} \tag{16}$$

so that, if we substitute for dR/dt making use of (10) we get

$$G = (1 - \alpha)\frac{dM}{dt} \tag{17}$$

or

$$G = (1 - \alpha)k\lambda Y \tag{18}$$

after making use of (13) and (14). If (18) is now put in (14) we get

$$B = \alpha k \lambda Y \quad \text{or} \quad \frac{B}{Y} = \alpha k \lambda. \tag{19}$$

In other words, the balance of trade surplus, expressed as a proportion of income, that is required to satisfy both the community's appetite for money and the authorities' appetite for reserves, is proportionate to the rate of growth, the factor of proportionality being αk, the ratio of foreign reserves to national income.

But we must take account of the fact that interest may be paid on the foreign reserves held by the monetary authorities; let us assume it is paid at the rate r. Then interest becomes a foreign exchange receipt and the balance-of-payments equation, instead of (9), becomes

$$B + rR = \frac{dR}{dt}. \tag{20}$$

The increase in the money supply is then determined by the equation

$$G + \frac{dR}{dt} = rR + \frac{dM}{dt} \tag{21}$$

because the interest payments now represent a source of government finance supplementary to money creation. In this case the required balance of trade expressed as a proportion of national income, turns out to be

$$\frac{B}{Y} = (\lambda - r)\alpha k \tag{22}$$

while the budget deficit is

$$\frac{G}{Y} = -(\lambda - r)\alpha k + k\lambda. \tag{23}$$

To summarise, the balance of trade must be positive or negative, for monetary growth equilibrium, including growth of exchange reserves, depending on whether the domestic rate of growth exceeds or falls short of the rate of interest paid on foreign exchange reserves. By leaving its reserves on deposit, in a foreign centre such as New York or London, a country may well finance the bulk of its additional reserve needs.

CONCLUSIONS

I have attempted to extend some of the theoretical conclusions of classical international trade theory in a wider framework using a simple model that can be reconciled with classical and Keynesian concepts. The basic assumption, that there are no securities, means that monetary and fiscal policies are not distinct from one another and that balance-of-payments problems persist because of the failure of the authorities to balance the budget. This model is not irrelevant to many of the less developed countries, and it contains insights into the adjustment process for developed countries as well.

Devaluation is a means by which a country, whose prices and costs have got out of line internationally, can restore equilibrium without the less attractive alternatives of deflation or trade and exchange controls. Bygones have to be accepted as bygones. However, looking prospectively rather than retrospectively, incipient deficits can be prevented by a monetary policy that is directed at preserving equilibrium in the balance of payments rather than at financing budget deficits.

International capital movements or foreign aid need not present balance-of-payments difficulties for either the receiving or transfer-ring country. The bulk of the transfer may be effected in real terms by direct expenditure effects, and it may even be over-effected. In any case the residual gap to be corrected by the adjustment process is necessarily smaller than the initial transfer.

A growing country should make some provision for increasing its international reserves over time to provide the extra safety, convenience, choice of adjustment measures, and cushioning for bad harvests that foreign reserves can provide. But a secular growth of reserves does not require a balance of trade surplus if reserves are held in the liquid assets of a deposit centre and interest is paid on them. In this connection, it should be remarked that the attachment to a major currency area such as the dollar area or a sterling area presents, for a smaller country, an opportunity that many current plans for international monentary reform do not provide.

As a rule of thumb, for a growing country, provision should be made for an increase in the money supply every year. But the proper rule is not to fix attention on a constant rate of growth of the money supply, as suggested by Friedman; the spirit of this rule is maintained only if the Friedman's companion proposal of flexible exchange rates is accepted. Instead, the authorities should keep in mind a rate of central bank *credit expansion* more or less equal to the rate of growth after making due allowance for income elasticities of credit demand differing from unity and altering needs for real money balances in the economy. This leaves room for the adjustment process to operate under fixed exchange rates, because it implies that the money supply will grow at a slower or faster rate than central bank credit expansion depending on whether there is a deficit or surplus in the balance of payments.

Fixed exchange rates, coupled with an absence of controls and a monetary policy that pays close attention to the balance of payments, can be a powerful instrument for generating the confidence needed to attract foreign capital. For the smaller countries there is no alternative system better adapted for generating a climate in which rapid growth can take place. It is difficult to see how the policies currently adopted by many of the smaller less developed countries, with the proliferation of controls, inflated budgets, and excessive inflation can be conducive to attracting needed capital imports or encouraging private investment to proceed in a stable environment of confidence. A restoration of freer commodity and exchange markets, fewer controls over the private sector of the economy, and greater automaticity in the balance-of-payments adjustment process could lay an improved foundation for a properly run, efficiently managed country.

APPENDIX

Three Monetary Standards

The text restricts the analysis to the case of a fixed exchange system. The method, however, is easily generalised to alternative monetary standards. This appendix is designed to illustrate a method of analysing these alternative standards and to show how the results can be generalised.

For purposes of analysis let us identify three markets—goods, foreign exchange, and money—in the economic system and let X, F, and L denote, respectively, the flow excess supplies in these markets. Assume that the conditions of market equilibrium depend on the domestic price level, the price of foreign exchange, and the stock of money. Then we have three conditions of equilibrium as follows:

$$X(P, \pi, M) = 0 \tag{24}$$

$$F(P, \pi, M) = 0 \tag{25}$$

$$L(P, \pi, M) = 0 \tag{26}$$

Under suitable assumptions we can identify $X = 0$ with $Y = E + B$, $F = 0$ with $B = T$, and $L = 0$ with $Y = E + T$, where Y, E, B, and T are now all interpreted in a behavioural (*ex ante*) sense. On the basis of this identification it can be seen that the three equations are interdependent, since $X = 0 = F$ implies $Y = E + T$, $X = 0 = L$ implies $B - T$, and $F = 0 = L$ implies $Y = E + B$. The equations are homogeneous of the first degree if X, F, and L are interpreted in value terms, and homogeneous of zero degree if they are expressed in real terms.

There are three cases of special interest worth isolating: (1) M is constant and π and P are variable, (2) π is constant and M and P are variable, and (3) P is constant and M and π are variable. The first case may be referred to as the monetary standard (the stock of money is fixed), the second as the international standard (this is the case analysed in the text), and the third as the commodity standard.

The three standards are illustrated by Figures 3A.1, 3A.2, and 3A.3 on the assumption that goods, money, and foreign exchange are all substitutes for one another. This information is sufficient to establish the condition of disequilibrium true for each diagram indicated in Table 3A.1.

Table 3A.1

Market Zone	Excess supply of goods (X)	Excess supply of foreign exchange (F)	Excess supply of money (L)
I	+	+	−
II	+	−	−
III	+	−	+
IV	−	−	+
V	−	+	+
VI	−	+	−

The arrows in the zones indicate the movement of the (two) variables for each of the three standards under the most plausible dynamic assumptions. Thus, if the supply of money is fixed (Figure 3A.1), the exchange rate will appreciate (depreciate) when there is an excess demand for (supply of) both goods and money; the price level will rise (fall) when there is an excess supply of both money and foreign exchange; and both the price level and the price of foreign exchange will rise (fall) when there is an excess demand for (supply of) both domestic goods and foreign exchange. A similar analysis applies when the money supply is variable and either the price of domestic goods or the exchange rate is stabilised once it is recognised that stabilisation policy implies that the authorities are purchasing or selling the stabilised object and thus increasing or decreasing the money supply whenever there is, respectively, an excess demand or supply of the stabilised object.

This development provides a general framework within which balance-of-payments problems can be studied under various

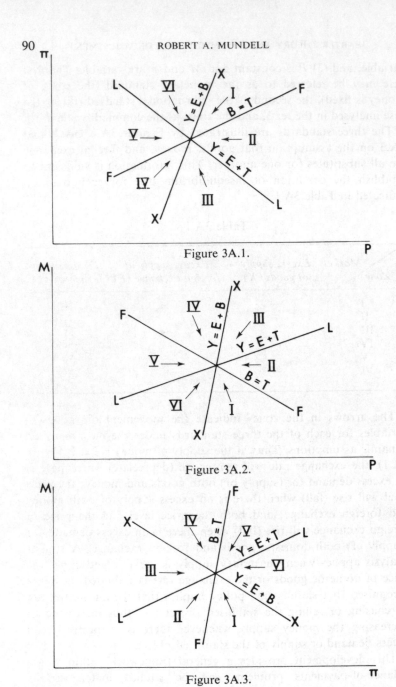

Figure 3A.1.

Figure 3A.2.

Figure 3A.3.

exchange systems. In each of the diagrams the balance of payments is in disequilibrium whenever the domestic price level, the exchange rate, or the money supply does not generate a point on the *FF* lines in any of the graphs. Cases of disequilibrium in the balance of payments imply disequilibrium in other markets, and after the counterparts are identified the direction of the equilibrium points, and therefore the required movements of the other variables in the system, can be ascertained.

The analysis, moreover, is readily generalised to any number of commodities, following traditional general equilibrium lines. In the foregoing, for example, it is implicitly assumed that wages and domestic prices move together. Suppose, however, that there are excess demands for the l types of goods, $X_1, \cdots, X_l$; m types of labour, $N_1, \cdots, N_m$; n types of foreign exchange, $F_1, \cdots, F_n$; and domestic money. Then the homogeneity and interdependent properties of the above system are retained in the following generalised case:

Goods:
$$X_1(P_1, \cdots, P_l; W_1, \cdots, W_m; \pi_1, \cdots, \pi_n; M) = 0$$
$$X_l(P_1, \cdots, P_l; W_1, \cdots, W_m; \pi_1, \cdots, \pi_n; M) = 0$$

Labour:
$$N_1(P_1, \cdots, P_l; W_1, \cdots, W_m; \pi_1, \cdots, \pi_n; M) = 0$$
$$N_m(P_1, \cdots, P_l; W_1, \cdots, W_m; \pi_1, \cdots, \pi_n; M) = 0$$

Foreign exchange:
$$F_1(P_1, \cdots, P_l; W_1, \cdots, W_m; \pi_1, \cdots, \pi_n; M) = 0$$
$$F_n(P_1, \cdots, P_l; W_1, \cdots, W_m; \pi_1, \cdots, \pi_n; M) = 0$$

Money:
$$L(P_1, \cdots, P_l; W_1, \cdots, W_m; \pi_1, \cdots, \pi_n; M) = 0$$

where the P's denote prices, the W's wages, and the π's exchange rates.

III. FURTHER DEVELOPMENTS

4

The International Distribution of Money in a Growing World Economy[1]

ROBERT A. MUNDELL

The purpose of this chapter is to analyse the conditions of world monetary equilibrium in a comprehensive bi-country framework that links inflation, interest rates, money stocks, rates of credit expansion, and the balance of payments in a growing world.

THE CONDITIONS OF MONETARY EQUILIBRIUM

The model we shall use for this purpose[2] requires balance in two markets: a market for claims against money and a market for capital against money. It assumes that in making the choice between holding money, claims, and capital the typical investor balances expected yields on each asset, where expectations are based on an extrapolation of current rates of change. Thus, if prices of commodities are rising at the rate π it is assumed that they will go on rising at

---

[1] Reprinted from R. A. Mundell, *Monetary Theory* (Pacific Palisades: Goodyear, 1971), 147–69.

[2] A simple version of the model at the micronational level is given in my *International Economics* (New York, Macmillan, 1968), chap. 9; and in a somewhat different version at the macronational level, 'Real Gold, Dollars and Paper Gold', *American Economic Review* 59 (May 1969), 324–31. Related theoretical work can be found in *Monetary Problems of the International Economy*, edited by Robert Mundell and Alexander Swoboda (Chicago, University of Chicago Press, 1969) and the contributions there of Grubel, Schmidt, Sjaastad and Johnson; also R. Komiya, 'Economic Growth and the Balance of Payments: A Monetary Approach', *Journal of Political Economy* 77 (Jan.–Feb. 1969), 35–48; and a paper by Arthur Laffer, including empirical tests.

that rate; and similarly for changes in the prices of claims. This assumption, which would be fully justified only in consideration of an economy in growth-inflation equilibrium, enables us to isolate some important comparative dynamic properties of an international economic system and to develop a convenient representation of it in graphical form.

The line *ii* in Figure 4.1 refers to the money-claims market in which the nominal interest rate is taken to be a declining function of real money balances, plotted on the abscissa. At low interest rates the community is willing to hold the outstanding stock of securities only if the quantity of real money balances is high. When the rate of interest rises people shift out of money into claims, raising the price level and lowering the real value of money balances. We shall write this function as

$$i = i(m),$$

where $m = M/P$, the real value of money holdings, and i is the rate of interest paid on claims.

The *rr* schedule plots the relation between the real interest and the stock of real money balances at which the money-capital market is in equilibrium. It can be derived by making use of the extension of the diagram in the left-hand quadrant. The abscissa in this quadrant

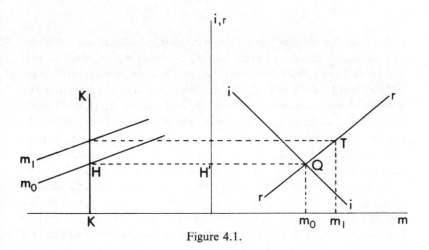

Figure 4.1.

measures the quantity of capital, and the schedule KK indicates the stock of capital, a magnitude which is marching to the left over time under conditions of growth, but which at any instant can be regarded as given. The line m_0 identifies the schedule of the marginal product of capital corresponding to the quantity of real money balances m_0. This intersects the capital stock schedule KK at the point H and establishes the real rate of interest corresponding to the level of real money balances m_0. Thus Q is one point on the rr schedule.

Consider now an increase in the quantity of real money balances to, say, m_1. This raises the marginal product of capital and shifts the H line upwards, establishing a new point of equilibrium on the rr line at the point T. In a similar way all the points on rr can be established, and it is readily seen that this schedule must have a positive slope. We shall write this function in the form

$$r = r(m),$$

where r is the real rate of interest.

The equilibrium interest rate and level of real balances is determined, in the absence of growth of capital or money, by the intersection of the two schedules, that is, at the point Q. The equilibrium condition is that $i = r$, so that

$$i\left(\frac{M}{P}\right) = r\left(\frac{M}{P}\right)$$

determines the equilibrium level of real money balance, m_0. At levels of real money balances lower than m_0 the marginal product of real capital is lower than the marginal product of money, and asset holders would shift out of commodities into money, lowering the price level and raising the quantity of real money balances. To put the question differently, raising the rate of interest above r_0 would create an excess supply of money and capital and an excess demand for securities, inducing a fall in the rate of interest and a return to the equilibrium at Q. Thus Q is an equilibrium that is stable.

Now consider the effects of taking growth explicitly into account (Figure 4.2). Growth induces an increased desire for liquidity (hoarding) and thus an increase in spending less than the increase in real output. If we define the rate of growth in the demand for real money balances as a proportion of the capital stock, we can subtract it from the rr line to get $\lambda\lambda$. For simplicity of exposition we shall also identify this schedule with the rate of growth of output, an identification which is probably a valid approximation for certain types of output increases, but is precise only under specific assumptions about the income elasticity of demand for real money balances.[3]

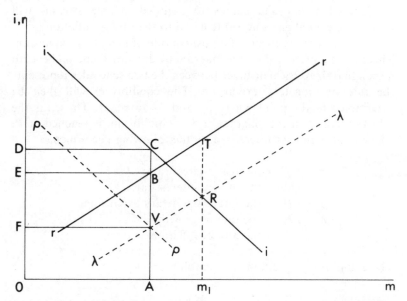

Figure 4.2. Inflationary growth equilibrium.

When the economy is growing but the stock of money is constant, the equilibrium will be at R. The price level will be falling at a rate equal to the rate of growth, and the real rate of interest will be

---

[3] Real money balances are a component of wealth and thus affect saving and the rate of interest [see my 'Inflation and Real Interest', *Journal of Political Economy* 71 (June 1963), 280–3] while the rate of growth of output itself will be affected by the productivity of capital; on the basis of these considerations the hoarding could be made endogenous to the system. My concern in this chapter, however, is with the international aspects of a long-term model, and it seemed appropriate to avoid over-burdening the exposition with details I have worked out for publication elsewhere: hence my technique of treating growth exogenously.

higher than the nominal rate of interest by the deflation rate RT. The condition of equilibrium is that

$$i\left(\frac{M}{P}\right) - r\left(\frac{M}{P}\right) = \pi = -\lambda,$$

where π is the rate of inflation and λ is the given rate of growth. Holders of money and claims to nominal income streams will experience capital gains at a rate equal to the rate of inflation.

Now consider the effects of a positive rate of monetary expansion. This can be represented on the diagram by drawing a line $\rho\rho$ beneath ii such that the vertical distance between the two schedules represents the rate of monetary expansion. The equilibrium will then be determined at the point where $\rho\rho$ and $\lambda\lambda$ intersect. Thus, for the schedule drawn in the diagram, a new equilibrium is reached at V. The equilibrium is characterised by the following phenomena:

$$r = OE = \text{the real interest rate;}$$
$$i = OD = \text{the money interest rate;}$$
$$\rho = FD = \text{the rate of monetary expansion;}$$
$$\lambda = FE = \text{the rate of growth;}$$
$$\pi = BC = \text{the rate of inflation.}$$

The equilibrium conditions are as follows:

$$i\left(\frac{M}{P}\right) - r\left(\frac{M}{P}\right) = \pi;$$

$$\rho = \pi + \lambda;$$

$$\lambda = \lambda_0;$$

$$\rho = \rho_0.$$

The comparative 'statics' of the system are thus established. An increase in the rate of monetary expansion lowers the real interest rate, raises the money interest rate, and lowers the level of real money balances. This is readily seen by differentiating the above system and noting that $\partial i/\partial(M/P) < 0$ and $\partial r/\partial(M/P) > 0$.

MONETARY INTERACTION BETWEEN ECONOMIES

Let us now consider the situation that arises when it becomes necessary or useful to divide the world economy into two or more distinct parts. Assume that the two parts use the same money and freely trade in goods but do not lend to one another. What monetary relationships would we expect to emerge? Let us assume first that the money supply in the world as a whole is fixed.

The first relationship is that money will move from slow-growing to fast-growing regions. The inhabitants of the fast-growing country will keep expenditure below output to generate a balance-of-payments surplus in order to finance money accumulation. This will exert deflationary pressure on the world as a whole. The effect, therefore, will be capital gains to the non-growing region as the real value of their cash balances appreciates, permitting them to export over time a fraction of their money stock to the other region. Equilibrium will be achieved when the world price level is declining at the rate sufficient to satisfy the desired increase in the real money stock in the growing country. The growing country finances its accumulations of new real money balances from two sources: (a) imports of money from the other region and (b) rising real value of hoards. The growing region's balance-of-trade surplus represents a transfer of resources to the non-growing part analogous to the seigniorage gain when one country alone is the issuer of money.

The equilibrium is represented in Figure 4.3. Let us denote the two countries by A and B, the latter being the growing region. Equilibrium in the absence of growth would be established by the intersection of the *rr* and *ii* schedules in the two countries. Growth in B now involves a reduction in expenditure and releasing of goods for export (or reduction of imports) to finance money accumulation. Deflationary pressure in B then results in a flow of goods to A in return for more imports of money, while the loss of money from A and the hoarding of money in B combine to produce deflationary pressure in the world as a whole. The conditions of equilibrium require that deflation in both countries goes on at the same rate because of the connected markets, meaning that the difference between real and nominal interest rates must be the same in both countries. A second condition is that the desired increase in real money balances in the growing country B be equal to the actual increase generated by the sum of the capital gains on their existing stock of real money balances and B's balance-of-trade surplus. The latter must be equal to the trade deficit of country A, which in turn has to equal the increase in the real value of existing money balances in A. Taken together, these conditions imply that

$$\frac{\lambda_b + \pi}{\pi} = -\frac{m_a}{m_b},$$

where the subscripts identify the countries. This means that the rate of world deflation due to growth in country B is

$$\pi = -\lambda_b \frac{m_b}{m_a + m_b},$$

that is, the rate of growth in B weighted by the size of B in relation to the world as a whole, the weights being the stocks of money. This result can easily be derived from the diagram since it implies that the two hatched areas are equal in area: they represent the real value of B's trade surplus and A's trade deficit.

It is a short step to take into account growth in country A. Growth in A creates more deflation in the world as a whole and diminishes A's deficit and B's surplus. When A and B grow at the same rate the deficit becomes zero, the appetite for real money balances in both countries being satisfied by the deflation in the world as a whole. This is readily seen from the generalisation of the above formula:

$$\pi = -\frac{\lambda_a m_a + \lambda_b m_b}{m_a + m_b}.$$

MONETARY EXPANSION IN ONE COUNTRY

Let us now elaborate the model by allowing for monetary expansion. If, in Figure 4.3, country B had the right to issue money, the authorities could create it by purchasing domestic assets, fully satisfy the hoarding demand occasioned by growth, and eliminate the balance-of-payments surplus. In so far as the balance-of-payments surplus may be regarded as a tax, the monetary independence implied by the right to issue money would enable the residents of B to avoid paying the tax.

It will be somewhat more instructive, however, if we first analyse the equilibrium that results when country A has the sole right to

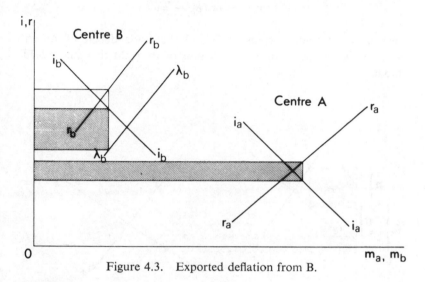

Figure 4.3.   Exported deflation from B.

issue money. Consider in Figure 4.4 a given rate of money expansion in A equal to the vertical distance between $\rho_a\rho_a$ and $i_a i_a$. If A were isolated this would result in inflation in A equal to the rate of monetary expansion and a transfer of resources from A residents to the government of A. But when country B is taken into account the rate of inflation in A is mitigated: the tax that A's government levied upon its citizens by the issuing of money will be paid partly by B.

The exact position of equilibrium will again depend on the relative sizes of the two countries. The conditions of equilibrium require that the rates of inflation in the two countries must be the same, and that A's deficit equals B's surplus. Thus the two hatched areas must be equal and

$$\rho m_a = \pi(m_a + m_b)$$

or

$$\frac{\pi}{\rho} = \frac{m_a}{m_a + m_b}.$$

This ratio measures the percentage of the tax that is borne by the residents of A, whereas

$$m_b\pi = m_a(\rho_a - \pi)$$

measures the trade surplus of B and the trade deficit of A—the seigniorage tax accruing to A because of its right to issue 'world' money.

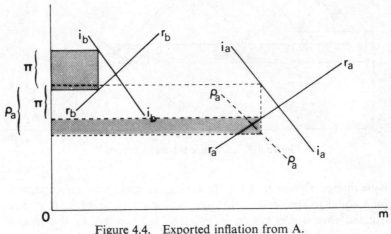

Figure 4.4.   Exported inflation from A.

Let us now analyse the more complete system that emerges when A is issuing money and both countries are growing. How will the new money be distributed between the two countries, and what balance-of-payments configuration will result?

The answers are provided in Figure 4.5. It will be convenient to identify five types of seigniorage arising from the monetary expansion in A. The total seigniorage is $\rho_a m_a$, which represents the purchasing power obtained by A's government when it issues money at the rate ρ_a, expressed as a fraction of money held in A. Internal seigniorage is the tax on A's residents, and external seigniorage is the tax on B's residents:

I πm_a = internal inflation seigniorage. This is due to the need of residents in A to rebuild cash balances eroded by price inflation.

II $\lambda_a m_a$ = internal growth seigniorage. This is due to the need of residents in A to add to real cash balances because of growth. External seigniorage is the tax on B's residents and is equal to A's balance-of-payments deficit.

III $(\rho_a - \pi - \lambda_a)m_a$ = external seigniorage. This can be interpreted as the flow excess supply of money in A, her balance-of-payments 'deficit'.

IV $\lambda_b m_b$ = external growth seigniorage. This arises from the desire of residents in B to acquire money to finance growth.

V πm_b = external inflation seigniorage. This represents the real value of the desired increment in nominal money balances required to compensate for the capital losses suffered on existing balances.

Clearly, when A's *ex ante* deficit is equal to B's *ex ante* surplus

$$III = IV + V$$

and the system is in 'equilibrium'.

It will be convenient to have a symbolic characterisation of some of these results. First, from the fact that total seigniorage

$$\rho_a m_a = I + II + III$$

we have

$$\rho_a m_a = \pi m_a + \lambda_a m_a + (\pi + \lambda_b)m_b,$$

so

$$\frac{m_a}{m_b} = \frac{\pi + \lambda_b}{\rho_a - \pi - \lambda_a}.$$

Now B's 'desired surplus' is

$$(\pi + \lambda_b)m_b$$

and A's 'desired deficit' is

$$(\rho_a - \pi - \lambda_a)m_a,$$

so that, when the two are in equilibrium the rate of inflation is

$$\pi = \frac{(\rho_a - \lambda_a)m_a - \lambda_b m_b}{m_a + m_b} = \frac{(\rho_a - \lambda_a)\dfrac{m_a}{m_b} - \lambda_b}{\dfrac{m_a}{m_b} + 1} = \frac{(\rho - \lambda_a)\sigma - \lambda_b}{\sigma + 1},$$

where σ is the ratio of money held in A to money held in B. The non-inflationary rate of monetary expansion in A is thus

$$\rho = \frac{\lambda_b}{\sigma} + \lambda_a$$

Thus when $\lambda_b = 0$, A's money supply must grow at a rate equal to

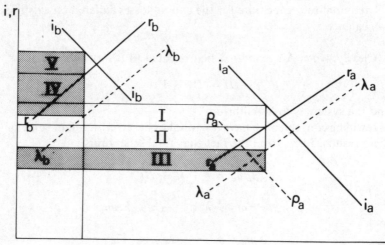

Figure 4.5.   The incidence of the seigniorage.

  I A's internal inflation seigniorage.
 II A's internal growth seigniorage.
III A's deficit.
IV A's external growth seigniorage.
 V A's external inflation seigniorage.

III = IV + V

the rate of growth of her economy if price stability is to be preserved. Other results of this kind are readily obtained from the formula.

'DEFENSIVE' MONETARY EXPANSION IN B

The monopolised right to issue money grants to A the possibility, not only the right, of determining the rate of expansion of the means of exchange and therefore, indirectly, the rate of change in the world price level; and also the means of taxing real resources from the rest of the world in addition to her own citizens. We shall refer to this right as the *issue privilege*. To offset it or to ameliorate its more outrageous effects, country B will create her own currency and confine her losses to the foreign exchange component of the banking assets which are the counterpart of the monetary liabilities. What effect will this have on the equilibrium?

It should be apparent that, for any given rate of monetary expansion in A, an increase in the rate of *credit* expansion in B is inflationary for the world as a whole. When there is an *ex ante* deficit in A the monetary authorities in B accumulate reserves. To resist undesired reserves they extend domestic credit and, in a sense, engage in competition for seigniorage that would otherwise accrue to A. The result is that the world price level as a whole rises at a more rapid rate than would otherwise occur. Suppose that, from a position of initial equilibrium, growth in B accelerates. This would ordinarily result in a surplus in B as residents hoard, and the result would be a deflation (or a slower rate of inflation) in the world as a whole as the *ex ante* surplus bids money away from A. But the demand-induced surplus in B can be prevented if B's authorities extend credit, assuming that B's money is convertible into A's money and is therefore a perfect substitute for it for internal transactions, and provide residents in B with the money they want through domestic banking operations. This prevents deflation or accelerates inflation, for if the government in B had not expanded, residents in B would have had to finance growth by sucking money away from the rest of the world.

We might also consider the effects of a credit expansion in B without any initiating increase in hoarding. The effect is to create an excess supply of money and an *ex ante* deficit in B so that its central bank will lose reserves. Unless the extension of credit in B is large, most of its effect will be taken up by a loss of reserves. But if B has initially very large reserves and can therefore afford a large extension of credit, the effects on the world money supply may be substantial, and there would result a significant effect on the world price level. For a given rate of monetary expansion in A, the potential increase in the world price level that could be induced by credit expansion in B depends on the ratio of the stock of reserves in B as a proportion of the world money supply. As this fraction increases the power of B to raise world prices is increased.

These results are useful first approximations, but they are not exact. To formulate more exact propositions it will be useful first to present the effects of credit expansion in B diagrammatically and then to develop the analysis in symbolic terms. It will simplify the diagrammatic exposition somewhat, without loss of essential generality, if we start off (Figure 4.6) with a situation in which the rate of credit expansion in B is zero and where the rate of monetary expansion in A is such as to ensure price stability in the world at large. A's rate of monetary expansion is AC, which exceeds A's rate of growth BC by enough (AB) to finance B's rate of growth DE without any changes in the price level.

Now suppose that from this position, where B is running a surplus to accumulate desired real balances, the central bank in B expands credit by the full amount of the surplus, i.e. at the rate ED. If A now reduced her rate of monetary expansion to BC, A's deficit and B's surplus would be corrected. But suppose instead that A maintains her rate of monetary expansion at the rate AC. Then the deficit in A is 'unwanted' in B, and there is an excess supply of money equal to the area $FGDE = ABHJ$, and a corresponding excess demand for goods. The price level must therefore rise to absorb the excess money.

Where will the new equilibrium be? The answer is found by establishing that level of real balances in A at which two conditions are met. First, the excess of the money over the real rate of interest in A must equal the excess in B. Second, the excess of A's rate of monetary expansion over the sum of her rate of growth and the rate of inflation multiplied by her stock of real money balances (A's *ex ante* deficit) must equal the excess of the sum of the inflation rate and B's growth rate over B's rate of credit expansion multiplied by the stock of real balances in B (B's *ex ante* surplus). The second condition means that the two hatched areas are equal.

We see, therefore, that B's attempt to eliminate her surplus is not wholly successful. The rate of credit creation DE causes inflation which increases the demand for additional money to compensate for the depreciation on existing balances.

To formulate the results exactly let us write the equilibrium conditions:

$$i_a(m_a) - r_a(m_a) = \pi = i_b(m_b) - r_b(m_b)$$

$$m_a(\rho_a - \lambda_a - \pi) = B = (\pi + \lambda_b - \delta_b)m_b$$

where B is the balance of payments deficit in A (surplus in B), and δ_b is the rate of credit expansion in B.[4] Now it is possible to see that when, initially, $\delta_b = 0$ and $\pi = 0$ the balance of payments deficit of A is

$$(\rho_a - \lambda_a)m_a = B = \lambda_b m_b.$$

When B now expands credit at the rate determined by the rate of growth of output, A's deficit becomes

$$(\rho_a - \lambda_a - \pi)m_a = B = (\pi)m_b,$$

[4] Differentiation of these equations with respect to δ_b yields

$$\frac{dm_a}{d\delta_b} = m_b\frac{(i_b' - r_b')}{\Delta} < 0,$$

$$\frac{dm_b}{d\delta_b} = m_b\frac{(i_a' - r_a')}{\Delta} < 0,$$

$$\frac{d\pi}{d\delta_b} = \frac{(i_a' - r_a')(i_b' - r_b')}{\Delta} > 0,$$

$$\frac{dB}{d\delta_b} = \frac{m_b(\rho_a - \lambda_a - \pi) - m_a(i_a' - r_a')}{\Delta}(i_b' - r_b'),$$

where

$$\Delta = \begin{vmatrix} i_a' - r_a' & r_b' - i_b' & 0 \\ \rho_a - \lambda_a - \pi & \delta_b \div \pi - \lambda_b & -m_a - m_b \\ 0 & i_b' - r_b' & -1 \end{vmatrix};$$

the inequalities are based on the assumption that $\Delta > 0$.

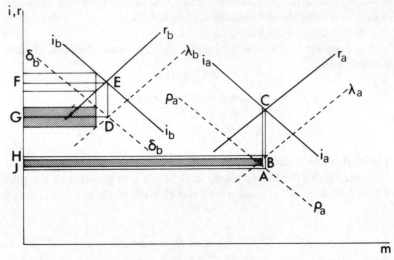

Figure 4.6.   Defensive measures in B.

which is still positive if B's credit expansion results in inflation, as
indeed it must since it reduces the *excess* flow demand for money in
A. To correct her surplus by her own actions alone B must expand
credit at the rate

$$\delta_b = \lambda_b + \pi.$$

Now

$$\pi = (\rho_a - \lambda_a) \frac{m_a}{m_a + m_b} + (\delta_b - \lambda_b) \frac{m_b}{m_a + m_b},$$

or simply

$$\pi = \rho_a - \lambda_a.$$

Thus

$$\delta_b = \lambda_b + \rho_a - \lambda_a.$$

Country B's expansion rate must exceed her growth rate by the
excess of A's rate of monetary expansion over A's growth rate. This
is because the inflation itself induced by B's credit expansion increases the hoarding demand for money.

CONCLUSION

This chapter has presented an image of the world payments situation different from that found in the literature and currently used to interpret balance-of-payments statistics. For a given rate of credit creation in each of the countries the balance of payments is determined by the rates of growth of transactions and output.

In the real world, of course, rates of credit expansion are policy variables and will in most cases be positive functions of domestic growth rates. Domestic growth creates in the first instance a desire for increasing money which reduces expenditure below income, puts pressures on the credit markets, and generates a balance of payments surplus. The additional money will be automatically created as the central bank intervenes in the exchange market to prevent currency appreciation, thus creating domestic money at the same time that it adds to its holdings of foreign exchange reserves. To prevent unnecessary accumulations of reserves the central bank will purchase domestic assets, e.g. government bonds, and satisfy, by internal monetisation, the growth-induced increases in desired cash. Different central banks, of course, will pursue different policies; some, for example, will try to maintain the same ratio of foreign reserves to central bank liabilities; others may vary the reserve ratio to keep domestic reserves a given fraction of imports. But in each case the autonomous variable in monetary policy is the rate of internal credit creation (the purchase of domestic assets), while the passive element is the rate of reserve increase. The public determines the quantity of money it wants to hold and the rate at which it is to be increased, while the central bank determines that part of it which will be backed by foreign reserves.

When we take into account interactions with the rest of the world, these propositions need to be adjusted. At the microeconomic level credit expansion has no effect on the money supply. But in the world as a whole a dollar's worth of money created anywhere in the system adds exactly that much money to the money supply of the system as a whole. At the microeconomic level the national communities determine the quantity of money they want. But at the macroeconomic level the nominal quantity of money is determined by the collective policies of the various central banks, while the world community as a whole determines its real value. If the collective money supply of the world economy is greater than the quantity desired, the world price level will rise until its real value has been adjusted to the level the community wants to hold.

This is not to say, of course, that the policies of various countries are symmetrical with respect to one another. Positions of dominance and subordination arise with respect to the different currencies. In the present configuration of the world economy the other nations keep their currencies convertible into the dollar, not the other way around. The U.S. monetary authorities are not constrained to govern their monetary policy by other than domestic considerations, since the only way the foreign central banks can avoid accumulating dollar holdings is by inflating themselves. The struggle on the part of the dominant country to acquire external inflation seigniorage at the expense of foreign countries and the resistance to paying the imposed tax on dollar balances can thus readily lead to a situation of competitive inflation.

5

A Dynamic Analysis of the Balance of Payments in a Model of Accumulation[1]

JACOB A. FRENKEL

1 INTRODUCTION

Traditionally, the theory of international economics has been divided into the real sector on the one hand and the monetary sector on the other. This somewhat artificial dichotomy has led to the development of theories in which the monetary and the real sectors of the economy have not been sufficiently integrated.

This chapter attempts to develop a theory of the secular evolution of the balance of payments which integrates the monetary and the real sectors in both production and consumption. Special attention is given to the influence of the real growth of the economy on the monetary behaviour underlying balance-of-payments developments. The analysis is confined throughout to the 'small-country' case, i.e. the case of a country whose terms of trade can be taken as fixed regardless of its growth.

Section 2 draws on previous work by Leontief (1958) and Liviatan (1965, 1966) to develop a simple model of the savings and accumulation behaviour of an individual over a succession of time periods. Section 3, which is the core of the chapter, extends this model to the aggregate behaviour of an open economy. Its main contribution is a technique for the incorporation of liquidity services in a 'generalised Rybczynski line'; this generalised Rybczynski line is then used to determine the secular evolution of the overall balance of payments, the current account and the capital account. A key assumption is that

[1] This chapter is adapted from Frenkel (1971). It modifies the factor intensity assumption used in the earlier paper so as to conform with the more conventional assumption.

only claims to income streams from capital equipment and not capital goods themselves can be internationally exchanged. The analysis is extended to include the role of money as a producers' good as well as the source of liquidity services for consumers. Section 4 alters the previous assumptions about savings behaviour— so as to make savings self-limiting—and discusses the existence and characteristics of a long-run steady state equilibrium of consumption and production. Section 5 concludes the text. The appendix provides the formal structure of the barter model and a framework for the analysis of its dynamics.

2 A MODEL OF ACCUMULATION: THE INDIVIDUAL'S BEHAVIOUR

To facilitate the diagrammatic analysis, a modified version of Leontief's technique is used. The essence of the technique is to generalise Fisher's asymmetric two-period model to a multi-period model which is capable of being visualised as a two-dimensional diagram. This is done by representing the 'future' as a perpetual stream of future consumption.[2]

Consider an individual consumer with a given wealth W_0, who plans to consume over $n + 1$ periods by maximising a utility function $U(C_0, C_1, \ldots, C_n)$ subject to the wealth constraint. It is assumed that he acts in a competitive market and faces a given set of prices and interest rates which are expected to stay constant. The budget constraint (in terms of present consumption) at the beginning of the horizon is:[3]

$$W_0 = C_0 + \frac{C_1}{1 + i} + \frac{C_2}{(1 + i)^2} + \cdots \qquad (1)$$

Since by assumption the rate of interest (i) is the same for all periods, the relative price of consumption between any two consecutive periods is constant. This constancy permits use of Hicks' composite good theorem. Define:

[2] For a rigorous treatment, see Liviatan (1966).
[3] It is assumed that income is received and consumed at the beginning of each period.

$$F = \sum_{t=1}^{\infty} \frac{C_t}{(1+i)^t}, \tag{2}$$

where F is the composite good of future consumption. Thus, solution of a reduced system in a two-dimensional diagram is possible. In a (C_0, F) plane, the tangency between a utility function $V(C_0, F)$—which is assumed to be independent of time—and a budget line $W = C_0^* + F$, solves for the optimal values of consumption in the first period and of capital accumulation. This route is taken by Liviatan (1966).

In the following analysis, the problem is discussed in terms of present and future consumption, where the latter can be maintained indefinitely. The perpetual future consumption C_p must satisfy the budget constraint. Thus:

$$\frac{C_p}{1+i} + \frac{C_p}{(1+i)^2} + \ldots = \frac{C_1}{1+i} + \frac{C_2}{(1+i)^2} + \ldots, \tag{3}$$

or equivalently,

$$C_p \sum_{t=1}^{\infty} \frac{1}{(1+i)^t} = \sum_{t=1}^{\infty} \frac{C_t}{(1+i)^t}. \tag{4}$$

The left-hand side of (4) is the product of C_p and the present value of a perpetuity of one dollar, beginning with the next period. Thus the constant potential stream of future consumption is:

$$C_p = i \sum_{t=1}^{\infty} \frac{C_t}{(1+i)^t} \tag{5}$$

and the budget constraint (1) becomes:

$$W_0 = C_0 + \frac{C_p}{i}. \tag{6}$$

Figure 5.1 describes this constraint. As can be seen, the absolute value of its slope exceeds unity as long as the rate of interest is below 100 per cent. A sacrifice of one dollar of present consumption enables the consumer to consume $i in *every* future period. The individual is in a long-run equilibrium if he neither adds to nor subtracts from his wealth. His wealth at the beginning of the second period is W_1:

$$W_1 = (1 + i) \frac{C_p}{i}. \tag{7}$$

Subtracting (6) from (7) yields

$$W_1 - W_0 = C_p - C_0. \tag{8}$$

Equating (8) to zero yields the *locus* of the long-run stationary equilibrium points. The 45° line in Figure 5.1 describes this *locus*.

The short-run equilibrium point is determined at the tangency of the indifference curve with the budget line E_0E_0. If the tangency is such that $C_p > C_0$ (point A), the individual is accumulating capital, and the budget constraint for the next period becomes E_1E_1. If, however, $C_p < C_0$ (point B), the opposite holds and the next period's constraint becomes E_2E_2. By shifting the budget line to alternative positions, we derive the *locus* of tangencies *ICC* (the income–consumption curve), which combines all possible short-run equilibrium points. Two alternative short-run equilibrium schedules are drawn. A *locus* like *OBL* results in a monotonic decline in wealth, and a *locus* like *OAK* results in a monotonic accumulation. A long-run stationary equilibrium exists if the *ICC* intersects with the 45° line, and, as can be verified, the stability of such an equilibrium requires that the *ICC* be steeper than the 45° line. In other words, the existence of a stationary equilibrium requires that the marginal propensity to consume out of permanent income exceeds unity around the stationary equilibrium. If it does not exceed unity an *ICC* of the *OAK* type is implied, which in turn implies that a secular accumulation takes place.

The analysis hitherto has not specified the exact form in which the individual holds his wealth and consumes the services. Since at the level of the aggregate economy the composition of wealth and consumption plays a crucial role, it is helpful to incorporate it at the present stage.

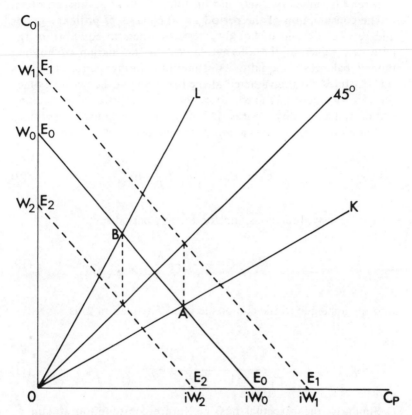

Figure 5.1.   Equilibrium of consumption and the path of accumulation.

The marketable wealth of the individual consists of his ownership of common stock (claims upon permanent income streams) and his real cash balances, which are assumed to be his only marketable assets. The ratio in which the individual wants to hold the components of his portfolio is assumed to depend upon the difference between what could have been earned from the holding of physical capital (claims on its yield), and what will be earned from holding real cash balances. This difference is the nominal rate of interest. It follows that for a given rate of interest there is a given desired ratio between his monetary assets and his total wealth. Let this ratio be l.

The consumption of the period $t = 0$ consists of ordinary goods and services C_0 and of liquidity services where in equilibrium the latter are valued at the alternative cost at the margin of holding money balances.[4] Liquidity consumption during period $t = 0$ is $(i/(1 + i))$ $(M/P(0))$ (evaluated at the beginning of the period). Since the rate of interest is fixed, so is the relative price of consuming ordinary and liquidity services. This fixity allows aggregating ordinary and liquidity services into a composite good $\bar{C}_0$ defined as:[5]

$$\bar{C}_0 = C_0 + \frac{i}{1+i} \frac{M}{P}(0). \tag{9}$$

Analogously, total consumption for any period t is:

$$\bar{C}_t = C_t + \frac{i}{1+i} \frac{M}{P}(t) \tag{10}$$

and the analogue to the composite good F (equation 2) is $\bar{F}$.

$$\bar{F} = \sum_{t=1}^{\infty} \frac{C_t + \dfrac{i}{1+i} \dfrac{M}{P}(t)}{(1+i)^t} = \sum_{t=1}^{\infty} \frac{\bar{C}_t}{(1+i)^t}. \tag{11}$$

Similarly, the perpetual possible future consumption stream $\bar{C}_p$ becomes:

$$\bar{C}_p = i \sum_{t=1}^{\infty} \frac{\bar{C}_t}{(1+i)^t}, \tag{12}$$

and an analysis similar to the previous follows. The only difference is that now in addition to the previous analysis, equilibrium requires that wealth be held in the desired forms.

---

[4] It is assumed that only money yields liquidity services.
[5] For the theory and application of such aggregations, see Patinkin (1965, ch. 5 and pp. 411–16), and Liviatan (1965, 1966).

3 THE AGGREGATE ECONOMY

3.A Dynamics of Accumulation in the Barter Model

In passing from the analysis of the individual to the analysis of the economy as a whole, several changes have to be recognised. Firstly, the economy has an aggregate production function—therefore, the technical transformation between C_0 and C_p must be considered. Secondly, prices in general are not given to the economy as a whole. Thirdly, the existing stocks of money and other assets may not be optimal, and therefore exchanges with other economies will result and will be reflected in the balance of payments.

The following analysis of the effects of accumulation on the balance of payments assumes a small country which is completely dominated by the world's commodity and capital markets. This implies that prices and interest rates are given exogenously by their world level.[6] The economy produces a consumption good and an infinitely durable capital good with two factors of production, labour and capital, subject to constant returns to scale. The production function of the capital good can be viewed as a process by which permanent income streams are produced. Thus, a transformation function in terms of C_0 and C_p can be defined, having the usual properties.[7]

Since the capital market is dominated by the world interest rate, the price of a permanent income stream in terms of the consumption good is given. Production takes place at the tangency between the transformation curve and the given price line. Consumption is determined at the tangency point between the budget constraint and an indifference curve which maps the trade-off between present consumption and future perpetuities of consumption commencing from the next period. In principle an economy can acquire a permanent income stream from abroad either by purchasing and transfer-

[6] A framework for the analysis of the 'large' country for which prices and interest rates are determined endogenously is provided in Fischer and Frenkel (1974).

[7] Technically, the production possibility curve in the (C_0, C_p) plane is derived from the corresponding curve in the (C_0, K) plane (where K is the capital good), by multiplying the abscissa (along which K is measured) by the constant i. By this construction the slopes of the price line, the production possibility curve and the Rybczynski line (the output expansion-contraction locus as the endowment of capital is changed at constant prices) in the (C_0, C_p) plane are $1/i$ times their respective slopes in the (C_0, K) plane.

ring the source of the stream or by purchasing a claim upon the perpetuity. It is assumed that capital goods are not traded internationally.[8] Thus, trade in permanent income streams does not change the location in which production takes place. The transaction is reflected in a purchase of a claim upon future permanent flows of income. In terms of the balance of payments, the immediate effect of such a purchase is to create a deficit in the capital account rather than a deficit in the trade account.[9]

The fact that claims upon income streams are traded internationally implies the possibility of a divergence between the value of output produced by resources *located* in the economy and the value of the rewards to resources *owned* by the economy. The difference between the two corresponds to the difference between gross domestic product and gross national product. Gross domestic product, which is represented by the price line which is tangent to the transformation curve, is more relevant for analyses of production, investment, and the factor market. Gross national product, which is represented by the budget constraint, is more relevant for analyses of consumption and portfolio choices. The budget constraint naturally includes the yield from the net ownership of foreign income streams. Only if the economy's net debtor–creditor position is zero will the budget constraint coincide exactly with the price line which is tangent to the transformation curve.

In Figure 5.2 which corresponds to the point in time at which the economy's net debtor–creditor position is zero, TT is the transformation function between C_0 and C_p. EE is the world price line (with the slope of $-1/i$), ICC is the 'income-consumption curve' of the economy, and RR is the Rybczynski line. The linearity and the slope of ICC reflect the assumptions that the preference map is homothetic and that the marginal propensity to consume out of permanent income is less than unity. The slope of RR with reference to the price line reflects the assumption that $\dot{C}_p$ is labour intensive compared with C_0.

In the equilibrium described by Figure 5.2, capital goods are being produced, i.e. positive investment takes place. It is assumed that firms issue new securities to finance their investment. On the other

---

[8] This assumption is further discussed in section 4.D below.

[9] In addition, the annual stream is reflected in the service account of the balance of payment.

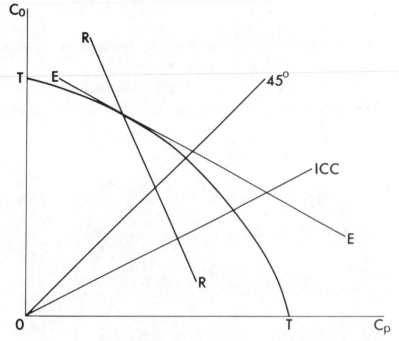

Figure 5.2. Production and consumption equilibrium when the
net debtor–creditor position is zero.

hand, the existence of positive savings implies that asset holders wish
to add to their holdings of securities. Only if the flow demand and
the flow supply of securities happen to equal each other will the
country's net ownership of foreign income streams be unchanged. If,
however, the flow supply of securities—representing the investment
implied by the production point—falls short of the flow demand for
securities—representing the savings implied by the consumption
point—asset holders buy permanent income streams from abroad.
If asset holders do buy permanent income streams from abroad,
then the next period's budget constraint lies to the right of the
production point, and vice versa.

Figure 5.3 describes the case in which the economy becomes a net
creditor. The transformation curve TT and the Rybczynski line RR
are reproduced from Figure 5.2, and the initial budget line passes
through the initial production point P^0. As capital goods are being

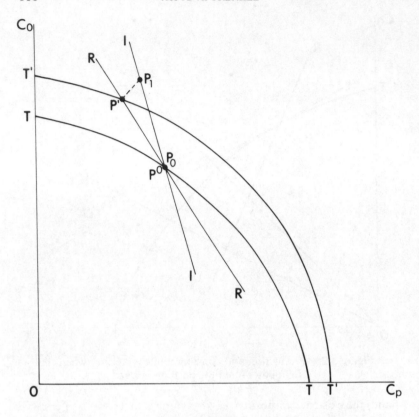

Figure 5.3.   Production and the budget constraint for alternative
stocks of capital and net debtor–creditor positions.

produced, two changes occur. Firstly, the increased stock of capital
causes a rightwards shift of the transformation curve TT to, say,
$T'T'$ and thus a new production point P' is implied. Secondly, since
by assumption there exists an excess flow demand for securities,
some permanent income streams are being purchased from abroad.
The net ownership of foreign income streams implies in turn that
the budget line describing the yield on resources owned by the
economy lies to the right of the price line passing through the production point P'. The new budget line is obtained by adding to the price
line that is tangent to the transformation curve the returns on the
net ownership of foreign securities. To add these returns, a two-

dimensional vector whose components are $(i/(i + 1))Z(t)$ is added to each point on the price line where $Z(t)$ denotes net ownership of foreign securities. Thus, the length of the north-eastern displacement is proportional to the economy's net creditor position and corresponds to the service account of the balance of payments. Therefore, when production is at P', the budget constraint passes through P_1 (where P^i denotes production along the ith period transformation curve and P_i denotes the corresponding point along the ith period budget line). Thus, when production by resources located in the economy (GDP) is at P', the 'production' of C_0 and C_p by resources owned by the economy (GNP) is at P_1. Combining points like P_0 (which coincides with P^0) and P_1 yield the II curve which is the locus of 'production' along the budget constraints that incorporate net ownership of foreign income streams.

Changes in the net ownership of foreign income are reflected by changes in the distance between the tangent to the transformation curve and the budget constraint. If accumulation is associated with an excess flow demand for securities, then the budget line is to the right of the tangent to the transformation curve since claims on part of the foreign output are owned by domestic residents. In such a case, the II curve is to the right of the Rybczynski line and accumulation is associated with a deficit in the capital account (and the economy is a net recipient of interest and dividends).

The rate of investment, and therefore the flow supply of securities, is determined endogenously by the annual production of C_p which has to be produced in order to assure full employment at the given price ratio. The assumption that C_p is labour intensive implies that as accumulation proceeds full employment requires a reduction in the production of C_p and an increase in that of C_0 which implies in turn that the flow supply of securities is falling with the process of accumulation. Since the value of GNP is rising, eventually the flow supply of securities must fall short of the flow demand induced by savings. Thus, eventually the II curve must be to the right of the RR curve.

Since the relationship between the flow demand and flow supply of securities determines the capital account and since the cumulative capital account determines the service account, a further investigation into the relationship between the RR curve and the II curve is useful.

In an early stage of the country's economic development when the capital stock is relatively small, full employment at the given terms of trade is achieved when the production of C_0 is relatively small and that of C_p is large. Therefore, this point in time $(t = t_1)$ is characterised by an excess of investment over savings which creates an excess flow supply of securities and thus a surplus in the capital account.

As time passes the flow supply of securities declines (as the economy moves along the Rybczynski line) while the flow demand for securities rises (as the value of GNP is rising). During that period, the surplus in the capital account declines and the deficit in the service account increases. At some point in time (at $t = t_2$) the capital account is balanced (at this point firms issue exactly the quantity of securities that asset holders want to add to their portfolio). At this point in time the cumulative ownership of foreign securities is being maximized and therefore the deficit in the service account reaches its maximum value. Thereon, the capital account deficit is rising and the service account deficit is falling. At a still later period of time (at $t = t_3$) the cumulative deficit in the capital account equals the

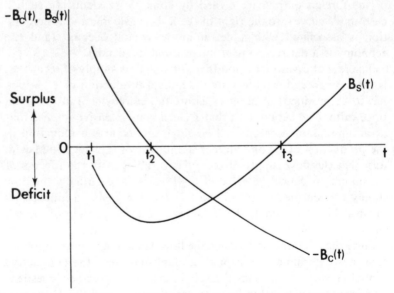

Figure 5.4. Time path of the capital account and the service account.

cumulative past surpluses, thereby bringing the net debtor–creditor position to zero. The service account which is balanced at that period switches into a surplus as the economy is switching from being a net debtor to being a net creditor. From this point on, the capital account deficit and the service account surplus are rising.

The paths describing the capital account $- B_c(t)$ and the debt service account $B_s(t) = i \int_0^t B_c(\tau) \, d\tau$ in accordance with the above analysis are presented in Figure 5.4.

The same analysis also implies a certain relationship between the RR and the II curves. Since the distance between these curves corresponds to the annual flow of interest and dividends, the higher is the surplus in the service account, the further to the right is the point on the II curve as compared with the production point on the

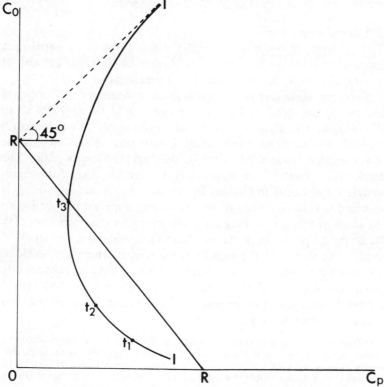

Figure 5.5.   The Rybczynski line and the II curve.

RR curve. Since the process of accumulation implies moving leftwards along the Rybczynski line, eventually the small economy ceases to produce investment goods and it specialises in the production of C_0. Thereon, the capital stock is constant but income continues to grow as the economy continues to save. Since there is no domestic flow supply of securities, the whole of savings is reflected in purchases of foreign securities, the yield on which induces a continuous rightwards movement of the income line. Since ordinary production continues to be the same once the economy specialises in the production of consumption goods, the slope of the *II* curve becomes 45° and the only change that occurs through time is in the length of the debt service vector whose components are $(i/1 + i) Z(t)$. Figure 5.5 describes the implied relationship between the *RR* and the *II* curves. In what follows, points along the *II* curve are referred to as points of 'production of GNP'.

3.B Introducing Money

The existence of money as an asset which produces a permanent income stream (liquidity services) at the rate of i per year per unit of money must now be incorporated in the analysis.

Since the world rate of interest is given, consumption of ordinary income streams and of liquidity services could be aggregated. In this way, C_0 and C_p would be defined analogously to equations (9) and (12). Assume that the individual dealt with in section 2 is the 'representative individual', that is, that aggregation is valid. The marketable wealth of the economy is the same as that of the representative individual multiplied by the number of individuals. It is assumed that the quantity of money is tied in a rigid proportion to the stock of foreign exchange. For simplicity let the proportionality factor be unity. To keep the portfolio in equilibrium, the stock of money has to rise at the same relative rate at which the stock of non-monetary wealth grows. Since the price level is exogenously given, the only way the monetary stock can rise is by 'importing' money. It follows that in the process of growth, the economy runs an over-all balance of payments surplus.[10]

[10] The need to 'import' money reflects the assumption that the quantity of money is rigidly tied to the stock of foreign exchange; this issue is further discussed in section 4.C below. On related issues, see Mundell (1968, 1971), Komiya (1969), Laffer (1969), Dornbusch (1971), Johnson (1972), Boyer (1971), Purvis (1972), and Frenkel and Rodriguez (1975).

The fraction of monetary wealth in total wealth is l. Therefore:

$$\frac{M}{P}(t) = l\,W_t. \tag{13}$$

The balance of payments $B(t)$ is defined as:[11]

$$B(t) \equiv \frac{M}{P}(t) - \frac{M}{P}(t-1) = l(W_t - W_{t-1}), \tag{14}$$

which from equation (8) becomes

$$B(t) = l(C_p - C_0). \tag{15}$$

The above discussion is represented in Figure 5.6.

At the initial period $B(0) = l(\overline{AB})$. As a result of the accumulation, the budget constraint E_0E_0 shifts to E_1E_1, and the balance of payments becomes $B(1) = l(\overline{CD})$. As is clear from the diagram, $B(t)$ is proportional to the *volume* of savings at period t, the proportionality factor being l, the marginal (average) propensity to hoard.

Disposable income is defined as the value of output plus the return on net ownership of foreign securities plus the flow of imputed liquidity services from real cash balances.[12] The services of real balances are income that has to be consumed thereby (assuming an over-all constant consumption ratio $\bar{c}$) reducing the proportion of physical output consumed and raising the ratio of real investment to output.[13]

---

[11] Note that by this definition, the recorded balance of payments $B(t)$ represents the cumulative flow over a specified period of time as measured at t—the end of the specified period; thus, it is a stock. Since the framework of this paper is that of a period-analysis, it cannot emphasise the important stock-flow distinction. This distinction can be better emphasised within the framework that is provided in the appendix in which the analysis is conducted in terms of continuous time.

[12] On the issue of imputing liquidity services, see Johnson (1967, ch. IV) and Levhari and Patinkin (1968).

[13] Let C denote physical consumption, $\bar{c}$ the over-all marginal propensity to consume Y_d disposable income, Y output owned by the economy and l the fraction of monetary wealth in total wealth. The ratio of incomes from monetary to non-monetary assets is $(l/1 - l)$. $C = \bar{c}\,Y - i(M/P)\,(1 - \bar{c})$ and $C/Y = \bar{c} - (l/1 - l)(1 - \bar{c}) < \bar{c}$. Note that for positive consumption of ordinary goods, we have to assume that $\bar{c} > l$.

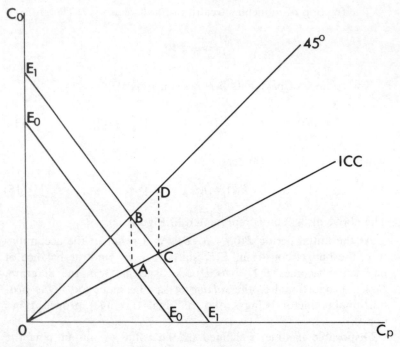

Figure 5.6. The balance of payments is proportional to the
volume of savings.

As was argued, economic expansion is associated with an over-all surplus in the balance of payments. The following discussion analyses the patterns of the components of the over-all balance.

We must distinguish between the ordinary budget constraint (GNP) and the economy's generalised budget constraint. Since money is assumed to be a consumer's good, the production possibility curve does not include liquidity services. However, the budget constraint which is relevant for consumption choices must include the liquidity services rendered by money. Thus, the generalised budget constraint includes possible combinations of C_0 and C_p rendered by ordinary goods and services (GNP) plus the value of the liquidity services rendered to households by their holdings of real cash balances.

The method of the analysis is to find the equilibrium combinations of over-all 'production' and over-all consumption and to calculate the implied pattern of trade after allowing for satisfaction of liquidity needs.

Consider Figure 5.7. E_0E_0 is the ordinary budget line. $\bar{E}_0\bar{E}_0$ is the relevant budget constraint when liquidity services are added to E_0E_0 (to add the imputed liquidity services, a two-dimensional vector whose components are $(i/1 + i)$ (M/P) (t) is added to each point on E_0E_0 to obtain $\bar{E}_0\bar{E}_0$). The other curves have the same meaning as in the previous discussion.

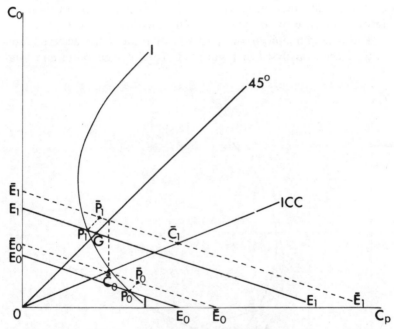

Figure 5.7.   Derivation of the *locus* of total production points
which include liquidity services.

Ordinary production (of GNP) in $t = 0$ is at P_0; thus total production (including liquidity services) is at $\bar{P}_0$. Total consumption is at $\bar{C}_0$ and thus by the implied accumulation, the generalised budget constraint for $t = 1$ is $\bar{E}_1\bar{E}_1$ for which the over-all consumption is at $\bar{C}_1$. To find the total production point $\bar{P}_1$, the ordinary production point (of GNP) P_1 must be found. The latter is achieved by identifying the ordinary budget line at the period $t = 1$. From the intersection of $\bar{E}_1\bar{E}_1$ with the 45° line subtract the vector whose components are $(i/1 + i)$ $[\{M/P\,(0)\} + l\{C_p - C_0\}]$ which are the liquidity services at $t = 1$. This procedure yields the point G.

The line through G which is parallel to the generalised budget line is E_1E_1, the ordinary budget line at $t = 1$, whose intersection with the II curve determines the ordinary production point P_1. Finally, the total production point $\bar{P}_1$ is obtained by adding to P_1 the same liquidity services vector.

This procedure could be continued to derive an FF curve which combines all total production points (ordinary production by resources owned by the economy plus liquidity services).

The determination of the patterns of trade when accumulation takes place is analysed in Figure 5.8. Total consumption and total

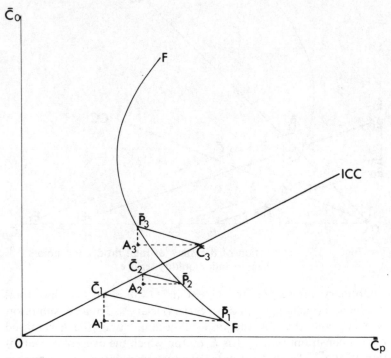

Figure 5.8. Determination of the patterns of trade and the components of the balance of payments in the process of accumulation.

production points lie along the *ICC* and the *FF* curves, respectively, where subscripts denote the time period. The line combining each period's total production and total consumption points is a segment of that period's generalised budget constraint. The trade triangle in the *t–th* period is $A_t \bar{P}_t \bar{C}_t$.

Consider the period $t = 1$. Total production is at $\bar{P}_1$, total consumption at $\bar{C}_1$, net imports of current goods and services are $A_1 \bar{C}_1$, and net exports of permanent income streams are $\bar{P}_1 A_1$. However, these magnitudes include purchases of liquidity services acquired through the balance of payments. To determine the net balance on the various accounts, the transactions involving liquidity services must be deducted.

Thus for $t = 1$ the deficit in the current account $- T(1)$ must be smaller than $A_1 \bar{C}_1$ by the purchase of liquidity services embodied in the over-all balance-of-payments surplus. Therefore:

$$- T(1) = A_1 \bar{C}_1 - \frac{i}{1 + i} B(1) =$$

$$= A_1 \bar{C}_1 - \frac{il}{1 + i} [\bar{C}_p(1) - \bar{C}_0(1)].$$

(16)

By the same token, the surplus in the capital account is equal to the total net sales of permanent future income excluding the part which is embodied in the over-all balance of payments, and thus it must exceed $\bar{P}_1 A_1$ by that part. Thus, the period $t = 1$ is characterised by a surplus in the capital account and a smaller deficit in the current account so as to yield a surplus in the over-all balance of payments.

As time passes, the over-all balance must improve since the volume of savings rises with time. This can be seen from the fact that the vertical distance between the *ICC* and the 45° line grows with time. The capital account must deteriorate since while the flow demand for securities rises with time, the flow supply declines (due to the Rybczynski theorem). Since, however, the over-all balance improves with time, the current account must improve at a rate that is faster than the rate at which the capital account deteriorates. As far as the components of the current account are concerned, it is clear that (as long as there is a surplus in the capital account), the trade account must improve with time since the current account improves while the service account deteriorates; the improvement in the balance of trade must proceed at a faster rate than the deterioration in the service account so as to result in an improvement in the current account.

When $t = t_2$, another production–consumption combination occurs $(\bar{P}_2, \bar{C}_2)$. At this point, the capital account is still in a surplus (which exceeds $\bar{P}_2 A_2$ by the purchase of permanent future income embodied in the over-all surplus) but the current account is balanced since net imports of $\bar{C}_0$ equal the purchase of liquidity services through the over-all surplus, i.e. $A_2 \bar{C}_2 = (i/1 + i) B(2)$. Since, however, at $t = t_2$ there is a cumulative surplus in the capital account, it follows that the service account is in a deficit which is equal to the surplus in the balance of trade.

At a still later period, $t = t_3$ (which occurs after the ICC intersects the FF schedule), a combination like $\bar{P}_3 \bar{C}_3$ occurs. At this period— which corresponds to the point in time in which the service account deficit reaches its largest value—the capital account is balanced. Net purchases of permanent income streams are exactly equal to the liquidity services acquired through the over-all balance-of-payments surplus. At that point, the surplus on the current account equals the over-all surplus. Since after $t = t_3$ the capital account switches into a deficit, there must still be a later period at which the cumulative deficits in the capital account equal the past cumulative surpluses. At that point, the service account balances and the surplus in the trade balance equals the surplus in the current account. At any later period, the deficit in the capital account rises, the surpluses in the service account and the current account increase as the over-all balance of payments improves.

Figure 5.9 describes the paths of the various balance-of-payments accounts that are implied by the above discussion.

To summarise the above analysis, as accumulation takes place, liquidity needs require an over-all balance-of-payments surplus. With respect to the components of the balance of payments, after some periods the capital account will be in deficit and the current account will be in surplus. The capital account deficit and the current account surplus will increase over time. However, it is imprecise to say that growth *per se* is associated with a surplus in the current account and a deficit in the capital account, since in early stages the opposite occurs.

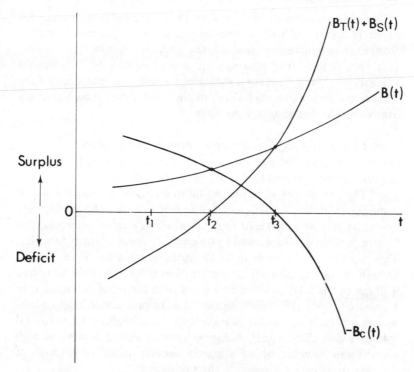

Figure 5.9.   The time paths of the balance of payments, the current account, and the capital account.

3.C Money as Both a Consumer's and a Producer's Good

The situation becomes more complex when money is treated as serving as a factor of production in addition to its role in generating services for consumers. In such a case, money holdings of firms lend themselves to analysis via the production function, and those of households via the utility function. Since the relative price of money and other factors of production is assumed to be a given constant, again a composite good could be defined aggregating money and other factors. Now the over-all balance of payments associated with growth is determined simultaneously by the liquidity needs of consumers and producers. The needs of producers depend upon the output elasticity of the demand for money as a factor of production along the output expansion path.

Complexities arise from the fact that accumulation of capital which is associated with a non-zero balance of payments implies changes in two factors of production—ordinary capital and money. This fact implies that assumptions regarding the relative capital intensity of C_0 and C_p are not sufficient to determine the slope of the Rybczynski line, since capital is not the only factor which changes over time. Several cases are possible:

(a) C_0 is both capital and money intensive relative to C_p. This is the simplest case, because the general characteristics of the RR line are unchanged compared with the previous analysis.

(b) The commodity which is capital intensive is not the one which is money intensive. In such a case, the slope of the RR line depends upon the relative change in the capital/money ratio in production (where production is assumed to be under constant returns to scale). This ratio in turn depends upon the ratio of g—which is the rate of growth of the capital stock to the fraction θ—which is the weighted average of the relative share of money as a factor of production in C_0 and C_p. Thus the capital/money ratio in production rises or falls as g/θ is greater or smaller than unity. Accordingly, if C_0 is capital intensive and C_p is money intensive, growth will be associated with an absolute increase or an absolute decline in the production of C_0, according as g is greater or smaller than θ.

Once the slope of the RR line is determined, the II curve can be derived by incorporating net ownership of foreign income streams. Once the II curve is determined, the FF curve can be derived by incorporating the liquidity services imputed from money held by households, and the analysis of the implications of accumulation for the current and capital accounts is analogous to that of the simpler case where money is not regarded as a factor of production.

4 RELAXATION OF SOME OF THE ASSUMPTIONS

4.A The Consumption Assumption

The foregoing analysis assumed constancy of the over-all consumption ratio. As a consequence, the economy did not converge to a stationary state but rather a continuing process of secular accumulation took place. Stationariness in consumption could be reached by modifying the assumptions about consumption behaviour to make it depend upon the magnitude of non-human wealth *per capita* or equivalently upon liquid assets *per capita*. Accordingly, the higher becomes the stock of marketable assets, the lower becomes the need for additional precautionary savings, and therefore the marginal propensity to consume rises as accumulation of marketable wealth proceeds. The resulting *ICC* is presented in Figure 5.10.

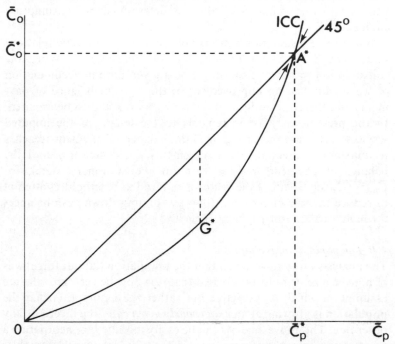

Figure 5.10.   The *ICC* schedule when the marginal propensity to consume rises as accumulation proceeds.

The system converges to a stationary state in consumption in which the average propensity to consume is unity (point A^*). The stability of the equilibrium is assured by the fact that in its neighbourhood, the marginal propensity to consume exceeds the average propensity. The stationary values of the variables are $\bar{C}_0^*$ and $\bar{C}_p^*$, and the long-run stationary balance of payments B^* is zero.[14]

[14] These results are modified in section 4.B when growth of the labour force is allowed for.

The vertical distance between the *ICC* and the 45° line is proportional to the balance of payments. It is clear in view of Figure 5.10 that the balance of payments considered as a function of $\bar{C}_p$ possesses a unique positive maximum. This maximum corresponds to the point G^* at which the marginal propensity to consume is unity.[15]

Figure 5.11a describes the balance of payments as a function of $\bar{C}_p$. Figure 5.11b and Figure 5.11c describe the convergence of the variables to their stationary values as determined by consumption choices.

When the consumption ratio is not constant, the simple relationship between *II* and the *FF* schedules no longer exists. When the consumption ratio was assumed to be a given datum, accumulation of wealth implied an improvement in the over-all balance of payments and therefore additional liquidity services had to be imputed. In the present case, the increments to the length of the imputed services vector are increasing until the balance of payments reaches its maximum value; then the increments are decreasing until the balance of payments reaches zero (at the stationary state), for $\bar{C}_p > \bar{C}_p^*$, the length of the vector is reduced as assetholders attempt to reduce the size of their portfolio by running down cash balances through a balance-of-payments deficit.

4.B The population assumption

The analysis hitherto assumed that the population (labour force) was of a given size. It must be stressed that it is not the zero growth-rate assumption which is restrictive but rather the assumption that the population is growing at an *exogenously given rate*—be it zero or any other rate. The above analysis can be easily modified to incorporate a positive constant rate of population growth by defining the variables in *per capita* terms and discussing convergence to a steady state growth path rather than to a stationary state.

In the following discussion, lower-case letters denote the *per capita* values of the variables and n is the constant rate of growth of population.

[15] Since money is not assumed to serve as a factor of production, the analysis of the over-all balance of payments depends only upon the shape of the *ICC*. If the homotheticity assumption is relaxed and money is assumed to be a 'luxury good', the fraction l is an increasing function of wealth and the balance of payments reaches its maximum at a point to the right of G^*, that is, at a point where the marginal propensity to consume exceeds unity.

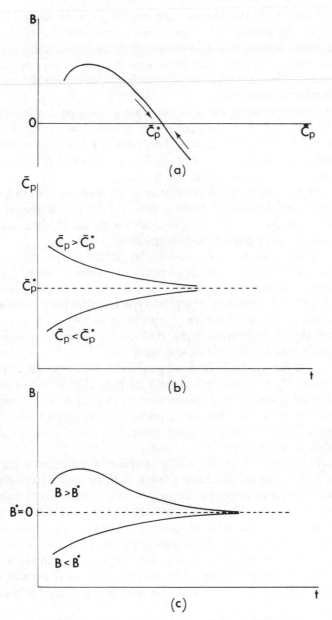

Figure 5.11.   Convergence of the variables.

In Figure 5.12, the ray through the origin with slope $(1 - n)$ represents the function $(1 - n)\bar{c}_p$, and forms with the 45° line an angle whose tangent is n. The vertical distance between this ray and the 45° line is $n\bar{c}_p$—the new permanent income stream *per capita* required to equip the additions to the population with the same $\bar{c}_p$ as the existing population.

The system converges to a steady state growth-path in consumption with $\bar{c}_p^*$ and $\bar{c}_0^*$ as the equilibrium values. The vertical distance between E^* and the 45° line is the steady state *per capita* savings $n\bar{c}_p$ and its product with the fraction l corresponds to b^*, the steady state *per capita* balance of payments.

As can be seen, a rise in the rate of growth of population lowers the steady state values of both $\bar{c}_0$ and $\bar{c}_p$, and in the special case where $n = 0$ the ray $(1 - n)\bar{c}_p$ coincides with the 45° line and the stationary state in consumption is reached.

Changes in n do not have such a clear effect on the steady state value of the *per capita* balance of payments. Since $b^* = ln\bar{c}_p$, a rise in n operates directly to raise b^* but operates indirectly—by reducing $\bar{c}_p^*$—to reduce it. As n rises, b^* starts to rise and then falls, reaching its maximum value when the rate of growth of population is such that the ray $(1 - n)\bar{c}_p$ intersects the *ICC* at the point in which the marginal propensity to consume is unity.

Since the *per capita* balance of payments converges to a steady state value b^*, the recorded over-all surplus B (not in *per capita* terms) must converge to a steady growth rate equal to the rate of growth of population. This ever-growing surplus is just sufficient to equip the increment to the labour force with just the same money *per capita* as the existing labour force.

Recent literature on growth and the balance of payments suggested that a higher rate of economic growth is associated with a higher over-all balance-of-payments surplus.[16] Since the over-all balance converges to the steady growth rate n, the higher is the rate of growth of the economy (the rate of growth of population), the higher becomes the rate at which the steady state surplus grows. However, as was shown, the *per capita* steady state surplus may *fall* as the rate of growth of population rises. This suggests that for some period of time following the rise in the rate of population growth, the over-all

---

[16] See, for example, Mundell (1968, chs 8–9) and Laffer (1969).

balance B might be *below* what it would have been had the lower rate of growth prevailed.

4.C Credit Creation

So far it has been assumed that the quantity of money is rigidly tied to the stock of foreign exchange, and therefore changes in the stock of money had to be reflected in the over-all balance of payments. In addition, the growth rate of the rest of the world has been ignored. We now assume that the monetary authority follows an active policy of credit creation and we consider the rate of growth of the rest of the world.

Technically, in terms of Figure 5.12, the ray with the slope of $(1 - n)$ should be replaced by a ray with a slope of $1 - (n - \bar{n}) + (\mu - \bar{\mu})$, where n and μ are domestic rates of growth of population

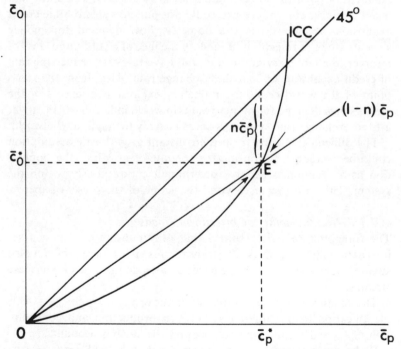

Figure 5.12. The steady state equilibrium when population is growing.

and credit creation, respectively, while $\bar{n}$ and $\bar{\mu}$ are the corresponding average values for the world. Whenever $n - \mu$ is greater (smaller) than $\bar{n} - \bar{\mu}$, the ray lies below (above) the 45° line and the economy is running a balance-of-payments surplus (deficit).

One of the unappealing implications of the assumption that the growth rate is exogenously given is that unless it happens to be the same in several countries, the one with the highest rate of growth must eventually comprise the whole world. If, however, the growth rate does happen to be identical in two countries, they will keep growing on a balanced growth path. Since in this case $n = \bar{n}$, the slope of the ray is $1 + \mu - \bar{\mu}$ and if $\mu = \bar{\mu}$, the steady state balance of payments is zero. If $\mu > \bar{\mu}(\mu < \bar{\mu})$ the ray is above (below) the 45° line and the economy is running a steady state deficit (surplus). Of course, if the ray of one country lies below the 45° line, the ray of the other country must lie above it so that the sum of all the balances of payments is zero (Cournot law). Clearly, a country that is not a reserve currency centre could not pursue a steady state credit expansion which exceeds the domestic flow demand for money since its stock of reserves is limited. In the face of a continuous loss of reserves, the monetary authorities will have to either reduce the rate of credit expansion or float the exchange rate. Also, from the viewpoint of the world economy, monetary expansion in excess of the world's flow demand for money results in world inflation which, under a fixed exchange-rate system, is spread evenly throughout the world.

The difficulties arising from the constant growth-rate assumption could be overcome by considering the rate of gowth of the population as an economic variable determined endogenously within the system. This, however, is beyond the scope of the present paper.

4.D The Non-tradability of Investment Goods
The foregoing analysis assumed that only consumption goods are internationally traded while transactions in sources of income streams were assumed to be reflected in a trade in claims upon these streams.

This assumption has permitted (after allowing for liquidity services) identification of the differences between production and consumption of $\bar{C}_0$ and $\bar{C}_p$ with the balances on the various accounts.

If the other extreme case is assumed—that is, if all trade in permanent income streams involves investment goods—all the transactions are reflected in the trade account. In this case, the analysis yields information regarding the composition of the output (as between the investment good and the consumption good) and the composition of the trade account.[17] In this case, the *II* curve coincides with the *RR* line, the technique by which money is incorporated into production and consumption is unaffected, and so is the analysis of the over-all balance of payments. However, the analysis regarding the components of the balance of payments is affected. Figure 5.9 describes in this case net exports of the investment good and of the consumption good instead of describing the capital account and the current account, respectively.[18]

5 CONCLUDING REMARKS

This chapter has attempted to develop a theory of the secular evolution of the balance of payments in a model of accumulation. In general, the approach emphasises the role of the budget constraint and views the various accounts of the balance of payments as the 'window' through which the various excess flow demands and supplies are cleared. Accordingly, surpluses in the trade account or in the capital account reflect excess flow supply of goods or of securities, respectively, and a surplus in the money account (the over-all balance of payments) reflects an excess flow demand for money.

Viewing the balance of payments as reflecting simultaneous decisions of the various sectors of the economy calls for the application of a general equilibrium analysis. The basic building blocks of the model have been a Fisherian analysis of savings together with the standard two-sector technology. Within this framework, a technique for the explicit incorporation of liquidity services in the analysis has been developed and then used to determine the secular evolution of the over-all balance of payments and its components.

[17] See Stiglitz (1970) and Johnson (1971).

[18] The main difficulty in modelling trade in both investment goods and securities using a two-sector model of a small economy for which the terms of trade are fixed, is that if a country can both import securities and investment goods, then it is a matter of indifference what its capital stock is. Its income will be the same whether it acquires income streams from abroad by buying securities or whether it owns physical capital. This indeterminacy can be overcome by introducing a demand for investment goods. One possibility of deriving such a demand function is from considerations of the effects of the rate of investment on the efficiency of production; see Fischer and Frenkel (1972).

APPENDIX

The Structure and the Dynamics of the Model[1]

This Appendix provides the formal structure of the barter model and a framework for the analysis of its dynamics. The analysis is conducted in terms of continous time.

A.I. The Model

The labour force is assumed to grow at a constant rate n. *Per capita* outputs of the consumption good (q_c) and the investment good (q_I) (which are produced under constant returns to scale) depend on the capital–labour ratio (k) and on the price of capital in terms of consumption (p_k). The assumption that the economy is small and that it is non-specialised implies that the price of capital, the rate of interest and factor rentals are fixed. The value of output (*per capita*) is equal to the income of domestic factors:

$$q_c(k) + p_k q_I(k) = rk + v \qquad (A.1)$$

where r is the rental on capital and v is the wage rate (all in terms of the consumption good). The assumptions that investment goods are labour intensive and that the economy is not specialised imply that:

$$\delta q_c/\delta k > 0, \ \delta q_I/\delta k < 0, \ \delta q_c/\delta k > r, \ \delta^2 q_c/\delta k^2 = 0. \qquad (A.2)$$

Consumption *per capita* (c) is assumed to be a constant fraction[2] (γ) of income (iw)

$$c = \gamma \, i \, w; \ 0 < \gamma < 1 \qquad (A.3)$$

---

[1] The formal structure and the framework of this appendix draw on Frenkel and Fischer (1972) and Fischer and Frenkel (1974).

[2] The analysis can be extended to accommodate a consumption function with variable propensity to consume as in section 4 of the text. For an extension along these lines, see Fischer and Frenkel (1974).

where income is defined as the return on wealth, i is the constant rate of interest and w is *per capita* wealth. In the absence of expected capital gains, $i = r/p_k$. Wealth in turn consists of ownership of capital $(p_k k)$, net ownership of foreign equities (z) and human capital (v/i):

$$w = p_k k + z + v/i. \tag{A.4}$$

The capital stock and the value of wealth (all *per capita*) grow through time according to:

$$\dot{k} = q_I(k) - nk \tag{A.5}$$

$$\dot{w} = (1 - \gamma) w - n(w - v/i). \tag{A.6}$$

Since investment goods are assumed to be labour intensive it follows from (A.5) that $\delta \dot{k}/\delta k < 0$. Similarly, from (A.6) $\delta \dot{w}/\delta w < O$ if and only if $n > i(1 - \gamma)$—a condition that is assumed to be satisfied. Note that the latter condition is identical to the stablity condition in the standard Solow-type one-sector growth model. It follows, therefore, that both the capital stock and the value of wealth (all *per capita*) approach their steady state values (k^*, w^*) monotonically. Given the wage rate and the interest rate, equation (A.4) implies that corresponding to k^* and w^* there is a steady state value of z^*—the net creditor position.

A.II. The Dynamics of the International Accounts
The *per capita* deficit in the capital account (b_c) equals the *per capita* net purchases of foreign securities $\dot{z} + nz$. The *per capita* surplus in the trade account (b_T) equals the excess of domestic production of consumption goods over domestic consumption $(q_c(k) - c)$. The surplus in the service account (b_s) equals the return on net *per capita* holdings of foreign securities (iz). Since $b_c = b_T + b_s$, it follows that the balance of indebtedness changes through time according to:

$$\dot{z} = q_c(k) - c + (i - n)z. \tag{A.7}$$

Figure 5A.1, a phase diagram in the (k, z) space, is the basic diagram that is used for the analysis of the dynamics. From (A.5) it is clear that there is only one value of k ($k = k^*$) for which $\dot{k} = 0$. This *locus* is described by the vertical ($\dot{k} = 0$) *locus* in Figure 5A.1. The directions of the horizontal arrows are implied by the fact that $\delta\dot{k}/\delta k < 0$.

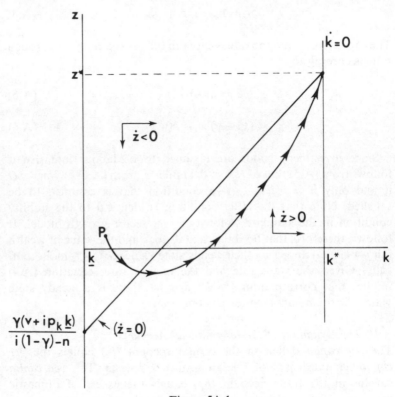

Figure 5A.1.

From (A.7) the (constant) slope of the *locus* along which $\dot{z} = 0$ is:

$$\left(\frac{dz}{dk}\right)_{\dot{z}=0} = -\frac{\delta\dot{z}/\delta k}{\delta\dot{z}/\delta z} = \frac{-\delta q_c/\delta k + p_k\gamma i}{i(1 - \gamma) - n} > 0. \qquad (A.8)$$

The directions of the vertical arrows in Figure (5A.1) are implied by the fact that $\delta\dot{z}/\delta z < 0$.

Since from (A.4) $\dot{w} = p_k \dot{k} + \dot{z}$, the intersection of the ($\dot{k} = 0$) *locus* with the ($\dot{z} = 0$) *locus* occurs at the steady-state values k^* and z^* for which $\dot{w} = 0$ and $w = w^*$. Without loss of generality, Figure 5A.1 is drawn under the assumption that the small country becomes a net creditor in the steady state so that $z^* > 0$. Alternative assumptions can be made by appropriate rescaling of the ordinate in Figure 5A.1. Since the economy is assumed to be non-specialised, the lowest value of k in Figure 5A.1 is $\underline{k}$ at which the economy just specialises in the production of investment goods. From (A.7) it follows that at $k = \underline{k}$ (at which $q_c(\underline{k}) = 0$), $z = \gamma(v + ip_k\underline{k})/\{i(1 - \gamma) - n\} < 0$.

The path that is drawn in Figure 5A.1 corresponds to the initial conditions that are denoted by point P. Starting from these initial conditions (low k and low z), the economy initially borrows and thereby reduces its net creditor position. As it continues to borrow, it becomes a net debtor. After some time (once the path crosses the $\dot{z} = 0$ *locus*) the economy starts lending and thereby reducing its net debtor position. Eventually (when the path crosses the abscissa) the economy becomes a net creditor until it reaches the steady state value of z^*. Clearly, the exact characteristics of the path depend on the initial conditions, but it can be seen that independent of the initial condition, no path can cross the ($\dot{z} = 0$) *locus* more than once.[3]

It can be noted in passing that since the value of wealth approaches its steady-state value monotonically, it is clear that even if $\dot{z} < 0$, capital must be growing sufficiently fast to increase wealth. In terms of Figure 5A.1, this can be illustrated by drawing iso-wealth *loci* with a slope of $-p_k$; it follows that in the region for which $\dot{z} < 0$, the path must be flatter than such iso-wealth *loci* (not drawn) so as to result in a monotonic motion to higher iso-wealth lines.

Figure 5A.2 describes the path of the (*per capita*) balance of indebtedness corresponding to initial conditions P.

The analysis of the path of the balance of indebtedness also provides the path of its counterpart in the balance of payments— the service account (b_s). Since the latter is iz, it is obtained by rescaling the ordinate of Figure 5A.2 by multiplying by the rate of interest i.

We turn now to the analysis of the path of the capital account and

[3] When the consumption function is that of section 4, the path can not cross the ($\dot{z} = 0$) *locus* more than twice. See Fischer and Frenkel (1974).

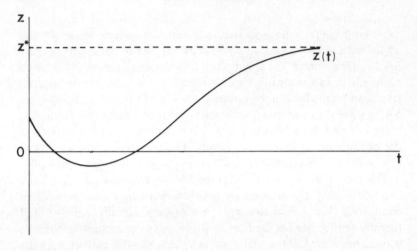

Figure 5A.2.

the trade account (all *per capita*). The deficit in the capital account (b_c) is $\dot{z} + nz$, and thus from (A.7):

$$b_c = q_c(k) - c + iz. \tag{A.9}$$

It follows that the slope of the $(b_c = 0)$ *locus* in Figure 5A.3 is:

$$\left(\frac{dz}{dk}\right)_{b_c = 0} = \frac{-\delta b_c/\delta k}{\delta b_c/\delta z} = \frac{-\delta q_c/\delta k + p_k \gamma i}{i(1 - \gamma)} < 0. \tag{A.10}$$

Since at the steady state $\dot{z} = 0$, the steady state deficit in the capital account is nz^* which is positive or negative, depending on whether z^* is positive or negative.

The intersection of the $(\dot{z} = 0)$ *locus* with the abscissa occurs at $k = \tilde{k}$. Since at this point $\dot{z} + nz = 0$, it follows that the $(b_c = 0)$ *locus* must also pass through $\tilde{k}$. These are the considerations on the basis of which the b_c loci are drawn in Figure 5A.3. Note also that equation (A.10) can be written as:

$$\left(\frac{dz}{dk}\right)_{b_c = 0} = -p_k \left[\frac{\dfrac{1}{p_k}\dfrac{\delta q_c}{\delta k} - \gamma i}{i - \gamma i}\right] < -p_k \tag{A.10'}$$

thus implying that the $(b_c = 0)$ *locus* is steeper than the iso-wealth *locus*. Since when $\dot{z} < 0$ the path must be flatter than $-p_k$, it must also be flatter than the $(b_c = 0)$ *locus* implying, therefore, that the capital account (*per capita*) deteriorates monotonically along the path.

The surplus in the balance of trade (b_T) is:

$$b_T = q_c(k) - c \qquad (A.11)$$

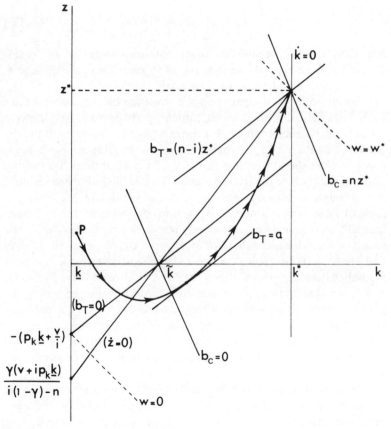

Figure 5A.3.

and thus the slope of the $(b_T = 0)$ *locus* is:

$$\left(\frac{dz}{dk}\right)_{b_T=0} = \frac{-\delta b_T/\delta k}{\delta b_T/\delta z} = \frac{-\delta q_c/\delta k + p_k \gamma i}{-\gamma i} > 0. \quad (A.12)$$

The comparison between this slope and the slope of the $(\dot{z} = 0)$ *locus* reveals that the $(b_T = 0)$ is flatter or steeper than the $(\dot{z} = 0)$ depending on whether i is larger or smaller than n. Figure 5A.3 is drawn under the assumption that $i > n$. Using (A.7), the balance of trade can also be written as:

$$b_T = \dot{z} - (i - n)z \quad (A.12')$$

and therefore the steady-state trade balance surplus is: $(n - i)z^*$. Equation (A.12′) reveals that the $(b_T = 0)$ must also pass through $\tilde{k}$ at which both $\dot{z}$ and z are equal to zero.

Since when $\dot{z} > 0$ the path and the iso-trade balance contours are both positively sloped, it might appear that the path may cross a given trade balance contour an arbitrary number of times. It can be shown, however, that no path can cross a given trade balance contour more than twice, and thus there may be at most one turning point in the path of the trade balance. To establish this proposition, it is enough to observe that the path in Figure 5A.3 crosses the $(\dot{z} = 0)$ *locus* with a slope of zero, and its slope increases monotonically as it approaches the steady state. The path approaches the steady state with a slope that lies in between the slopes of the $(\dot{z} = 0)$ and the $(\dot{k} = 0)$ *loci*. Since the slope of the iso-trade balance contour is smaller than the slopes of both of the $(\dot{z} = 0)$ and the $(\dot{k} = 0)$ *loci*, it follows that there is a unique intermediate point at which the path is tangent to an iso-trade balance contour $(b_T = \alpha)$, a tangency which corresponds to the turning point of the path of b_T.

Figures 5A.4 and 5A.5 describe the implied paths of the capital account and the balance of trade corresponding to initial conditions P.

The analysis in this appendix was confined to a barter economy. It could, however, be extended to a monetary economy by adding a portfolio relationship which in turn implies that part of the flow of savings manifests itself as a flow demand for money. The behaviour of the monetary authorities determines the flow supply of money, and the excess flow demand corresponds to the surplus in the monetary account of the balance of payments.

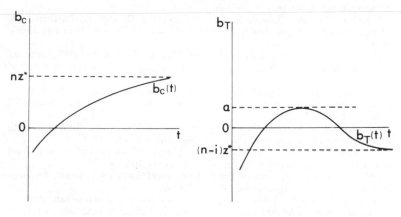

Figure 5A.4.   Figure 5A.5.

REFERENCES

Boyer, Russell, 'The Dynamics of an Open Economy: Growth and the Balance of Payments', unpublished doctoral dissertation, University of Chicago (1971).

Dornbusch, Rudiger, 'Notes on Growth and the Balance of Payments', *Canadian Journal of Economics, 4* (August 1971), 389–95.

Fischer, Stanley, and Frenkel, Jacob A., 'Investment, the Two-Sector Model and Trade in Debt and Capital Goods', *Journal of International Economics, 2* (August 1972), 211–33.

Fischer, Stanley, and Frenkel, Jacob A., 'Economic Growth and Stages of the Balance of Payments: A Theoretical Model', in G. Horwich and P. A. Samuelson (eds.), *Trade Stability and Macroeconomics: Essays in Honor of Lloyd A. Metzler* (New York, Academic Press, 1974), 503–21.

Fischer, Stanley, and Frenkel, Jacob A., 'Interest Rate Equalization, Patterns of Production, Trade and Consumption in a Two-Country Growth Model', *Economic Record, 50* (December 1974), 555–80.

Frenkel, Jacob A., 'A Theory of Money Trade and the Balance of Payments in a Model of Accumulation', *Journal of International Economics, 1* (May 1971), 159–87.

Frenkel, Jacob A., and Fischer, Stanley, 'International Capital Movements Along Balanced Growth Paths: Comments and Extensions', *Economic Record, 48* (June 1972), 266–71.

Frenkel, Jacob A. and Rodriguez, Carlos A., 'Portfolio Equilibrium and the Balance of Payments: A Monetary Approach', *American Economic Review, 65* (September 1975).

Johnson, Harry G., *Essays in Monetary Economics* (Cambridge, Mass., Harvard University Press, 1967).

Johnson, Harry G., *Further Essays in Monetary Economics* (London, George Allen & Unwin, 1972).

Johnson, Harry G., 'Trade and Growth: A Geometrical Exposition', *Journal of International Economics, 1* (February 1971), 83–101.

Komiya, Ryutaro, 'Economic Growth and the Balance of Payments: A Monetary Approach', *Journal of Political Economy, 77* (January/February 1969), 35–48.

Laffer, Arthur B., 'An Anti-Traditional Theory of the Balance of Payments Under Fixed Exchange Rates', unpublished manuscript, University of Chicago (1969).

Leontief, Wassily, 'Theoretical Note on Time-Preference, Productivity of Capital, Stagnation and Economic Growth', *American Economic Review, 48* (March 1958), 105–11.

Levhari, David, and Patinkin, Don, 'The Role of Money in a Simple Growth Model', *American Economic Review, 58* (September 1968), 713–53.

Liviatan, Nissan, 'On the Long-Run Theory of Consumption and Real Balances', *Oxford Economic Papers, 17* (July 1965), 205–18.

Liviatan, Nissan, 'Multiperiod Future Consumption as an Aggregate', *American Economic Review, 56* (September 1966), 828–40.

Mundell, Robert A., *International Economics* (New York, Macmillan, 1968).

Mundell, Robert A., *Monetary Theory* (Pacific Palisades, Goodyear, 1971).

Patinkin, Don, *Money, Interest and Prices*, 2nd edn (New York, Harper and Row, 1965).

Purvis, Douglas D., 'More on Growth and the Balance of Payments', *Canadian Journal of Economics, 5* (November 1972), 531–40.

Stiglitz, Joseph E., 'Factor Price Equalization in a Dynamic Economy', *Journal of Political Economy, 78* (May/June 1970), 456–88.

6

The Monetary Approach to Balance-of-Payments Theory[1]

HARRY G. JOHNSON

My purpose in this chapter is to present the main outline of a new approach to the theory of the balance of payments and of balance-of-payments adjustment (including devaluation and revaluation) that has been emerging in recent years from several sources. Concretely, this new approach is to be found on the one hand in the change in policy orientation adopted by the British government under pressure from the International Monetary Fund after the failure of the devaluation of 1967 to produce the expected improvement in the British balance of payments, the theoretical basis for the new orientation being traceable back to the work of the Dutch economist J. J. Koopmans; and on the other hand to the theoretical work of my colleague at the University of Chicago, R. A. Mundell, and his students—though it is only fair to note that economists elsewhere have been working along similar lines. Its essence is to put at the forefront of analysis the monetary rather than the relative price aspects of international adjustment.

To put the new approach in perspective, it is helpful to go back to the origins of balance-of-payments theory in the work of David Hume, and specifically to his contribution of the analysis of the price-specie-flow mechanism. Hume was concerned to refute the concentration of the mercantilists on the objective of accumulating precious metals within the country, and their consequent recommendation of policies designed to bring about a surplus on the balance of payments. His analysis, couched in terms relevant to the

[1] Reprinted from H. G. Johnson, *Further Essays in Monetary Theory* (London, George Allen & Unwin, 1972).

emerging new approach to balance-of-payments theory, showed that the amount of money in a country would be adjusted automatically to the demand for it, through surpluses or deficits in the balance of payments, induced by the effects on relative national money price levels of excess supplies of or excess demands for money. Hence the mercantilist desire to accumulate 'treasure' was in conflict with the basic mechanism of international monetary adjustment and could only be *ephemerally* successful.

Three points are worth noting about the price-specie-flow mechanism at this stage. Firstly, in contemporary terminology, it assumes (in line with the stylised facts of that time) that all money is 'outside' money (precious metals); i.e. there is no commercial or central banking system capable of creating money not backed by international reserves, domestic money and international reserves being the same thing. Secondly, the mechanism of adjustment focuses on international transactions in goods, as distinguished from securities, a characteristic that has remained dominant in balance-of-payments theory. Thirdly, in the detailed analysis of the mechanism there is a rather awkward compromise between the assumption of a closed and of an open economy, in which it is assumed that domestic prices can vary from purchasing-power parity under the influence of imbalances between money demand and money supply, but that such variations give rise to changes in trade flows which alter the balance of payments and hence the domestic stock of money in the longer run. As we shall see, the new approach to balance-of-payments theory, while basically Humean in spirit, places the emphasis not on relative price changes but on the direct influence of excess demand for or supply of money on the balance between income and expenditure, or more generally between total acquisition and disposal of funds whether through production and consumption or through borrowing and lending, and therefore on the over-all balance of payments.

Hume's analysis ran in terms of an automatic mechanism of international adjustment motivated by money flows and consequential changes in national money price levels. The subsequent elaboration of the theory, up to and partly through the 1930s, retained the general notion of automaticity while adding in the complications required by the existence of credit money provided by commercial banks and of central banking based on partial international reserve holdings, and by the possibility of attraction or otherwise of international short-term capital movements through international interest-rate differentials. In addition, Cassel contributed the purchasing-power-parity theory of the equilibrium determination of the values of floating exchange rates.

In the 1930s, under the stimulus on the one hand of the collapse of the international regime of fixed exchange rates and the emergence of mass unemployment as a major economic problem, and on the other hand of the Keynesian revolution—which altered the basic assumptions of theory from wage and price flexibility with full employment to wage rigidity with normal mass unemployment—a new approach to balance-of-payments theory emerged, one which viewed international adjustment not as an automatic process but as a policy problem for governments. The key problem, the classic article on which is Joan Robinson's essay on the foreign exchanges, was the conditions under which a devaluation would improve a country's balance of payments. On Keynesian assumptions of wage rigidity, a devaluation would change the real prices of domestic goods relative to foreign goods in the foreign and domestic markets, thereby promoting substitutions in production and consumption. On Keynesian assumptions of mass unemployment, any repercussions of these substitutions on the demand for domestic output could be assumed to be met by variations in output and employment and repercussions of such variations on to the balance of payments regarded as secondary. Finally, on the same assumption, together with the general Keynesian denigration of the influence of money on the economy and concentration on the short run, the connections between the balance of payments and the money supply, and between the money supply and aggregate demand, could be disregarded. Attention was therefore concentrated on the 'elasticity conditions' required for the impact effect of a devaluation—i.e. of the associated change in relative real prices—to be an improvement in the balance of payments. These conditions were, for a simple model with perfectly elastic supplies and initially balanced trade, that the sum of the elasticities of home and foreign demand for imports should exceed unity (the so-called 'Marshall–Lerner condition'); and for more complex models assuming independent elasticities of demands for imports and supplies of exports, a fearfully complex algebraic expression, cumbersome but challenging to derive and explore.

(Much of the interest in this body of work lay in the related questions of whether a devaluation that improved the balance of payments would necessarily turn a country's terms of trade against it, and increase domestic employment.)

The so-called 'elasticity approach' to devaluation proved demonstrably unsatisfactory in the immediate post-war period of full and over-full employment, owing to its implicit assumption of the existence of unemployed resources that could be mobilised to produce the additional exports and import substitutes required to satisfy a favourable impact effect. Recognition of this by the profession came in three versions. One was carping at the irrelevance of 'orthodox theory' (which the elasticity approach really was not), generally associated with the recommendation of exchange controls and quantitative import restrictions as an alternative to devaluation. The second was S. S. Alexander's 'absorption approach', which argued essentially that a favourable effect from devaluation alone, in a fully-employed economy, depends not on the elasticities but on the inflation resulting from the devaluation in these conditions producing a reduction in aggregate absorption relative to aggregate productive capacity. One part of the mechanism that might bring this about in Alexander's analysis is worth mentioning as foreshadowing the new approach to be discussed below; the 'real balance effect', by which the rise in prices consequent on the excess demand generated by devaluation deflates the real value of the domestic money supply and so induces a reduction in spending out of income.

The presentation of the 'absorption approach' as an alternative to the 'elasticity approach' led to considerable controversy and extensive efforts to reconcile the two. The truth lies, however, in recognition that a fully employed economy cannot use devaluation alone as a policy instrument for correcting a balance-of-payments deficit. It must use a combination of devaluation—to obtain an allocation of foreign and domestic demand among domestic and foreign output consistent with balance-of-payments equilibrium—and deflation—to match aggregate domestic demand with aggregate domestic supply. More generally, it must use a proper combination of what I have elsewhere called 'expenditure-reducing' and 'expenditure-switching' policies. This general principle is developed at length in James Meade's classic book on *The Theory of International Economic Policy:*

The Balance of Payments, though it was known before. It constitutes the third, and most useful, version of recognition of the inadequacies of the 'elasticity approach' as well as providing a synthesis between that approach and the 'absorption approach', that is logically satisfactory (though not economically satisfactory from the point of view of the new monetary approach). Unfortunately, Meade presented his analysis in terms of a short-run equilibrium analysis, and on the assumption that the policy-makers understood the theory as well as he did, both of which characteristics made the book extremely inaccessible to policy-makers and may help to account for the bumbling of British demand-management policy after the devaluation of 1967. Also, following the tradition of British central banking and monetary theory, Meade identified monetary policy with the fixing of the level of interest rates, a procedure that automatically excludes consideration of the monetary consequences of devaluation by assuming them to be absorbed by the monetary authorities (this is the reason for the economic objection to the Meade synthesis mentioned above).

Subsequent to the work of Meade and others in the 1950s, the main development in conventional balance-of-payments theory has been the development of the theory of the fiscal-monetary policy mix, following the pioneering contributions of R. A. Mundell. In the general logic of the Meade system, a country has to have two policy instruments if it is simultaneously to achieve internal and external balance (full employment and balance-of-payments equilibrium). In Meade's system, the instruments are demand management by fiscal and/or monetary policy, and the exchange rate (or controls or wage-price flexibility). What if wages are rigid, and controls and exchange rate changes are ruled out by national and international political considerations? A solution can still be found, at least in principle, if capital is internationally mobile in response to interest rate differentials. Fiscal expansion and monetary expansion then have the same effects on the current account, increasing imports and possibly decreasing exports, but opposite effects on the capital account, fiscal expansion increasing domestic interest rates and attracting a capital inflow and monetary expansion having the opposite effect, so that the two policies can be 'mixed' so as to achieve a capital account surplus or deficit equal to the current account deficit or surplus at the level of full employment of the economy. This extension of the Meade approach has lent itself to almost infinite mathematical product differentiation, with little significant improvement in quality of economic product, and will not concern us further, except to note that theoretical investigation of the model led naturally into the question of what would happen if capital were perfectly mobile, and specifically the implications of this assumption for the ability of the monetary authority to control the domestic money supply.

To recapitulate, the essential structure of what may be termed the standard model of balance-of-payments theory is a Keynesian model of income determination, in which flows of consumption and investment expenditure are determined by aggregate income and demand-management policy variables (taxes and expenditures, and interest rates), and the level of exports and the division of total expenditure between domestic and foreign goods (imports) are determined by the exchange rate which fixes the relative real prices of exports relative to foreign prices and of imports relative to domestic prices. By choosing a proper mix of demand-management policies and the exchange rate, the authorities can obtain full employment consistently with any current account surplus or deficit. The net current account surplus (or deficit) is equal to the excess (or deficiency) of the economy's flow of production over its flow of absorption, or to the excess (or deficiency) of its exports over its imports, or to its net excess (deficiency) of the flow of savings in relation to the flow of investment. By convention, but by no means necessarily, the current account surplus or deficit is identified with the overall balance-of-payments position; it is easy enough to add in the determination of the balance on capital account by the differential between domestic and foreign interest rates, as is in fact done in the theory of the fiscal–monetary policy mix.

The basic assumption on which this system of balance-of-payments analysis rests, and which forms the point of departure of the new 'monetary' approach to balance-of-payments theory, is that the monetary consequences of balance-of-payments surpluses or deficits can be and are absorbed (sterilised) by the monetary authorities so that a surplus or deficit can be treated as a flow equilibrium. The new approach assumes—in some cases, asserts—that these monetary inflows or outflows associated with surpluses or deficits are not sterilised—or cannot be, within a period relevant to policy analysis—

but instead influence the domestic money supply. And, since the demand for money is a demand for a stock and not a flow, variation of the supply of money relative to the demand for it associated with deficit or surplus must work towards an equilibrium between money demand and money supply with a corresponding equilibration of the balance of payments. Deficits and surpluses represent phases of stock adjustment in the money market and not equilibrium flows, and should not be treated within an analytical framework that treats them as equilibrium phenomena.

It should be noted, however, that this criticism applies to the use of the standard model for the analysis and policy prescription of situations involving deficits or surpluses; where the standard model is used for the analysis of the policies required to secure balance-of-payments equilibrium, it is generally not subject to this criticism because by assumption the domestic money market will be in equilibrium. But even in this case the fiscal–monetary mix version of it is open to criticism for confusing stock adjustment in the market for securities, in response to a change in interest-rate differentials between national capital markets, with a flow equilibrium.

In order to obtain flow-equilibrium deficits or surpluses on the basis of stock adjustments in the money market (and also possibly the securities market) it is necessary to construct a model in which the need for stock adjustments is being continuously re-created by economic change—in other words, to analyse an economy or an international economy, in which economic growth is going on. This is one of the important technical differences between the new 'monetary' models of the balance of payments and the standard Keynesian model—and a potent source of difficulty in comparing the results of the two types of analysis.

A further difference between the two types of models is that the 'monetary' models almost invariably assume—in contrast to the emphasis of the standard model on the influence of relative prices on trade flows—that a country's price level is pegged to the world price level and must move rigidly in line with it. One justification for this assumption is that, at least among the advanced industrial countries, industrial competition is so pervasive that elasticities of substitution among the industrial products of the various countries approximate more closely to infinity than to the relatively low numbers implicit in the standard model. Another and more sophisticated justification is derivable from the general framework of the monetarist approach, namely that changes in relative national price levels can only be transitory concomitants of the process of stock adjustment to monetary disequilibrium and that in the longer-run analysis of balance-of-payments phenomena among growing economies attention should be focused on long-run equilibrium price relationships—which for simplicity can most easily be taken as constant.

This point has sometimes been put in terms of the positive charge that the standard model rests on 'money illusion', in the sense that it assumes that workers will accept a reduction in their real standard of living brought about by a devaluation which they would not accept in the form of a forced reduction of domestic money wages. An alternative version of this charge is that the standard model assumes that workers can be cheated out of their real marginal product by devaluation. The charge, however, is incorrect: if rectification of a balance-of-payments deficit requires that the domestic marginal product of labour in terms of foreign goods falls, because the price of domestic goods relative to foreign goods must be reduced in the foreign and home markets to induce substitution between these goods favourable to the balance of payments, it requires no money illusion but only economic realism for the workers to accept this fact. Applications of the standard model to the case of devaluation, however, do require the assumption of money illusion if the elasticities of substitution between domestic and foreign goods are in fact high (approximately infinite), and it is nevertheless assumed that wages will remain unchanged in terms of domestic currency. For in this case it is being expected that workers will be content to accept wages below the international value of their marginal product, and that employers will not be driven by competition for labour in the face of this disequilibrium to bid wages up to their marginal productivity levels. The issue therefore is not one of the standard model wrongly assuming the presence of money illusion on the part of the workers, but of its possibly wrongly assuming low elasticities of substitution between domestic and foreign goods—which is an error in empirical assumptions rather than in model construction.

One further difference between the two types of model of balance-of-payments theory is worth noting. Whereas the Keynesian model assumes that employment and output are variable at (relatively) constant prices and wages, the monetary models assume that output and employment tend to full-employment levels, with reactions to changes taking the form of price and wage adjustments. This difference mirrors a broader difference between the Keynesian and quantity theory approaches to monetary theory for the closed economy. The assumption of full employment in the monetary balance-of-payments models can be defended on the grounds that these models are concerned with the longer run, and that for this perspective the assumption of full employment is more appropriate than the assumption of general mass unemployment for the actual world economy since the end of the Second World War.

I now turn from the discussion of theoretical issues in model construction to an exposition of some monetarist models of balance-of-payments behaviour in a growing world economy. The models to be constructed are extremely simple, inasmuch as they concentrate on the overall balance of the balance of payments, i.e. on the trend of international reserve acquisition or loss, and ignore the composition of the balance of payments as between current account, capital account and over-all balance, as well as the question of changes in the structure of the balance-of-payments accounts that may occur as a country passes through various stages of economic growth. Nevertheless they will, I hope, provide some interesting insights into balance-of-payments phenomena.

To begin with, it is useful to develop some general expressions relating the growth rates of economic aggregates to the growth rates of their components or of the independent variables to which they are functionally related. These can be established by elementary calculus, and are merely stated here. In the formulas, g is the growth rate per unit of time of a subscripted aggregate or variable, A and B are components of an aggregate, $f(A, B)$ is a function of A and B, and η denotes the elasticity of the aggregate defined by the function with respect to the subscripted variable. Then we have

$$g_{A+B} = \frac{A}{A+B} g_A + \frac{B}{A+B} g_B$$

$$g_{A-B} = \frac{A}{A-B} g_A - \frac{B}{A-B} g_B$$

$$g_{AB} = g_A + g_B$$

$$g_{A/B} = g_A - g_B$$

$$g_{f(A, B)} = \eta_A g_A + \eta_B g_B$$

(where η denotes an elasticity).

I begin with a discussion of monetary equilibrium in a single country, maintaining a fixed exchange rate with the rest of the world, assumed to be growing over time, and small enough and diversified enough in relation to the world economy for its price level to be the world price level, and its interest rate the world interest rate. (Differentials between domestic and foreign price indices, or between domestic and foreign interest rates, could readily be allowed for, provided they are assumed fixed by economic conditions.) In addition, it is assumed that the supply of money is instantaneously adjusted to the demand for it, because the residents of the country can get rid of or acquire money either through the international market for commodities or through the international securities market. Which mechanism of adjustment of money supply to money demand prevails will determine the way in which monetary policy affects the composition of the balance of payments, but that is a question not pursued in the present analysis.

The consequence of these assumptions is that domestic monetary policy does not determine the domestic money supply but instead determines only the division of the backing of the money supply the public demands, between international reserves and domestic credit. Monetary policy, in other words, controls the volume of domestic credit and not the money supply; and control over domestic credit controls the balance of payments and thus the behaviour of the country's international reserves.

The demand for money may be simply specified as

$$M_d = pf(y, i)$$

where M_d is the nominal quantity of domestic money demanded; y is real output; i is the interest rate or alternative opportunity cost of holding money; p is the foreign and therefore domestic price level; and multiplication of the demand for real balances, $f(y, i)$, by p

assumes the standard homogeneity postulate of monetary theory. The supply of money is

$$M_s = R + D$$

where R is the international reserve and D the domestic credit or domestic assets backing of the money supply. Since by assumption M_s must be equal to M_d,

$$R = M_d - D$$

and

$$g_R = \frac{1}{R} B(t) = \frac{M_d}{R} g_{M_d} - \frac{D}{R} g_D$$

where $B(t) = dR/dt$ is the current overall balance of payments. Letting $r = R/M_s = R/M_d$, the initial international reserve ratio, and substituting for g_{M_d},

$$g_R = \frac{1}{r}(g_p + \eta_y g_y + \eta_i g_i) - \frac{1-r}{r} g_D.$$

Simplifying by assuming constant world prices and interest rates,

$$g_R = \frac{1}{r} \eta_y g_y - \frac{1-r}{r} g_D$$

i.e. reserve growth and the balance of payments are positively related to domestic economic growth and the income elasticity of demand for money, and negatively related to the rate of domestic credit expansion. Simplifying still further by assuming no domestic growth ($g_y = 0$),

$$g_R = -\frac{1-r}{r} g_D$$

i.e. reserve growth and the balance of payments are inversely related to the rate of domestic credit expansion.

These results are to be contrasted with various Keynesian theories about the relation between economic growth and the balance of payments. According to one such theory derived from the multiplier analysis, economic growth must worsen the balance of payments through increasing imports relative to exports; this theory neglects the influence of demand for money on export supply and import demand and on the international flow of securities. According to another and more sophisticated theory, domestic credit expansion will tend to improve the balance of payments by stimulating investment and productivity increase and so lowering domestic prices in relation to foreign prices and improving the current account through the resulting substitutions of domestic for foreign goods in the foreign and domestic markets. This theory begs a number of questions even in naïve Keynesian terms; in terms of the present approach it commits the error of attempting to deduce the consequences of domestic credit expansion from its presumed relative price effects without reference to the monetary aspect of balance-of-payments surpluses and deficits.

Henceforth the analysis will be simplified by assuming that world interest rates are constant, so that the growth of demand for real balances depends only on the growth of real output (the growth of demand for nominal money balances depends of course also on the rate of change of the price level). This assumption can be justified on the grounds that real rates of return on investment are relatively stable, and that money rates of interest in a longer-run growth context will be equal to real rates of return plus the (actual and expected) rate of world price inflation or minus the (actual and expected) rate of world price deflation.

The foregoing model was concerned with one small country in a large world economy. The next model considers monetary equilibrium in the world system as a whole. For initial simplicity it is assumed that there is a single world money, i.e. there is no national credit money supplementing international reserves. This assumption does considerable violence to reality, but it can be rationalised on the assumption that each national economy's domestic banking system can be compressed into a functional relation between its real output and its demand for real international reserves. The essential difference between this model and the preceding one is that the world price level becomes endogenous instead of exogenous, determined by the relation between the growth rates of demand for and supply of international reserves.

For the world economy, the growth rate of demand for international money, assuming the homogeneity postulate as before, is

$$g_{M_d} = \sum_i w_i \eta_{y_i} g_{y_i} + g_p$$

where the w_i are initial country shares in the world money supply. Equilibrium requires $g_{M_d} = g_{M_s}$, where g_{M_s} is the growth rate of the world money supply. This requirement determines the rate of change of world prices,

$$g_p = g_{M_s} - \sum_i w_i \eta_{y_i} g_{y_i}.$$

The growth rate of an individual country's holdings of international money (which is also its balance-of-payments surplus, or deficit if negative, as a proportion of its initial reserves) is

$$\begin{aligned}
g_{M_j} &= \eta_{y_j} g_{y_j} + g_p \\
&= \eta_{y_j} g_{y_j} + g_{M_s} - \sum_i w_i \eta_{y_i} g_{y_i} \\
&= g_{M_s} + (1 - w_j)\left(\eta_{y_j} g_{y_j} - \sum_{i \neq j} \frac{w_i}{1 - w_j} \eta_{y_i} g_{y_i} \right) \\
&= g_{M_s} + (1 - w_j)(\eta_{y_j} g_{y_j} - \overline{\eta_{y_i} g_{y_i}})
\end{aligned}$$

where the bar denotes the average product of income elasticity of demand for real balances and rate of growth of real income in the rest of the world, or

$$g_{M_j} = g_{M_s} + \eta_{y_j} g_{y_j} - \overline{\eta_y g_y}$$

when the bar denotes the average product of the two terms for the whole world economy.

A country will acquire world money (through a balance-of-payments surplus) faster or slower than the rate of world monetary expansion according as the product of its income elasticity of demand for real balances and its growth rate of output exceeds or falls short of either this average product for the rest of the world or this average product for the whole world including itself. In the latter event it may lose international reserves even though total world reserves are growing.

If for further simplification it is assumed that the growth rate of world reserves is zero, the condition just stated determines whether the country has a surplus or a deficit. If for further simplification the income elasticity of demand for real balances is assumed to be everywhere unity, the expression reduced to

$$g_{M_j} = (1 - w_j)(g_{y_j} - \overline{g_{y_i}}) = g_{y_j} - \overline{g_y}$$

the bars successively denoting the average growth rate in the rest of the world and the average growth rate of the world as a whole, and the country gains or loses reserves according as its real growth rate is greater or less than the world average.

The preceding model aggregated national monetary systems into a demand for international money derived from real output. I now turn to a model in which the world economy possesses an international reserve money, but in which the residents of the various countries demand national monies which are based partly on international money reserves and partly on domestic credit. In the model, the total money supply for the world economy is

$$M = R + \sum_i D_i$$

$$= \sum_i w_i r_i M + \sum_i w_i (1 - r_i) M$$

where R is total international reserve money; D_i is domestic credit in country i; w_i is country i's share in the total world stock of money; and r_i is country i's ratio of international reserve money to its domestic money supply.

As before, the rate of growth of world demand for money is

$$g_{M_d} = \sum_i w_i \eta_{y_i} g_{y_i} + g_p.$$

The rate of growth of the world money supply is

$$g_{M_s} = \sum_i w_i r_i g_R + \sum_i w_i (1 - r_i) g_{D_i}.$$

These two equations determine the rate of change of world prices, through the requirement that $g_{M_d} = g_{M_s}$:

$$g_p = \sum_i w_i r_i g_R + \sum_i w_i (1 - r_i) g_{D_i} - \sum_i w_i \eta_{y_i} g_{y_i}.$$

From previous results, the growth rate of an individual country's reserves is

$$g_{r_j} = \frac{1}{r_j} (g_p + \eta_{y_j} g_{y_j}) - \frac{1 - r_j}{r_j} g_{D_j}$$

$$= \frac{1}{r_j} \sum_i w_i r_i g_R + \frac{1}{r_j} \sum_i w_i (1 - r_i) g_{D_i} + \frac{1}{r_j} \eta_{y_j} g_{y_j}$$

$$- \frac{1}{r_j} \sum_i w_i \eta_{y_i} g_{y_i} - \frac{1 - r_j}{r_j} g_{D_j}$$

$$= \frac{1}{r_j} \left\{ \sum_i w_i r_i g_R + (\eta_{y_j} g_{y_j} - \overline{\eta_y g_y}) - [(1 - r_j) g_{D_j} - \overline{(1 - r) g_D}] \right\}$$

where the bars again indicate the average product of the barred terms for the world economy.

This expression indicates that a country's reserves will grow faster the lower its initial reserve ratio, the faster the growth of total world reserves, the higher its income elasticity of demand for money and its real growth rate relative to other countries, and the lower its international reserve ratio and rate of domestic credit expansion relative to other countries.

Simplifying by assuming that income elasticities of demand for money are everywhere unity, and that international reserve ratios are also the same everywhere, we obtain

$$g_{R_j} = g_R + \frac{1}{r} (g_{y_j} - \overline{g_y}) - \frac{1 - r}{r} (g_{D_j} - \overline{g_D})$$

which shows that the growth rate of a country's reserves will on these assumptions tend to be faster than the world average if its real growth rate is greater than the world average, and slower than the world average if its rate of credit expansion is greater than the world average, and vice versa.

An alternative approach in this model is to formulate the money supply for the world in terms of the ratio of international reserves to total money stock r, initial shares in international reserves s_i, and initial ratios of domestic credit to reserves d_i. (Note that $r = 1/(1 + d)$, where d is the ratio of credit to reserves.) Then

$$M = \sum_i s_i R + \sum_i d_i s_i R$$

$$g_{M_d} = \sum_i s_i (1 + d_i) \eta_{y_i} g_{y_i} + g_p$$

$$g_{M_s} = r(g_R + \sum_i d_i s_i g_{D_i})$$

$$g_p = r(g_R + \sum_i d_i s_i g_{D_i}) - \sum_i s_i (1 + d_i) \eta_{y_i} g_y$$

$$g_{R_j} = (1 + d_j)(g_p + \eta_{y_j} g_{y_j}) - d_j g_{D_j}$$

$$= (1 + d_j) r g_R + [(1 + d_j) \eta_{y_j} g_{y_j} - \sum_i s_i (1 + d_i) \eta_{y_i} g_{y_i}]$$

$$- [d_j g_{D_j} - (1 + d_j) r \sum_i d_i s_i g_{D_i}]$$

$$= (1 + d_j) r g_R + [(1 + d_j) \eta_{y_j} g_{y_j} - \sum_i s_i (1 + d_i) \eta_{y_i} g_{y_i}]$$

$$- \left[d_j g_{D_j} - \frac{1 + d_j}{1 + d} \sum_i d_i s_i g_{D_i} \right].$$

This alternative formulation, which will not be explored further here, naturally produces the same qualitative results as the one presented above.

The next stage in making the 'monetary' model of balance-of-payments behaviour more realistic is to introduce a reserve-currency country whose currency is held as a substitute for the basic international money. The interesting problem in this case is the behaviour of the reserves of the reserve-currency country. The total world money supply is as before the sum of reserves and domestic credit created by the individual countries; but the reserve-currency role enables the reserve-currency country to induce other countries to hold its domestic money, backed by its own domestic credit, instead of or in addition to providing their own money by domestic credit creation.

As before we have

$$g_{Ms} = \sum_i w_i r_i g_R + \sum_i w_i (1 - r_i) g_{D_i}$$

$$g_p = \sum_i w_i r_i g_R + \sum_i w_i (1 - r_i) g_{D_i} - \sum_i w_i \eta_{y_i} g_{y_i}.$$

But now the behaviour of the reserve currency country's reserves is determined by the relation between the growth of both foreign and domestic demand for its money, and its domestic credit expansion. Assuming homogeneity in money demand still,

$$g_{R_j} = \frac{1}{r_j} [g_p + h\eta_{y_j} g_{y_j} + (1 - h)g_f] - \frac{1 - r_j}{r_j} g_{D_j}$$

where h is the proportion of the reserve currency country's currency held by residents and g_f is the rate of growth of foreign demand for its money as a reserve currency, in real terms.

$$g_{R_j} = \frac{1}{r_j} [(1 - h)g_f + \sum_i w_i r_i g_R + (h\eta_{y_j} g_{y_j} - \overline{\eta_y g_y})] -$$
$$- [(1 - r_j)g_{D_j} - \overline{(1 - r)g_D}].$$

If the real foreign demand for the reserve country's currency is assumed to be a constant proportion of the foreign money supply, the expression simplifies to

$$g_{R_j} = \frac{1}{r_j} [\sum_i w_i r_i g_R + h(\eta_{y_j} g_{y_j} - \overline{\eta_y g_y})] - [(1 - r_j)g_{D_j} - \overline{(1 - r)g_D}].$$

Assuming unitary income elasticities of demand for real balances everywhere and the same initial ratios of international reserves to domestic money, it simplifies further to

$$g_{R_j} = g_R + \frac{h}{r}(g_{y_j} - \overline{g_y}) - \frac{1-r}{r}(g_{D_j} - \overline{g_D}).$$

That is, the reserve currency country will gain reserves faster than the rate of growth of total reserves if its real growth rate exceeds the world average or its rate of domestic credit expansion is below the world average, and vice versa.

An alternative formulation of the problem, using the same two assumptions for simplicity, is to ask what rate of growth of foreign holdings of the reserve currency is necessary to enable the reserve currency country's reserves to grow at the world rate. The answer is

$$g_f = \frac{1}{1-h}[(1-r)(g_{D_j} - \overline{g_D}) - (hg_{y_j} - \overline{g_y})].$$

That is, foreign demand for the reserve currency must grow faster, the faster the reserve currency country's rate of domestic credit expansion relative to the rate of credit expansion abroad and the slower its real rate of growth relative to the real world growth rate.

Finally, I apply the general class of monetary models of the balance of payments developed above to the problem of the effects of a devaluation of a currency. The application is not entirely theoretically satisfactory, since the mathematics employed relate to continuous change whereas a devaluation is a once-over affair. Still, the results are suggestive.

For this problem, retain the assumption that domestic prices must keep in line with foreign prices, but introduce an exchange rate that can be changed, representing devaluation by an instantaneous rate of change of the exchange rate. The demand for money now becomes

$$M_d = \rho \, p_f f(y, i)$$

where p_f is the foreign price level and ρ is the price of foreign currency in terms of domestic. The rate of growth of reserves then becomes

$$g_R = \frac{1}{r}(g_p + g_{p_f} + \eta_y g_y + \eta_i g_i) - \frac{1-r}{r}g_D.$$

(Note that this formula reintroduces the interest rate as a determinant of the demand for money; for analysis, g_i may be interpreted as an expected rate of change of the money interest rate.)

There are several points to notice about the formula, with specific reference to the British devaluation of the pound in 1967 and the initial failure of that devaluation to improve the balance of payments.

Firstly, aside from the scale factor $(1 - r)$, devaluation is equivalent to domestic credit contraction; its function is to deflate domestic real balances and thereby to cause domestic residents to attempt to restore their real balances through the international commodity and security markets.

Secondly, since devaluation is a one-shot affair, it can be only a transitory factor for improvement in the balance of payments. Lasting improvement can only be achieved via a decrease in the rate of domestic credit expansion.

Thirdly, the beneficial transitory effects of devaluation on reserves and the balance of payments can be offset or neutralised by any one or more of the following developments: (i) an increase in the rate of domestic credit expansion, which the authorities may allow either unwittingly or as a consequence of efforts to hold down interest rates on government debt; (ii) a fall in the growth rate (though this requires modifying the model to allow unemployment, which may be induced by deflationary official policies or by lags in the adjustment of production to demand); (iii) a rise in interest rates inducing a fall in the demand for real balances relative to income: here interest rates have to be interpreted to include the expected money rate of return on holdings of goods, which may be expected to rise temporarily as a consequence of devaluation and the inflationary expectations generated by it.

It may be noted in passing that the equation for devaluation can be converted into an equation for the motion of a freely floating exchange rate as a function of policy variables, as follows:

$$g_\rho = rg_R + (1 - r)g_D - g_{Pf} - \eta_y g_y - \eta_i g_i.$$

The monetary models of the balance of payments surveyed in this chapter are long-run models, inasmuch as they assume full employment of resources and the necessity for domestic price levels to keep in line with the world price level. The Keynesian model with which they have been contrasted applies to a shorter run in which these assumptions do not necessarily, or commonly, hold. The Keynesian model has become the basis for policy-thinking and policy formulation. The monetary models suggest that it may be very misleading to rely on the Keynesian model as a guide to policy-making over a succession of short periods within each of which the Keynesian model may appear to be a reasonable approximation to reality.

ADDENDUM

The formulas presented in the text can be applied to a number of other problems than those mentioned, simply by rearranging terms. Thus, if a small country in an open international economy wishes to maintain a certain balance-of-payments surplus (growth rate of reserves), it must control the growth rate of domestic credit according to the formula

$$g_D = \frac{1}{1-r}(g_p + \eta_y g_y + \eta_i g_i - r g_R^*)$$

where g_R^* is the desired growth rate of reserves.

Similarly, in a world economy without a reserve-currency country, if there is an international monetary authority that has control over the growth of world reserves, and it seeks to maintain world price stability, the formula it must follow (assuming stability of interest rates) is

$$g_{MS}^* = \sum_i w_i \eta_{y_i} g_{y_i}.$$

Note that this formula will not imply a constant growth rate of world reserves over time, if income elasticities of demand for money, or growth rates of real output, vary among countries.

The formula is still more complex if the fractional-reserve character of domestic money supplies is allowed for, being

$$g_R^* = \frac{\sum_i w_i \eta_{y_i} g_{y_i} - \sum_i w_i (1 - r_i) g_{D_i}}{\sum_i w_i y_i}.$$

Note that the presence of a reserve-currency country does not affect this formula; however, it affects the empirical value of it indirectly through the effects of reserve-currency status on the willingness of the reserve-currency country to expand domestic credit, and the possible desires of other countries to expand domestic credit in order to avoid accumulating excess stocks of the reserve currency.

Finally, for a country on a floating exchange rate, the movement of the exchange rate over time is related to domestic credit expansion and exchange-market intervention intended to (or having the effect of) altering the country's international reserves by the formula

$$g_\rho = rg_R^* + (1 - r)g_D^* - g_{Pf} - \eta_y g_y - \eta_i g_i.$$

(The last term should probably be dropped, as a transitional factor.) *Note.* Arturo Brillembourg has pointed out to me an implicit assumption in the analysis of the effects of devaluation presented above, namely that the capital gains on the domestic value of international reserves are sterilized and have no effect on the money supply. For the longer run it would be more reasonable to assume that these gains are lent or transferred to the government and spent. In that case, $M_S = R + D$, $r = \dfrac{\rho R}{\rho R + D}$, and $g_R = \dfrac{1 - r}{r}(g_\rho - g_D) + \dfrac{1}{r}$ $(\eta_y g_y + \eta_j g_j + g_p)$. This formulation brings out more clearly than mine the symmetry between devaluation and domestic credit contraction, since there is no 'scale factor' as in my analysis. In this case

$$g_\rho = \frac{1}{1 - r}(\eta_y g_y + \eta_j g_j + g_p) - \frac{r}{1 - r}g_R - g_D,$$

in which equation the movement of the exchange rate can be thought of as determined by the authorities' desired rate of growth of reserves g_R. In a truly floating rate case, r goes to zero and $g_\rho = \eta_y g_y + \eta_j g_j + g_p - g_D$.

7

Devaluation, Money, and Non-Traded Goods[1]

RUDIGER DORNBUSCH

This chapter develops a monetary approach to the theory of currency devaluation.[2] The approach is 'monetary' in several respects. The role of the real balance effect is emphasised and a distinction is drawn between the relative prices of goods, the exchange rate and the price of money in terms of goods. Furthermore, money is treated as a capital asset so that the expenditure effects induced by a monetary change are spread out over time and depend on the preferred rate of adjustment of real balances.[3] The latter aspect gives rise to the analytical distinction between impact and long-run effects of a devaluation.

The first part of this chapter develops a one-commodity and two-country model of devaluation. The simplicity of that structure is chosen quite deliberately to emphasise the monetary aspect of the problem as opposed to the derivative effects that arise from induced changes in relative commodity prices. Trade is viewed as the exchange of goods for money or a means of redistributing the world supply of assets. A devaluation is shown to give rise to a change in the level of trade and the terms of trade, the price of money in terms of goods.

[1] University of Chicago. This paper draws on my dissertation and I am indebted to the members of my thesis committee, Harry Johnson, Stanley Fischer, and Robert Mundell. In revising the material I had the benefit of comments from Karl Brunner, George Borts, Stanley Engerman, and Murray Kemp. I am particularly indebted to Ronald W. Jones and Michael Mussa with whom I enjoyed extended discussion of the topic [Reprinted from *The American Economic Review*, lxii, 5 (December 1973), 871–83].

[2] This approach is by no means novel. For formal developments see Frank Hahn, Jones (1971), Kemp (1969, 1970), Mundell, and Takashi Negishi (1972). Acceptance of that approach has nevertheless remained limited.

[3] A 'capital-theoretic' approach to the real balance effect is developed by Alvin Marty.

In the second part the implications of the existence of non-traded goods are investigated, and induced changes in the relative prices of home goods enter the analysis.

1. DEVALUATION IN A ONE-COMMODITY WORLD

In this part we develop a purely monetary approach to devaluation in discussing a two-country, two-monies, and one-commodity model.[4] This stripped down model abstracts from the complexities of distribution and substitution effects that may arise from changes in relative commodity prices and places primary emphasis on the real balance effect.

A. The Model

We assume that money is the only marketable asset and that real income (output) is in fixed supply in each country. The demand for nominal balances in each country is assumed to have the Cambridge form.[5]

$$L = kP\bar{y}, \quad L^* = k^*P^*\bar{y}^* \tag{1}$$

where

k, k^* = the desired ratios of money to income
$\bar{y}, \bar{y}^*$ = real outputs
P, P^* = the money price of goods in terms of domestic and foreign currency

and where an asterisk denotes the foreign country. Given the exchange rate, e, the domestic currency price of foreign exchange, arbitrage ensures that

$$P = P^*e. \tag{2}$$

---

[4] The notion of trade in one commodity may alternatively be interpreted as trade in a composite commodity, so that relative goods prices remain unchanged. Such conditions may obtain either because of perfect substitution or else because of the absence of distribution effects.

[5] The particular functional form of the demand for money obviously lacks generality. It is chosen here in order not to detract from the main line of argument. Alternative specifications would assume the demand for money proportional to expenditure as in Jones (1971) or else derive the demand for money from intertemporal utility maximisation. Provided the underlying utility function is separable in consumption and real balances the qualitative conclusions of this paper carry over to such a formulation.

With respect to monetary policy we assume that the nominal quantity of money in each country M, M^*, is initially given and that governments abstain from changing domestic money supplies except as it is necessary to maintain a pegged exchange rate. Accordingly the rate of increase in the domestic money supply is given by the trade balance surplus, B.

$$\dot{M} = B = -e\dot{M}^*. \tag{3}$$

Desired nominal expenditure in each country, Z, Z^*, is equal to money income less the *flow* demand for money, H, H^*, where the latter is assumed proportional to the *stock* excess demand

$$Z = P\bar{y} - H, \tag{4}$$

$$Z^* = P^*\bar{y}^* - H^*,$$

$$H = \pi(L - M) = H(P, M); \tag{5}$$

$$H^* = \pi^*(L^* - M^*) = H^*(P^*, M^*),$$

and where π and π^* are the domestic and foreign rates of adjustment. The expenditure functions in (4) imply a short-run marginal propensity to spend out of income smaller than unity while in the long-run, when monetary stock equilibrium is attained, the average propensity to spend equals unity.

In Figure 7.1 we show the domestic rate of hoarding, H, and the foreign rate of *dis*hoarding, $-H^*$, as a function of P the domestic currency price of goods. The schedules are drawn for given nominal money supplies in each country and an exchange rate e^0. With the nominal quantity of money given, hoarding in the home country is an increasing function of the price level. An increase in the price level creates a stock excess demand for money and causes expenditure to decline relative to income as the community attempts to restore the real value of cash balances. It follows that we may view the hoarding schedule alternatively as the flow demand for money or the excess supply of goods (in nominal terms). By the same reasoning the foreign rate of *dis*hoarding, given the exchange rate, is a decreasing function of the home price level. We note that the distribution of the money supplies underlying Figure 7.1 is not compatible with balance-of-payments equilibrium. Foreign monetary stock equilibrium would obtain at P' while for domestic monetary equilibrium the price level would have to be equal to P''.

Consider now the conditions of short-run equilibrium. In order for the world goods market to clear, we require that world income equal

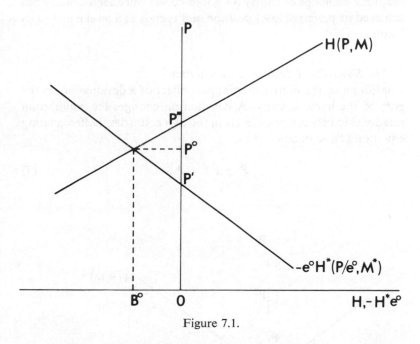

Figure 7.1.

world expenditure or equivalently that the home country's rate of hoarding equal the foreign country's rate of dishoarding.

$$H = - H^* e^0. \tag{6}$$

The equilibrium is shown in Figure 7.1 at a domestic currency price of goods P^0; a higher price level would leave a world excess supply of goods and a lower price level a world excess demand for goods. We observe, too, that the short-run equilibrium at P^0 implies a trade balance deficit for the home country equal to B^0. That deficit, in the absence of sterilisation, as we assume, redistributes money from the home country to the rest of the world. The reduction in the domestic nominal quantity of money reduces real balances at the initial price level and thereby causes planned hoarding to increase and conversely abroad. In terms of Figure 7.1 this implies that the hoarding and dishoarding schedules shift to the right, a process that continues over time until they intersect between P'' and P' on the vertical axis. At that time exchange of money for goods ceases since each country has achieved its preferred asset position and spends at a level equal to its income.

B. The Short-Run Effects of a Devaluation

Consider now the short-run or impact effect of a devaluation on the part of the home country. A devaluation changes the equilibrium relationship between price levels in the two countries. Differentiating equation (2) we obtain

$$\hat{P} = \hat{P}^* + \hat{e} \qquad (7)$$

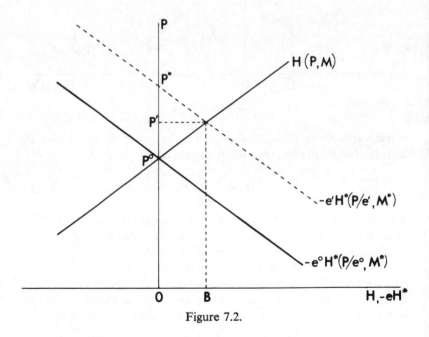

Figure 7.2.

where a circumflex (^) denotes a relative change in a variable. Equation (7) informs us only about the relationship between changes in the price levels at home and abroad; we have to investigate the equilibrium condition in the world goods market in order to determine what the actual change in the price level in each country will be. For that purpose we turn to Figure 7.2 where we show the world economy in initial long-run equilibrium at a domestic currency price of goods P^0.

The effect of a devaluation is shown in Figure 7.2 by an upward shift in the foreign dishoarding schedule. For foreign monetary stock equilibrium to obtain, given the nominal quantity of money, the foreign currency price of goods would have to remain constant which in turn by (7) implies that the domestic price level would have to increase in the same proportion as the exchange rate, a price change equal to $(P'' - P^0)/P^0$. The domestic hoarding schedule, on the contrary, is unaffected and domestic monetary stock equilibrium would continue to obtain at a domestic price level P^0. It is observed from Figure 7.2 that at an unchanged domestic price level there would be a world excess demand for goods due to the increase in foreign real balances and expenditure while at an unchanged foreign price level there would be a world excess supply of goods due to the decrease in domestic real balances and expenditure. It follows that in order for the world goods market to clear the price level changes will have to be distributed in such a manner as to reduce domestic absorption and increase foreign absorption by an equal amount.

The equilibrium increase in the domestic price level is equal to $(P' - P^0)/P^0$ while the foreign price level declines in the proportion $(P'' - P')/P^0$. We note that both the domestic and foreign currency price of goods change less than proportionately to the rate of devaluation and that the distribution of price changes depends on the relative slopes of the hoarding schedules.

Given these price changes foreign real balances have increased and the real value of domestic balances has decreased thereby causing foreigners to dishoard in order to decumulate their capital gains and domestic residents to save in order to restore the real value of their cash balances. The home country's balance of payments surplus is equal to OB and causes a redistribution of the world money supply.

The formal criterion for the price changes and the balance of payments can be developed by differentiating the goods market equilibrium condition

$$\pi(kP\bar{y} - M) + e\pi^*(k^*P\bar{y}^*/e - M^*) = 0 \qquad (6')$$

with respect to P and e holding the nominal quantity of money constant in each country. The relative change in the domestic price level is

$$\hat{P} = \frac{\pi^* M^* e}{\pi M + \pi^* M^* e}\, \hat{e}. \qquad (8)$$

Defining the world money supply, measured in terms of domestic currency $\bar{M}$,

$$\bar{M} = M + eM^* \qquad (9)$$

and the domestic and foreign country's share in the money world supply, σ and σ^*, we can rewrite (8) as

$$\hat{P} = \frac{\pi^* \sigma^*}{\pi\sigma + \pi^*\sigma^*}\, \hat{e} \geq 0. \qquad (8')$$

Substituting (8') in (7) we obtain the effect of a devaluation on the foreign price level:

$$\hat{P}^* = \frac{-\pi\sigma}{\pi\sigma + \pi^*\sigma^*}\, \hat{e} \leq 0. \qquad (10)$$

Equations (8') and (10) show the distribution of price changes to depend on relative effective size where effective size is the product of the speed of adjustment and the share in the world money supply. In the small country case ($\pi\sigma/\pi^*\sigma^* = 0$) the home country price level increases in the same proportion as the exchange rate.

The home country's trade balance surplus is obtained by differentiating the flow demand function for money with respect to the price level and substituting (8) to yield

$$dB = dH = \pi M\left[\frac{\pi^* M^* e}{\pi M + \pi^* M^* e}\right] \hat{e} > 0. \qquad (11)$$

Equation (11) confirms that the balance of payments unambiguously improves.

C. The Long-Run Effects of Devaluation

The long-run effects of devaluation on nominal money supplies and price levels may be interpreted with the help of Figure 7.3. In quadrants II and IV we show the domestic and foreign demand for real balances as hyperbolae; quadrant III shows the equilibrium price relationship $P^*e = P$ for the initial exchange rate as the ray OA. Lastly in quadrant I the world money supply at the initial exchange rate is given by $\bar{M}\bar{M}^*$, where $\bar{M}^* = \bar{M}/e$.

Initial long-run equilibrium is indicated by point E where the distribution of the world money supply is such that each country

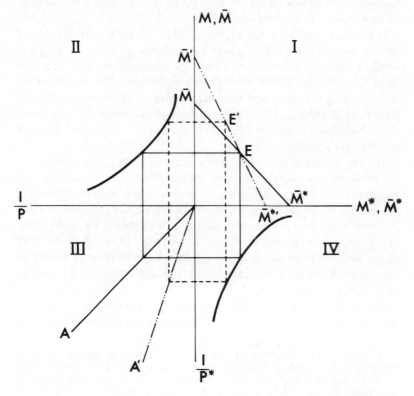

Figure 7.3.

holds the desired quantity of real balances and where the equilibrium relationship between price levels is satisfied.[6]

A devaluation on the part of the home country affects both the price relationship and the world money supply. To each domestic price level corresponds now a lower equilibrium foreign price level; this is indicated in quadrant III by a rotation of the arbitrage line to OA'. Furthermore, given the initial nominal quantities of money in each country indicated by point E, the world money supply measured in terms of either currency changes: it decreases when measured in terms of foreign currency by the initial domestic quantity of money times the exchange rate change and it appreciates in terms of domestic currency by the initial foreign quantity of money times the exchange rate change. Accordingly the world monetary constraint rotates around point E—the initial endowment of currencies—to become $\bar{M}'\bar{M}^{*\prime}$.

It is readily verified from Figure 7.3 that the initial distribution of money supplies at point E is no longer appropriate as a long-run equilibrium position since it would be inconsistent with the new price relationship. The new long-run equilibrium is shown by point E' indicating an increased domestic quantity of money and price level and a decreased foreign quantity of money and price level. Real balances obviously remain unchanged, between the new equilibrium and the old.

We should emphasise that our assumption about the absence of national money supply changes other than by the balance-of-payments mechanism is only one possible assumption about the behaviour of money supplies. If we had assumed on the contrary that the home country accompanied the devaluation by an equiproportionate increase in its nominal quantity of money the only short- and long-run effect of the combination of policies would be an equiproportionate increase in the domestic price level and no effect whatsoever abroad.[7]

The latter monetary assumption would be appropriate if the home country wished to run a transitory budget deficit financed by money

---

[6] For a similar geometric treatment, see Arnold Collery.

[7] In terms of Figure 7.3 the policy combination would imply that the world monetary constraint both rotates and shifts outward passing through $\bar{M}^*$ since the world money supply measured in terms of foreign currency would remain unchanged. The conclusions in the text are readily verified from the fact that the new equilibrium point would lie vertically above point E.

creation without impairing its foreign exchange position; the former assumption corresponds to the case where a country uses a devaluation to increase its foreign exchange holdings.

2. DEVALUATION AND NON-TRADED GOODS

In this part we consider an extension of the monetary model to introduce flexibility in relative prices. Following Jones (1972), Michael Michaely, Mundell, and Anne Krueger, we assume that there are two classes of goods produced and consumed in each country, traded goods and non-traded goods. Each class of goods itself is taken to be a composite commodity so that the relative prices of goods within each group are invariant. The aggregation chosen here places emphasis on the relative price of non-traded in terms of traded goods rather than on the terms of trade between internationally traded goods; it emphasises the effects of changes in absorption on relative prices rather than the income effect of changes in the relative prices of traded goods.

This extension has two implications for the effects of a devaluation: changes in hoarding or equivalently changes in expenditure relative to income change the equilibrium relative price of home goods and these changes in relative prices in turn affect the equilibrium rates of hoarding.

We will show that in this more disaggregated structure the conclusions of the one-commodity model continue to hold for the effects of a devaluation on the balance of payments and the prices of traded goods; the additional element that arises is that the reduction in domestic absorption and the increase in foreign absorption cause the relative price of home goods to decline at home and to rise abroad. This result may be viewed as a special case of transfer analysis and arises in that perspective since each country's marginal propensity to spend on foreign home goods is by definition zero.[8]

A. The Model
Denoting traded and non-traded commodities as goods one and two, respectively, we assume that production takes place along a

---

[8] The relationship between the transfer problem and devaluation is more extensively analysed in Dornbusch (1973) and Jones (1971).

concave transformation curve and that supplies are a function only of the relative price:

$$X_i = X_i(q), \, i = 1, 2 \tag{12}$$

where q is the relative price of non-traded goods—the ratio of the domestic currency prices of non-traded and traded goods, P_2 and P_1, respectively:

$$q = P_2/P_1. \tag{13}$$

Demand for the two commodities is assumed to depend on money prices and nominal expenditure, or, using the homogeneity property and adopting traded goods as a numeraire, on relative prices and real expenditure measured in terms of traded goods, $\tilde{Z}$.[9]

$$C_i = C_i(q, \tilde{Z}), \, i = 1, 2. \tag{14}$$

Real expenditure is defined as real income less real hoarding, all measured in terms of traded goods as a numeraire:

$$\tilde{Z} = \tilde{Y} - \tilde{H} \tag{15}$$

where real income or the real value of output is defined as follows:

$$\tilde{Y} \equiv X_1 + qX_2 = \tilde{Y}(q). \tag{16}$$

Monetary considerations affect the goods markets via the expenditure function and in particular via the planned rate of hoarding. Maintaining our assumption that the demand for nominal balances is proportional to money income and that hoarding is proportional to the stock excess demand for money we may write the desired real rate of hoarding, measured in terms of traded goods, as a function of the relative price and the real quantity of money measured in terms of traded goods:

$$\tilde{H} = \tilde{H}(q, \tilde{M}) \tag{17}$$

[9] In the remainder of this chapter a tilde will denote the fact that a quantity is measured in terms of traded goods. When these quantities are referred to as 'real' this will not imply measurement in terms of a price index.

where $$\tilde{M} = M/P_1. \qquad (18)$$

Our assumptions about the stock demand for money ensure that an increase in either domestic currency price raises the desired rate of real hoarding so that the following properties hold:

$$q\frac{\partial\tilde{H}}{\partial q} \equiv \alpha > 0, \quad -\tilde{M}\frac{\partial\tilde{H}}{\partial\tilde{M}} \equiv \beta > 0. \qquad (19)$$

The definition of real expenditure in (15) may be rewritten as the budget constraint in a manner that reveals the disaggregation of the model:

$$q(X_2 - C_2) + (X_1 - C_1) = \tilde{H}. \qquad (20)$$

It is evident from the budget constraint that when the home-goods market clears ($X_2 = C_2$) the excess supply of traded goods identically equals the planned rate of hoarding.

Given a corresponding set of behavioural relations and constraints for the foreign country we can now turn to the conditions of short-run equilibrium in this model. Short-run equilibrium obtains when for a given exchange rate and given money supplies, all goods markets clear; that is, when the market for non-traded goods clears in each country and when the world market for traded goods clears. Such an equilibrium, by the budget constraint in each country, implies that one country's planned rate of hoarding equals the other country's planned rate of dishoarding. Equations (21) formally state these equilibrium conditions of the model

$$E_2 \equiv X_2(q) - C_2(q, \tilde{Z}) = 0, \qquad (21)$$

$$E_2^* \equiv X_2^*(q^*) - C_2^*(q^*, \tilde{Z}^*) = 0,$$

$$\tilde{H}(q, \tilde{M}) + \tilde{H}^*(q^*, \tilde{M}^*) = 0,$$

where

$$\tilde{M}^* \equiv M^*/P_1^*; \quad q^* \equiv P_2^*/P_1^*; \quad P_1^*e = P_1.$$

The first two conditions in (21) state that in equilibrium the excess

demand for home goods is zero in each country while the third
equation is the market clearing condition in the market for traded
goods.

B. The Impact Effect of a Devaluation

To examine the modifications in the effects of devaluation brought
about by the introduction of non-traded goods we consider first the
relationship between the relative price of home goods and real
hoarding. In particular we want to show that an increase in real
hoarding lowers the relative price of home goods. That result
obtains since an increase in real hoarding represents a decrease in
real expenditure relative to real income so that at constant relative
prices and given a positive marginal propensity to spend on home
goods the demand for home goods decreases. A decline in the
relative price of home goods is required in order to eliminate the
excess supply generated by an increase in hoarding. More formally
the relationship between the relative price of home goods and real
hoarding may be derived by differentiating the first market
equilibrium condition in (21) to obtain

$$\hat{q} = - \frac{m_2}{(\eta_2 + e_2)qC_2} \, d\tilde{H} \tag{22}$$

where

$$m_2 \equiv q \, \frac{\partial C_2}{\partial \tilde{Z}} > 0,$$

$$\eta_2 \equiv - \frac{q}{C_2} \left[\frac{\partial C_2}{\partial q} + \frac{\partial C_2}{\partial \tilde{Z}} \frac{\partial \tilde{Y}}{\partial q} \right] > 0,$$

$$e_2 \equiv \frac{\partial X_2}{\partial q} \frac{q}{X_2} > 0.$$

The terms m_2, η_2, and e_2 denote, respectively, the marginal propensity
to spend on home goods, the compensated elasticity of demand for
home goods, and the elasticity of supply.

In Figure 7.4 we show the market equilibrium schedule for the
home country's non-traded goods market as the *locus* $E_2 = 0$; to

maintain market equilibrium the expenditure reducing effects of an increase in hoarding have to be offset by the substitution effects of a decrease in the relative price of home goods.

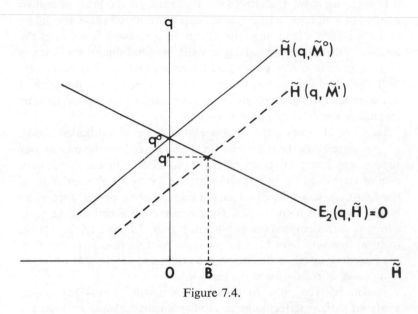

Figure 7.4.

So far we have treated hoarding as the exogeneous variable and have enquired into the relative price effects of changes in hoarding. We wish next to develop an expression that relates the rate of hoarding, given the nominal quantity of money, to price changes. Differentiating the hoarding function in (17) we obtain

$$d\tilde{H} = \alpha\hat{q} + \beta\hat{P}_1 \tag{23}$$

and substituting for the change in the relative price of home goods, $\hat{q}$, from (22), we obtain

$$d\tilde{H} = \gamma\beta\hat{P}_1 \tag{24}$$

where the terms

$$\gamma \equiv \frac{1}{1 + \alpha\delta} > 0, \; \delta \equiv \frac{m_2}{(\eta_2 + e_2)qC_2} > 0$$

are introduced for notational convenience. To gain further understanding of the relationship between hoarding, relative prices and
the money price of traded goods derived in (24) we turn to Figure
7.4 where we show the effect of an increase in the price of traded
goods. In addition to the market equilibrium schedule for home
goods we draw a hoarding schedule as an increasing function of the
relative price of home goods, given the nominal quantity of money
and the price of traded goods and hence the real quantity of money,
$\tilde{M}^0$. The schedule is upward sloping since an increase in the price of
home goods raises income and hence the demand for money, thereby
increasing the desired rate of hoarding.

Initial equilibrium is shown at a relative price of non-traded goods,
q^0. An increase in the price of traded goods reduces the real money
supply and hence increases at constant relative prices the desired
rate of hoarding. This is shown in Figure 7.4 by a rightward shift of
the hoarding schedule. Since at constant relative prices there is an
excess supply of home goods, their relative price will decline to q'
which in turn dampens the equilibrium rate of hoarding, $\tilde{B}$, relative
to what it would have been at constant relative prices. The shift in
the hoarding schedule corresponds to the term $\beta \hat{P}_1$ in (24) while the
dampening effect shows in the term γ.

It will be recognised that in the composite commodity model
analysed earlier perfect substitutability ensured that $\delta = 0$. In the
present formulation the absence of perfect substitution and the
requirement that home-goods markets clear ensure that absorption
changes are reflected in changes in relative prices; furthermore these
induced changes in relative prices affect the equilibrium rate of
hoarding tending to reduce the hoarding response associated with a
given change in the price of traded goods.

Having developed the basic relationships of the model we can now
proceed to investigate the effects of a devaluation. For that purpose
we turn to Figure 7.5. In the upper part of that figure we draw the
domestic and foreign home goods market equilibrium schedules,
where the latter is drawn as a function of the foreign rate of *dis*-
hoarding and hence is negatively sloped. We assume, arbitarily and
without consequence, that initially the relative prices of home goods
are the same in both countries. In the lower part of Figure 7.5 we
draw the domestic hoarding schedule and the foreign dishoarding
schedule. It is important to note that along these hoarding schedules

the relative price of home goods is allowed to adjust in order to clear the home-goods market so that by the budget constraint these hoarding schedules may alternatively be interpreted as the domestic excess supply of traded goods and the foreign excess demand for traded goods. Analytically the schedules are defined by equation (24) and its counterpart for the foreign country.

Initial equilibrium obtains at a domestic currency price of traded goods P_1^0 and equilibrium relative prices of home goods $q^0 = q_0^*$. A devaluation by the home country may be analysed in a manner similar to the composite commodity model developed above. At an unchanged domestic currency price of goods foreign real balances increase causing foreigners to dishoard which is shown in Figure 7.5 by a rightward shift of the foreign dishoarding schedule to $\tilde{H}^{*'}$. Short-run equilibrium will obtain at a domestic currency price of goods $\bar{P}_1$ where the world market for traded goods clears. The increase in the domestic price of traded goods causes the home country to reduce expenditure relative to income and run a trade balance surplus equal to $\bar{B}$. Corresponding to the reduction in domestic absorption we find a decline in the relative price of non-traded goods at home to $\bar{q}$ while the increase in foreign absorption raises the relative price of non-traded goods in that country to $\bar{q}^*$.

These results can be derived more formally by consideration of the equilibrium in the world market for traded goods. Recalling that (24) allows explicitly for market clearing in the home-goods market that expression is identically equal to the excess supply of traded goods. Accordingly we may use (24) and its counterpart for the foreign country to determine the effects of a devaluation on the domestic currency price of traded goods:

$$\beta\gamma\hat{P}_1 + \beta^*\gamma^*(\hat{P}_1 - \hat{e}) = 0 = d\tilde{H} + d\tilde{H}^* \qquad (25)$$

Solving for the relative change in the domestic currency price of traded goods yields

$$\hat{P}_1 = \frac{\beta^*\gamma^*}{\beta\gamma + \beta^*\gamma^*} \, \hat{e} \equiv \theta\hat{e}. \qquad (26)$$

The solution for the effect of a devaluation on the domestic currency price of traded goods shows that this price will increase less

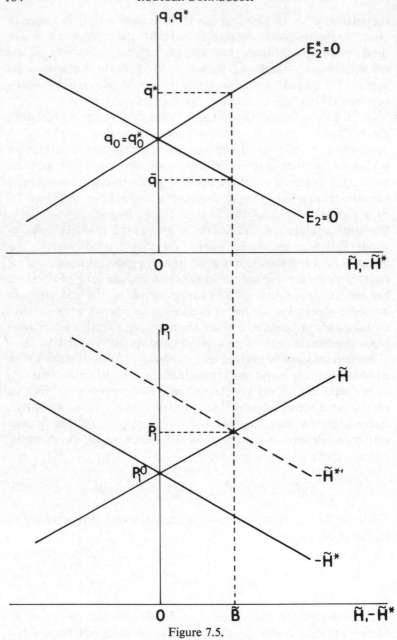

Figure 7.5.

than proportionately to the rate of devaluation $(0 < \theta < 1)$. Differentiating the price relationship $P_1^* = P_1/e$ it is seen that the foreign currency price of traded goods will fall less than proportionately to the rate of devaluation. Subsitution of (26) in (24) shows that the devaluing country's balance of payments unambiguously improves:

$$d\tilde{H} = \beta\gamma\theta\hat{e}. \tag{27}$$

So far our results correspond qualitatively to those obtained in the composite commodity model. The departure arises from the fact that changes in absorption in the two countries change the equilibrium relative prices of home goods. Substituting (27) in (22) we find that a devaluation lowers the relative price of nontraded goods in the home country and raises it abroad:

$$\hat{q} = - \delta\beta\gamma\theta\hat{e}; \quad \hat{q}^* = \delta^*\beta^*\gamma^*(1 - \theta)\hat{e}. \tag{28}$$

While, as in the first part of this chapter, short-run equilibrium is characterised by an exchange of traded goods for real balances and hence the absorption effects of a devaluation are emphasised, the role of the relative price of home goods is nevertheless crucial in the adjustment mechanism. Given imperfect substitutability between home goods and traded goods on the production side it is the adjustment in the relative price of home goods that translates changes in absorption into an excess supply of traded goods at home and an excess demand for traded goods abroad.

3. CONCLUDING REMARKS

Rather than summarise here the conclusions of this chapter we wish to emphasise some of the issues raised by the present formulation of devaluation analysis.

The first and primary issue concerns the role of money in models of devaluation. The stance taken here is that a devaluation is foremost a monetary phenomenon and that its effects derive from the reduction in the real value of money attendant upon a devaluation. If it is believed that the effects of a reduction of real balances on expenditure, by whatever transmission mechanism, are negligible, then it may stand to reason that the effects of a devaluation are negligible not that there must be other powerful avenues through which it exerts its effects.

The second issue that deserves attention is that of aggregation. The formulation developed here suggests that it is helpful to view traded goods as a composite commodity and thus to highlight the distinction between money and goods and between classes of goods that are respectively traded and nontraded.

REFERENCES

Collery, A. *International Adjustment, Open Economies and the Quantity Theory of Money*, Princeton Studies in International Finance, no. 28 (Princeton, 1971).

Dornbusch, R. 'Aspects of a Monetary Theory of Currency Depreciation', unpublished doctoral dissertation, Univ. Chicago, 1971.

Dornbusch, R., 'Currency Depreciation, Hoarding and Relative Prices', *J. Polit. Econ.* (July/Aug. 1973), *81*, 893–915.

Hahn, F. 'The Balance of Payments in a Monetary Economy', *Rev. Econ. Stud.*, Feb. 1959, *26*, 110–25.

Jones, R. W. 'A Role for Money in the Exchange Model', unpublished, Univ. Rochester, 1971.

Jones, R. W. 'Alternative Models of Devaluation', unpublished, Univ. Rochester, 1972.

Kemp, M. 'The Balance of Payments and the Terms of Trade in Relation to Financial Controls', *Rev. Econ. Stud.*, Jan. 1970, *37*, 25–31.

Kemp, M., *The Pure Theory of International Trade and Investment* (Englewood Cliffs, 1969), ch. 14.

Krueger, A. O., 'The Role of Home-Goods in Exchange Rate Adjustments', unpublished, 1971

Marty, A., 'The Real Balance Effect: An Exercise in Capital Theory', *Can. J. Econ. Polit. Sci.*, Aug. 1964, *30*, 360–7.

Michaely, M., 'Relative-Prices and Income-Absorption Approaches to Devaluation: A Partial Reconciliation', *Amer. Econ. Rev.*, Mar. 1960, *50*, 144–7.

Mundell, R. A., *Monetary Theory* (Pacific Palisades, 1971), chs. 9–11.

Negishi, T., *General Equilibrium Theory and International Trade* (Amsterdam, 1972), 15–17.

8

Tariffs and the Balance of Payments[1]

A Monetary Approach

MICHAEL MUSSA[2]

INTRODUCTION

The purpose of this chapter is two-fold: firstly, to expound the basic features of the 'monetary approach' to the balance of payments; secondly, to provide a specific example of the monetary approach by analysing the effects of a tariff on the balance of payments. The exposition of the basic features of the monetary approach will emphasise general principles rather than specific models and specific results. At this level of generality, it will be argued that a monetary approach is essential for sensible discussion of the behaviour of the balance of payments. The analysis of the effects of a tariff will use a specific, formal model. The results will depend on the assumptions of the model. The basic principles of the monetary approach, however, will be shown to be robust to a variety of respecifications of the model.

The question of the effects of a tariff on the balance of payments, rather than the more standard question of the effects of a devaluation, will be discussed because the analysis of this question brings out most forcefully the essentially monetary character of the balance of payments. A tariff is a 'real' policy which has its primary effects on 'real' variables such as relative prices, levels of production and

[1] This chapter is a substantially revised and shortened version of a paper of the same title which was delivered at the Fourth Konstanz Conference on Monetary Theory and Policy 1973; see also Mussa (1974).

[2] I would like to thank Rudiger Dornbusch for his many helpful comments and suggestions.

consumption, and the volume of trade. These 'real' effects can be analysed in an exclusively 'real' model (i.e. a model in which money is not present). It will be argued, however, that the effect of a tariff on the balance of payments cannot be analysed except in an explicitly monetary model. The common-sense view that a tariff improves the balance of payments because it discourages imports will be shown to be fallacious.

The general view which we will develop of the effect of a tariff on the balance of payments may be summarised as follows: in the long run, a tariff has no effect on the balance of payments, thought of as a flow, but does have an effect (under fixed exchange rates) on the level of a country's foreign exchange reserves, brought about by a temporary change in the balance of payments. The reason for this long-run change in reserves and temporary change in the balance of payments is that the tariff affects the long-run demand for nominal money balances. A tariff increases the domestic money prices of imported goods and import substitutes. In general, this increase in prices reduces the real value of the country's initial nominal stock of money relative to the demand for real money balances and, thereby, sets in motion a process of adjustment which, in the absence of an expansion of the domestic source component of the money supply, leads to an increase in the money supply brought about by an inflow of foreign exchange. The exact nature of the process of adjustment will vary from model to model. The only necessary feature is that the balance-of-payments surplus must always be equal to the excess of income over expenditure. Assuming that prices and wages adjust to clear markets and maintain full employment, the long-run effect of a tariff on the level of foreign exchange reserves (i.e. the cumulative effect on the balance of payments) depends on the properties of the money demand function, on the effect of the tariff on the arguments of the money demand function, and on the response of the domestic source component of the money supply to the change in money demand.

In addition, our analysis will show that there are circumstances in which a tariff can lead to a cumulative balance of payments deficit (even if the domestic source component of the money supply is held constant). Further, we will analyse a 'Keynesian' model in which the money wage is assumed to be fixed, and show that in such a model, a tariff will result in an increase in the level of output, thus providing an additional reason for an increase in money demand and a larger, cumulative balance of payments surplus. Finally, the analysis for the case of a tariff will be extended to other commercial policies.

1 THE MONETARY APPROACH TO THE BALANCE OF PAYMENTS

The monetary approach to the balance of payments consists of a set of broad principles which are shared by a wide class of specific theoretical models. In this section, these broad principles will be summarised into three basic features of the monetary approach.[3]

A. An Essentially Monetary Phenomenon

The first feature is summarised in the fundamental proposition: *the balance of payments is an essentially (but not exclusively) monetary phenomenon*. In this proposition, the term 'the balance of payments' refers specifically to the Official Settlements Balance, that is, to the 'money account'. The official settlements balance is in surplus (deficit) when the monetary authorities of a country are purchasing (selling) foreign exchange assets in order to prevent their own money from appreciating (depreciating) relative to other monies. Thus, analysis of the balance of payments only makes sense in an explicitly monetary model, and, in this sense, the balance of payments is an essentially monetary phenomenon.[4] Or, to give the point a more provocative tone, analysis of the balance of payments in a theoretical framework where money is not explicitly present is, prima facie, nonsense.

The monetary approach has a limited perspective. It does not attempt to provide a theory of the balance-of-payments accounts. These accounts include the trade account, the service account, the

---

[3] The monetary approach to the balance of payments is not a new approach: the basic ideas date back at least to David Hume and his discussion of the price specie flow mechanism. Indeed, up to the 1930s, the monetary approach was *the* recognised approach to the analysis of the balance of payments. For a particularly penetrating discussion of the basic features of the 'monetary approach', see Marshall (1926). Also see Keynes (1971).

[4] Under a system of freely floating rates, attention is shifted from the balance of payments, which is always zero, to the exchange rate, which moves up and down to absorb the consequences of policy and parametric changes which, under a system of fixed rates, would affect the balance of payments.

short-term and long-term capital accounts, and the private and government transfer accounts, as well as the official settlements account. The monetary approach concentrates on the official settlements account and lumps everything else into a single category: 'items above the line'. The rules of double entry book-keeping require that the net sum of all items which appear above the line equal the official settlements balance. The monetary approach attempts to provide only a theory of this net sum, not to explain its decomposition.

The narrowness of the monetary approach in its concentration on the official settlements account is complemented by the breadth of the monetary approach in its conception of 'an essentially monetary phenomenon'. To say that something is 'an essentially monetary phenomenon' says that money plays a vital role, but does not imply that *only* money plays a role. The monetary approach takes explicit account of the influence of 'real' variables such as levels of income and interest rates on the behaviour of the balance of payments. Indeed, a primary purpose of the present article is to explain how what is usually thought of as a 'real' variable, the tariff rate, can have an effect on the balance of payments, and thus to dispel the confusion which has associated the monetary approach with the view that 'only money matters'.

B. The Demand for Money and the Supply of Money

To some extent, this confusion has been generated because of a second basic feature of the monetary approach: *the use of the money supply process and, particularly, the demand for money function as the central theoretical relationships around which to organise thought concerning the balance of payments.* The basic rationale for this principle of organisation is that we are interested in the behaviour of the money account for which the demand for money and the supply of money should be of prime importance. The same principle would apply if we were interested in the steel account; we would organise the analysis around the demand for and supply of steel.

The importance of the principle of organisation is dramatised by contrasting it with the frequently employed procedure of treating the balance of payments as the excess of exports over imports. Given the rules of double entry book-keeping, this procedure is formally correct, provided that the import demand and the export supply functions are correctly specified. But, it does not focus on the prime determinants of the behaviour of the money account; and, in practice, it is rarely the case that the demand and supply functions are correctly specified. Usually, the import demand function and the export supply function abstract from monetary variables with the result that the demand for money and the supply of money are either ignored or treated as passive in the analysis of the money account.

Of course, if the organisation of the analysis of the balance of payments around the demand for money function and the money supply process is to make much sense, the demand for money and the money supply process must be stable functions of a limited set of variables. Fortunately, extensive empirical analysis has established the existence of both a stable money demand function and a stable money supply process. Given these stable relationships, it follows that if any policy or parametric change is to have an effect on the balance of payments, it must cause a divergence between what the demand for money would have been in the absence of the policy or parametric change and what the supply of money would have been in the absence of any change in the level of official holdings of foreign exchange. If there is no such divergence, then there can be no long-run, cumulative effect on the balance of payments. Any initial surplus must be wiped out by a later deficit and any initial deficit must be wiped out by a later surplus because people will not be willing to hold either more or less money than they were previously holding.

If money demand were passive, i.e. if the economy was in a liquidity trap, the monetary approach would have no predictive power. The cumulative balance-of-payments surplus would be whatever was dictated by exclusively non-monetary considerations, and the demand for money would simply adjust to that fact and a non-monetary approach would not only be justified, it would be required.

A stable money supply process is, in some ways, less essential to the monetary approach to the balance of payments than a stable money demand function.[5] That part of the money supply process which deals with the behaviour of the monetary authorities need not be stable since the focus of the analysis is usually on the policy

[5] For a discussion of the money supply process in an open economy, see Brunner (1973).

choices which are open to the monetary authority. For this purpose, the behaviour of the monetary authorities is taken as exogeneous, and the question that is asked is: what would be the effect on the balance of payments if the monetary authorities pursued policy X rather than policy Y? A sensible and useful answer to this type of question depends only on the assumption of reasonably stable behaviour on the part of other actors in the money supply process.

The monetary approach does not always assume a constant domestic source component of the monetary base, nor does it always assume that the monetary authorities follow the gold standard rules of the game by maintaining a constant ratio of foreign exchange reserves to the monetary base. If the monetary authorities expand the domestic source component of the base in excess of the growth in the implied demand for the base, then the monetary approach predicts that there will be a balance-of-payments deficit equal in magnitude to the excessive expansion of the domestic source component of the base. If the monetary authorities sterilise the balance-of-payments surplus created by, say, the imposition of a tariff, then the monetary approach predicts that there will be a further surplus, equal to the reduction in the domestic source component of the base which is implied by sterilisation, and so on, until the sterilisation operations cease.[6]

The monetary approach forces into the open the question of what the monetary authorities are doing and, hence, isolates effects which arise from a particular policy of parametric change, *per se*, and effects which arise from the induced (and frequently implicit) responses of the monetary authorities. Thus, the monetary approach avoids the unsound and objectionable procedure of concealing the basic determinants of the behaviour of the balance of payments behind such assumptions as 'a neutral monetary policy' or 'a

[6] Some care must be taken in analysing the effects of a policy of sterilisation. If the monetary authorities are selling domestic interest-bearing assets out of their portfolio in order to sterilise a foreign exchange inflow, then the stock of such assets in private hands must be rising and the interest which the government will be required to pay on the privately held government debt will be rising. The effects of a change in the stock of privately held debt and the effects of the change in government interest payments and of the means which are used to finance these interest payments must be dealt with in order to have a complete analysis of the effects of sterilisation. The issue here is akin to the issue of what happens to the budget surplus in a closed economy macro model. For further discussion, see Mussa (1976).

monetary and fiscal policy which maintains internal balance' or 'an accommodating monetary policy'.

C. The Long Run and the Short Run

The empirical evidence which justifies the assumption of a stable money supply process and a stable money demand function applies to periods of a year or more, rather than to periods of a month or a quarter. These empirical facts account for the third basic feature of the monetary approach: *a concentration on the longer-run consequences of policy and parametric changes for the behaviour of the balance of payments, coupled with an eclectic view of the processes through which these longer-run consequences come about.*

This concentration on 'longer-run consequences' does not imply that the nature of the process of adjustment is unimportant or that specific models which lie within the monetary approach can and should ignore the process of adjustment. Rather, the monetary approach takes an eclectic view of the process of adjustment because it seems unlikely that any single model of the process of adjustment will be relevant to all countries, at all time periods, and under all institutional arrangements. The monetary approach seeks to combine a relatively general theory of long-run behaviour with a number of different models of the process of adjustment.

Concerning the concentration of the monetary approach on 'longer-run consequences', four comments should be made. Firstly, if these 'longer-run consequences' take years or decades to materialise, the monetary approach will not be very useful. It will not be useful for discussing current policy problems because the horizon of the policy maker is typically much shorter than a decade. It will not be useful for empirical analysis because there is great difficulty in sorting out empirical relationships which involve very long lags. Therefore, the advocacy of a monetary approach to the balance of payments necessarily involves the assertion that these 'longer-run consequences' materialise within a time horizon of two or three years.

Secondly, while the monetary approach explicitly denies the possibility that the demand for money is passive in the long run, it admits the possibility that the demand for money may be more or less passive in the short run. In the short run, money might operate as a buffer stock which serves to absorb the changes in other variables. In such an event, essentially non-monetary factors would determine the behaviour of the balance of payments in the very short run. The monetary approach, however, denies that this very short run could last very long before monetary factors began to assert themselves and explicitly raises the question of how long the very short run is. Thus, the monetary approach focuses attention on the critical role which monetary factors must play in the process of adjustment.

Thirdly, the monetary approach emphasises that as a fact of accounting, the balance-of-payments surplus is identically equal to the excess of income over expenditure. Hence, any analysis of the process of adjustment must explain how the policy or parametric change which is under investigation generates a divergence between income and expenditure.[7] The monetary approach does not insist that such a divergence may be created only by a real balance effect working directly on expenditure. Expenditure may be affected by changes in interest rates or changes in the values of non-monetary assets. In a world of capital mobility, the requirements of portfolio balance may lead to purchases or sales of assets to the rest of the world.[8] In a variable employment model, the divergence between income and expenditure may come as a result of changes in income rather than changes in expenditure. All of these mechanisms, and conceivably others, can play a role in the process of adjustment. The point is that there must be at least one such mechanism. This mechanism should be explicit, rather than implicit, in the formal model of the process of adjustment.

Fourthly, since the monetary approach establishes the long-run balance-of-payments effects of a policy change, it places limits on what is a reasonable analysis of the process of adjustment. If a tariff causes a finite change in foreign exchange reserves in the long run, then an analysis which suggests that a tariff creates a permanent (flow) balance-of-payments surplus is clearly incorrect. The analysis of the process of adjustment must show that as foreign exchange reserves accumulate, the flow balance-of-payments effect of the

---

[7] The fact that a balance-of-payments surplus requires an excess of income over expenditure is the fundamental principle of the 'absorption approach' to balance-of-payments analysis. The monetary approach incorporates this basic principle of the absorption approach in so far as the analysis of the process of adjustment is concerned. For further discussion of the absorption approach, see Alexander (1952) and Johnson (1958).

[8] Note that purchases of assets are included with expenditures, and sales of assets are included with income in the calculation of the balance-of-payments surplus as the difference between income and expenditure.

tariff is gradually reduced and ultimately eliminated. The cumulative balance-of-payments surplus which is implied by the process of adjustment must be equal to the required long-run change in foreign exchange reserves.

2 THE EFFECTS OF A TARIFF INCREASE IN A SMALL, FULLY EMPLOYED ECONOMY

In order to illustrate the basic features of the monetary approach to the balance-of-payments analysis, we will consider the specific problem of analysing the effect of an increase in the tariff in a small, fully employed economy which will be referred to as 'the home

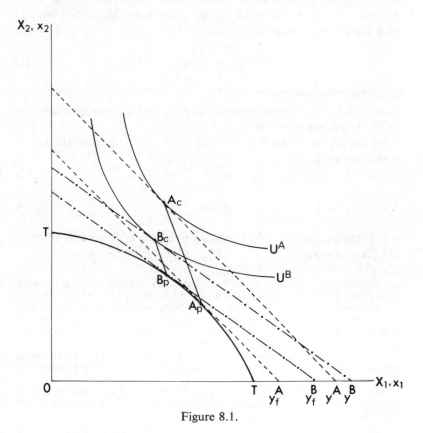

Figure 8.1.

country'. The home country produces and consumes two goods: an exportable, good 1, and an importable, good 2. Production of the two goods will be denoted by x_1 and x_2, respectively; and consumption of the two goods will be denoted by X_1 and X_2, respectively. The assumption of full employment means that the economy's production point is constrained to lie along the transformation curve TT which is shown in Figure 8.1. The assumption that the home country is small means that the prices of the two goods in the rest of the world, P_1^* and P_2^*, respectively, will be taken as given, and all repercussions of the home country's behaviour on the rest of the world will be ignored.[9] The relative price of good 2 in terms of good 1 in the rest of the world is denoted by $q^* \equiv P_2^*/P_1^*$.[10] The domestic relative price of good 2 which faces producers and consumers in the home country, $q \equiv P_2/P_1$, is equal to the world price multiplied by one plus the *ad valorem* tariff rate, i.e.

$$q = (1 + \tau) . q^*. \tag{1}$$

A. A Model of the Real Sector

The model of the real sector of the home country's economy consists of the following elements:

(i) Supply functions for the two goods derived from the transformation curve,

$$x_1 = x_1^s(q) \tag{2}$$

$$x_2 = x_2^s(q); \tag{3}$$

(ii) Demand functions for the two goods derived from a community indifference map,[11]

---

[9] The assumption that the home country is 'small' is useful because it permits us to obtain a clear view of the roles of real and monetary factors in determining the balance-of-payments effects of a tariff increase, without having to deal with the complexities that arise when the home country is of substantial size relative to the rest of the world. These complexities are discussed in some detail in a separate paper; see Mussa (1974).

[10] An asterisk (*) superscripted to a symbol indicates that the variable in question refers to the rest of the world. Symbols without asterisks refer to the home country.

[11] It is convenient for purposes of graphical analysis to assume that the demand functions arise from a community indifference map. This assumption is not essential for the formal analysis.

$$X_1 = X_1^d(q, c), \tag{4}$$

$$X_2 = X_2^d(q, c), \tag{5}$$

where c is total consumption expenditure measured in terms of good 1 and where the demand functions satisfy

$$X_1^d(q, c) + q . X_2^d(q, c) = c; \tag{6}$$

(iii) The budget constraint

$$c = y \tag{7}$$

which requires that consumption expenditure (measured in terms of good 1) equal the income of consumers (measured in terms of good 1), y, where income is equal to factor income, y_f (which is equal to the value of output at domestic prices, $x_1 + q . x_2$), plus redistributed tariff proceeds (which are equal to the tariff rate multiplied by the value of imports at world prices),[12] i.e.

$$y = x_1^s(q) + q . x_2^s(q) + \tau . q^*(X_2^d(q, c) - x_2^s(q)), \tag{8}$$

$$= y_f(q) + \tau . q^*(X_d^2(q, c) - x_s^2(q)).$$

Imposing the condition (7), we obtain the equation

$$y - x_1^s(q) - q . x_2^s(q) - \tau . q^* . (X_2^d(q, y) - x_2^s(q)) = 0 \tag{9}$$

which may be solved to determine the level of income, $\bar{y}(\tau)$, as a function of the tariff rate, given the world price ratio, q^*. Substituting $\bar{y}(\tau)$ into the demand functions we determine the consumption point as a function of the tariff rate.

Diagrammatically, this procedure amounts to the following: for a given value of the tariff rate, say, τ^A, determine the production point, A_p. From this point, move up and to the left along a line which has slope (relative to the x_2 axis) equal to minus the world

---

[12] The government is deriving revenue from the tariff. The disposal of this revenue must be accounted for. The simplest assumption is that the government distributes the tariff proceeds as lump sum transfers.

price ratio until a point, A_c, is reached at which the slope of the tangent to the community indifference curve is equal to minus the domestic price ratio. The intercept of the tangent to this community indifference curve with the horizontal axis determines the level of income and expenditure, y^A. This level of income is equal to the sum of factor income, y_f^A, which is given by the horizontal intercept of the tangent to the transformation curve at the production point A_p, and the tariff proceeds, $y^A - y_f^A$, which are equal to the vertical distance between the consumption point A_c and the production point A_p multiplied by the difference between the domestic relative price of good 2 and the world relative price of good 2.

B. The Long-Run Real Effects of an Increase in the Tariff

Now consider the effects of an increase in the tariff rate. As illustrated in Figure 8.1, an increase in the tariff rate from τ^A to τ^B increases the domestic relative price of good 2 and shifts the production point from A_p to B_p. The value of output measured in terms of good 1 rises from Y_f^A to Y_f^B.[13] The new consumption point, B_c, lies along the line passing through B_p with slope equal to the given value of the world price ratio. At B_c, the slope of the community indifference curve, U^B, is equal to the new domestic price ratio. The new indifference curve, U^B, necessarily lies below the initial indifference curve, U^A.[14] The volume of trade, both imports and exports, declines, as indicated by the fact that the distance from B_p to B_c is shorter than the distance from A_p to A_c.[15] The level of income and expenditure, measured in terms of good 1, is seen to rise from y^A to y^B.[16]

Formally, the effects of an increase in the tariff rate on various magnitudes may be determined by differentiating the relevant

[13] The value of output must rise provided that some positive amount of good 2 is produced.

[14] Since the home country has no monopoly power in trade and since there are no other distortions present in the economy, an increase in the tariff must make the home country worse off.

[15] Provided that the import good is 'normal' in the ordinary demand theory sense, the volume of trade must decline. In this case the income and substitution effects in demand and the production substitution effect all operate to reduce imports of good 2.

[16] This is not a necessary result. The level of income and expenditure could fall if the reduction in tariff proceeds is greater than the increase in the value of output. The possibility will be discussed in greater detail below.

expressions. In particular, the change in total income and total expenditure is[17,18]

$$d\bar{y}/d\tau = \frac{X_2 \cdot q^* + \tau \cdot ((\delta X_2^d/\delta q) - (dx_2^s/dq)) \cdot q^{*2}}{1 - \tau \cdot q^* \cdot (\delta X_2^d/\delta c)} \quad (10)$$

The effect of the tariff increase on the balance of trade and on the difference between income and expenditure requires emphasis. In the equilibrium which prevails before the tariff increase and in the equilibrium which prevails after the tariff increase, trade is balanced and income is equal to expenditure. The increase in the tariff reduces imports, but it reduces the value of exports (at world market prices) by exactly the same amount. The increase in the tariff increases income (measured in terms of good 1), but it also increases expenditure by the same amount. From these facts it follows that, within the context of the exclusively real theory model, an increase in the tariff rate cannot be seen to have any effect on the balance of payments. For this reason, the real theory model, by itself, cannot provide the basis for an adequate analysis of the balance-of-payments effects of tariff changes.

C. A monetary model

In order to analyse the balance-of-payments effects of an increase in the tariff rate, it is necessary to extend the real theory model to include behaviour with respect to money. In the monetary model, the money prices, P_1^* and P_2^*, denote the prices of the two goods in terms of world money. The domestic money prices of the two goods are determined by the home country's exchange rate (the price of a unit of world money in terms of units of domestic money), ϵ, and the tariff rate, τ, viz.

$$P_1 = \epsilon \cdot P_1^*, \quad (11)$$

$$P_2^* = (1 + \tau) \cdot \epsilon \cdot P_2^*. \quad (12)$$

---

[17] To derive this result, totally differentiate equation (9) and solve for $d\bar{y}/d\tau$. Using the fact that since the value of output is maximised at the initial value of q, it follows that $(dx_1^s/dq) + q \cdot (dx_2^s/dq) = 0$.

[18] Note, for future reference, that when the initial tariff is zero, the value of $d\bar{y}/d\tau$ is $X_2 \cdot q^*$.

The exchange rate will be assumed to be fixed by the monetary authorities in the home country. Further, it will be assumed that the only way in which the money supply of the home country changes is as a result of balance-of-payments surpluses and deficits. It follows that the rate of change of the home country's money supply, $\dot{M}$, is equal to the flow balance-of-payments surplus, B, i.e.

$$\dot{M} = B, \tag{13}$$

and that the total change in the money supply between time t_0 and time t_1 is

$$M(t_1) - M(t_0) = \int_{t_0}^{t_1} B(s)ds. \tag{14}$$

We will assume that the nominal demand for money, $L(Y, P_1, P_2, r)$ is a function of nominal income, $Y \equiv P_1 \cdot y$, the domestic money prices of the two goods, P_1 and P_2, and the interest rate on domestic securities, r; and has the usual properties including homogeneity of degree one in Y, P_1, and P_2.[19,20] Dividing through by P_1, we can write the demand for money measured in terms of good 1 as

$$L(Y, P_1, P_2, r)/P_1 = 1(y, q, r). \tag{15}$$

A useful special form of this money demand function arises when the demand for money is proportional to income with a factor of proportionality, $k(r)$, which depends only on the interest rate, i.e.

$$1(y, q, r) = k(r) \cdot y. \tag{16}$$

[19] The stock of domestic securities is fixed, and securities are not internationally tradeable. The demand for securities need not be dealt with directly because, following Metzler (1951), it is possible to argue that since the asset demand functions satisfy the asset constraint, equilibrium in the money market implies equilibrium in the securities market.

[20] It is convenient to think of the money demand function L as a reduced form demand function which incorporates the effects of changes in the interest rate on the real value of domestic securities. If the stock of domestic securities is thought of as the financial counterpart of the economy's stock of capital, then we would want the domestic relative price in the reduced form money demand function in order to pick up the effects of changes in relative prices on the income of capital and, hence, on the value of securities.

In the monetary model, in contrast to the exclusively real model, consumption expenditure is not automatically set equal to income. Rather, nominal desired expenditure $C^d(Y, P_1, P_2, r)$, is assumed to depend on nominal income, money prices, and the interest rate; and is assumed to be increasing as a function of Y, decreasing as a function of r, and homogeneous of degree one in Y, P_1, and P_2.[21] Dividing by P_1, we obtain desired consumption expenditure measured in terms of good 1;

$$C^d(Y, P_1, P_2, r)/P_1 = c^d(y, q, r). \qquad (17)$$

It is assumed that for each pair of values of y and q, there is a value of r, say $\bar{r}(y, q)$, for which desired consumption expenditure is equal to income. Necessarily,

$$d\bar{r}/dy = (1 - (\delta c^d/\delta y))/(\delta c^d/\delta r), \qquad (18)$$

$$d\bar{r}/dq = -(\delta c^d/\delta q)/(\delta c^d/\delta r). \qquad (19)$$

A useful special form of the desired expenditure function is given by

$$c^d(y, q, r) = b(r) \cdot y. \qquad (20)$$

For this special form there is a unique value of the interest rate, say, ρ, for which desired expenditure will be equal to income; that is, for the special form, $\bar{r}(y, q) = \rho$ for all y and q.

In discussing the monetary model, it is necessary to distinguish two concepts of equilibrium: 'instantaneous equilibrium' and 'long-run equilibrium'. For both types of equilibrium, producers must be on their supply functions, consumers must be on their demand functions, and the demand for money must be equal to the supply of money. For instantaneous equilibrium, the supply of money, M, is taken as given, at a moment of time, and equilibrium is analysed conditional on the given value of M. For instantaneous equilibrium, it is *not* required that consumption expenditure be equal to income. The excess (deficiency) of nominal income over nominal expenditure

---

[21] The desired expenditure function should be thought of as a reduced form behaviour function, in the same sense as the money demand function.

will be equal to the home country's balance-of-payments surplus (deficit) and, hence, to the rate at which the home country's money supply is growing (declining). In the analysis of long-run equilibrium, the nominal money supply is treated as a variable. The value of this additional variable is determined by imposing the requirement that, in long-run equilibrium, expenditure must be equal to income. In long-run equilibrium, the flow balance-of-payments surplus is zero, and there is no tendency for the money supply to grow or decline.

D. The cumulative balance-of-payments effect of a tariff increase

It is convenient to start with the analysis of long-run equilibrium. Given the requirement that consumption expenditure must be equal to income, it follows that the conditions which prevail in the real sector of the monetary model, in long-run equilibrium, must be exactly as described by the real theory model of subsection A.[22] Given the domestic price ratio and the level of income determined in the real sector, the long-run equilibrium level of nominal money balances, $\bar{M}(\tau)$, is determined by calculating the long-run equilibrium value of the interest rate, $\bar{r}(\bar{y}(\tau), (1 + \tau) . q^*)$, and evaluating money demand for this value of the interest rate and for $y = \bar{y}(\tau)$ and $q = (1 + \tau) . q^*$, i.e.

$$\bar{M}(\tau) = P_1 . 1(\bar{y}(\tau), (1 + \tau) . q^*, \bar{r}(\bar{y}(\tau), (1 + \tau) . q^*)). \quad (21)$$

Under our assumptions regarding the money supply process, the cumulative balance-of-payments effect of a tariff increase is equal to the difference between $\bar{M}$ at the new value of τ and $\bar{M}$ at the initial value of τ.[23] Formally, differentiating $\bar{M}$ with respect to τ,

---

[22] The supplies of commodities have been assumed to depend only on relative prices and not on the interest rate or on the level of real money balances. Demands for commodities have been assumed to depend on relative prices and on total desired expenditure. Total desired expenditure is affected by the interest rate and the interest rate is affected by the level of money balances, but neither the interest rate nor the level of money balances has any direct effect on the demands for individual commodities. In long-run equilibrium, where the level of expenditure must be equal to the level of income, commodity demands are independent of the interest rate and of the level of money balances. Thus, in so far as long-run equilibrium is concerned, money is a 'veil'.

[23] Even if the stock of nominal money balances is not equal to its initial long-run equilibrium value at the moment when the tariff is increased, it may be appropriate to equate the change in $\bar{M}$ to the cumulative balance-of-payments

we obtain the cumulative balance-of-payments effect of a 'small' change in the tariff rate:

$$\frac{d\bar{M}}{d\tau} = P_1 \left\{ \left[\frac{\delta 1}{\delta y} + \frac{\delta 1}{\delta r} \frac{\delta \bar{r}}{\delta y} \right] \frac{d\bar{y}}{d\tau} + \left[\frac{\delta 1}{\delta q} + \frac{\delta 1}{\delta r} \frac{\delta \bar{r}}{\delta q} \right] \cdot \frac{dq}{d\tau} \right\},$$

$$= P_1 \left\{ \left[\frac{\delta 1}{\delta y} + \frac{\delta 1}{\delta r} \left(\frac{1 - \dfrac{\delta c^d}{\delta y}}{\dfrac{\delta c^d}{\delta r}} \right) \right] \frac{d\bar{y}}{d\tau} + \right.$$

$$\left. + \left[\frac{\delta 1}{\delta q} + \frac{\delta 1}{\delta r} \left(\frac{-\dfrac{\delta c^d}{\delta q}}{\dfrac{\delta c^d}{\delta r}} \right) \right] \cdot q^* \right\}, \tag{22}$$

where $d\bar{y}/d\tau$ is given by (10).

When the money demand function and the desired expenditure function have the proportional forms given in (16) and (20), $\bar{M}(\tau)$ is given by

$$\bar{M}(\tau) = k(\rho) \cdot P_1 \cdot \bar{y}(\tau); \tag{23}$$

and starting from a zero initial tariff, the effect of a 'small' increase in the tariff is given by

$$d\bar{M}/d\tau = (k(\rho) \cdot P_1) \cdot (X_2 \cdot q^*). \tag{24}$$

The change in $\bar{M}$ is equal to the increase in the cost, at domestic prices, of purchasing the initial consumption bundle, multiplied by $k(\rho)$. The interpretation of this result is that the increase in the tariff leads to a cumulative balance-of-payments surplus because it reduces the real value of initial nominal money balances while leaving the real demand for money unchanged and, hence, requires

---

effect of the tariff increase. In the absence of the tariff increase, M would have gradually adjusted to its initial, long-run equilibrium value. The tariff increase forestalls this adjustment and, instead, causes M to adjust to the long-run equilibrium value which is appropriate for the new tariff rate.

an increase in nominal money balances which is exactly proportional to the increase in the price level.

These results for the proportional case are rather special, but the principle which they illustrate is quite general: given the assumption that the money supply changes only through the balance of payments, an increase in the tariff rate leads to a cumulative balance-of-payments surplus if and only if it increases the long-run equilibrium level of nominal money balances.

This analysis of the cumulative balance-of-payments effects of a tariff increase illustrates the first two features of the monetary approach to balance-of-payments analysis. Firstly, that money is essential to balance-of-payments analysis is apparent from the fact that when money is excluded from the model, it is not possible to derive any balance-of-payments consequences from an increase in the tariff rate. That the balance of payments is not an exclusively monetary phenomenon is apparent from the fact that, in general, it is necessary to know the changes in the real variables y and q in order to determine the change in the long-run equilibrium level of nominal money balances. Secondly, the central role of the money demand function and the money supply process is apparent from the way in which the cumulative balance-of-payments effect of an increase in the tariff rate has been calculated using the long-run relationship between money balances and the tariff rate which is given in (21). Note, however, that the money demand function is not the only relationship which is involved in the long-run relationship $\bar{M}(\tau)$. Rather, the money demand function is used as a vehicle to determine the effects on the balance of payments of the changes in the interest rate, income, and relative prices which are induced by the tariff increase.

3 THE PROCESS OF ADJUSTMENT

It remains to be shown how an increase in the tariff operates, in the short run, to generate the balance-of-payments surplus (or deficit) which produces the required long-run change in the nominal money supply. The mechanism which governs this process of adjustment is already present in the monetary model specified in section 2C. In the monetary model, the actual level of consumption expenditure is determined by the desired expenditure function and is not necessarily cqual to income. If the increase in the tariff rate increases the long-run equilibrium level of money balances above the money balances which are held at the moment when the tariff rate is increased, then, in the instantaneous equilibria which prevail after the increase in the tariff, expenditure will be less than income. The reduction in expenditure relative to income will come at the expense of consumption of *both* exportables and importables. The difference between income and expenditure is equal to the balance-of-payments surplus. As these surpluses accumulate, the money supply grows, and the excess of income over expenditure declines. Eventually, when the cumulative balance-of-payments surplus is equal to the required increase in the stock of nominal money balances, expenditure will equal income and the inflow of money will cease.

A. A Formal Analysis

For any given value of the tariff rate, domestic relative and absolute prices are completely determined and remain constant during the process of adjustment. It follows that the outputs of the two goods and the value of total output are completely determined by the tariff rate and remain constant throughout the process of adjustment. Thus, if we consider the effect of an increase in the tariff rate from, say, τ^A to τ^B, the effect must be, as illustrated in Figure 8.2, to shift the production point immediately from A_p to B_p and to increase the value of output (level of factor income) from y_f^A to y_f^B. Further, since the relative price which faces consumers responds immediately to the increase in the tariff, the consumption point must shift immediately to some point along the Engel curve for the new domestic relative price. The position of this point along the Engel will depend on the level of expenditure which households wish to make immediately after the increase in the tariff. If households wish to spend all of their income, the consumption point would be at its new long-run equilibrium position B_c. If households wish to spend less than their new long-run equilibrium level of income, y^B, the consumption point will lie below B_c, and, conversely, if they wish to spend more than y^B.

To determine the level of expenditure, proceed as follows: firstly, substitute the function $c^d(y, q^* \cdot (1 + \tau), r)$ for the variable c, which appears in (8), and solve the resulting equation to obtain a functional relationship, $\bar{y}(r; \tau)$, between the level of income and the interest

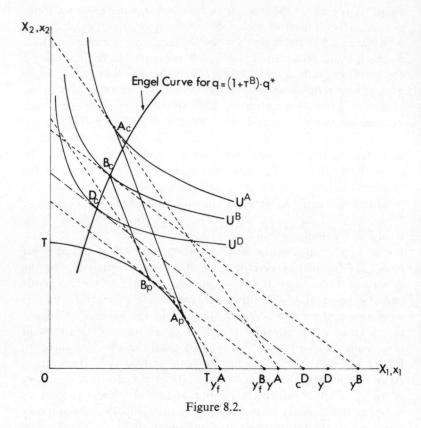

Figure 8.2.

rate, taking the tariff rate as given. The partial derivative of $\tilde{y}$ with respect to r is given by

$$\delta\tilde{y}/\delta r = \frac{\dot{\tau} \cdot q^* \cdot (\delta X_2^d/\delta c) \cdot (\delta c^d/\delta r)}{1 - \tau \cdot q^* \cdot (\delta X_2^d/\delta c) \cdot (\delta c^d/\delta y)}, \tag{25}$$

and is less than zero provided that both goods are normal and the marginal propensity to spend, $\delta c^d/\delta y$, is smaller than $(1/(\tau \cdot q^* \cdot (\delta X_2^d/\delta c))) > 1$. Substituting $\tilde{y}(r; \tau)$ for the variable y which appears in the desired expenditure function yields

$$\tilde{c}(r; \tau) \equiv c^d(\tilde{y}(r; \tau), q^* \cdot (1 + \tau), r). \tag{26}$$

Necessarily,[24]

$$\tilde{y}(r; \tau) \gtreqless \tilde{c}(r; \tau) \text{ according as } r \gtreqless \bar{r}(\bar{y}(\tau), q^* . (1 + \tau)) \quad (27)$$

where $\bar{r}(\bar{y}(\tau), q^* . (1 + \tau))$ is the long-run equilibrium value of the interest rate associated with the tariff rate τ.

Secondly, to determine the value of the interest rate, substitute $\tilde{y}(r; \tau)$ for the variable y which appears in the money demand function, and obtain

$$\tilde{l}(r; \tau) \equiv l(\tilde{y}(r; \tau), q^*(1 + \tau), r). \quad (28)$$

The instantaneous equilibrium value of the interest rate, $\hat{r}(\bar{M}; \tau)$, is determined by the condition that the demand for money must equal the existing supply, i.e.

$$\tilde{l}(r; \tau) = M/P_1. \quad (29)$$

Differentiating equation (29), yields

$$\delta\hat{r}/\delta M = \frac{1}{P_1 . (\delta\tilde{l}/\delta r)} = \frac{1}{P_1 . (\delta l/\delta y)(\delta\tilde{y}/\delta r) + P_1 . (\delta l/\delta r)}. \quad (30)$$

From the properties of the money demand function, it follows that $\delta\hat{r}/\delta M$ must be negative provided that $\delta\tilde{y}/\delta r$ is negative.

Substituting $\hat{r}(M; \tau)$ for the variable r which appears in the functions $\tilde{y}(r; \tau)$ and $\tilde{c}(r; \tau)$, we obtain

$$\hat{y}(M; \tau) \equiv \tilde{y}(\hat{r}(M; \tau); \tau), \quad (31)$$

$$\hat{c}(M; \tau) \equiv \tilde{c}(\hat{r}(M; \tau); \tau). \quad (32)$$

---

[24] By definition of the function $\bar{r}(y, q)$, $c = y$ when $r = \bar{r}$. An increase in $\hat{r}$ above $\bar{r}$ leads to a reduction in both c and y, but, provided good 1 is normal, the reduction in c must be greater than the reduction in y. y falls only because of the reduction in the tariff proceeds. The reduction in the tariff proceeds is proportional to the reduction in expenditure on good 2, with a factor of proportionality of less than one. Provided that good 1 is normal, the reduction in expenditure on good 2 is only a fraction of the reduction in total expenditure, and it follows that the reduction in income must be smaller than the reduction in expenditure. Clearly, this argument works in reverse for a decrease in the interest rate.

where, necessarily,[25]

$$\hat{y}(M;\tau) \gtreqless \hat{c}(M;\tau) \text{ according as } M \gtreqless \bar{M}(\tau). \qquad (33)$$

The reduced form relationships $\hat{c}(M;\tau)$ and $\hat{y}(M;\tau)$ determine the levels of expenditure and income as functions of the money supply, given the tariff rate.

The difference between the value of the home country's exports at world market prices, $p_1^* \cdot (x_1 - X_1)$, and the value of the home country's imports at world market prices, $P_2^* \cdot (X_2 - x_2)$, all multiplied by the exchange rate, ϵ, is equal to the home country's balance-of-payments surplus measured in terms of domestic currency, i.e.

$$\hat{B}(M;\tau) = \epsilon \cdot [P_1^* \cdot (x_1^s(q^* \cdot (1 + \tau)) - \hat{X}_1(M;\tau)) -$$
$$- P_2^* \cdot (\hat{X}_2(M;\tau) - x_2^s(q^* \cdot (1 + \tau)))]. \qquad (34)$$

This balance-of-payments surplus is identically equal to the excess of nominal income over nominal expenditure,[26] i.e.

$$\hat{B}(M;\tau) = P_1 \cdot (\hat{y}(M;\tau) - \hat{c}(M;\tau)). \qquad (35)$$

Under the assumption that the domestic money changes only as a result of balance-of-payments surplus and deficits, we obtain from equations (13) and (35) a differential equation which characterises the adjustment of the money supply over time, viz.

$$\dot{M} = \hat{B}(M;\tau). \qquad (36)$$

Since $\hat{B}$ is positive for values of M less than $\bar{M}(\tau)$ and negative for values of M greater than $\bar{M}(\tau)$, it follows that the money supply will converge to its long-run equilibrium value starting from any initial value, and, hence, that the economy will converge to its

[25] This result follows from (27) and from the fact that r is $\gtreqless \hat{r}$ according as M is $\lesseqgtr \bar{M}$.

[26] This is true as an accounting identity. Formally, the right hand side of (34) divided by $P_1 = \epsilon \cdot P_1^*$ is equal to $(x_1 - X_1) - q^* \cdot (X_2 - x_2)$ which equals $(x_1 + q \cdot x_2 + \tau \cdot q^*(X_2 - x_2)) - (X_1 + q \cdot X_2)$ which is equal to the right hand side of (35) multiplied by P_1.

long-run equilibrium position starting from any initial instantaneous equilibrium position.[27]

B. A Graphical Representation

The determination of the instantaneous equilibrium values of r, y, and c is illustrated in Figure 8.3. The curve labelled $L_{\tau B}$—M_0 shows the combinations of y and r for which the nominal demand for money, given the tariff rate τ^B, $L_{\tau B} \equiv P_1 \cdot 1(y, q^* \cdot (1 + \tau^B), r)$, is equal to the nominal money supply M_0 (which is less than $\bar{M}(\tau^B)$). The curve labeled $\tilde{y}(r; \tau^B)$ shows the level of income as a function of the interest rate, given the tariff rate τ^B. The intersection of the $L_{\tau B}$—M_0 curve and the $\tilde{y}(r; \tau^B)$ curve determines the interest rate, $\hat{r}(M_0; \tau^B)$, and the level of income, $\hat{y}(M_0; \tau^B)$, at which equation (29) is satisfied, given a money supply of M_0. $\hat{r}(M_0; \tau^B)$ is greater than the long-run equilibrium value of the interest rate associated with the tariff rate τ^B, $\bar{r}(\tau^B)$, which is shown by the intersection of $\tilde{y}(r; \tau^B)$ curve and the $\tilde{c}(r; \tau^B)$ curve. The intersection of the horizontal line $\hat{r}(M_0; \tau^B)$ and the $\tilde{c}(r; \tau^B)$ curve determines the instantaneous equilibrium level of consumption expenditure, $\hat{c}(M_0; \tau^B)$, which is less than the instantaneous equilibrium level of income, $\hat{y}(M_0; \tau^B)$. An increase in the money supply to M_1 shifts the LM curve down to $L_{\tau B}$—M_1 and results in a decrease in the instantaneous equilibrium interest rate to $\hat{r}(M_1; \tau^B)$ and an increase in the instantaneous equilibrium levels of income and expenditure to $\hat{y}(M_1; \tau^B)$ and $\hat{c}(M_1; \tau^B)$, respectively.

The determination of the balance-of-payments surplus as a function of M, for a given value of the tariff rate, is illustrated in Figure 8.4. In the upper panel, the functions $\hat{y}(M; \tau^B)$ and $\hat{c}(M; \tau^B)$ which are derived from Figure 8.3 are shown as the solid lines which intersect at the point $(\bar{M}(\tau^B), \bar{y}(\tau^B))$. For values of M greater than $\bar{M}(\tau^B)$, the $\hat{c}$ curve lies above the $\hat{y}$ curve, and, for values of M less than $\bar{M}(\tau^B)$, the $\hat{c}$ curve lies below the $\hat{y}$ curve, as is required by (33). The vertical difference between the $\hat{y}$ curve multiplied by the domestic money price of good 1 determines the $\hat{B}$ curve which is plotted in the lower panel of Figure 8.4. This curve lies above the horizontal axis for M less than $\bar{M}(\tau^B)$, crosses at $M = \bar{M}(\tau^B)$, and lies below the horizontal axis for M greater than $\bar{M}(\tau^B)$.

[27] The fact that the sign of B is the same as the sign of $\bar{M} - M$ is implied by (33) and (35).

The analysis of the process of adjustment subsequent to an increase in the tariff may now be completed with the aid of Figures 8.3 and 8.4. Suppose that the increase in the tariff from τ^A to τ^B increases the long-run equilibrium level of income and the long-run equilibrium level of money balances. Then, as illustrated in Figure 8.4,

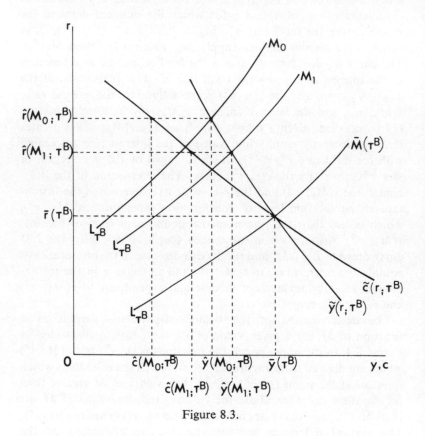

Figure 8.3.

the $\hat{c}$, $\hat{y}$, and $\hat{B}$ curves shift from the dashed lines to the solid lines. Suppose that at the moment when the tariff rate is increased, nominal money balances are at their initial long-run equilibrium level, $\bar{M}(\tau^A)$. Then, after the increase in the tariff, money balances will be below their new long-run equilibrium level, $\bar{M}(\tau^B)$. The interest rate which prevails in the instantaneous equilibrium immediately following the tariff increase, $\hat{r}(\bar{M}(\tau^A); \tau^B)$, may be determined in Figure 8.3 by constructing the LM curve which is appropriate for a nominal money supply of $\bar{M}(\tau^A)$ and a tariff rate of τ^B. This interest rate determines a level of consumption expenditure $c^D = \tilde{c}(\hat{r}(\bar{M}(\tau^A)); \tau^B) = \hat{c}(\bar{M}(\tau^A); \tau^B)$ and a level of income $y^D = \tilde{y}(\hat{r}(\bar{M}(\tau^A); \tau^B)) = \hat{y}(\bar{M}(\tau^A); \tau^B)$. c^D is less than y^D, and both c^D and y^D are

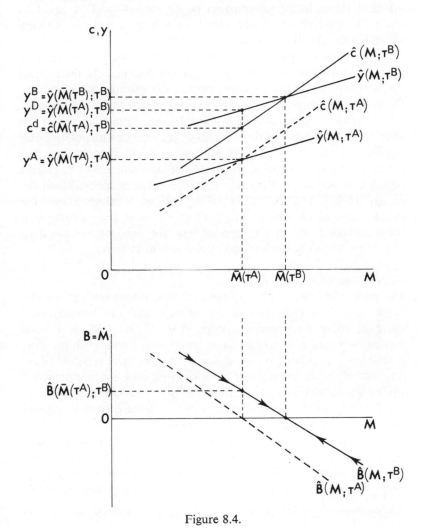

Figure 8.4.

less than the long-run equilibrium level of income $y^B = \bar{y}(\tau^B)$. The level of expenditure c^D determines the consumption point D_c in Figure 8.2, which lies on the Engel curve appropriate for the price ratio, $q^B = q^* . (1 + \tau^B)$, below the long-run equilibrium consumption point B_c. The difference between y^D and c^D, multiplied by P_1, is equal to the balance-of-payments· surplus $\hat{B}(\bar{M}(\tau^A); \tau^B)$ which is shown in the lower panel of Figure 8.4, and is equal to the rate at which the home country's money supply is growing immediately after the increase in the tariff.

As the money supply grows, the interest rate which is required to maintain equilibrium in the money market declines. As the interest rate declines, the level of consumption expenditure rises, moving the consumption point up along the Engel curve from D_c to B_c. The increase in expenditure on good 2 leads to an increase in the tariff proceeds which, in turn, increases income toward its long-run equilibrium value of y^B. Expenditure remains less than income, but the gap between the two narrows. Hence, the balance of payments remains in surplus, but the size of this surplus declines. When the money supply reaches its new long-run equilibrium value, the interest rate reaches $\bar{r}(\bar{y}(\tau^B), q^* . (1 + \tau^B))$ and the consumption point arrives at B_c. At B_c, expenditure and income are equal to y^B and the (flow) balance-of-payments surplus is zero.

C. The Role of Reduced Forms

The entire analysis of the process of adjustment (except for the discussion of the behaviour of the interest rate) can be conducted using the reduced form relationships, $\hat{c}(M; \tau)$ and $\hat{y}(M; \tau)$ without making any reference to the basic behavioural relationships, $c^d(y, q, r)$ and $l(y, q, r)$, or to the condition of money market equilibrium. Any set of basic behavioural relationships and equilibrium conditions which give rise to the reduced form relationships, $\hat{c}(M; \tau)$ and $\hat{y}(M; \tau)$, will lead to the same analysis of the process of adjustment as that described in the last subsection.

For instance, consider a model in which there are no marketable securities (other than money) and, hence, no interest rate which may enter into either the desired expenditure function or the money demand function.[28] There is still a demand for money function which

[28] See Dornbusch (1973) for an analysis of the type of model which is discussed in this paragraph.

specifies the amount of money people want to hold as a function of income and prices. Further, the difference between the amount of money which people have and the amount of money which they wish to hold will be an argument in the expenditure function, since the only way in which people can achieve their desired money balances is by spending less or more than their income. At the level of basic behaviour functions and equilibrium conditions, this model is very different from the model described in subsection 2C. Nevertheless, it leads to the same type of reduced form relationships between the level of money balances and the tariff rate and the levels of expenditure and income. It follows that the analysis of the process of adjustment using this new model is essentially the same as that described at the end of subsection 3B.

D. The Speed of Adjustment v. the Cumulative Result

The analysis of the process of adjustment uses properties of the basic behaviour functions and of the implied reduced forms which are irrelevant in the analysis of long-run equilibrium. This fact comes out most clearly for the case where the money demand function and the expenditure function have the proportional forms given in (16) and (20). For long-run analysis all we need to know is $k(\rho)$. The behaviour of $b(r)$ and $k(r)$ for values of r other than ρ is important only for the speed with which a given long-run equilibrium is achieved.[29]

A clear distinction between the determinants of long-run behaviour and short-run behaviour is vital for answering many important questions. For instance, suppose that a country is experiencing a balance-of-payments deficit and wishes to impose a tariff in order to eliminate this deficit. The tariff must be chosen so as to make the long-run equilibrium stock of nominal balances equal to the existing nominal money supply. Hence, it is the relationships which govern long-run equilibrium behaviour, rather than the relationships which govern the speed of adjustment, which are important for determining the required tariff. The required tariff could be quite large, even if the

[29] Holding ρ and $k(\rho)$ constant, if we increase the interest elasticity of desired expenditures, $-(r/b(r)) \cdot (db(r)/dr)$, and decrease the interest elasticity of the demand for money, $-(r/k(r)) \cdot (dk(r)/dr)$, we will have no effect on the cumulative balance-of-payments surplus generated by an increase in the tariff, but we will increase the speed with which this surplus comes about.

initial deficit were rather small, if the speed of adjustment were low; and conversely. For this reason, it would be wrong to infer the size of the required tariff from the size of the (flow) deficit which it was supposed to eliminate.

The distinction between things which matter for the long-run and things which matter for the process of adjustment, and the distinction between basic behavioural relationships and reduced form relationships relate to the third basic feature of the monetary approach: an emphasis on a unified theory of long-run behaviour coupled with an eclectic view of the process of adjustment. Since a number of different specifications of the basic behavioural relationships give rise to the same type reduced form relationships, a number of different models of the adjustment process can be successfully integrated into a single theory of long-run equilibrium. For some specifications the speed of convergence to long-run equilibrium will be fast, for other specifications it will be slow. But, across a wide class of models of the process of adjustment, the long-run results remain the same.

4 A TARIFF WHICH CREATES A DEFICIT

The phenomenon of a tariff increase which creates a deficit is most conveniently illustrated for the special case in which the home country produces only a fixed amount, $\bar{x}_1$, of good 1, and in which the money demand function and the desired expenditure function have the proportional forms given in (16) and (20).[30] For this special case, the home country's transformation curve collapses to the point $\bar{x}_1$ along the horizontal axis of Figure 8.5. Since P_1 is not affected by changes in the tariff rate, nominal income, $Y = P_1 \cdot y$, varies directly and only in response to variations in the redistributed tariff proceeds. Since the long-run equilibrium level of money balances, $\bar{M}(\tau)$ is equal to $k(\rho) \cdot Y$, it follows that $\bar{M}(\tau)$ varies directly and only in response to variations in the redistributed tariff proceeds. Now suppose that the initial value of the tariff rate, τ^A, is set at the revenue maximising value, that is, at the value which maximises the tariff proceeds measured in terms of good 1. An increase in the tariff rate to τ^B necessarily reduces the tariff

[30] Since the home country does not produce the import good, a tariff is equivalent to a consumption tax levied on good 2.

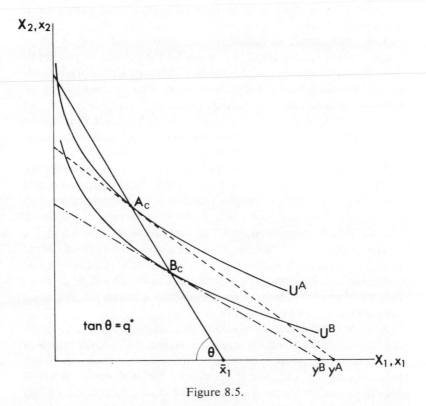

Figure 8.5.

proceeds, reduces y and Y, reduces $\bar{M}$, and, hence, generates a cumulative balance-of-payments deficit.[31]

Note that in this example, the increase in the tariff brings about a *deficit* in the balance of payments because, and only because, the increase in the tariff strongly *reduces* the demand for imports. Holding imports constant, an increase in the tariff will increase the tariff proceeds. Only if the reduction in demand is sufficiently strong

[31] An increase in the tariff can produce a deficit even when both goods are produced, but the response of factor income to changes in domestic relative prices implies that the conditions which must be satisfied for this result are more stringent than in the present case. In particular, at the revenue maximising tariff, a small increase in the tariff will result in a surplus if some positive amount of the import good is produced at home and the money demand function and the expenditure function are given by (16) and (20).

to outweigh this effect, will an increase in the tariff reduce tariff proceeds.

This result stands in opposition to conventional wisdom which suggests that reducing imports is good for the balance of payments. The common-sense view of the way in which tariffs affect the balance of payments is formalised in the standard, textbook analysis of the demand for, and supply of, foreign exchange.[32] Exports provide the supply; imports represent the demand; the difference is equal to the balance-of-payments surplus. An increase in the tariff discourages imports and, hence, produces a balance-of-payments surplus.

The fallacy in this common-sense view comes from neglect of the budget constraint. In a two-good model, holding income and expenditure constant, if people spend less on imports, then they must spend more on goods which would otherwise be exported. Hence, holding expenditure and income constant, the supply of foreign exchange will fall by the same amount as demand. More generally, since the balance-of-payments surplus is identically equal to the excess of income over expenditure, a tariff can affect the (flow) balance of payments only to the extent that it affects the difference between income and expenditure.

Another fallacy arises from taking an exclusively monetary view of the balance of payments. It might be argued that a tariff improves the balance of payments because it increases the domestic money price of imports and, thereby, reduces the real value of initial nominal money balances. To restore real money balances to desired levels, a balance-of-payments surplus is required.

The difficulty with this argument is that it neglects the effects which an increase in the tariff, operating on the real sector of the economy, may have on the demand for real money balances. The potential importance of this neglect is apparent in the example considered at the beginning of this section. Starting at the revenue maximising tariff, an increase in the tariff reduces income measured in terms of good 1 and, hence, reduces the demand for money measured in terms of good 1. Since the money price of good 1 is fixed, it follows that the nominal demand for money falls. Thus, the reduction in the real demand for money dominates the reduction in the real value of the existing supply. To derive and interpret this

---

[32] The better textbooks recognise that there is a fallacy in the 'common-sense view'. See, for instance, Kindleberger (1963).

result, it is necessary to analyse the response of the real sector to an increase in the tariff. The money demand function, and the argument about the price level, by themselves, are not enough.

5 A 'KEYNESIAN' MODEL

In order to demonstrate that the monetary approach is not limited to fully employed economies, it is useful to consider a 'Keynesian' model which retains all of the behaviour functions and equilibrium conditions of the model of section 2, except for the supply functions (2) and (3). Rather than assuming that production of the two goods is confined to the points which lie along the transformation curve, assume that there is a fixed money wage rate, w, at which the supply of labour is infinitely elastic.[33] Assuming that labour is the only variable factor of production in both industries, that there is a declining marginal physical product of labour in both industries, and that firms produce up to the point where the value of the marginal product of labour is equal to the money wage rate, it follows that the supply functions for the two goods can be written as

$$x_1 = \tilde{x}_1 (P_1/w), \ \delta\tilde{x}_1/\delta P_1 > 0, \tag{37}$$

$$x_2 = \tilde{x}_2 (P_2/w), \ \delta\tilde{x}_2/\delta P_2 > 0. \tag{38}$$

Given these supply functions, and given the assumption of a constant money wage rate, it follows that an increase in the tariff increases the output of good 2, while leaving output of good 1 unchanged. The increase in the value of output is greater in the 'Keynesian' model than in the full employment model because it is no longer necessary to reduce output of the export good in order to increase output of the import good. This larger increase in the value of output implies a larger increase (or smaller decrease) in the long-run equilibrium level of money balances and, hence, a larger cumulative balance-of-payments surplus (or smaller cumulative deficit) than in the full employment model. In all other respects, the analysis

---

[33] Other assumptions such as a two-sector, Hecksher-Ohlin-Samuelson technology, or a rising supply price of labour could be made. These assumptions would complicate the analysis, but would not affect the basic point that the monetary approach can be applied to less than fully employed economies.

of the 'Keynesian' model remains the same as the analysis of the full employment model.

6 ALTERNATIVE COMMERCIAL POLICIES

Finally, it is worthwhile to demonstrate that the monetary approach is not limited to the analysis of tariffs. It can be applied to any commercial policy. For instance, using the model of section 2, consider the imposition of an export tax at an *ad valorem* rate λ.[34] In terms of its effect on the price ratio, an export tax at the rate λ has the same effect as a tariff at the rate $\tau = (\lambda/(1 - \lambda))$. It follows that an export tax at the rate λ has the same effect on the real sector of the economy, in long-run equilibrium, as the equivalent tariff. This result is a manifestation of Lerner's symmetry theorem which states that export taxes and import taxes which are applied at equivalent rates have the same real effects since both operate as taxes on trade.[35]

The symmetry between export taxes and import taxes, however, does not extend to their long-run monetary effects or to the short-run real effects which are associated with the process of adjustment. Relative prices and the long-run equilibrium level of income measured in terms of either good must be the same under the two taxes. But, the money prices of the two goods and the level of nominal income are lower, by a percentage amount λ, under the export tax than they are under the tariff. It follows that the long-run equilibrium level of nominal money balances is lower, by a percentage amount λ. This implies that an export tax generates a cumulative balance-of-payments deficit, as compared with the equivalent tariff. It follows that during the adjustment to an increase in the export tax, consumption of both commodities will be greater than during the process of adjustment to an increase in the tariff.

The imposition of an export tax which is not accompanied by an equivalent tariff is generally thought to worsen the balance of payments. For the case where the desired expenditure function and the

[34] The proceeds which the government derives from the export tax are assumed to be redistributed in the form of lump-sum transfers. More generally, in this discussion of alternative commercial policies, it is always assumed that the government's budget is balanced by means of lump-sum taxes and transfers.

[35] Lerner (1936) establishes this proposition for the standard, two-country two-commodity model of international trade.

money demand function have the proportional forms given in (16) and (20), it can be shown that this must be the case. Figure 8.1, which was constructed for the case of the tariff, is still relevant, except it is the domestic money price of the import good, P_2, which remains constant when an export tax is imposed. Hence, nominal income is proportional to income measured in terms of good 2. Since the imposition of an export tax necessarily reduces income measured in terms of good 2, it necessarily reduces nominal income and hence the long-run equilibrium level of nominal balances, generating a cumulative balance-of-payments deficit.[36]

This result accords with the common-sense view that taxing exports is bad for the balance of payments. It is important to recognise, however, that the balance-of-payments deficit does not come about because of the reduction of exports. In the new long-run equilibrium, exports will be lower, but so will imports. The deficits which occur during the process of adjustment occur because people spend more than their income. This expenditure is distributed across both goods in accord with consumers' marginal propensities to spend.

An export subsidy is a negative export tax. When such a subsidy is combined with a tariff of the same rate, relative prices are left unchanged. Nominal prices, however, are both increased by the percentage amount of the tariff and export subsidy. The result is exactly the same as would be achieved by a devaluation of the amount of the tariff and subsidy; that is, by an increase in ϵ equal in percentage terms to tariff and subsidy rates. This leaves the real long-run equilibrium position of the economy unchanged, but increases the long-run equilibrium level of nominal money balances proportionately with the tariff and subsidy rates. This implies a cumulative balance-of-payments surplus which is brought about, in the short run, by a reduction of expenditure relative to income.[37, 38]

Consumption and production taxes and subsidies can also be

[36] When income is measured in terms of good 2, the production substitution effect, the consumption substitution effect, and the consumption income effect of either a tariff or an export tax all operate in the direction of reducing income.

[37] It is conceivable that the demand for money will be affected somewhat differently by the tariff cum export subsidy than by the equivalent devaluation. In the tariff cum subsidy case, the government is collecting and then redistributing the tax proceeds and subsidy payments. This increase in transactions could increase the demand for money.

[38] See Dornbusch (1973) for further discussion of the monetary approach to the analysis of devaluation.

analysed within the framework of the model of section 2. However, since such taxes and subsidies create differences between the domestic price ratio as seen by producers and the domestic price ratio as seen by consumers, more care must be taken in specifying the general forms of the money demand function and the desired expenditure function.[39] If the proportional forms (16) and (20) are used with the understanding that income refers to income at final consumer prices, then the following conclusions hold, starting from a position of no taxes of any kind: (i) A consumption tax applied to either good increases the nominal demand for money and generates a cumulative balance-of-payments surplus;[40] (ii) A production tax applied to either good reduces the nominal demand for money and generates a cumulative balance-of-payments deficit.[41]

CONCLUSION

This chapter has summarised the basic principles of the monetary approach to the balance of payments and has indicated how these principles manifest themselves in relatively simple models. The general principles, however, are much broader than any model. Capital mobility, non-traded goods, sticky prices, inventory accumulation, 'disequilibrium' behaviour, growth, and many other issues remain for future research. But none of these complications will

[39] Firstly, there is the issue of the additional transactions which are required in order to collect and pay various taxes and subsidies. Secondly, household demands may depend on prices facing consumers because these prices affect the level of utility which households are able to achieve. Thirdly, producer prices may be relevant to the demand for money by firms, and also, indirectly to the money demand and desired expenditure of households through the effect of producer prices on income of capital and the real value of the stock of securities.

[40] Consumption will occur at some point along the line determined by the tangent to the home country's transformation curve with slope equal to minus the world price ratio. A tax on one good (with redistribution of the proceeds) will always increase income measured in terms of the other good, as compared with the no tax situation. Since the money price of the other good is held constant, the increase in income measured in terms of this good translates into an increase in nominal income. In general, it is not true that an *increase* in a consumption tax leads to an increase in nominal income.

[41] A production tax does not affect the prices which face consumers. Since such a tax results in a reduction in the value of output at world market prices by driving the production point away from the tangency of the world price line to the transformation curve, it follows that it reduces the nominal income of households and, hence, reduces the nominal demand for money.

provide any escape from the essentially monetary character of the balance of payments, or from the central role which the money demand function and the money supply process must play in balance-of-payments analysis, particularly for the long run.

REFERENCES

Alexander, S. S. (1952) 'Effects of a Devaluation on the Trade Balance', *IMF Staff Papers*, vol. II (April 1952), 263–78.

Brunner, Karl (1973) 'Money Supply Process and Monetary Policy in an Open Economy' in M. Connolly and A. Swoboda (eds.) *International Trade and Money* (London, George Allen & Unwin, 1973), 127–66.

Dornbusch, Rudiger (1973), 'Currency Depreciation, Hoarding and Relative Prices', *JPE*, vol. 81, no. 4 (July/August, 1973), 843–915.

Johnson, H. G. (1958), 'Towards a General Theory of the Balance of Payments', in H. G. Johnson, *International Trade and Economic Growth* (London, George Allen & Unwin, 1958), 153–68.

Keynes, John M. (1971), *Tract on Monetary Reform* (London, Macmillan, 1971).

Kindleberger, Charles P. (1963), *International Economics*, 3rd edn (Homewood, Irwin, 1963).

Lerner, Abba P. (1936), 'The Symmetry between Import and Export Taxes', *Economica*, N.S. vol. III, no. 11 (August 1936), 306–13.

Marshall, Alfred (1926), *Official Papers* (London, Macmillan, 1926), 170–95.

Metzler, Lloyd A. (1951), 'Wealth, Saving and the Rate of Interest', *JPE*, vol. 59 (April 1951), 93–116.

Mussa, Michael (1974), 'Trade and the Balance of Payments: a Two-Country Monetary Model', unpublished manuscript, 1974.

Mussa, Michael (1974), 'A Monetary Approach to Balance of Payments Analysis,' *JMCB*, vol. 6 (August 1974).

Mussa, Michael (1976), *A Study in Macroeconomics* (Amsterdam, North Holland, forthcoming 1976).

9

Money and Wealth in an Open Economy Income–Expenditure Model[1]

CARLOS A. RODRIGUEZ

The purpose of this chapter is to analyse some of the dynamic implications of the endogeneity of the money supply implicit in a trading world with fixed exchange rates.[2] The world we choose to represent is a Keynesian one where prices are constant and outputs are responsive to changes in aggregate demands. Models where prices are fully flexible and outputs are constant or growing at an exogenous rate can be found in Prais (1961), Mundell (1968), and Johnson (1972). Despite the wide difference in assumptions, both types of models bear the common characteristic that the balance of payments is one of the channels through which countries can adjust their actual to their desired holdings of real cash balances.

The principal features of the model used are:

(a) A liquidity preference function which expresses the desired ratio of holdings of real cash balances to other financial assets as a function of the interest rate. Any given size of the portfolio is assumed to be always held in the desired ratio (composition equilibrium); the size of the portfolio itself, however, need not be always equal to the long-run desired value.

(b) An expenditure function which depends on both the level of income and the magnitude of the discrepancy between the actual and the desired holdings of financial assets.

[1] I want to thank Rudiger Dornbusch and Jacob Frenkel for their comments and suggestions on a previous version of this paper.
[2] Swoboda and Dornbusch (1973) analyse essentially the same problem. This model differs from theirs in that it includes a more detailed specification of the role of assets and liquidity preference in the determination of aggregate expenditures.

(*c*) The possibility that domestic income and—when capital is immobile—the interest rate adjust in response to domestic monetary disturbances.

Our main results could be summarised as follows: domestic monetary policy affects income and the interest rate in the short run. In the long run, the endogeneity of the domestic money supply implies that domestic monetary policy will have a permanent effect on other domestic variables—in addition to international reserves—only if it contributes to changes in the world's supply of money. Thus, in the case of a small country—whose repercusions on the rest of the world are ignored—an expansion in the domestic money supply will not be feasible in the long run and any attempt to do it by printing new money will be matched by an equivalent reduction in the stock of international reserves with no effective change in the domestic money supply.

Section 1 develops the basic structure of the model. Section 2 applies it to a small country. The concept of the 'small country' used in this chapter is not defined in the traditional sense as a country facing a perfectly elastic foreign demand for its exports since usually it is incompatible with the existence of a fixed supply price of exportables (in terms of domestic currency) and a fixed exchange rate. Rather, the country is 'small' in that changes in its level of imports or reserves have a negligible effect on the rest of the world's aggregate expenditures and thus on the demand for the country's exports. Under those circumstances, given the exchange rate and the fixed domestic supply price of exportables, the quantity demanded of exports is a constant, X_0. Section 3 abandons the small-country assumption and studies the monetary interactions of a two-country world economy. Throughout the chapter it is assumed that securities are not traded internationally.[3]

1 THE DESCRIPTION OF THE ECONOMY

It is assumed that output in each country is in perfectly elastic supply at a given price level. To abstract from the effects of economic

[3] Trade in securities will not affect the main long-run predictions of the model. If it were to be considered, national income and not domestic income would have to be the relevant variable in the determination of expenditure decisions; on this see Frenkel (1971).

growth it is assumed that the demand for net investment is zero at all times.

A. Aggregate Expenditures

Whenever the existing stock of financial assets is equal to the desired long-run stock, it is assumed that individuals will want to spend all of their current income. We will therefore define the following expenditure function:

$$Z = Y + a(A - A^d), a > 0, \tag{1}$$

where

$\quad$ Z: Aggregate domestic expenditures,
$\quad$ Y: Current domestic income,
$\quad$ A: Actual stock of financial assets,
$\quad$ A^d: Desired stock of financial assets,
$\quad$ a: Desired speed of adjustment of an excess stock demand for assets.

Of total expenditures, a constant fraction, m, is spent on foreign goods and the rest on domestic goods.[4]

B. Financial Assets and Liquidity Preference

The stock of financial assets is the sum of three elements:

(i) The stock of money, H.
(ii) The value of common stock owned by the private sector: $p_e E_0 = cY/r$ where E_0 is the number of pieces of common stock (it is fixed due to the absence of net investment); c is the fraction of profits in income (assumed constant); p_e is the price of each piece of common stock and r is the interest rate.
(iii) The value of government debt held by the private sector: $p_B B$, where p_B is the price of each government bond and B is the quantity of such bonds.

---

[4] In the two-country case analysed in section 2 it is assumed that imports depend on income rather than on expenditures. This assumption simplifies considerably the presentation and does not affect any of the long-run results. The short-run dynamics, however, could be different from the one obtained in that section if imports were to depend on expenditures.

Government debt is assumed to be a perfect substitute for common stock, so the interest rates on both types of assets are the same. Each government bond pays $1 per year so $p_B = 1/r$ and B represents the annual stream of payments on government debt. It is assumed that the service of the public debt is financed from income taxes so that a change in B does not affect personal income.

It has been argued that if individuals capitalise the future stream of taxes necessary to pay interest on that debt then government debt should not be included in the calculation of the wealth of the private sector—see Mundell (1971). We will assume that the market does not capitalise future taxes on income streams and thus we consider the full amount B/r as wealth. Notice that even if B/r were not considered as wealth, it would anyway affect other variables of the economy through liquidity preference. The total stock of financial wealth of the private sector is therefore:

$$A = H + (B + cY)/r. \tag{2}$$

Individuals are assumed to decide on the composition of their portfolio only on the basis of the returns on the available assets. We thus postulate a liquidity preference function similar to the one used in Metzler (1951), where the desired ratio of money holdings to other financial assets is a declining function of the interest rate,

$$H = L(r) . (B + cY)/r, \ L'(r) < 0. \tag{3}$$

It is further assumed that the interest rate adjusts such that the liquidity preference is always satisfied. From equations (2) and (3) it follows that the value of financial assets at any moment will depend on the value of money holdings, the number of outstanding government obligations and the level of income,

$$A = A (H, B, Y) \tag{4}$$

where $\delta A/\delta H > 0$

$\delta A/\delta B \gtrless 0$

$\delta A/\delta Y \gtrless 0.$

An increase in H always raises A since, in addition to its own impact —in (2)—it also depresses the interest rate—by (3)—and thus raises the value of other financial assets outstanding. This however does not hold for increases in the supply of other financial assets since the change in their total value will depend on the elasticity of demand; this accounts for the indeterminacy of the sign of $\delta A/\delta B$ and $\delta A/\delta Y$.

The desired stock of financial assets is taken to be a constant fraction, k, of income,

$$A^d = kY. \tag{5}$$

From (1), (4) and (5) we get the expression for aggregate expenditures,

$$Z = Y + a[A(H, B, Y) - kY] \tag{6}$$

Finally, it is assumed that the short-run marginal propensity to spend out of an increase in income is positive, but less than unity:

$$0 < \delta Z/\delta Y = 1 + a(\delta A/\delta Y - k) < 1.$$

This in turn implies that

$$-1 < a(\delta A/\delta Y - k) < 0.$$

2 THE SMALL-COUNTRY CASE

At any moment B and H are given and thus short-run equilibrium is obtained at that level of income which is demanded. The demand for domestic output, in turn, is the sum of the demands by domestic consumers—total expenditures minus imports—and by foreigners— X_0. Thus short-run equilibrium is attained when $(1 - m)Z + X_0 = Y$ or, rearranging terms, when:

$$Z - Y = mZ - X_0 \tag{7}$$

which implies that any excess of domestic expenditure over income must be validated by a trade deficit.

In the absence of capital mobility or private holdings of foreign exchange, the fixed exchange rate system requires that any trade deficit (surplus) be financed by an equivalent loss (gain) in international reserve holdings of the monetary authority. If those changes in international reserves are not sterilised by the monetary authority, the domestic money supply must change by the same magnitude as the stock of reserves—assuming for simplicity that the exchange rate and the high power money multiplier are unity. It follows that the path of the domestic money supply, in the absence of other sources of money creation, is given by:

$$\dot{H} = dH/dt = X_0 - mZ = X_0 - mY - ma\,[A(H, Y, B) - kY].\ (8)$$

From equations (6) and (7), the condition for internal balance can be written as:

$$a(1 - m)[A(H, Y, B) - kY] = mY - X_0;\qquad(9)$$

this condition determines the level of income for any given H, B and X_0. This level of income, in turn, determines—from (8)—the rate at which H will be changing. The model is described graphically in Figure 9.1 where the domestic money supply (H) is depicted along the horizontal axis and domestic income (Y) along the vertical axis. The curve $Y = Y(H)$ represents the combinations of Y and H—given B and X_0—that are consistent with internal balance and it corresponds to the *locus* of short-run equilibria. This schedule is upward sloping since a larger H increases aggregate demand by raising the value of assets; to restore equilibrium, output must be raised.[5]

The $\dot{H} = 0$ *locus* represents the combinations of Y and H—given B—that are consistent with a zero trade balance and thus the supply of money remains unchanged. This schedule is downward sloping since an increase in H raises expenditures and imports, generating a trade deficit. A reduction in expenditures through a lower income restores trade balance.[6]

[5] The slope of this schedule is:
$$dY/dH = \frac{\delta A/\delta H}{(k - \delta A/\delta Y) + m/a(1 - m)} > 0.$$

[6] The slope of this schedule is:
$$dY/dH = \frac{-\delta A/\delta H \cdot a}{1 + a(\delta A/\delta Y - k)} < 0.$$

The long-run values Y^* and H^* are obtained at the unique intersection of the $Y(H)$ and $\dot{H} = 0$ schedules. It should be noted that at this intersection $X_0 = mY^*$. This can be easily verified by inspection of equations (7), (8) and (9). Thus the long-run level of income (Y^*) is solely determined by the amount of exports and the propensity to import.

Consider the effect of raising the quantity of money from H^* to H_1 in Figure 9.1. Initially, income must rise to Y_1 according to the relation $Y = Y(H)$. Since at this higher income and money supply there is a trade deficit—any point to the right of the $\dot{H} = 0$ schedule implies a trade deficit—the domestic money supply starts to decrease. This process continues as long as $Y > Y^*$. Thus an increase in H above H^* will raise income only for a transitional period. Eventually

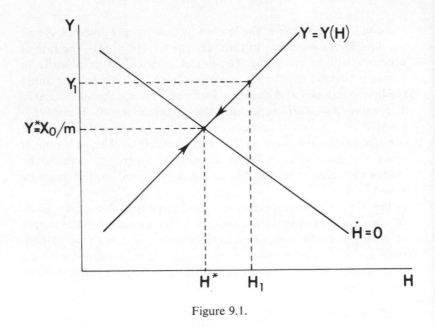

Figure 9.1.

all of the original rise in H will be offset by a cumulative loss in international reserves through the balance-of-payments deficits. On the other hand, a policy of government expenditures financed by printing money will succeed in raising income in the long run but at the cost of a continuous loss in reserves that is equal to the amount of government expenditures. In this case the internal balance condition becomes:

$$a(1 - m) [A(H, Y, B) - kY] = mY - X_0 - G,$$

where G is the level of government expenditures. The money supply will change according to:

$$\dot{H} = G + X_0 - mY - am [A(H, Y, B) - kY];$$

thus when eventually $\dot{H} = 0$, the country will be losing reserves at the rate $G = mY - X_0$ although income has now been raised to the higher level $(X_0 + G)/m$. Clearly this higher level of income can be sustained only as long as the country has enough reserves to cope with the continuous implied trade deficit.

A once and for all increase in the amount of government debt outstanding will not affect the long-run level of income, although it will affect the long-run holdings of money and the interest rate. It will, however, affect income in the short run and this effect depends on the sign of $\delta A/\delta B$ which in turn determines whether the schedule $Y = Y(H)$ shifts up or down due to a change in B.[7]

If $\delta A/\delta B$ is positive, an increase in B will raise the interest rate but the over-all value of financial assets will be higher so that expenditures, and thus income, will also rise. This initial rise in income will, however, be transitory since at this higher level there is a trade deficit and H will be falling until income is back at the equilibrium level $Y^* = X_0/m$. At this point the interest rate must be higher than its value prior to the increase in government debt since now, at the same income, there is less money and more bonds. We conclude that in the case of a small country, monetary policy or the stock of government debt outstanding can affect the level of income only in the short run—unless a continuous loss in reserves is allowed for.

[7] Whatever the direction of the shift in the $Y = Y(H)$ schedule, the $\dot{H} = 0$ schedule will shift horizontally by the same magnitude such that their intersection will remain at the same level of income $Y^* = X_0/m$. The horizontal shift in both schedules due to changes in B is $\delta H/\delta B = -(\delta A/\delta B)/(\delta A/\delta H)$.

3 A TWO-COUNTRY WORLD

We now generalise the model of the last sections by considering the interaction between the home country and the rest of the world. If the home country does not have a negligible size, changes in its imports or in its holdings of international reserves will affect other countries' incomes and money stocks. Given fixed exchange rates, changes in the money supply of any one country, in the absence of capital movements, can be due either to a non-zero trade balance or to a pure monetary creation by the monetary authorities. Since a trade surplus for one country must be a trade deficit for the rest of the world, it follows that, in so far as no government resorts to pure monetary creation, the world money supply will remain constant over time. To the extent that some government(s) do resort to a pure monetary creation, their actions will increase the world supply of money and therefore will have a permanent effect on the income levels of all countries. These effects will, however, be independent of the country in which the changes in the money supply originated.

For simplicity, consider the rest of the world as a single country and assume that demands for imports depend on income rather than on expenditures. The magnitudes for the rest of the world are referred to by an asterisk (*). Since exports of the home country must be imports of the rest of the world—and vice versa—the internal balance conditions for the home country and the rest of the world are, respectively:

$$a[A(H, B, Y) - kY] = mY - m^*Y^*, \qquad (10)$$

$$a^*[A^*(H^*, B^*, Y^*) - k^*Y^*] = m^*Y^* - mY. \qquad (11)$$

In the absence of a pure monetary creation, an increase in the domestic money supply must be matched by an equal decrease in the foreigner's money supply, which in turn must be equal to the trade surplus at home and the trade deficit abroad. We can thus postulate:

$$\dot{H} = m^*Y^* - mY = -\dot{H}^* \qquad (12)$$

with the implication that, at any moment,

$$\bar{H} = H + H^*, \qquad (13)$$

where $\bar{H}$ is the world's supply of money and is constant.

It then follows from $(10) - (13)$ that long-run equilibrium is defined by:

$$A(H, B, Y) = kY, \qquad (14a)$$

$$A^*(\bar{H} - H, B^*, Y^*) = k^* Y^*, \qquad (14b)$$

$$mY = m^* Y^*. \qquad (14c)$$

These conditions imply that for long-run equilibrium, all countries must be satisfied with their asset holdings—by (14a) and (14b)—and, in addition—by (14c)—those assets are not changing over time. From $(14a) - (14b)$ we obtain a relation between Y and Y^* indicating the levels of income for which both countries satisfy their demand for assets—given the world's money supply and the stocks of government bonds. This relationship (in Figure 9.2) is downward

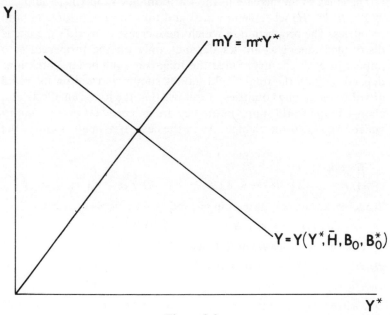

Figure 9.2.

sloping since an increase in domestic income requires an increase in the domestic money supply and thus a reduction in the foreigner's money supply, which in turn implies a reduction in income abroad.[8]

Equation (14c) describes the pairs of Y and Y^* for which the distribution of the money supply between countries is unchanged. As can be seen, this relation depends only on the propensities to import in each country and is independent of the world's supply of money.

The world long-run equilibrium for a given set $(\bar{H}, B, B^*)$ is shown in Figure 9.2. The upward sloping schedule, $Y = Y^* m^*/m$ describes the *locus* for which $\dot{H} = 0$. The downward sloping schedule $Y = Y(Y^*, \bar{H}, B, B^*)$ represents the *locus* of Y and Y^* for which both countries are on their desired demands for assets. Long-run equilibrium is, of course, attained at the intersection of both schedules.

The stability of the long-run solution is guaranteed by our assumption that the short-run marginal propensities to spend are positive but less than unity.[9]

The effect of an increase in the world money supply is to shift the $Y(Y^*, B, B^*, \bar{H})$ schedule upwards and thus to raise income in both countries. The proportion in which the increase in world's income is distributed among countries depends only on the propensities to import in each country. Since the long-run equilibrium conditions depend only on the total world money supply and not on its initial distribution among countries, it follows that the long-run effects of a change in the world supply of money are independent of the country which originated the change. As in the case of a small country, the

---

[8] The slope of this curve is:

$$dY/dY^* = -\delta A/\delta H \cdot (k^* - \delta A/\delta Y^*)/(\delta A^*/\delta H^*) \cdot (k - \delta A/\delta Y) < 0.$$

The schedule shifts with changes in the world money supply according to:

$$dY/d\bar{H} | Y^* = \delta A/\delta H \cdot (k^* - \delta A^*/\delta Y^*)/(k - \delta A/\delta Y) > 0.$$

[9] From differentiation of (10), (11), and (13) and using (12) we obtain:

$$d\dot{H}/dH = (aa^*/D) \cdot [m\delta A/\delta H(\delta A^*/\delta Y^* - k^*) + m^*\delta A^*/\delta H^*(\delta A/\delta Y - k)] < 0$$

since

$$D = aa^*(\delta A/\delta Y - k)(\delta A^*/\delta Y^* - k^*) - am^*(\delta A/\delta Y - k) -$$
$$- a^*m(\delta A^*/\delta Y^* - k^*) > 0.$$

effects of changes in the stocks of outstanding government debts depend on the signs of $\delta A/\delta B$ and $\delta A^*/\delta B^*$.

Having shown the nature and the stability of the long-run solution, we now turn to the dynamics of adjustment. From equation (10) we obtain a relation $Y = f(Y^*, H, B)$ describing the combinations of domestic and foreign income that are consistent with internal balance at home, given the domestic money supply. The slope of this schedule is

$$\delta f(.)/\delta Y^* = \frac{m^*}{m + a(k - \delta A/\delta Y)} < m^*/m.$$

Similarly, from (11) we obtain:

$$Y = g(Y^*, B^*, H^*),$$

which shows the pairs of incomes consistent with internal balance abroad, given the foreign money supply. The slope of this schedule is:

$$\delta g(.)/\delta Y^* = \frac{m^* + a^*(k^* - \delta A^*/\delta Y^*)}{m} > m^*/m.$$

It is easy to verify that increases in H will shift the $f(.)$ schedule upwards and increases in H^* will shift the $g(.)$ schedule downwards.[10]

Given any initial distribution of the world supply of money between countries, short run equilibrium is obtained when:

$$f(Y^*, B, H) = g(Y^*, B^*, H^*) = Y$$

Figure 9.3 shows such a short-run equilibrium position at point Q. Since, as depicted, short-run equilibrium is in the region where $m^*Y^* > mY$, H must be rising over time and H^* decreasing. Thus, as time passes, both schedules must shift upwards until long-run equilibrium is obtained when their intersection is on the $\dot{H} = 0$ line—when $mY = m^*Y^*$. Starting from a long-run equilibrium

---

[10] These shifts are given by:
$$\delta f(.)/\delta H = a(\delta A/\delta H)/m + (ak - a\delta A/\delta Y) > 0 \text{ and}$$
$$\delta g(.)/\delta H^* = -(a^*/m) . \delta A^*/\delta H^* < 0.$$

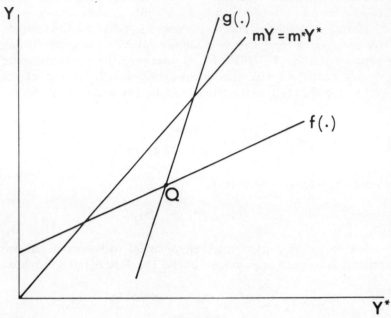

Figure 9.3.

position, Figure 9.4 shows the effects of a once and for all increase in the money supply in the home country. Starting at point A, an increase in H will shift the $f(.)$ schedule upwards from f_0 to f_1 and thus will generate a short-run equilibrium at point B where both incomes are higher than before. At B, however, the home country will be running a trade deficit and thus $\dot{H} < 0$, $\dot{H}^* > 0$, and both the $f(.)$ and the $g(.)$ schedules will start shifting to the right. Over time, it is clear that what happens with both incomes depends crucially on the speed at which both schedules are shifting. In particular, it is interesting to note the role of the speeds of adjustment to stock disequilibrium (a and a^*) in the determination of the behaviour of both incomes over time. After the new short-run equilibrium at B, a redistribution of money from the home country to the rest of the world will take place until a new long-run equilibrium position is attained. Thus the path of Y and Y^* will depend on how this redistribution of money affects aggregate demands in both countries.

There are three main possible outcomes indicated as paths 1, 2, and 3 in Figure 9.4:

(a) *Path 1*: Both Y and Y^* continue to rise after B has been attained. This case is more likely the larger is a^* and the smaller is a. This is so because as H decreases, a small a implies a small reduction in aggregate expenditures at home and conversely, a large a^*

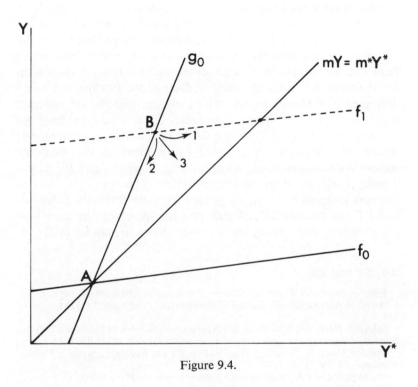

Figure 9.4.

induces a large increase in aggregate expenditures abroad, since H^* is rising. In this case, it is more likely that the increased foreign demand for domestic products will outweigh the reduced demand by domestic residents with the net effect that both incomes tend to rise.

(b) *Path 2*: Both Y and Y^* start to decrease. This case is more likely the larger is a and the smaller is a^*. This is so because a reduction in H induces a large decline in domestic expenditures while the rise in H^* does not induce a large increase in foreign expenditures.

(c) *Path 3*: Y decreases and Y^* increases: This is an intermediate case between (a) and (b) and its likelihood will depend on the precise relationship between all of the variables involved.

CONCLUSIONS

In this chapter we have analysed the implications of a system of fixed exchange rates on the short- and long-run effects of monetary policy. The main conclusion is that, independently of the size of the country, the domestic money supply cannot be controlled, in the long run, by the monetary authorities unless a continuous loss in international reserves is allowed for. Despite the fact that the world described is a Keynesian one where income and the interest rate adjust in response to domestic monetary disturbances, the long-run effects of monetary policy are similar to the ones obtained in models where the real sector is assumed independent of the monetary sector. We have described, both for a small country and for a two-country world, the short-run (impact) effect of changes in the domestic money supplies and the long-run effects together with a description of the dynamic adjustment process, in which the speeds of adjustment to assets disequilibrium were shown to play a ciucial role.

REFERENCES

Frenkel, Jacob, 'A Theory of Money, Trade and the Balance of Payments in a Model of Accumulation', *Journal of International Economics*, I (2) (May 1971), 159–87.

Johnson, Harry G., 'The Monetary Approach to Balance of Payments Theory', *Journal of Financial and Quantitative Analysis*, vii (March 1972), 1555–72.

Metzler, Lloyd A., 'Wealth, Saving and the Rate of Interest', *Journal of Political Economy*, 59 (1951), 93–116.

Mundell, Robert A., *International Economics* (Macmillan, 1968).

Mundell, Robert A., *Monetary Theory* (Goodyear, 1971).

Prais, S. J., 'Some Mathematical Notes on the Quantity Theory of Money in an Open Economy', IMF Staff Papers, 8, no. 2 (1961).

Swoboda, A., and Dornbusch, R., 'International Adjustment, Macroeconomic Policy and Monetary Equilibrium in a Two-Country Model of Income Determination', in *International Trade and Money*, edited by A. Swoboda and M. B. Connolly (London, George Allen & Unwin, 1973), 225–65.

10

Monetary Policy under Fixed Exchange Rates

Effectiveness, the Speed of Adjustment, and Proper Use[1]

ALEXANDER K. SWOBODA

Some, though far from total, agreement has begun to emerge as to the role and effects of monetary policy in a closed economy. At least major issues have been delineated and the battle joined in terms of fairly well-defined analytical frameworks. The impact of changes in the stock of money (or its rate of change) on prices, output and interest rates has been discussed at the theoretical level and investigated empirically. Much dispute remains as to the lag-structure of response to monetary disturbances, as to the division into output and price effects, and as to proper monetary targets and policy indicators. Nevertheless, most economists would agree that monetary policy can be used as a counter-cyclical device, and that the stock of money (or its rate of growth) can, in some average sense over the medium run, be controlled, however difficult it may be to exercise such control in the very short run and however poorly monetary authorities have actually performed in this respect.

Discussion of monetary policy in the open economy, on the other hand, has proceeded at a higher level of abstraction (or over-simplification) and empirical work has remained scarce. The reason

[1] Reprinted from *Economica* (May 1973), 136–54. Preliminary versions of this chapter were presented at the Second Konstanz Seminar on Monetary Theory and Policy (June 1971) and at the February 1972 Money Study Group Conference held at Bournemouth. I am indebted to Leonall Anderson and Karl Brunner for their incisive discussion at Konstanz and to Harry G. Johnson for helpful comments.

is close at hand: with some notable exceptions, recent developments in monetary theory and policy analysis have been, largely, the work of economists based or trained in the United States; and, from an American vantage point (especially a Middle-Western one and before the so-called 'dollar' crises), what more natural simplifying assumption than that of the closed economy? Yet, in recent years, under the pressure of events and following the rediscovery of Hume and Ricardo and the work of, among others, Meade, Alexander, Polak, Prais, Tsiang, Johnson, and Mundell, the analysis of monetary policy in the open economy has made much progress, at least on a theoretical plane. The focus and conclusions of that work, especially that of Mundell, have been rather different from those of analyses dealing with the closed economy: the monetary balance-of-payments adjustment mechanism and the role of capital mobility and of the size of countries are emphasised; severe limits to the use (and controllability) of the money stock as a counter-cyclical device are found and one asks not only whether monetary policy can, but also whether it should, be used for anti-cyclical purposes.

This chapter attempts a brief summary of the analytical conclusions reached as to the effectiveness and proper use of monetary policy in an open economy under fixed exchange rates. Its usefulness, if any, should lie in clarification of some implicit assumptions and conclusions that have perhaps received insufficient attention in the literature. Much confusion and controversy can be avoided by precise specification of definitions and assumptions on the one hand, and by explicit delineation of the exact aims and limits of a particular piece of analysis or conclusion, on the other hand.

The first section below discusses the proposition that the money supply is an endogenous variable in an open economy under fixed exchange rates in terms of comparative-statics analysis. The second section focuses on the determinants of the length of time required to regain equilibrium after a monetary disturbance. The third deals with the proper use of monetary policy under fixed exchange rates, while some concluding remarks are offered in the last section.

1 THE EFFECTIVENESS OF MONETARY POLICY

In a fundamental sense, monetary policy can have no lasting impact on the income level of a small open economy under fixed exchange rates. It is important to understand the meaning and limitations of this proposition as well as the assumptions required to make it hold.

Firstly, monetary policy must be defined as an exogenous once-and-for-all change in the domestic assets of the consolidated banking system (or of the domestic source component of the base) and *not* as an exogenous change in the money supply or the rate of interest (as the point of the analysis is to show that these two variables are endogenous and not exogenous). Secondly, an economy will be said to be small if it cannot influence foreign interest rates, income levels, and so forth. Thirdly, by lasting influence is meant a permanent change in income after the economy has adjusted fully to the change in the domestic assets of the banking system (i.e. the proposition is stated in terms of full-equilibrium comparative statics). Fourthly, by fixed exchange rates is meant that the spot rate is rigidly fixed by the exchange-stabilisation operations of the government. For simplicity, assume that spot rates, and all other variables, are expected to remain at current levels so that the forward rate coincides with the spot exchange rate.[2]

Given these definitions, only three assumptions are needed to prove the proposition stated at the beginning of this section, namely: (1) that the economic system is stable; (2) that an increase in the money supply, from equilibrium, tends to create a balance-of-payments deficit; and (3) that the associated reserve loss tends to reduce the money supply.[3] For, suppose that, starting from a position of full equilibrium in the economy, the monetary authorities increase the domestic assets of the consolidated banking system; for a given stock of foreign-exchange reserves the money supply increases and a balance-of-payments deficit emerges (by assumption 2); reserves fall and the money supply contracts (by assumption 3); as long as the money supply has not returned to its initial value there must be a balance-of-payments deficit and a further contraction of the money

[2] This assumption is not strictly necessary to the proof of the proposition stated at the beginning of this section. If we assume that the system is stable and that people learn, the full equilibrium to which the system eventually converges will not be affected. However, some assumptions result in an unstable model.

[3] Under most 'reasonable' dynamic postulates, if the third assumption is satisfied, then satisfaction of the second becomes a necessary condition for stability of the system, i.e. for satisfaction of the first. This interdependence is merely noted here but plays a fundamental role in the analysis of section 3, below.

stock; final equilibrium will occur when the system has returned to its initial equilibrium position, as it will under assumption 1. In the final equilibrium, the money supply is returned to its initial level, as are all real variables and prices. Only the composition of the consolidated banking system's assets has changed, the increase in domestic assets being matched by an equal decrease in foreign reserves.[4]

Note that this conclusion has been reached independently of any specific assumptions as to the existence of capital movements, the responsiveness of the latter to interest-rate changes, the ratio of traded to non-traded goods, or the extent to which transitional changes take the form of real output or price variations. These factors will affect the path of adjustment (and their role in this context will be discussed in the next section) but not the final equilibrium. That this should be so is readily explained. Our assumptions imply that the money supply in an open economy and under fixed exchange rates is an endogenous variable in the 'long run', that is that, other things equal, there is only one money stock compatible with payments equilibrium, and that the monetary mechanism of adjustment works properly, i.e. that it will ensure that the money stock converges to its equilibrium value. In an important sense, our conclusion is nothing but the small-country counterpart of the Ricardian 'natural distribution of specie'.

It may be useful to illustrate the above general proposition in the specific context in which it was originally put by Mundell and amplified by the present writer.[5] Figure 10.1 represents the combinations of interest rate and income level that equate the supply of domestic output with the demand (the sum of domestic spending and the balance of trade) along XX, the demand for money with the

---

[4] This assumes, of course, that the composition of the banking system's assets does not *per se* affect the public's behaviour. In addition, it is assumed implicitly that open-market operations do not engender wealth effects in full equilibrium (XX in Figure 10.1 does not shift) as they would not if changes in future tax liabilities are entirely discounted by the public. Furthermore, for a small open economy, the assumption that the relationship between real variables and the payments balance is unaffected by changes in the level or composition of wealth is sufficient to ensure fixity of FF in Figure 10.1 and, in the case of capital immobility, invariance of full-equilibrium income to monetary policy, whatever happens to XX. In a world model this need not be the case as wealth effects would affect aggregate world expenditure.

[5] See Mundell [8], as reprinted in [10]; and Swoboda [13], from which Figure 10.1 is reproduced with minor changes.

supply along *LL*, and for which the trade balance is equal but opposite in sign to the capital account, leaving the balance of payments in equilibrium, along the curves *FF*. These last three curves correspond to various degrees of capital mobility (defined as the interest sensitivity of capital inflows), ranging from capital immobility

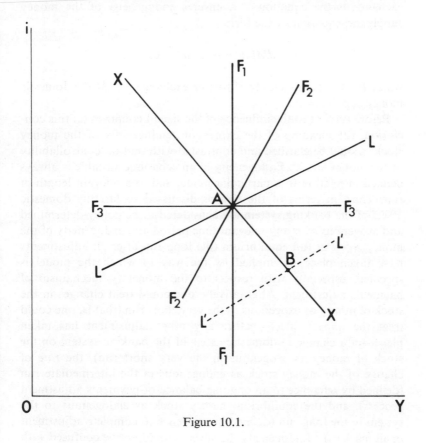

Figure 10.1.

along F_1F_1 to perfect capital mobility along F_3F_3. Three interpretations can be given to variations in 'income': changes in real output with prices constant, changes in domestic prices (foreign prices assumed constant) with real output constant,[6] or a mixture of both.

[6] For the variable price case see, in particular, Mundell [9], also reprinted in [10].

An increase in the domestic assets of the banking system temporarily pushes LL out and to the right to, say, $L'L'$. A payments deficit emerges and the money supply contracts until LL is re-established. That is, an integral component of this type of model, in addition to the excess demand functions for money, domestic output and foreign exchange is the equation that ensures endogeneity of the money supply, an equation of the form:

$$dM/dt = h(F), h' > 0,$$

where F is the excess supply of foreign exchange and M the domestic money supply.

Before turning to the influence of the size of countries on this conclusion, the meaning of the expression 'endogeneity of the money stock' should be clarified and contrasted with that of 'controllability of the money stock'. Endogeneity of an economic variable is always defined in relation to a particular model and to a relevant length of run. Thus, in terms of the models discussed so far, the domestic assets of the banking system are considered to be policy-determined and exogenous over any relevant time period and endogeneity of the money stock in full equilibrium (the long run after all adjustments have taken place) is implied by the way in which the model is specified, especially with respect to the monetary mechanism of payments adjustment. Alternatively, one could treat changes in the stock of money as exogenous in the very short run (that is, one could treat the impact effect—before any other adjustment has taken place—of a change in domestic assets of the banking system on the stock of money as exogenous in the very short run), the *rate* of change of the money stock as endogenous in the intermediate run (defined by reference to an ongoing balance-of-payments adjustment process), and the equilibrium money stock as endogenous to the system in the long run (defined by reference to complete adjustment in all markets).[7] Endogeneity, however, should not be confused with 'uncontrollability'. In buffer-stock analysis, the quantity and price of coffee bought and sold are endogenous variables, yet they may or may not be 'controllable' depending on the buffer stock's inventories of coffee and money relative to flow private excess demands or

---

[7] This three-fold classification follows on a suggestion made by Karl Brunner at the Konstanz meeting.

supplies. In the present context, controllability of the money stock will depend (a) on the limits set to the decumulation or accumulation of foreign-exchange reserves by the availability of foreign-exchange reserves on the one hand and that of domestic assets on the other hand, and (b) on the speed of adjustment of the system to a discrepancy between the actual and equilibrium money stock. This topic will be pursued further in section 2 below.

Finally, note once again that the conclusion that monetary policy affects only the composition of the assets of the banking system is of course valid only for the definition of monetary policy adopted here, namely, a once-and-for-all change in the stock of domestic assets of the consolidated banking system. This definition rules out systematic neutralisation operations by the monetary authorities, that is, the creation of a *flow* of domestic assets equal in size but opposite in sign to the flow of foreign-exchange reserves.

The above conclusion as to the ineffectiveness of monetary policy in terms of the full-equilibrium values of real variables depends crucially also on the 'small country' assumption. Defining the effectiveness of monetary policy as the change in domestic income or interest rate that results from a one 'dollar' change in the domestic assets of the banking system, it is possible to show that this effectiveness is directly proportional to the relative size of the country undertaking the open-market operation. This proposition has been advanced by Mundell for the case of perfect capital mobility within a 'Keynesian' framework.[8] We will show that it is in fact quite general and that it follows from the proposition that, under fixed exchange rates, the final impact on all variables, except the distribution of the world's reserves, of an increase in the domestic assets of country A is the same as that of an equivalent increase in domestic assets in any other country. That is, the final outcome is entirely determined, with the exception noted above, by the impact of the increase in domestic assets on the 'world money supply'—the sum of the money stocks in the hands of the publics of various countries.

In terms of a two-country model, we can write:

$$M_w = M_1 + M_2 = D_1 + D_2 + R_1 + R_2 = \tag{1}$$
$$D_1 + D_2 + R_1 + (R_w - R_1) = D_1 + D_2 + R_w,$$

[8] See [10], appendix to ch. 18.

where M refers to money supply, D to the domestic assets of the consolidated banking system, R to foreign exchange reserves, the subscripts 1, 2, and w refer to country 1, country 2, and the world, respectively, and where world reserves R_w are assumed to be given. The proof of our statement is particularly simple if we can assume

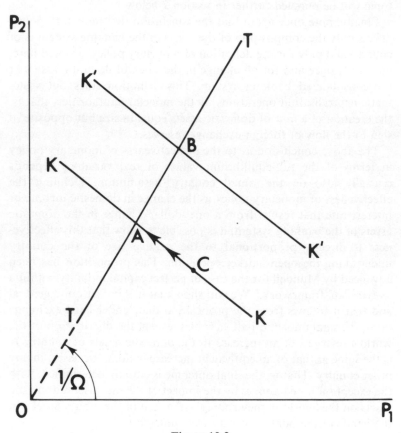

Figure 10.2.

that each country is specialised in the production of one good, that full employment prevails in both countries, and that the income elasticity of the demand for money is unity in both countries. This case is illustrated in Figure 10.2. TT shows those combinations of the money prices of the two goods which keep the balance of trade in equilibrium (this line goes through the origin and stays fixed as long as 'real' forces do not change the equilibrium terms of trade). KK shows those combinations of the two money price levels that would keep the world money supply equal to the sum of the demands for money in the two countries. A movement along KK corresponds to a redistribution of the world money supply between the two countries. For a given world money supply, the distribution of specie is unique; suppose we take money away from the residents of country 2 to give it to those of country 1 and let prices vary so that we are at C. At that point there would be an excess demand for the goods of country 2 (a trade surplus for country 2) and money would flow from 1 to 2 until equilibrium is re-established at A. Suppose now that the central bank in country 1 increases the domestic assets of its banking system. By equation (1) this increases the world money supply and KK shifts up to $K'K'$. Country 1 experiences a temporary balance-of-payments deficit until the world money supply is redistributed and prices are adjusted to make B the new equilibrium point. Note that the final equilibrium would also be at B had country 2 initiated the money supply increase.

It is now a simple matter to prove that the impact of a given change in the money supply of country 1 is proportional to the size of that country. The quantity equation for the two countries is given by (2) and (3) below, and trade equilibrium requires (4):

$$P_1 Y_1 = M_1 V_1; \tag{2}$$

$$P_2 Y_2 = M_2 V_2; \tag{3}$$

$$P_1/P_2 = \Omega, \tag{4}$$

where V_1 and V_2 are income velocities of circulation, Y_1 and Y_2 are real income levels, and Ω is a constant. Substituting from (2) and (3) into (4) and carrying out log differentiation yields

$$d \log M_1 + d \log V_1 +$$
$$+ d \log Y_2 - d \log M_2 - d \log V_2 - d \log Y_1 = 0. \tag{5}$$

Noting that Y_1, Y_2, V_1 and V_2 are assumed constant (we assumed unit income elasticity of the demand for money), (5) yields: $d \log M_1 = d \log M_2$; the increase in the world money supply is distributed proportionately to existing money stocks, the latter being obviously related to the size of countries (and exactly related if $V_1 = V_2$). For instance suppose that, initially, the money stock of country 1 is $10 and that of country 2 is $90. Now let country 1 increase the money supply by $1; in the final equilibrium the money supply of country 1

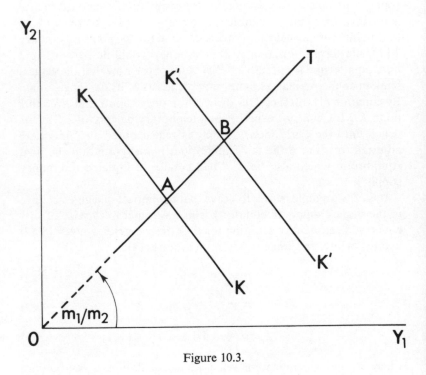

Figure 10.3.

will have increased by $0·10, the other $0·90 spilling out to country 2 to increase the latter's money stock. Money prices will have increased by only 1 per cent, even though the stock of money was *initially* increased by 10 per cent in country 1.

Much the same type of result can be obtained in a 'Keynesian world' where each country's economy is represented by the type of model depicted in Figure 10.1 above. The bare bones of such a model[9] are given in Figure 10.3. Income levels replace prices on the abscissa and ordinate, and the slope of the balance-of-payments equilibrium schedule TT is equal to m_1/m_2, the ratio of marginal propensities to import. Assuming that the income elasticity of the demand for imports is unity in both countries and that the capital account is initially balanced, an increase in the world money supply (whatever its origin) again shifts the KK curve to $K'K'$ and changes income levels in the two countries in the same proportion. If we now assume that the income and the interest elasticities of the demand for money are the same in the two countries, the increase in the world money supply is again distributed among the two countries in proportion to their income levels (and initial money stocks) as the system moves from A to B. This result is independent of the degree of capital mobility since, as Dornbusch and the present writer have shown [15], the shift in KK is independent of the degree of capital mobility and the equilibrium interest-rate *differential* is invariant with respect to changes in the world money supply.[10]

To summarise, the effectiveness of monetary policy, defined as the full-equilibrium impact on domestic money income of a one dollar open-market operation, is directly proportional to the size of the home country relative to that of the rest of the world, this effectiveness tending to zero as the country becomes very small in relative terms.

So far, the analysis has been carried out under the assumption of stationary expectations and once-and-for-all changes in the money supply. As has been shown by Mundell, similar results hold in terms of the comparative dynamics of equilibrium growth and inflationary paths.[11] Assuming for simplicity that all goods are perfect substitutes in the world economy and that the money-income elasticity of the demand for money is unity, the *equilibrium* percentage rate of growth of the money supply is equal to the sum of the percentage rates of growth of output and prices (in the short run, stock adjustments make for a more complicated result). Any attempt at increasing (decreasing) the rate of monetary expansion above (below) its

---

[9] A complete analysis of this model can be found in Swoboda and Dornbusch [15].

[10] See [15], section IV.

[11] The most important contribution is Mundell [11], ch. 15. See also Mundell [10], ch. 9; Komiya [4]; Johnson [2]; and a forthcoming paper by A. Laffer.

equilibrium level through changes in the rate of domestic credit expansion results only in a balance-of-payments deficit (surplus) in the small open economy. Equilibrium in the balance of payments (no change in the stock of reserves) requires a rate of domestic credit expansion,

$$\frac{1}{D}\frac{dD}{dt},$$

equal to

$$\frac{M}{D}\left(\frac{1}{P}\frac{dP}{dt} + \frac{1}{Y}\frac{dY}{dt}\right),$$

with symbols defined as before.[12] Note that in this type of model, inflation in the small country is always of the imported type, except in the very short run. Prices of goods and services are determined in the international market and domestic monetary policy has but a negligible influence on international prices. Inflation (or deflation) is imported through goods arbitrage; capital movements are neither necessary nor sufficient for the process to take place. They will, however, in practice influence the speed of adjustment to inflationary or non-inflationary equilibrium, the subject to which we now turn.

2 THE SPEED OF ADJUSTMENT

The discussion so far has been concerned with full-equilibrium comparative statics and once-and-for-all changes in the domestic source component of the monetary base. For practical purposes, it is important to ask how long it will take for full equilibrium to be re-established after an initial monetary disturbance and whether and to what extent disequilibrium policies can be effected. In terms of Figure 10.1, the questions we want to ask are (a) how long will it

---

[12] The expression in the text is obtained simply by differentiating $M = D + R = L(Y, P)$ proportionally with respect to time, setting dR/dt equal to zero, and noting that the elasticity of the demand for money with respect to each of its arguments is assumed equal to 1. With given growth rate of output and (world) rate of inflation, the balance of payments as a proportion of the stock of reserves $(1/R)(dR/dt)$ is entirely determined by the percentage rate of domestic credit expansion $(1/D)(dD/dt)$.

take to restore the initial equilibrium after a shift of LL to, say, $L'L'$;
(b) how feasible is it, and what is required, to keep the money
supply at a level consistent with maintenance of the system at a
point such as B? To answer these questions satisfactorily would
require, at the analytical level, building a complete dynamic model of
the adjustment process and, empirically, determining the value of the
parameters that enter the analytical model. The approach below is a
much more modest one; we discuss, intuitively and separately, the
probable influence of two factors—the degree of capital mobility and
the proportion of traded to non-traded goods—on the speed of
adjustment of the system. We also consider briefly the role of
exchange-rate margins. The analysis is non-rigorous and subject to
all the usual caveats about implicit dynamics.

One possible procedure to obtain partial answers to the questions
raised above is as follows: suppose that somehow the system
temporarily settles at point B in Figure 10.1; then ask how the
magnitude of the disequilibrium at B (in a flow per unit of time sense)
is affected by the two factors mentioned above. Presumably, the
larger the disequilibrium at B, the more speedily, other things equal,
would the (stable) system tend to return to equilibrium and the
harder would policies have to be applied to maintain it at B.[13] One
way of analysing this issue is to ask what policies are required to
turn the temporary disequilibrium point B into a 'quasi-equilibrium'
point.

Consider point B: the demand for domestic output is equal to the
supply, and the demand for domestic money by residents is equal to
the supply, but there is a balance-of-payments deficit. Other things
equal, there would be a tendency for the money supply to decline as
the monetary authorities intervene in the foreign-exchange market to
prevent a depreciation of the home currency. However, the authorities can keep the money supply at the level implied by $L'L'$ by
neutralising the monetary effects of reserve losses.[14] Denoting the

---

[13] This statement is approximate rather than exact since the length of time
required to reach equilibrium after a temporary disturbance depends not only
on the speeds of adjustment in various markets but also on whether the approach
to equilibrium is direct or cyclical.

[14] It may seem, at first, that treating points like B as quasi-equilibria violates
Walras' Law. For how can there be a disequilibrium in the foreign-exchange
market when both the money and goods markets are in equilibrium? The answer
is that a *flow* excess supply of securities by the public matches their flow excess

base by B, the money multiplier (assumed constant at the given interest rate) by m, foreign-exchange reserves by R and the domestic securities held by the central bank by D^*, we have:

$$M = mB = m(R + D^*);\tag{6}$$

$$\frac{1}{M}\frac{dM}{dt} = \frac{1}{B}\left\{\frac{dR}{dt} + \frac{dD^*}{dt}\right\}.\tag{7}$$

Thus, keeping the money supply constant requires

$$dD^*/dt = -\,dR/dt.\tag{8}$$

In words, the monetary authorities must increase (decrease) the domestic source component of the base by the same amount per unit of time as the foreign source component decreases (increases), namely, by an amount equal to the balance-of-payments deficit (surplus), dR/dt. Thus, the extent of the balance-of-payments disequilibrium at B determines the rate of neutralisation operations required to keep the system in a state of quasi-equilibrium, and, in the absence of neutralisation, will determine in part the time interval needed to restore full equilibrium.

In this context, consider, first, the role of capital mobility, defined for simplicity as the interest-rate responsiveness of international flows of capital.[15] In the simple, variable real income 'Keynesian', framework of Figure 10.1, the balance-of-payments disequilibrium at a quasi-equilibrium point like B is given by expression (9):

$$\frac{dR}{dt} = \frac{mE_i - (s + m)K_i}{-(s + m)L_i - L_yE_i}\,(M - M^*) < 0,\tag{9}$$

---

demand for foreign exchange. The authorities prevent these disequilibria from affecting the goods and money markets by absorbing the flow excess supply of securities at the existing rate of interest through their neutralisation operations and by satisfying the excess private demand for foreign exchange at the existing exchange rate through their exchange-stabilisation operations.

[15] Conceptually, it would be preferable to treat capital movements as resulting from a stock-adjustment process. The flow approach could be considered as a special short-run version of the stock-adjustment one, the interest sensitivity of flows depending, in part, on the speed at which portfolios are adjusted.

where s and m are the marginal propensities to save and import, respectively, E is domestic expenditure, L the demand for money, K net capital imports, Y money income, i the rate of interest, M and M^* are, respectively, the actual and full-equilibrium stocks of money ($M > M^*$), and subscripted variables denote partial derivatives with respect to the subscript.[16] Obviously, the higher the interest responsiveness of capital flows, K_i, the larger the payments disequilibrium created by a discrepancy between the actual and full-equilibrium money stock. In the limit, the payments disequilibrium tends to infinity as capital mobility becomes perfect ($K_i \to \infty$). This is the case where neutralisation becomes impossible and self-contradictory as it would require open-market operations to be undertaken at an infinite rate; this is inconsistent with positive and finite reserve stocks—a deficit country would rapidly lose all its reserves, a surplus country accumulate the world's entire stock of reserves. To summarise, the higher the degree of capital mobility the less scope for the disequilibrium effects of monetary policy and the larger the rate of neutralisation operations required to maintain a given quasi-equilibrium stock of money.[17]

Consider, next, the role of non-traded goods. To focus on the point at issue, imagine that there are only three goods in the system; traded or international goods, non-traded or domestic goods, and money. Assume that the three goods are substitutes. Assume further that the foreign-currency price—and hence the domestic-currency price at a given exchange rate—of international goods is fixed or exogenously determined. From equilibrium, let the monetary authorities increase the money supply; the impact effect is to create an excess supply of money and an excess demand for both domestic and international goods. The excess demand for foreign goods is reflected in an excess demand for foreign exchange, and the money supply will tend to decrease as the authorities sell foreign exchange to stabilise the exchange rate. In the end, full equilibrium will be re-established when the money supply has returned to its original

---

[16] For a derivation and further explanation see Swoboda [13].

[17] If the stock-adjustment view of capital movements is adopted, the required extent of neutralisation policies becomes independent of the degree of capital mobility in the long run; after the stock adjustment has been completed, the neutralisation rate depends only in the trade disequilibrium associated with the quasi-equilibrium point B.

level, with international prices and domestic prices unchanged. However, there will have been a transitory increase in domestic goods prices. The length of time it will take for the system to return to equilibrium will depend partly on the size of the impact effect on the excess demand for foreign exchange and hence on the balance of payments and the rate of change of the money supply. To the extent that part of the excess supply of money is absorbed by a rise in the prices of domestic goods, the excess demand (per unit of time) for international goods will be smaller than it otherwise would be (by Walras' Law). Therefore, other things equal, we would expect the rapidity with which the system adjusts to a monetary disturbance to be directly related to the ratio of traded to non-traded goods, even though the final equilibrium is not.

The same type of reasoning can be applied to the analysis of the role of non-traded goods in the transmission of 'imported inflation'. We will show that, contrary to a belief sometimes expressed, the presence of non-traded goods does not affect the full transmission of inflation in the long run and in the absence of neutralisation policies; it does, however, affect the 'length of the short run' and the rate at which neutralisation operations need to be carried out to maintain the domestic below the international rate of inflation.

These points are illustrated in Figure 10.4, which is based on a diagram used by Mundell to analyse the effects of devaluation (an issue with which we are not concerned here).[18] The curve DD shows those combinations of domestic-goods prices, P_D, and international-goods prices, P_I, that equate the demand and supply of non-traded goods, II those combinations of P_I and P_D that leave the excess demand for international goods equal to zero, and MM those combinations of the two prices that equate the demand for money with the existing stock. The three curves are drawn on the assumption that the three goods are substitutes; in addition, assume that the real excess demand functions are homogenous of degree zero in the two money prices and the nominal quantity of money. Initial equilibrium is at Q. Suppose now that the price of international goods rises in the rest of the world; the domestic-currency price of international goods must rise in the same proportion, say from P_I^0 to P_I^*, if the rate of exchange is fixed and if goods arbitrage takes

18 See Mundell [11], ch. 9.

place. Before the price of domestic goods changes, the impact effect of the rise in foreign prices is to move the commodity prices to point R; there is now an excess demand for money and domestic

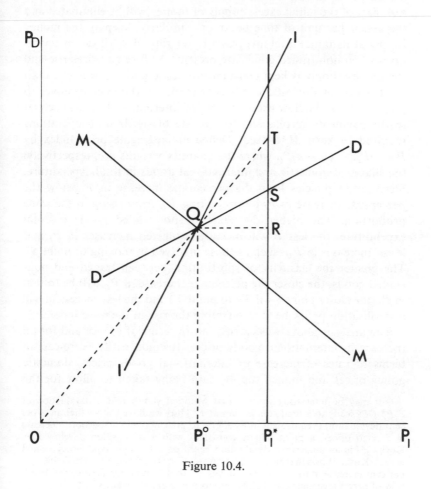

Figure 10.4.

goods and an excess supply of foreign goods. The price of domestic goods begins to rise, and the country experiences a balance-of-payments surplus that shifts the MM curve up and to the right pulling the DD and II curves in its wake. Final equilibrium is established at

T; by the homogeneity postulate the money prices and the money supply will all have increased by $P_I^0 P_I^*/OP_I^0$.[19]

The movement to T, however, will tend to be slower with non-traded goods present in the system. For, as domestic-goods prices rise, part of the initial excess supply of money will be eliminated and the deficit per unit of time be lower. Similarly, keeping the money supply at its initial level involves a lower rate of sterilisation operations when non-traded goods are present. As foreign prices rise and the money supply is kept constant, domestic goods prices rise until the market for domestic goods is cleared, i.e. the system moves to point S. At S, the flow excess supply of international goods is equal to the payments surplus and to the rate of sterilisation operations required to keep MM fixed. Define an aggregate price index by $P = aP_D + (1 - a)P_I$, where the quantity weights are, respectively, the shares of domestic and international goods in total expenditure. Sterilisation policies keep the percentage increase in P below the percentage increase in P_I by preventing P_D from rising in the same proportion. The higher the share of non-traded goods in total expenditure, the less P will increase for given increases in P_I and lesser increases in P_D (such as those involved in moving to point S). The greater the elasticity of substitution between traded and non-traded goods, the closer the percentage increase in P_D will be to that in P_I (the closer point S will lie to point T) and the less successful will a sterilisation policy be in moderating the rise in the price index P.[20]

The analysis above was carried out in terms of a once-and-for-all increase in international goods prices. It could easily be re-cast in terms of rates of increase of international goods prices, domestic goods prices and money supply, care being taken to allow for the

[19] It may be interesting to note that Mundell shows that a devaluation of $P_I^0 P_I^*/OP_I^0$ leads to a final equilibrium at T. Thus we have shown that an x per cent devaluation is equivalent in its effects to an x per cent 'exogenous' increase in foreign prices, a point that is consistent with a proposition developed by Kuska [5] in an analysis of devaluation based on a Patinkin-type disaggregated model. Kuska shows that an x per cent devaluation is equivalent to $a(100x/100-x)$ per cent increase in foreign money stocks. With due attention paid to the definition of percentage changes, the two propositions are equivalent.

[20] In the discussion in the text capital movements were neglected. If we allow for the existence of a bond market, the excess demand for money created by the imported inflation at point Q would tend to result in a rise in the interest rate. As the rate of interest would be higher when the system is at S than when it is in full equilibrium, capital inflows will tend to take place and make the task of keeping the domestic below the world rate of inflation more difficult.

effects on the stock demand for real balances of changes in the expected rate of inflation.

Finally, it has been assumed so far that the spot rate of exchange was perfectly fixed and expected to remain so, and that there was no difference between the spot and forward rates. This is clearly an 'unrealistic' assumption and an inappropriate one in certain circumstances. In the real world, the spot rate is allowed to fluctuate, albeit within narrow intervention limits, and the forward rate is not systematically pegged. Complete discussion of the complications introduced by this flexibility is impossible here. Suffice it to say that exchange-rate margins make it possible for the system to behave somewhat like a flexible rate system as long as the margins are not reached. For instance, an increase in the money supply would lead to a permanent increase in prices or income (with fixed money wages and money illusion) as the home currency depreciates, that is, as long as the price of foreign exchange does not rise to the upper intervention point; moreover, the higher the degree of capital mobility, the greater the effectiveness of monetary policy under flexible exchange rates.[21] The flexibility of *forward* rates gives some additional scope for the use of monetary policy even in the face of a high degree of capital mobility and pegged spot rates. For, if the flow of arbitrage capital is in perfectly elastic supply with respect to the *covered* interest-rate differential, it is still possible to create a divergence between domestic and foreign interest rates by affecting the premium or discount on forward exchange. However, the scope for affecting premiums on forward exchange is severely limited as long as confidence in the parity is maintained; for the speculative supply or demand for forward exchange will tend to become perfectly elastic at the exchange-rate margins.

The main strands of the argument up to this point can be summarised by four propositions: (1) The full-equilibrium effect on incomes, prices and interest rates of a once-and-for-all change in the domestic assets of the banking system of an open economy is directly proportional to the economic size of the country relative to the rest of the world. A corollary of this proposition is that the effectiveness of monetary policy thus defined tends to zero as the country becomes smaller and smaller. (2) This conclusion is indepen-

[21] See Mundell [10], chs. 17 and 18; and Sohmen [12].

dent of the degree of capital mobility and the proportion of traded to non-traded goods. (3) In the short run, however, it is possible for a country to affect its price and income level by maintaining the money stock at a given level through neutralisation policy, that is, by combining a money-*stock* policy with a *flow*-neutralisation policy— where the flow of open-market sales (purchases) equals the balance-of-payments surplus (deficit) implied by the maintenance of the money supply below (above) its full-equilibrium value. This possibility is not available when capital is perfectly mobile or when there are no non-traded goods as the required rate of neutralization policy would rapidly become infinite. (4) In the long run, however, the maintenance of quasi-equilibrium positions is incompatible with fixed exchange rates; the limits are reached in theory when only domestic assets back the money supply in case of a deficit, and when only foreign assets back the money supply in case of a surplus. As the ratio of domestic to foreign assets is usually larger than one, this means that a quasi-equilibrium involving a surplus can, potentially, be maintained for a longer lapse of time than one involving a deficit.[22]

The effects of monetary and neutralisation policy under fixed exchange rates have now been outlined. It remains to try to define the appropriate use of monetary policy in an open economy.

3 THE APPROPRIATE USE OF MONETARY POLICY[23]

There are, we have argued, severe limits to the effectiveness of monetary policy as a counter-cyclical device under fixed exchange rates except in the short run. However, within the limits set by the available stock of reserves and the openness of the economy as

[22] This statement is subject to at least two qualifications. Firstly, in practice, the limits are reached faster than in theory as speculation as to exchange-rate changes sets in. Secondly, as payments imbalances are usually defined, the foreign-exchange assets that are accumulated (decumulated) in the case of a surplus (deficit) are those of the monetary authorities; the ratio of domestic to foreign-exchange assets of the monetary authorities is quite low in several open economies; in this case the scope for neutralisation of a surplus through traditional open-market operations will be limited. A substitute to open-market operations is to induce commercial banks to absorb into their portfolios the foreign-exchange assets that would otherwise flow to the central bank; this is one of the goals of the German Bundesbank's policy of offering commercial banks special swap rates.

[23] In what follows, I abstract from the problem of the proper use of monetary policy by the centre or *n*th country of the system.

measured by its relative size, the degree of capital mobility and the ratio of traded to non-traded goods, monetary policy coupled with neutralisation of reserve flows can still be used to stabilise income and prices in the short run. Under what circumstances is it 'appropriate' to use the monetary instrument in such a fashion under fixed exchange rates?

The answer, I would argue, is 'in those cases where the balance of payments takes care of itself in the long run'. There are two principal cases where this statement would apply.

Firstly, suppose that the initial position is one of internal and external balance; then introduce cyclical variations in the balance of payments, deficits alternating with surpluses but averaging out to zero over a finite time period. In that case it may be appropriate to maintain the money supply at its long-run 'average' equilibrium level, neutralising temporary reserve changes through open-market operations. A prerequisite for the success of such a policy is that the reserve stock be large enough relative to disturbances to finance temporary deficits without causing anticipations of devaluation. Moreover, this policy will succeed in stabilising income and prices only if the payments disturbances originate predominantly in the capital account, that is, if in Figure 10.1 the curve *FF* shifts while the *XX* curve stays put. If this is not the case, stabilising the money supply will not suffice to stabilise prices and income.[24] Secondly, consider disequilibrium situations where the monetary policy requirements of internal and external balance coincide, that is, situations where inflation is coupled with a deficit or where deflation is accompanied by a payments surplus. In these cases, directing monetary policy towards internal balance will also relieve the existing payments disequilibrium.

On the other hand, the attempt to use monetary policy as a counter-cyclical device in so-called dilemma cases, unless these reverse themselves fairly rapidly, is incompatible with a regime of fixed exchange rates. For, suppose that deflation is accompanied by a deficit; using monetary policy (coupled with neutralisation operations) to restore full employment will eventually lead to exhaustion of foreign exchange reserves, and conversely for the case where a payments

[24] A case can also be made for the use of monetary policy to stabilise income and prices when disturbances originate in finite shifts in the public's portfolio preferences.

surplus is coupled with inflation. These are, of course, the dilemma cases emphasised in Meade's classic work [6].

The preceding remarks should not be interpreted to mean that there is no important role for monetary policy in the open economy under fixed exchange rates. For, though monetary policy is rarely appropriate as a counter-cyclical device and taken by itself, unless the level of reserves is of no concern, it does represent a very powerful instrument of balance-of-payments policy. In terms of full-equilibrium comparative statics, a \$1 open-market sale of securities increases the stock of foreign exchange reserves by \$1 $(M_w - M_1)/M_w$ under the assumptions listed in section 1 above. As M_1 becomes very small relative to M_w, the reserve gain tends to equality with the open-market sale.

This suggests that some other instrument be used for internal balance, leaving monetary policy to take care of residual payments imbalances. This is precisely the purpose of Mundell's well-known monetary-fiscal policy-mix analysis which consists of two separate (though related) propositions:[25] (1) that fiscal and monetary policies have different impacts on internal and external balance and hence represent two separate instruments with the help of which it is possible to achieve simultaneously internal and external balance, a comparative-statics proposition or possibility theorem; (2) that, in a decentralised system of policy responses, *assigning* monetary policy to external balance and fiscal policy to internal balance leads to convergence to the desired position of simultaneous internal and external balance while the reverse assignment of instruments to targets does not, a proposition in economic dynamics.

Whereas the first of these propositions suggests that to achieve internal and external balance simultaneously it is sufficient to find those values of the monetary and fiscal instruments that will do so and set these instruments accordingly, the second proposition asserts that in a system of decentralised response—or more fundamentally in a system of limited information—the proper use of monetary policy under fixed exchange rates is for external balance. The fundamental basis for this assignment of the monetary instrument resides in the automatic monetary mechanism of payments adjustment. As a matter of fact, it can be shown that stability of the

[25] See Mundell [7], reprinted in [10].

open economy requires as a necessary condition that an increase in the money supply, from equilibrium, leads to a deterioration of the balance of payments. It turns out that fulfilment of that condition is necessary and sufficient to insure stability of the assignment of monetary policy to the balance of payments and of fiscal policy to internal balance.[26]

To conclude this section, a few remarks on the interpretation of the expression 'appropriate' or 'proper' use of monetary policy are in order. The normative content of these expressions is limited even though, I would argue, important. The appropriateness of the particular recommendations discussed above is conditional on certain maintained hypotheses and restricted to a narrow concept of 'appropriateness'. The principal maintained hypothesis is that a fixed exchange regime prevails and that no alternative system is available. Appropriateness basically means (a) 'possible' in terms of a fixed-target framework limited to fairly narrow definitions of internal and external balance, and (b) convergent under a system of decentralised decision-making under limited information. In addition, tying monetary policy to the balance of payments is seen to be the only governing principle for monetary policy consistent with maintenance of a fixed exchange-rate system in the long run. These conclusions are quite consistent with (a) a stock-adjustment view of capital movements—the latter implying simply that reconciliation of internal and external balance through manipulation of the capital account is possible only in the short run but would imply ever-widening interest rate differentials in the long run, and (b) with the argument first advanced by Johnson and pursued by Williamson that the composition of the balance of payments that results from application of the policy mix may, or even is likely to, run counter to the dictates of the welfare considerations implied by maximisation of

[26] This point is demonstrated and related to the problem of limited information in Swoboda [14]. Note also that the expression 'effectiveness' has sometimes been used in the policy-mix literature in a different sense from that given to it in section 1 above. Thus, monetary policy is sometimes said to be more effective than fiscal policy in dealing with external balance (and vice versa for internal balance) under fixed exchange rates. This is a notion of relative effectiveness, or comparative advantage, that is most useful in a discussion of convergence of decentralised assignments. Formally, the assertion above about comparative effectiveness means that the ratio of the effect of a given change in monetary policy on external balance to its effect on internal balance is greater than the equivalent ratio for fiscal policy under fixed exchange rates.

a social welfare function over time.[27] In the context of the policy-mix model, this last consideration implies that a third instrument be found to make the composition of the balance of payments consistent with the steady-state one that maximises world welfare over time.

4 CONCLUDING REMARKS

The main thrust of this analysis has been to argue that monetary policy is an inappropriate instrument of anti-cyclical policy under fixed exchange rates in a small open economy in anything but the short run. That is, systematic use of monetary policy to stabilise incomes and prices is, save under exceptional circumstances, incompatible with the proper functioning of a system of fixed exchange rates. This argument does not require that the stock of money be uncontrollable; except under extreme circumstances (such as perfect mobility of all forms of capital), some measure of control over the stock of money can be retained in the short run; rather, the issue concerns the use to which the remaining measure of control should be put. The simultaneous pursuit of internal and external balance requires the use of at least two instruments of economic policy, say, fiscal and monetary policy, and the assignment of instruments to targets is not a matter of indifference, the monetary instrument having a clear comparative advantage in affecting the balance of payments and the stock of reserves.

These are well-known conclusions; this chapter has merely tried to make their basis quite explicit and to deal in more detail with the role of capital mobility and non-traded goods. Much further work needs to be done on these issues, notably, at an empirical level, on the role of size, capital mobility, forward markets and non-traded goods.[28] Finally, new issues for analysis and policy arise in an inflationary world where all goods are close substitutes; for, in such a world, fiscal policy of the counter-cyclical variety loses much of *its* power to affect income and price levels in small countries and the issue of control of the over-all inflationary process, and the role of large and reserve-issuing countries therein, becomes of paramount importance.

[27] See Johnson [3] and Williamson [16].
[28] For some interesting empirical work on the issue of controllability and endogeneity of the money stock, see Courchene [1] and Willms [17].

REFERENCES

[1] Courchene, T. J., 'The Price-Specie-Flow Mechanism and the Gold-Exchange Standard: Some Exploratory Empiricism Relating to the Endogeneity of Country Money Balances', in H. G. Johnson and A. K. Swoboda (eds.), *The Economics of Common Currencies* (1973).

[2] Johnson, H. G., 'The Monetary Approach to Balance-of-Payments Theory', in M. B. Connolly and A. K. Swoboda (eds.), *International Trade and Money* (1973).

[3] Johnson, H. G., 'Theoretical Problems of the International Monetary System', in *Further Essays in Monetary Economics* (1973).

[4] Komiya, R., 'Economic Growth and the Balance of Payments: A Monetary Approach', *Journal of Political Economy*, 77 (1969), 153–70.

[5] Kuska, E. A., 'The Pure Theory of Devaluation', *Economica*, xxxix (1972), 309–15.

[6] Meade, J. E., *The Balance of Payments* (1951).

[7] Mundell, R. A., 'The Appropriate Use of Monetary and Fiscal Policy under Fixed Exchange Rates', *IMF Staff Papers*, 9 (1962), 70–9.

[8] Mundell, R. A., 'The International Disequilibrium System', *Kyklos*, 14 (1961), 153–70.

[9] Mundell, R. A., 'The Monetary Dynamics of International Adjustment under Fixed and Flexible Exchange Rates', *Quarterly Journal of Economics*, 74 (1960), 227–57.

[10] Mundell, R. A., *International Economics* (New York, 1968).

[11] Mundell, R. A., *Monetary Theory: Inflation, Interest and Growth in the World Economy* (Pacific Palisades, 1971).

[12] Sohmen, E., *Flexible Exchange Rates*, rev. edn. (Chicago, 1969).

[13] Swoboda, A. K., 'Equilibrium, Quasi-Equilibrium, and Macro-Economic Policy under Fixed Exchange Rates', *Quarterly Journal of Economics*, 86 (1972), 162–71.

[14] Swoboda, A. K., 'On Limited Information and the Assignment Problem', in E. Claassen and P. Salin (eds.), *Stabilization Policies in Interdependent Economies* (Amsterdam, 1972).

[15] Swoboda, A. K., and Dornbusch, R. 'International Adjustment, Policy, and Monetary Equilibrium in a Two-Country Model', in Connolly and Swoboda (eds.), op. cit.

[16] Williamson, J. H., 'On the Normative Theory of Balance-of-Payments Adjustment', in G. Clayton, J. C. Gilbert and R. Sedgwick (eds.), *Monetary Theory and Policy in the 1970s* (Oxford, 1971).

[17] Willms, M., 'Controlling Money in an Open Economy: The German Case', *Federal Reserve Bank of St Louis Review*, 53 (1971).

11

The Monetary Theory of
Balance-of-Payments Policies

HARRY G. JOHNSON

While the term 'the balance of payments' is often used to refer to particular components of the balance-of-payments account, such as merchandise trade, the current account, or the 'basic balance', policy concern about aggregates so defined is a concern about the composition of a country's international accounts or the structure of its economic relations with the rest of the world. The definition relevant to balance-of-payments policy properly defined and to the corresponding instruments of macroeconomic policy—monetary policy, fiscal policy, exchange-rate policy, and controls on trade and payments imposed for balance-of-payments reasons—is the net resultant inflow or outflow of international reserves.

So defined, the balance of payments is a monetary phenomenon, representing a disequilibrium in the market for money. Such disequilibria carry with them their own corrective mechanisms, summarisable in the theory of real balance effects, and balance-of-payments policies should accordingly be analysed in terms of their impacts on money flows within this self-corrective framework. Yet the prevailing theory of the balance of payments and of balance-of-payments policies persists in applying the concepts of real (barter) equilibrium, often on a partial equilibrium basis, to the problem. This is particularly true of popular or policy-operational analysis, which almost invariably uses partial-equilibrium real analysis concepts, especially elasticities of demand and supply, but also of more sophisticated 'Keynesian' analyses incorporating multiplier effects, since such analysis also concentrates on 'real' analysis and abstracts from the monetary implications of real changes.

The purpose of this chapter is to develop an explicitly monetary approach to balance-of-payments theory and policy, though within the usual context of short-run analysis, in which the growth of real and financial assets and of potential full-employment income is ignored. Section 1 briefly summarises prevailing real theories of the balance of payments and points out their shortcomings. Section 2 develops some simple monetary models of balance-of-payments policy for a regime of fixed exchange rates. Section 3 uses the results to discuss the theory of a floating-rate system. Section 4 comments briefly on the application of the approach to the context of economic growth.

It should be emphasised that the chapter draws heavily on the ongoing work of the University of Chicago Workshop in International Economics. Throughout the analysis, for simplicity and in conformity with theoretical tradition but contrary to the facts of reality and much of recent work on the 'monetary approach' to balance-of-payments theory, international capital movements are ignored; this has the advantage of concentrating attention on the interaction between monetary and real phenomena.[1] It is also assumed for simplicity that, short of 'full employment', commodities are in perfectly elastic supply with their quantities determined by demand, and that each country is completely specialised on its export good.[2]

---

[1] As has been shown by a number of other writers, the assumption of the presence of international capital movements would make no difference to the results. They simply appear as another item 'above the line' dividing other transactions from the net international reserve flow. See R. Dornbusch (1971) and J. A. Frenkel (1971).

[2] The assumption of complete specialisation on exportable goods makes no substantial difference. Domestic production of importables affects the level and elasticity of demand for imports; substitution of domestic production for imports consequent on import duties introduces a production welfare loss in addition to the usual consumption welfare loss, but such welfare losses are assumed to be too small to bring into account. Some economists not familiar with the relevant theory make difficulties about non-traded goods; but since the analysis is concerned largely with general price level movements that restore the initial real equilibrium of the economy, there are no changes in the relative prices of non-traded goods to worry about (such changes can only be transitory, part of the mechanism of restoration of monetary equilibrium). Trade taxes and subsidies introduced for balance-of-payments reasons might alter the relative prices of non-traded goods and so affect the demand for money, but this possibility is ignored anyway in the subsequent analysis.

1 REAL THEORIES OF THE BALANCE OF PAYMENTS

A. *Popular theories*

Popular theories of the balance of payments, as presented in elementary textbooks and propounded in popular explanations and discussions of balance-of-payments policies, may be summarised in the following propositions.[3]

A tariff or other restriction on imports reduces a country's spending on imports in terms of foreign currency and so improves the balance of payments; and conversely for a subsidy on imports. An export subsidy increases foreign spending on a country's exports if the foreign elasticity of demand for those exports exceeds unity and so improves its balance of payments; if on the other hand the elasticity of demand for exports is less than unity, export earnings and the balance of payments will be improved by a tax on exports. A devaluation of the currency is simultaneously a tax on imports and a subsidy to exports and will improve the balance of payments if the net effect of these two on net foreign exchange receipts is positive. The condition for this, assuming initially balanced trade and perfectly elastic supplies of goods, is that the sum of the domestic elasticity of demand for imports and the foreign elasticity of demand for exports exceeds unity.[4] If the balance of payments is measured in domestic currency, as is appropriate if domestic activity and employment rather than the balance of payments is the object of analysis, export earnings including the subsidy must increase, but import expenditure including the tax proceeds may rise or fall depending on the elasticity of demand for imports, the condition for the balance of payments to be improved by devaluation from an initially balanced position being the same.

It should be noted in passing that the assumed identity of import duties and import restrictions is subject to qualifications on two grounds, both involving 'distribution effects'. Firstly, the scarcity value created by an import quota may be appropriated by the foreign suppliers rather than domestic residents, depending on how

---

[3] The analysis refers to the balance of payments on merchandise or current account, identified with the over-all balance through abstraction from international capital movements.

[4] The explanation is that a devaluation of one per cent gives the foreigner one per cent of the value of existing exports and increases export-earnings and reduces import expenditure respectively by percentages equal to the corresponding elasticity of demand.

quotas are assigned, or appropriated by domestic importers or consumers, with different effects on demand than if it were captured by the government as tariff proceeds. Secondly, the use of import restrictions rather than the tariff may involve a different response of domestic supply, the simplest example being that quotas and tariffs have different effects on the marginal revenue curve facing a domestic monopoly supplier.

This simple analysis is subject to three major criticisms, at increasing levels of abstraction, all concerned with its partial equilibrium, 'real equilibrium', nature.

Firstly, the analysis of export and import taxes and subsidies makes no reference to how these fiscal interventions are financed or disposed of. A tax is a net drain of purchasing power from the circular flow of income and expenditure, and a subsidy a net injection into the flow, involving respectively a cumulative shrinkage or expansion of the money supply if assumed to be 'financed' by destruction or creation of money, or a cumulative disturbance of portfolio balance if 'financed' by purchase or sale of assets. To maintain the conditions for real equilibrium, taxes and subsidies must be matched by purchases or sales of goods from current production, the simplest assumption being that taxes on trade are returned to the community as general income subsidies or remission of other existing general 'taxes and that subsidies on trade are financed by the imposition of general taxes.[5] This assumption in turn implies that the analysis must take account of both the effect of a trade tax or subsidy on demand for a given level of disposable income, and of its effect on disposable income itself. Thus an import duty has an income and a substitution effect, reducing imports demanded for a given level of income, and an income effect, increasing the quantity of imports demanded as a result of the addition of the tax proceeds of disposable income. The net effect is a reduction in imports demanded through the substitution effect (the income effect cancelling through the exclusion of 'redistribution effects'). Similarly, an export subsidy increases or reduces export earnings,

[5] An alternative assumption would be that government varies its own expenditures on goods and services; this assumption, or the assumption that certain specific taxes are altered to offset the effects of trade taxes or subsidies, raises the possibility of 'redistribution effects' from changes in the composition of a given total of taxes and of subsidies plus direct government expenditure, which should be ignored at this level of abstraction.

depending on whether the foreign elasticity of demand for exports is greater or less than unity, and reduces import expenditure through the income effect of the reduction of domestic disposable income by the taxation required to pay the subsidy. Thus an export subsidy will improve the balance of payments if the elasticity of foreign demand for exports is greater than unity *minus* the domestic marginal propensity to spend on imports (*not* simply unity), and an export tax will improve the balance if the foreign demand elasticity is less than this critical fraction.

Further, unity minus the domestic marginal propensity to spend on imports is the domestic marginal propensity to spend on home (exportable) goods, and the elasticity of foreign demand for exports can be decomposed into the sum of the foreign marginal propensity to spend on exportables and a positive substitution elasticity (compensated demand elasticity). Therefore, an export subsidy must improve the balance of payments unless the foreign propensity to spend on exportables is less than the domestic; that is, there is an adverse 'redistribution effect' involved in the transfer of income from residents to foreigners implicit in the export subsidy.

Turning to the analysis of devaluation, if trade is initially balanced the export subsidy is exactly financed by the import duty implicit in the devaluation, and neither passes through the government budget. The condition for trade balance improvement is the same sum–of–demand–elasticities–minus–unity criterion (which could be arrived at by explicit accounting and cancellation of the implicit income tax and subsidy). If trade is initially unbalanced, however, the income tax and subsidy implicit in the devaluation do not cancel out; with an initial export surplus, specifically, the criterion for trade balance improvement becomes more stringent because there is a net implicit subsidy to domestic income, and vice versa.

Secondly, the analysis implicitly assumes that changes in domestic income consequent on an increase in export earnings or a diversion of domestic expenditure from imports to home goods have no further effects on demand: both increased export earnings and reduced expenditures on imports are simply saved or hoarded. Behaviour postulates can obviously be devised that will ensure this result; for example, the postulate that there exists a 'leisure' or 'non-traded goods' sector which acts as a shock absorber so that there is a unique demand curve for imports as a function of their price, independent of domestic employment and income, and that exports are determined only by their price along a unique foreign demand curve. Such postulates, however, are obviously too unrealistic to be worth considering. This major defect of the popular 'elasticities' approach to balance of payments is remedied—though not satisfactorily, as will be explained—by the Keynesian multiplier approach discussed below, in which the impact effects of policy changes on demands and incomes generate multiplier effects which are limited to finiteness by the assumption that total expenditure changes by less than total income. This assumption, and not the elasticity criteria (which determine only the direction of the impact effect), is responsible for the outcomes of the policy changes.

Thirdly, the analysis, and its Keynesian improvement in common with it, ignores the monetary implications of both the initial disequilibrium situation calling for a policy change and the policy change itself. To anticipate more detailed subsequent analysis, a balance-of-payments deficit (or surplus, though the analysis will concentrate on a deficit as the typical case) involves a stock disequilibrium that will cure itself through international money flows unless the disequilibrium is continually renewed by monetary policy; for a given monetary policy, therefore, a balance-of-payments policy change can have only a transitory effect on the balance of payments—that is, on the international monetary flows required to restore stock equilibrium. Further, the policy change will generally alter the conditions of stock equilibrium between the demand for and supply of money by altering the stock demand, and this effect must be an integral part of the analysis.[6] Finally, monetary policy influences that part of the supply of domestic money which is provided from domestic sources, the remainder of the total being supplied from foreign sources, so that the effects of balance-of-payments policy changes on the balance of payments depend crucially on how domestic monetary policy (more accurately, domestic credit policy) is concurrently being managed.

To put the point of this criticism in the most challenging possible way, there is no reason whatsoever to assume that import restrictions, export subsidies, devaluation, or for that matter domestic deflation, will necessarily improve a country's balance of payments,

[6] This issue is elaborated further in ch. VI of Johnson (1958). For similar criticism of the 'popular model' see Dornbusch (1973).

or that, if it does so, the effect will be more than transitory. To assume otherwise is to assume either that real changes have monetary consequences of a simple and predictable kind, or that these consequences persist without reacting back on the real sector of the economy, or both.

B. Keynesian theories

As mentioned, Keynesian theories of the balance of payments and balance-of-payments policy treat the changes in the allocation of demand analysed by the elasticity approach as impact effects evoking multiplier effects on aggregate domestic incomes (and also foreign income, in closed world-economy models). They rely on the assumption that changes in income lead to less than equivalent changes in expenditure from that income to produce changes in the balance of payments.[7] Thus a policy change that produces an impact improvement of the trade balance will generate a multiplier increase in income which will tend to worsen the balance of payments, but, given a positive marginal propensity to save, the offset will be only partial.

A simple version of this type of model is:

$$
\begin{bmatrix}
0 & s_1 + m_1 & -m_2 \\
0 & -m_1 & s_2 + m_2 \\
1 & +m_1 & -m_2
\end{bmatrix}
\begin{pmatrix}
\dfrac{dB_1}{d\pi} \\[2mm]
\dfrac{dY_1}{d\pi} \\[2mm]
\dfrac{dY_2}{d\pi}
\end{pmatrix}
= -
\begin{pmatrix}
\dfrac{\delta B_1}{\delta \pi} \\[2mm]
\dfrac{\delta B_1}{\delta \pi} \\[2mm]
\dfrac{\delta B_1}{\delta \pi}
\end{pmatrix}
\qquad (1)\text{--}(3)
$$

where subscripts denote countries (country 1 being the policy actor and country 2 the rest of the world); Y represents income and s and m marginal propensities to save and to spend on imports;

---

[7] In the early 1950s there was a flurry of analytical interest in the possibility that balance-of-payments policy changes could have direct as well as indirect effects on aggregate expenditure—specifically, that the adverse real income effect of a devaluation, assumed by model-construction to worsen the terms of trade, would increase aggregate expenditure from a given level of output. That possibility has been dropped, however, as a consequence of both its analytical indeterminacy and its quantitative negligibility.

incomes are measured in units such that the exchange rate is initially unity; B_1 represents country 1's balance of trade measured in foreign currency and is assumed to be initially zero so that $(\delta/\delta\pi)(rB_1) = (\delta/\delta\pi)(B_1)$, where r is the exchange rate converting foreign into domestic currency as is required for analysis of the effects of exchange rate changes on country 1's domestic output, and π is a policy variable to be specified later, assumed not to affect the total expenditure from a given level of domestic or foreign income. The solutions for the effects of policy changes on incomes and the trade balance are

$$\frac{dB_1}{d\pi} = \frac{s_1 s_2}{\Delta} \frac{\delta B_1}{\delta\pi} \tag{4}$$

$$\frac{dY_1}{d\pi} = \frac{s_2}{\Delta} \frac{\delta B_1}{\delta\pi} \tag{5}$$

$$\frac{dY_2}{d\pi} = -\frac{s_1}{\Delta} \frac{\delta B_1}{\delta\pi} \tag{6}$$

where $\Delta = s_1 s_2 + m_1 s_2 + m_2 s_1$. Hence, if the impact effect of the policy change is to improve the trade balance, the total effect must be to improve the trade balance by a fraction of the impact effect, increase output in the policy-changing country, and reduce it in the rest of the world; and vice versa. The impact effects are:

$$\frac{\delta B_1}{\delta\pi} = X(\eta_2 - 1 + m_1) \quad \text{for an export subsidy financed by} \atop \text{a general income tax;} \tag{7}$$

$$\frac{\delta B_1}{\delta\pi} = X(\eta_1 - m_1) \quad \text{for an import duty redistribution} \atop \text{as a general income subsidy; and} \tag{8}$$

$$\frac{\delta B}{\delta\pi} = X(\eta_1 + \eta_2 - 1) \text{ for a devaluation of the currency.} \tag{9}$$

where η is the subscripted country's constant-expenditure price-elasticity of demand for imports and X is the initial quantity or value of exports or imports. (Recall that trade is assumed to be initially balanced.)

These results can be used to verify the discussion of export and import taxes and subsidies and currency devaluation (and implicitly appreciation) of the preceding subsection. The model can be extended further to consider the effects of deflationary or inflationary policies in the two countries by replacing the three expressions in $\delta B_1/\delta \pi$ on the right-hand sides of the original equations respectively by $(s_1 + m_1 - 1)T_1 - m_2 T_2$, $(s_2 + m_2 - 1)T_2 - m_1 T_1$, and $m_1 T_1 - m_2 T_2$, where T_1 and T_2 are respectively lump-sum taxes imposed by countries 1 and 2 on disposable incomes in those countries and are assumed to have the same effects on expenditures and saving as any other change in income. The results are:

$$. \Delta dB_1 = m_1 s_2 T_1 - m_2 s_1 T_2, \tag{10}$$

$$\Delta d Y_1 = \Delta T_1 - (s_2 + m_2)T_1 - m_2 T_2, \tag{11}$$

$$\Delta d Y_2 = \Delta T_2 - (s_1 + m_1)T_2 - m_1 T_1. \tag{12}$$

(Note that $\Delta = (s_1 + m_1)(s_2 + m_2) - m_1 m_2$ and so must be smaller than either $(s_1 + m_1)$ or $(s_2 + m_2)$, so that an increase in taxes in either country must reduce incomes in both).

By setting $T_2 = -T_1$ and defining disposable income as $dY - T$, it is easy to verify the Metzler results[8] that, with positive marginal propensities to save in the two countries, a transfer financed by income taxes and disposed of by income subsidies must lower disposable income in the transferor and raise disposable income in the transferee and must be 'under-effected' in the sense that the trade balance of the transferor improves by less than the amount of the transfer. Similarly, by setting $(1 - s_1)T_1 = -(1 - s_2)T_2 = T$ so that the transferor reduces and the transferee increases expenditure by an amount equal to the transfer, and re-defining $\delta B_1/\delta \pi$ as the impact effect of the transfer on the over-all balance of payments including the transfer as well as the trade balance, $\delta B_1/\delta \pi = (m_1/(1 - s_1) + m_2/(1 - s_2) - 1)$ can be substituted for $\delta B_1/\delta \pi$ in the foregoing policy-change equations to yield the Meade–classical result[9] that, if the sum of the proportions of the changes in ex-

[8] L. A. Metzler, 'Tariffs, the Terms of Trade, and the Distribution of Income', *JPE*, LVII, No. 1, Feb. 1949, pp. 1–29.

[9] See for example, J. E. Meade, *The Theory of International Economic Policy, Vol. I, The Balance of Payments* (London: Macmillan, 1951).

penditure directly due to the financing and disposal of the transfer which fall on imports exceeds unity, and vice versa, the transfer will be over-effected and income will rise in the transferor and fall in the transferee country.

The foregoing model assumes perfectly elastic supplies of exports at constant domestic-currency prices, implying Keynesian conditions of unemployment and price rigidity. Following Meade, however, it can easily be transformed into a model analysing the effect of a balance-of-payments policy change on the assumption that policies controlling total domestic expenditure are simultaneously changed to keep total foreign and domestic expenditure on each country's output constant. This implies changing domestic expenditure just sufficiently to offset the effect of the policy change on the balance of trade.

Assuming as before that this is accomplished through changes in lump-sum taxes on disposable income, and confining attention to the trade balance to the exclusion of the determination of the requisite expenditure changes, we have

$$\frac{dB_1}{d\pi} = \frac{m_1}{1 - s_1} \cdot \frac{dB_1}{d\pi} + \frac{m_2}{1 - s_2} \cdot \frac{dB_2}{d\pi} + \frac{\delta B_1}{\delta \pi} \tag{13}$$

or

$$\frac{dB_1}{d\pi} = \frac{\delta B_1/\delta \pi}{1 - m_1/(1 - s_1) - m_2/(1 - s_2)}. \tag{14}$$

Alternatively, $$d\pi = \frac{1 - m_1/(1 - s_1) - m_2/(1 - s_2)}{\delta B/\delta \pi} dB_1 \tag{15}$$

where dB_1 is to be interpreted as a target change in the trade balance and $d\pi$ is the change in the policy variable required to achieve it, once the changes in the relations between target output levels and domestic expenditures requisite to achieve the trade-balance change have been effected. It is apparent that the required change in the policy variable may be in either the positive or the negative direction, even assuming that the impact effect $\delta B/\delta \pi$ is positive (the conditions discussed above are fulfilled) depending on whether the sum of the proportions of the expenditure changes falling on imported goods is less than or greater than unity.

In fact, as is obvious, the results are simply a somewhat more generalised form of the analysis of the transfer problem and are identical with that analysis if the policy instrument is assumed to be the exchange rate and the exchange rate a means of changing the terms of trade. Thus an export subsidy, a tax, an import duty, or a devaluation may be associated with either a deficit or a surplus on the balance of trade, even if the conditions required for a positive impact effect in the trade balance are satisfied. The reason, heuristically, is that the associated expenditure-changing policies may produce either an excess supply of or an excess demand for the export good of the country implementing the balance-of-payments policy (an 'under-effected' or an 'over-effected' transfer) requiring respectively either a positive or a negative policy impact effect to offset it.

It is also obvious that in both this and its previous formulation the model makes two very peculiar, and mutually inconsistent, monetary assumptions. The first is that the fiscal operations involved in export or import subsidies or taxes, and the change in the domestic price of imports consequent on import duties or devaluation, together with induced changes in the levels of domestic output and expenditures allowed in the first version of the model, either have no effect on the domestic demand for money or have effects which are exactly offset by changes in the domestic money supply provided by domestic credit operations that have no implications for the international movement of money through the balance of payments. The second is that it is possible for there to be a continuing international equilibrium flow of money, determined in the first version of the model by a marginal propensity to save—more strictly speaking, to hoard international money—as a function of income, and in the second by the actions of the policy makers in setting the relation between domestic expenditure and target domestic output.[10]

To put these criticisms another and probably clearer way, the Keynesian analysis in general makes the inconsistent assumptions (a) that domestic credit policy accommodates any change in the

[10] Note that the second objection, but not the first, disappears if the policy analysis is confined to the analysis of policies designed to move the economy from an initial balance-of-payments disequilibrium position to a position of balanced payments with zero international reserve flows, because a zero reserve flow (alone) is consistent with stock equilibrium in the market for money; but for such problems the analysis cannot be simplified as above by assuming initial equality of export and import values, and the algebra becomes much clumsier.

domestic demand for money consequent on balance-of-payments policy changes (or, quite improbably, that no such changes occur); (b) that, contrary to the established monetary–theoretic approach to the demand for money in terms of a desired relationship of money stock to income flow, or of money stock to total wealth, for which income flow can be used as a proxy, there is a flow demand for *additions* to the stock of international money related, like flow demands for goods, to the flow of income.[11]

By contrast, a monetary–theoretic approach to the balance-of-payments theory and policy suggests that, in so far as domestic credit policy provides any additional money demanded (or subtracts any excess supply created) by balance-of-payments policy, aggregate expenditure on goods and services will equal aggregate income, and balance-of-payments policy changes will have no effect on the balance of payments, but only effects on the allocation of expenditures (and, though this matter will not be pursued here, on the efficiency of resource allocation and economic welfare). And in so far as domestic credit policy is not so accommodating, disequilibria between the demand for money and the initial stock will be corrected through a divergence of expenditure from income and a balance-of-payments surplus or deficit continuing until its cumulative effect has been to make the stock of money held by domestic residents equal to the quantity demanded, as determined by real income and the price level. These points can be illustrated, with reference to the first version of the Keynesian model above, by noticing that if s_1 is 0, $dB_1/d\pi$ also equals zero.

2 THE MONETARY THEORY OF THE BALANCE OF PAYMENTS

The essence of the monetary theory of the balance of payments and balance-of-payments policy has just been stated: balance-of-payments policies will not produce an inflow of international reserves unless they increase the quantity of money demanded and unless domestic credit policy forces the resident population to acquire the extra money wanted through the balance of payments via an excess of receipts over out-payments; the balance-of-pay-

---

[11] Again, the second assumption does not constitute grounds for objection *if* analytical attention is concentrated on cases in which the equilibrium flow demand for money is zero.

ments surplus will continue only until its cumulative effect in increasing domestic money holdings satisfies the domestic demand for money. This theory, of course, is simply a reformulated version of David Hume's price–specie–flow–mechanism[12] extended to include the case of exchange rate devaluation as well as the mercantilist policies of import substitution and export promotion he was attacking. In elaborating on this, it is convenient to begin with the classical price-flexibility–full-employment case, rather than the Keynesian price-rigidity–variable-output case. It is also convenient analytically, though unrealistic, to consider the initiation of various balance-of-payments policies from a starting position of balanced trade—recall that international capital movements have been excluded by assumption—and to assume that the rest of the world is so large relative to the country under analysis that monetary effects on it can be ignored, or that it is prepared to replace initial reserves by domestic credit as required to satisfy domestic demand for nominal money at an unchanged price level for its imports.

Consider first a devaluation of the currency. As is well known from elementary monetary theory and recent international monetary theory literature, restoration of the initial real equilibrium requires increases in the domestic prices of all goods approximately equi-proportional to the devaluation[13] which in turn requires an equi-proportional increase in nominal money balances for the maintenance of monetary equilibrium. If the nominal monetary increase is provided by helicopter distribution or domestic credit expansion, the outcome is inflation proportional to the devaluation with no gain of international reserves. If, on the contrary, domestic-asset-backed money is kept constant, reserves must increase by the amount of the increase in the quantity of nominal money demanded, via a cumulated balance-of-payments surplus of the same total amount in domestic money terms (or by this amount less the capital gain on existing international reserves if this gain is monetised). If

---

[12] The term 'price–specie–flow–mechanism', though sanctified by tradition, is misleading, because in a single world market national prices cannot diverge by more than tariffs and transport costs allow, and international monetary disequilibria produce expenditure flows directly, without intervening relative price changes.

[13] Approximately, since in finite as distinct from infinitesimal mathematics a ten per cent increase after a ten per cent decrease does not restore a variable to its initial value.

the country maintains a fixed ratio of value of international reserves to domestic money, the value of international reserves will rise proportionally to the devaluation; but this will involve a balance-of-payments surplus only if some or all of the capital gain on existing reserves is sterilised.

If the devaluation is assumed to occur from a position of balance-of-payments deficit, involving an initial excess supply of money and excess of international spending over international receipts, there are two further complications. Firstly, the devaluation will mop up part or all, or more than all, of the initially excess supply of money, leaving a net increase (which may still be negative) in the quantity of money demanded algebraically less than proportional to the devaluation. Secondly, if world demand for the country's exports and world supply of its exports are less than perfectly elastic, the expansion of its exports and contraction of its imports necessary to restore balance-of-payments equilibrium will lower the world prices of both compared with the initial (deficit) situation, so that its price level and equilibrium demand for nominal money will rise less than proportionally to the devaluation.

It should be emphasised that the analysis of the effects of a devaluation is completely independent of any critical-magnitude condition applying to the elasticities of international demand. The relevant stability condition is the monetary–theoretic one that a reduction in real balances produces a reduction in real expenditure from a given real income, and vice versa.

Now consider the imposition of an import duty, on the reasonable assumption of a perfectly elastic world supply of imports to the duty-imposing country. The resulting increase in the domestic price of imports will increase the demand for nominal money. The reduction in the quantity of imports will also in equilibrium mean a reduction in the quantity of exports required to pay for them; and if world demand for the country's exports is imperfectly elastic, their domestic currency price will increase, raising the demand for nominal money still further. Note, with respect to the increase in the domestic price of imports, that consumer disposable income has risen because redistributed tariff proceeds are now added to earned income; hence, in so far as nominal money demanded is a function of disposable income or expenditure, it must increase.

A more sophisticated way of arriving at the same conclusion is to assume that real balances are held for their utility or convenience yield, as represented by their purchasing power over real income, and are proportional to real income; then any rise in the price level, regardless of its composition, and in the money level of expenditure, will increase nominal money demanded in the same proportion. The demand for real balances is usually assumed to be a function also of the alternative opportunity cost of holding them, the money rate of interest; but the simple model employed here includes no rationale for a money rate of interest and no mechanism for such a rate to be affected by balance-of-payments policy. It might be thought that the authorities could influence the interest rate by altering the proportions of domestic money and domestic securities to be held, but presumably this interest rate would in the long run have to be consistent with equality of income and expenditure and a balanced trade account, or else be pegged to world interest-rate levels by the international mobility of capital.[14] In accordance with the general lines of previous analysis, the increase in the quantity of nominal money demanded, in consequence of the import duty, may be provided either by domestic credit creation or by a transitional balance-of-payments surplus.

Finally, consider an export subsidy, which assumes a less than perfectly elastic foreign demand for exports. It is convenient to begin with the dividing-line condition $\eta_2 = 1 - m_1$, which ensures that the additional exports demanded by the rest of the world are exactly provided by the reduction in domestic demand for exportables caused by the general taxation required to finance the subsidy. In this case, domestic currency prices, income and expenditure are unchanged, and so is the domestic demand for money. If η_2 is greater than $1 - m_1$, as may normally be assumed to be the realistic case, there is an excess demand for exportables and excess supply of importables at the initial level of domestic expenditure. The money price of exportables must therefore rise to shift foreign and domestic demand away from exportables and toward importables; the demand for nominal money must increase; and the additional money demanded must be supplied either by domestic credit expan-

[14] Equality of money interest rates among countries involves (1) equality of expected inflation rates—inflation is excluded by the static nature of the models of this chapter but, given the assumptions of a world market for goods, would proceed at the same pace in all countries; (2) equality of real interest rates. This would follow from mobility of securities or capital goods.

sion or by a transitional balance-of-payments surplus. In the unrealistic converse case of $\eta_2 < 1 - m_1$, the money price of exportables must fall and excess nominal money must be wiped out by domestic credit contraction or a transitional balance-of-payments deficit. The dividing-line case can be given some verisimilitude by assuming that, regardless of the foreign elasticity of demand for exports, domestic producers simply sell abroad whatever extra quantities are made available by the taxation that finances the export subsidy, charging the initial price less the subsidy and rationing supplies by queuing purchasers.

Where $\eta_2 < 1 - m_1$, the popular theory previously summarised indicates an export tax to improve the balance of payments. In this case the export tax creates an excess demand for exportables and raises their domestic price and the demand for money.[15] Moreover, the proceeds of the export tax constitute an addition to earned income, making disposable income greater than the value of output, further increasing the demand for money. In fact, taking this latter effect into account, an export tax must increase the demand for money, provided the elasticity of demand for exports is less than unity.[16]

We turn now to the Keynesian model of fixed domestic prices of exportables and variable output, taking first the case of a small policy-making country facing a large outside world. The essential analytical principle here is that in full equilibrium exports must exactly pay for imports, and the quantity of domestic money must be equal to the amount demanded at the domestic equilibrium output and price levels. For simplicity, we assume that the quantity of money demanded bears a fixed ratio k_1 to the money value of domestic output.

In this case, starting from initially balanced trade, the general expression for the effect of a balance-of-payments policy change on equilibrium money income would seem to be (by setting $s_1 = 0$),

$$\frac{dY_1}{d\pi} = \frac{1}{m_1} \frac{\delta B_1}{\delta \pi}, \qquad (16)$$

[15] This is, of course, a version of the well-known Metzler exception to the general proposition that a tariff turns the domestic price ratio against exportable goods and shifts production towards importables.

[16] The monetary approach to the analysis of tariffs is also elaborated in Mussa (1973) abridged and extended in Chapter 8 above.

and the expression for an increase in the quantity of domestic
money (C for cash) demanded

$$\frac{dC_1}{d\pi} = \frac{k_1}{m_1} \frac{\delta B_1}{\delta \pi}. \tag{17}$$

This answer is correct for the case of a devaluation, which involves
no fiscal transfers, and for an export subsidy, which includes drawing
taxes from consumers' earned incomes and paying them to producers
to make up the difference between export prices and domestic cost
of production. In both cases, there is a critical elasticity condition
for the balance-of-payments policy to improve the balance of
payments and attract foreign exchange reserves; these conditions
are the same as in the Keynesian analysis, but in each case the
balance-of-payments improvement is transitory and conditioned on
restraint of expansion of the money supply via domestic credit
expansion (including monetisation of capital gains on existing
international reserves).

In the case of an import duty, however, consumers' disposable
income and expenditure exceed their earned income by the amount
of the tariff proceeds collected and redistributed by the government.
In this case, disposable income increases by approximately

$$\frac{dY_1'}{d\pi} = \frac{dY_1}{d\pi} + X = X\frac{\eta_1}{m_1}, \tag{18}$$

and the increase in the quantity of domestic money demanded is

$$\frac{k_1\eta_1}{m_1} X. \tag{19}$$

In this case, there is no critical elasticity condition, other than the
exclusion of Giffen goods; but again the potential improvement
in the balance of payments is transitory and conditional on restraint
of domestic credit expansion.

In the case of an export tax, where tax proceeds enter into disposable income,

$$\frac{dY_1'}{d\pi} = \frac{1}{m_1} X(1 - m_1 - \eta_2) + X = \frac{1 - \eta_2}{m_1} X. \tag{20}$$

Even though total output falls ($\eta_1 > 1 - m_1$), the quantity of money demanded in this case will increase provided the foreign import demand elasticity is less than unity. Thus a country may gain reserves by imposing such a tax, even though prevailing theory would suggest that imposition of the tax will worsen the balance of payments.

Turning finally to a closed two-country world system, it is clear to begin with that the limitation imposed on the small open economy in a large world of the previous case, by the fixity of the demand curve for its exports and the world money price of its imports, must be replaced by a restriction on the total quantity of the world money supply, in the form obviously of a limited world stock of international reserves and desired ratios of international reserves to domestic money stocks. Otherwise, there would be nothing to fix the absolute, as distinct from the relative, levels of output and employment in the two countries. Such a restriction can be most conveniently represented by assuming a fixed total of world reserve money and suppressing the domestic money supply multipliers into the proportionality factor k between domestic money income and reserves demanded, though to do so excludes certain obvious analytical possibilities of substituting domestic credit expansion or contraction for reserve acquisition or reserve loss. (Note that the assumption implies monetisation of capital gains on international reserves from devaluation.)

The system can be represented by two equations, the trade balance equation:

$$B_1 = X_1 - rX_2 = 0, \qquad (21)$$

and the reserve-constraint equation:

$$k_1 \frac{Y_1'}{r} + k_2 Y_2' = \bar{C}, \qquad (22)$$

where r is the price of country 2's currency in terms of country 1's, X represents a country's exports, Y_1' its disposable income measured in its own currency, k_1 and k_2 the international reserve ratios, $\bar{C}$ the total of world reserves, and country 2's currency is measured in equivalent units of international money. Since country 1 is assumed to be the policy-changing country, country 2's disposable income can be identified with its output Y_2 and country 1 must gain or lose reserves accordingly as Y_2 falls or rises. Initially, $Y_1' = Y_1$; recall that, of the policies considered, only an import duty or an export tax causes disposable income to diverge from earned income or the value of output.

$$\frac{\delta B_1}{\delta \pi} + m_2 \frac{dY_2}{d\pi} - m_1 \frac{dY_1}{d\pi} = 0, \tag{23}$$

$$k_1 \frac{\delta Y_1'}{\delta \pi} - k_1 Y_1 \frac{dr}{d\pi} + k_1 \frac{dY_1}{d\pi} + k_2 \frac{dY_2}{d\pi} = 0, \tag{24}$$

and
$$\frac{dY_2}{d\pi} = \frac{k_1 m_1}{k_1 m_2 + k_2 m_1} \left[Y_1 \frac{\delta r}{\delta \pi} - \frac{\delta Y_1'}{d\pi} - \frac{1}{m_1} \frac{\delta B_1}{\delta \pi} \right]. \tag{25}$$

Substituting from previous results, $dY_2/d\pi < 0$ and country 1 gains reserves as a result of devaluation if

$$\eta_1 + \eta_2 - 1 > \frac{Y_1}{X_1}; \tag{26}$$

the condition that the sum of the elasticities of international demand should exceed unity plus the reciprocal of the initial trade to income ratio, a critical value necessarily above two and empirically somewhere in the neighbourhood of five or more, is obviously a stringent one. In the case of an export subsidy, country 1 will gain or lose reserves accordingly as $\eta_2 \gtrless 1 - m_1$, and conversely for an export tax. An import duty must increase country 1's reserves apart from the exceptional case of its imports being Giffen goods. And an export tax will increase country 1's reserves provided that $\eta_2 < 1$, even though if $\eta_2 > 1 - m_1$ standard theory would indicate a worsening of the balance of payments and a loss of reserves.

3 THE MONETARY THEORY OF FLOATING EXCHANGE RATES

Floating exchange rates rule out balance-of-payments deficits and surpluses and possibilities of reserve gain or loss from balance-of-payments policies. The interesting questions concern the effects of balance-of-payments policies on the exchange rate. For the analysis of these questions, attention will be confined to a classical full-employment world, in which the domestic price level is adjusted to give the existing stock of money the real value that the public desires given its real income; in other words, the price level is adjusted in relation to nominal money balances to secure the desired level of real balances. In this connection, it is obvious that the exchange rate (defined as the price of foreign currency in terms of domestic currency) must vary in proportion with the nominal quantity of domestic money and appreciate or depreciate as the country deflates or inflates its money supply, the money supply in the rest of the world being constant, appreciate or depreciate as the rest of the world inflates or deflates, the domestic money supply being constant; and appreciate or depreciate as the domestic money supply is inflated relatively more slowly or deflated relatively faster than the rest of the world's money supply. The more interesting questions, therefore, concern the effects of trade taxes or subsidies.

Before turning to these questions, a preliminary remark is in order concerning the familiar elasticity condition (sum–of–the–elasticities–of–demand–for–foreign–exchange–greater–than–unity) for exchange market stability. As has already been mentioned, this condition is completely irrelevant to a monetary international economy—unless esoterically reinterpreted to make it true—because it is the condition for stability of exchange in a barter economy. All it amounts to is the proposition that a barter market will be stable if a fall in a commodity's price produces an excess demand for it: the elasticity of demand for one good minus unity is identically equal to the elasticity of supply of the other, and the condition is simply that the sum of the demand and supply elasticities for a commodity be positive. In a monetary economy, as already mentioned, the stability condition is simply that a reduction in real balances leads to a fall in prices and vice versa. As applied to the foreign exchange market, given one world price level and nominal quantities of domestic money in the two countries (home country and rest of world) there will be only one exchange rate that will give each country the real balances it desires.

The classic analysis of the effects of balance-of-payments policies on the equilibrium exchange rate has been provided by James Meade.[17] However, Meade introduces money prices into what is essentially a real barter model by assuming that the monetary authority in each country stabilises the factor-cost price of the exportable good in terms of domestic currency, with the convenient result that for an import duty the exchange rate is identical with the barter terms of trade.[18] Besides being arbitrary (though understandable in Keynesian terms), this procedure in general allies a balance-of-payments policy change with a particular (and varying) monetary policy change. The theoretically more acceptable procedure is to assume a fixed quantity of domestic money and consider the effects of a trade policy change on the quantity of money demanded at a fixed exchange rate with balanced trade: if the quantity of money demanded increases the domestic price level must fall and the exchange rate appreciate, and vice versa.

The effects of trade policy changes on the exchange rate are immediately apparent from the analysis of the previous section provided that the policy-changing country can be assumed to be relatively small. An import duty must lead to an increase in the demand for money, a fall in the price level, and an appreciation of the currency. An export subsidy must have the same effect provided that the elasticity of foreign demand for exportables exceeds the policy-changing country's marginal propensity to consume them, and conversely. And an export tax must have the same effect providing that the elasticity of foreign demand for exports is less than unity. Moreover, the assumption that the policy-changing country is relatively small is not in fact necessary: since no policy change occurs in the rest of the world, and its quantity of domestic money is fixed, its money income is fixed and with it the domestic money price of its exportable good.

4 THE MONETARY THEORY OF BALANCE-OF-PAYMENTS POLICY UNDER CONDITIONS OF ECONOMIC GROWTH

The central point of the monetary approach to balance-of-payments policy theory is that balance-of-payments deficits or surpluses

---

[17] See for example Meade (1952).
[18] ibid., p. 47.

reflect stock disequilibrium between demand and supply in the market for money and must be transient in nature, as must the effects of balance-of-payments policies, unless stock disequilibrium is continually being re-created. In the short-run static context analysed in this chapter, such re-creation must involve progressive arbitrary shifts in the demand for money (changes in the desired money-to-income ratio or, in Keynesian cases, shifts in the autonomous components of aggregate demand) or in the quantity of money supplied by domestic credit policy. In a growing economy, however, the process of continuous growth produces steady stock shifts that may constitute flow disequilibrium.

Thus an economy growing steadily in real terms at constant prices and interest rates demands a growing stock of real and therefore of nominal money balances; and if the domestic credit component of the money supply grows at the same rate, so must the international reserve component, with the result that the country will run a balance-of-payments surplus equal to a constant proportion of its national income and growing at the same rate. A deficit will develop if domestic credit expands sufficiently more rapidly than real output at constant prices, or more generally for a world economy with a given growth rate of international reserves, if domestic credit expands sufficiently rapidly relative to the country's real growth rate and the rate of growth of international reserves.[19]

The central point relevant to this chapter, however, is that if a country is subject to a chronic condition of balance-of-payments deficit as a result of such a constellation of causal factors, it cannot hope to remedy the problem except transitorily by application of any of the conventional balance-of-payments policies: deflation of the money supply or of aggregate demand by fiscal policy, devaluation, import restriction or export subsidisation (or in exceptional circumstances export taxation). Even if these policies create a temporary balance-of-payments surplus—and the foregoing analysis indicates that it is not certain that they will, the strongest candidate being import taxation—the only possible long-run remedy within the control of the national policy-making authorities is reduction of the rate of domestic credit expansion.

[19] The relevant formal analysis is laid out in Johnson (1973, ch. 9).

REFERENCES

Dornbusch, Rudiger, 'Notes on Growth and the Balance of Payments', *Canadian Journal of Economics* iv, no. 3 (August 1971), 389–95.

Dornbusch, Rudiger, 'A Note on Exchange Rates in a Popular Model of International Trade', unpublished manuscript, University of Rochester (1973).

Frenkel, Jacob A., 'A Theory of Money, Trade and the Balance of Payments in a Model of Accumulation', *Journal of International Economics*, i, no. 2 (May 1971), 159–87.

Johnson, Harry G., *International Trade and Economic Growth* (London, George Allen & Unwin, 1958).

Johnson, Harry G., *Further Essays in Monetary Economics* (London, George Allen & Unwin, 1973).

Meade, James E., *A Geometry of International Trade*, 1st edn (London, George Allen & Unwin, 1952).

Mundell, Robert A., *Monetary Theory* (Pacific Palisades, California, Goodyear, 1971).

Mussa, Michael, 'Tariffs and the Balance of Payments', unpublished manuscript, University of Rochester (1973).

PART TWO

Empirical

IV. CASE STUDIES

12

Monetary Equilibrium and International Reserve Flows in Australia[1]

J. RICHARD ZECHER

The balance of payments in an open economy plays an important role in determining changes in the stock of domestic money. International reserve inflows, for example, will increase the domestic stock of money if they are added directly to the money balances of residents, or if they are exchanged for domestic currency at the central bank.[2] In Australia, reserve flows are an important factor, and occasionally a dominant one, in determining changes in the domestic stock of money.[3] This observation raises the question, what are the major determinants of Australian reserve flows and what role, if any, do policy actions play in affecting reserve flows?

Models of open economies that include a market for money have been developed by R. A. Mundell (1968, 1971), H. G. Johnson (1972), A. B. Laffer (1968), R. Komiya (1969), J. Frenkel (1971), and R. Dornbusch (1971), among others.

These models suggest two equivalent ways of describing a reserve flow. One asserts that reserves flow in when residents demand less goods, services, and non-monetary assets from non-residents than

---

[1] The author is indebted to the Australian Reserve Bank for supplying most of the data used in this study, and to Harry G. Johnson, Arthur B. Laffer, and members of the International Trade Workshop at the University of Chicago during Summer Quarter, 1972, for many helpful comments. Any remaining errors are the author's.

[2] International reserve flows are treated here as equivalent to the balance of payments. For this and other definitions of the balance of payments, see Kindleberger (1969).

[3] See McGregor, Burrows, and Zecher (1972).

non-residents demand from them, and the converse. The other description says that reserves flow in when residents desire to accumulate money balances faster than the rate at which policy actions and other domestic factors are increasing the stock of money. This highly simplified characterisation implies that reserve flows result from the states of equilibrium in all non-monetary markets or, equivalently, from the state of equilibrium in the money market.

In this chapter the latter, and simpler, approach is taken. Reserve flows are related to factors determining growth in demand for money, and to policy and other domestically determined factors that contribute to growth in the stock of money. This money-market approach to the balance of payments is a slightly modified version of a model developed by H. G. Johnson (1972).

1 INTERNATIONAL RESERVES, MONEY SUPPLY, AND MONEY DEMAND

When the monetary authorities in an open economy are willing to buy or sell international reserves at a fixed price, private citizens and businesses play a central role in determining the amount of high-powered money. If domestic supply of money exceeds demand, outlays rise above receipts, and part of the increased outlays is directed at foreign goods, services, and assets. Residents may acquire the reserve currencies to pay for the increased purchases from foreigners by buying reserves from the central bank in exchange for domestic money, thus generating a decline in the domestic money stock. This process can be formally stated in terms of a money supply identity.

$$
\begin{aligned}
M &\equiv a.H, \\
M &= \text{stock of domestic money}, \\
a &= \text{money multiplier}, \\
H &= \text{stock of high-powered money}.
\end{aligned}
\tag{1}
$$

The amount of high-powered money is derived from the consolidated balance sheet of the monetary authorities. In simplified form, this balance sheet contains the following items, in addition to high-powered money:[4]

---

[4] For a detailed discussion of Australian high-powered money, see McGregor, Burrows, and Zecher (1972).

Monetary Authorities' Balance Sheet

$$\begin{array}{c|c} R & H \\ OA & OL \end{array}$$

R = official holdings of international reserves,

OA = all other assets of the monetary authorities, such as domestic bonds, bank buildings, etc.,

OL = all liabilities of the monetary authorities other than high-powered money.

Define high-powered money in terms of the balance sheet items, such that

$$H \equiv R + (OA - OL) \equiv R + D. \tag{2}$$

Every change in high-powered money is associated with changes in R and/or changes in all domestic influences on the balance sheet, summarised by the variable D. Substituting (2) into (1) gives the money supply formula

$$M \equiv a.(R + D). \tag{3}$$

Demand for money is given the simple form:

$$\left(\frac{M}{P}\right)^d = \frac{y^{\alpha_1} e}{i^{\alpha_2}}, \tag{4}$$

where P = price index,

y = permanent income,

i = the rate of interest,

e = stochastic disturbance term.

Since demand for money is assumed to be homogeneous of degree one in the price level, (4) may be rewritten as:

$$M^d = \frac{P y^{\alpha_1} e}{i^{\alpha_2}}. \tag{5}$$

Continuous equilibrium in the money market implies:

$$a.(R + D) = \frac{Py^{\alpha_1}e}{i^{\alpha_2}} \qquad (6)$$

A final set of operations takes the logarithm of (6) and differentiates with respect to time. For simplicity, new notation is introduced such that $g_X = dlnX/dt$, $X = a$, R, D, y, P, and i. In addition, $(R/H)g_R$ is identified as the dependent variable:

$$\left(\frac{R}{H}\right)g_R = \alpha_1 g_y - \alpha_2 g_i + g_P - g_a - \left(\frac{D}{H}\right)g_D + e'. \qquad (7)$$

The coefficient (α_1) is the income elasticity of demand for money, and therefore it is expected to be positive and in the neighbourhood of unity. For given interest rate, price level, money multiplier, and domestic credit (D), growth in income is associated with reserve inflows, according to the hypothesis. Specifically, a 1 per cent growth in income generates an α_1 per cent increase in demand for money, and consequently a reserve inflow just sufficient to result in an α_1 per cent increase in nominal and real money stock.[5]

Increases in the interest rate are associated with reserve outflows in this hypothesis, a result that runs counter to intuition unless the interest rate variable is interpreted in a particular way. Namely, 'the' interest rate is viewed as a proxy for world interest rates, and changes in this interest rate are taken to reflect similar movements in rates all around the world. If this assumption is accurate, then estimates of α_2 should be negative and within the range that is reasonable for interest elasticities of demand for money. However, if changes in Australian interest rates are dominated by changes relative to the rest of the world, then estimates of α_2 are likely to be positive.[6]

In the regressions reported in the following section, coefficients for g_P, g_a, and $(D/H)g_D$ are estimated, and it may be helpful to

[5] This result may appear to be at variance with the absorption theory in which rising income increases imports and generates reserve outflows. However, the absorption theory is concerned with the balance of trade rather than the balance of payments. Whatever the effects on the balance of trade, rapid growth does appear on a causal basis to be associated with reserve inflows (Japan, Germany), and slow growth with reserve outflows (U.S.A., U.K.).

[6] That is, increases in Australian rates relative to world rates should attract capital and generate reserve inflows, and the converse.

consider here the conditions under which they will take the hypothesised values of $+1\cdot0$ for g_P, and $-1\cdot0$ for both g_a and $(D/H)g_D$.
In the extreme case where the error terms in equation (5), and hence
in equation (7) are everywhere equal to zero, the estimated coefficients
for g_P, g_a, and $(D/H)g_D$ would be precisely $+1\cdot0$, $-1\cdot0$, and $-1\cdot0$.

A second extreme case is where demand for money is unrelated
to income and the interest rate. Here, the terms $\alpha_1 g_y$ and $\alpha_2 g_i$ drop
out of equation (7), and we are left with a regression that makes
the contribution of one source of money growth a function of all
the other sources. In this case the estimated coefficients for g_P, g_a,
and $(D/H)g_D$ can in principle take any value, positive or negative.[7]
If the demand for money given by equation (5) is reasonably stable,
then the estimated coefficients for g_P, g_a, and $(D/H)g_D$ should
approach their hypothesised values.

Price changes are assumed to have a positive effect on reserve
flows. An X per cent increase in prices will reduce real money
balances by X per cent and, other things equal, lead to a reserve
inflow just sufficient to restore real money balances to their previous
level. As with interest rates, changes in prices are viewed primarily
as changes in all world prices rather than as changes in Australian
prices relative to the rest of the world prices.

The final two variables reflect all domestic influences on the
money stock, and both of these variables are responsive to policy
actions by the monetary authorities (McGregor, Burrows, and
Zecher, 1972). An increase in either variable tends to increase the
stock of money and, other things equal, should lead to an outflow
of reserves sufficient to restore money to its previous level.

2 ESTIMATES OF THE MONEY DEMAND EQUATION AND THE RESERVE FLOW EQUATION

Table 1 displays regression results for two equations: the reserve
flow equation:

$$\left(\frac{R}{H}\right)g_R = \hat{\alpha}_1 g_y - \hat{\alpha}_2 g_i + \hat{\beta}_1 g_P - \hat{\beta}_2 g_a - \hat{\beta}_3 \frac{D}{H} g_D + \hat{e}' \qquad (7')$$

[7] For instance, if g_P and g_a were always zero, and total money grew at 5 per
cent per year, and half of this growth was due to $(R/H)g_R$ and half to $(D/H)g_D$,
then the estimated coefficients for g_P and g_a would be zero, and for $(D/H)g_D$,
plus one.

and the demand for money equation:

$$g_m = \hat{\alpha}'_1 g_y - \hat{\alpha}'_2 g_i + u, \tag{8}$$

where g_m = growth rate of real money balances,
$\quad u$ = stochastic disturbance.

The data are for the period 1950–71.

y = permanent income: a sixteen-quarter weighted average of gross national product,
R = official international reserve holdings of the Australian Reserve Bank,
i = two-year Australian government bond rate,
P = consumer price index,
$D \equiv H - R$: where H is high-powered money,
M = currency plus all trading bank deposits owned by the public (roughly equivalent to U.S. M_2).[8]

A quarterly regression of money demand yields the results shown in the following equation:

$$g_m = 0\cdot74g_y - 0\cdot075g_i \quad \bar{R}^2 = 0\cdot30; D\text{–}W = 1\cdot04$$
$$\quad\;\;(6\cdot19)\;\;(-3\cdot35)$$

where the numbers in parentheses are t statistics.[9] The estimates of both the income and interest rate elasticities of demand for money conform to expectations, but the $\bar{R}^2$ shows that much of the variation in real money balances is not systematically related to changes either in income or in the interest rate. Estimation of the reserve flow equation reveals that even on a quarterly basis the demand for money is sufficiently stable to yield the expected results:

$$\left(\frac{R}{H}\right)g_R = 1\cdot11g_y - 0\cdot035g_i + 0\cdot65g_P - 0\cdot89g_a -$$
$$\qquad\quad(6\cdot54)\;\;(-1\cdot08)\qquad(3\cdot70)\;\;(-12\cdot77)$$

$$-1\cdot06\left(\frac{D}{H}\right)g_D \quad \bar{R}^2 = 0\cdot89; D\text{–}W = 1\cdot69.$$
$$(-20\cdot92)$$

[8] Readers interested in obtaining these data should contact the author.
[9] Sample period is 1951–II through 1971–I.

The estimated coefficients of g_P, g_a, and $(D/H)g_D$ are all within two standard errors of their hypothesised values of $+1 \cdot 0$ or $-1 \cdot 0$.

Expanding the discrete observation period from quarterly to yearly observations yields a much better fit for the money demand equation, and also shows rises in both estimated elasticities:

$$g_m = 0 \cdot 99 g_y - 0 \cdot 28 g_i \quad \bar{R}^2 = 0 \cdot 77; \ D\text{--}W = 2 \cdot 45.$$
$$\quad (7 \cdot 05) \ (-5 \cdot 73)$$

Estimation of the reserve flow equation using yearly observations shows that all estimated coefficients continue to conform to values implied by the hypothesis:

$$\left(\frac{R}{H}\right) g_R = 0 \cdot 92 g_y - 0 \cdot 11 g_i + 1 \cdot 38 g_P - 1 \cdot 14 g_a -$$
$$\quad\quad\quad (3 \cdot 54) \ (-0 \cdot 75) \quad (2 \cdot 56) \quad (5 \cdot 08)$$

$$- 1 \cdot 23 \left(\frac{D}{H}\right) g_D \quad \bar{R}^2 = 0 \cdot 93; \ D\text{--}W = 2 \cdot 13.$$
$$(-7 \cdot 97)$$

In Table 12.1 the same pairs of regressions are reported for various quarterly and semi-annual subperiods. The most interesting of these are the results in lines 3 and 4, which are based on quarterly data for the period 1961–II through 1971–I. Line 3 shows reasonable estimates of both income and interest rate elasticities, but a negative $\bar{R}^2_*$. The money market would appear to be far from equilibrium on a quarter-by-quarter basis over this period, at least given this simple money demand formulation. Estimation of the reserve flow equation for the same period, as might be expected, is unsatisfactory in almost every way. The income elasticity estimate is twice its expected value, while the interest elasticity estimate is positive, though not significantly so. The price coefficient is not only more than two standard errors from its hypothesised value, but also has the wrong sign. Estimates of the coefficients of the two domestic money supply variables (g_a and $(D/H)g_D$) are close to their hypothesised values, but $\hat{\beta}_2$ is slightly more than two standard errors from $-1 \cdot 0$. The semi-annual regressions for the same period, reported in lines 7 and 8, showed marked improvement in both equations, and are more consistent with the over-all results.

Table 12.1 Semi-Annual and Quarterly Estimates of the Reserve Flow Equation and of the Demand for Money

Sample	Equation no.	Dependent Variable	Income Elasticity of Money Demand	Interest Elasticity of Money Demand	β_1	β_2	β_3	$\bar{R}^2$	D-W
Quarterly 1951–II to 1961–I	1	g_m	0·62 (2·82)	−0·075 (−2·40)				0·23	0·99
	2	$\frac{R}{\bar{H}} g_R$	0·51 (2·44)	−0·19 (−2·66)	1·01 (6·43)	−1·02 (−14·44)	−1·05 (−18·84)	0·94	1·68
Quarterly 1961–II to 1971–I	3	g_m	0·84 (7·94)	−0·064 (−1·97)				−0·19	1·16
	4	$\frac{R}{\bar{H}} g_R$	2·07 (6·17)	+0·059x (0·55)	−0·87x (−1·31)	−0·64x (−5·05)	−1·13 (−17·08)	0·89	1·70
Semi-Annually 1955–I to 1966–I	5	g_m	0·85 (6·69)	−0·19 (−5·41)				0·58	1·57
	6	$\frac{R}{\bar{H}} g_R$	0·78 (2·70)	−0·28 (−3·46)	0·71 (1·37)	−1·17 (−8·95)	−0·77x (−11·34)	0·94	2·93
Semi-Annually 1962–III to 1971–I	7	g_m	0·90 (7·49)	−0·08 (−1·70)				0·18	1·76
	8	$\frac{R}{\bar{H}} g_R$	0·55 (1·78)	−0·14 (−1·62)	1·17 (1·72)	−1·17 (−7·73)	−0·82x (−14·73)	0·95	2·76

These results taken together suggest that the Australian reserve flow experience over the period 1950–71 has been broadly in conformity with the monetary approach to the balance of payments. The novel implications of the hypothesis that both economic growth and rises in the price level lead to *surpluses* are both supported by the evidence. The implication that rises in domestic interest rates lead to deficits, while not finding strong support, is certainly not inconsistent with the results of these regressions. Finally, the two variables reflecting domestic influences on the money stock (g_a and $(D/H)g_D$) appear to have a dependable, negative effect on reserve flows, and also appear to be the dominant influence on short-run fluctuations in reserve flows.

A few comments by way of summary and clarification are in order concerning the independence of the independent variables. In deriving a single equation model of reserve flows, a number of judgments had to be made concerning the dominant factors influencing each of the variables. The resulting hypothesis assumes that (1) Australian reserve flows are dominantly influenced by the state of equilibrium in the market for Australian money, and (2) that the five other variables are dominantly influenced by factors outside the market for Australian money. Growth in real, permanent income is assumed to result primarily from growth in technology and factors of production. Both interest rates and prices are assumed to be dominantly influenced by world market conditions. In addition, Australia being a small part of the world market, conditions in domestic markets should have little influence on these prices and interest rates.

The two remaining variables, the money multiplier and the domestically determined portion of high-powered money, are influenced by a variety of factors, including monetary policy actions. To the extent that policy actions are aimed at offsetting or 'sterilising' reserve flows, these two variables will be functionally dependent on reserve flows, thus partly reversing the direction of causation implied by the hypothesis. This objection remains an open question, although I find it unconvincing, particularly during the 1950s when policy actions were carried out by the Commonwealth Bank. After the formation of the Reserve Bank, policy actions were more aggressive, and reserve flows may have become a more important factor in policy decisions.

3 CONCLUSIONS

Australian international reserve flows over the past two decades are consistent with the pattern implied by the monetary approach to the balance of payments. When demand for money grows faster than the supply of money would have grown due to domestic sources alone, international reserves tend to accumulate and to bring actual growth in the money stock closer to desired growth, and the converse. As implied by the hypothesis, growth in output and the price level are associated with balance-of-payments surpluses, while growth in the domestically determined portion of the money stock tends to be associated with deficits and reserve outflows. Effects of the interest rate on reserve flows tend to be weak, but generally conform to the negative relation implied by the hypothesis.

If the present hypothesis captures a significant portion of the systematic factors involved in determining reserve flows in Australia, then the interpretation of reserve flows, and the policy actions required to control reserve flows, are clear. For example, consider the stormy, six-quarter period ending in the August 1971 international monetary crisis. Australian output and Australian (and world) prices rose at historically high rates over this period, while domestic monetary policies were restrictive, contributing little to growth in the domestic money stock. This combination of factors should have led to a rapid rate of reserve accumulation. Such an accumulation did occur, and at a rate sufficient to nearly double official reserve assets in Australia over the six-quarter period.

Two policy implications of the hypothesis concerning this episode are worth mentioning. Firstly, the reserve inflow could have been stemmed or reversed by a more expansionary domestic monetary policy. Secondly, an exchange rate adjustment such as the one in 1971 will at best provide temporary relief from undesirable reserve flows. Once Australian prices adjust to the new international price constellation, the Australian balance of payments will again tend to reflect the difference between growth in demand for money and growth in domestically determined supply of money.

REFERENCES

Dornbusch, Rudiger, 'Notes on Growth and the Balance of Payments', *Canadian Journal of Economics* (August 1971).

Frenkel, J., 'A Theory of Money, Trade and the Balance of Payments in a Model of Trade and Accumulation', *Journal of International Economics*, 1 (May 1971).

Hume, David, 'Of the Balance of Trade (1752), in his *Essays, Moral, Political and Literary*, vol. 1 (London, Longmans Green 1898).

Johnson, Harry G., *Macroeconomics and Monetary Theory* (Chicago, Aldine 1972).

Kindleberger, C. P., 'Measuring Equilibrium in the Balance of Payments', *Journal of Political Economy*, 77, no. 6 (November/December 1969), 873–91.

Komiya, Ryutaro, 'Economic Growth and the Balance of Payments', *Journal of Political Economy*, 77, no. 1 (January/February 1969), 35–48.

Krueger, Anne O., 'Balance of Payments Theory', *Journal of Economic Literature* (March 1969), 1–26.

Laffer, Arthur B., 'The Anti-Traditional General Equilibrium Theory of the Rate of Growth and the Balance-of-Payments under Fixed Exchange Rates', unpublished manuscript, University of Chicago (December 1968).

Laidler, David E. W., *The Demand for Money: Theories and Evidence* (Scranton, Pa., International Textbook Company, 1969).

McGregor, L., Burrows, C., and Zecher, R., 'Determinants of the Australian Money Supply since 1950'. Presented to the Australian and New Zealand Association for the Advancement of Science, Forty-fourth Congress, Sydney (August 1972).

Meade, J. E., *The Balance of Payments* (London, Oxford University Press, 1951).

Mundell, Robert A., *International Economics* (New York, Macmillan, 1968).

Mundell, Robert A., *Monetary Theory* (Pacific Palisades, Goodyear, 1971).

13

Aspects of the Monetary Approach to Balance-of-Payments Theory

An Empirical Study of Sweden[1]

A. HANS GENBERG

INTRODUCTION

In this chapter we shall attempt to provide an empirical analysis of some aspects of the monetary approach to balance-of-payments theory. We shall concentrate on a few but in our view crucial hypotheses regarding the nature of a small economy and its relationship with the world at large.

Firstly we take up the question of goods and asset market integration in the world. This is one of the building blocks of the monetary approach which stresses the importance of world rather than individual country equilibrium in the determination of prices and interest rates. Secondly we discuss the link between reserve flows and the domestic money stock and show that this is the avenue through which monetary equilibrium is reached in an open economy. After identifying and estimating empirical demand functions for money in Sweden, some conclusions with respect to the effect of monetary policy are discussed. The final section combines the obtained evidence in a monetary interpretation of reserve flows. Some questions regarding the possibility of lagged balance-of-payments adjustment and central bank sterilisation are also taken up.

---

[1] This chapter is based on my Ph.D. dissertation with the same title at the University of Chicago. I would like to express my gratitude to my advisers, Professors H. G. Johnson, A. B. Laffer, and J. R. Zecher, for their guidance and encouragement during the preparation of the dissertation.

MARKET INTEGRATION IN THE WORLD ECONOMY

Market integration and interdependence among national economies can be studied from several angles. In theoretical work it is common to link structural models of individual economies and to simulate the effects of policies allowing for interaction between countries.[2] In practice, when the true structures of the models are not known, this approach might lead to effectively specifying a certain type of interdependence rather than letting the data decide the issue. Hence we shall concentrate on a more pragmatic approach by directly comparing price series in goods and asset markets of several countries to determine how closely they move together. For each market we shall first consider intercountry comparisons and then look somewhat more closely at the Swedish data.

Goods Market
Comparison of consumer price indices between countries implicitly involves comparing prices of both internationally traded and non-traded goods. Thus, while we expect traded goods prices to be kept in line through arbitrage, there will be some room for variance in domestic goods prices. The degree of correspondence between countries will depend on the elasticity of substitution in consumption and/or production relative to the traded goods both at home and abroad.

Apart from the existence of non-traded goods, price indices might change at different rates due to non-conformity in weighing patterns, collection practices, timing, coverage, treatment of indirect taxes, etc. If, for instance, the price of heating oil carries a large weight in a Swedish consumer price index relative to an Italian one, an equal change in the price of oil in both countries will make for unequal change in the price indices. While this is a feature we wish a price index to have, it can not be used as evidence against the market integration hypothesis.

Assuming that the artificial differences introduced in constructing the indices can be approximated by a random disturbance term, we can test the market integration hypothesis as follows.

Let $(\dot{P}/P)_{i,t}$ be the inflation rate in country i at time t. Then we can write

[2] This route is also followed by the project LINK.

$$(\dot{P}/P)_{i,t} = \overline{(\dot{P}/P)_t} + a_{i,t} + u_{i,t} \tag{1}$$

where $\overline{(\dot{P}/P)_t}$ is the world rate of inflation and $a_{i,t}$ represents the systematic difference between country i's and the world's rate of inflation at time t due to the specific economic environment in country i. $u_{i,t}$ is a disturbance term. Under the hypothesis that all countries have the same rate of inflation, we see that

$$a_{i,t} = 0 \text{ for all } i \text{ and } t.$$

A simple analysis of variance procedure was used to examine this hypothesis for the period 1959–II to 1970–II. Quarterly rates of change in the consumer price index (as reported by the OECD)[3]

Table 13.1 F-*Statistics to Test Equality of Inflation Rates Between Various Countries*

Period	Average rate of price change (% per year)	F-ratio	Critical F-values
Period 1[a]	0–2%	$F_{15,47} = 0\cdot55$	25% point: $F_{15,60} = 1\cdot38$
Period 2[b]	2–4%	$F_{15,254} = 2\cdot63$	2·5% point: $F_{15,\infty} = 2\cdot40$
Period 3[c]	4–6%	$F_{15,183} = 1\cdot12$	25% point: $F_{15,\infty} = 1\cdot40$

[a]The 1962–III observation for the Netherlands was deleted from the sample due to the unusual behaviour of food prices. (Whereas the CPI including food fell from 101 to 97 between the 2nd and 3rd quarters, the index excluding food stayed constant at 97.)

[b]The 1962–I observation for Sweden and 1962–IV observation for Denmark were excluded since large changes in indirect taxes were made during these quarters.

[c]Three observations for Austria and the Netherlands, two for Ireland and one for Sweden were deleted so that breaks in the series (Austria and Ireland), indirect tax changes (the Netherlands and Sweden), and extraordinary food price changes (Austria, Ireland, and the Netherlands) would not distort the results.

[3] OECD (1970)

were computed for the following countries: Austria, Belgium, Denmark, Finland, France, Germany, Ireland, Italy, Japan, the Netherlands, Norway, Portugal, Sweden, Switzerland, United Kingdom, and U.S.A. Since some countries did alter their exchange rate during the sample period, we deleted the observations which were affected under the assumption that adjustment to the exchange rate change was complete within the quarter.[4] The sample period was also split into three groups according to the average rate of inflation of the whole set of countries. The relevant F-ratios for the analysis of variance procedure are presented in Table 13.1.

The analysis of variance technique calls for computing the ratio of the sum of squared differences of country means from the over-all mean to the sum of squared differences of within country observations from the country means.[5] Thus a high value of the F-ratio would indicate significant differences between the country mean rates of inflation. Under the null-hypothesis the ratio will have the F-distribution, given certain assumptions about the error term (normality and independence). Thus we can attach significance levels to the rejection or acceptance of the null-hypothesis. The critical F-values are given in the last column of Table 13.1.

By comparing the last two columns of Table 13.1 for the first and third periods we can reject the hypothesis that inflation rates differ significantly between countries. But for the second period we must conclude that a difference does exist. This appears to be due mainly to two factors. Firstly the average rate of inflation in Japan seems to be significantly larger than in the other countries during this period. Secondly, it might be that the many devaluations in 1967 had dissimilar price index movements associated with them lasting longer than a quarter as assumed above. The F-ratios of period 2 which

[4] Exchange rate changes were in other words treated as breaks in the price index series affecting only the quarter of the exchange-rate change.

[5] In terms of the notation in (1) the F-ratio is computed as:

$$F_{N-1,\,T-N} = \frac{\sum\limits_{i=1}^{N} T_i [(\dot{P}/P)_i - \overline{(\dot{P}/P)}]^2/(N-1)}{\sum\limits_{i=1}^{N} \sum\limits_{t=1}^{T_i} [(\dot{P}/P)_{i,t} - \overline{(\dot{P}/P)}_i]^2/(T-N)}$$

where $\overline{(\dot{P}/P)}_i$ is the mean rate of inflation in country i, N is the number of countries, T_i is the number of observations on country i, and $T = \sum\limits_{i=1}^{N} T_i$.

includes observations immediately before and after those devaluations would accordingly be affected. These speculations are supported
by the fact that when calculations were made for only the countries[6]
which maintained fixed exchange rates *vis-à-vis* the U.S.A. during
the whole sample period, the F-ratios[7] were $1 \cdot 98$ with Japan included
and $1 \cdot 07$ with Japan excluded.

Since the assumptions needed to apply the F-test might not be
met in our sample, a different kind of comparison was also carried
out. Rates of change in the quarterly consumer price index for
fifteen U.S. cities[8] were computed and the same ratios (see Table
13.2) were formed as in the country analysis.

It is evident from Tables 13.1 and 13.2 that the differences between
OECD countries are no greater on the average than those between
cities within the United States. Thus, if we believe that the whole of
the U.S. can be treated as a single market in a macroeconomic
context, then the area composed of the above countries can be
treated likewise.

Table 13.2 F-*Statistic to Test Equality of Inflation*
Rates Between U.S. Cities

Period	F-*ratio*
Period 1	$F_{14,375} = 0 \cdot 79$
Period 2	$F_{14,222} = 0 \cdot 75$
Period 3	$F_{14,195} = 1 \cdot 59$

For a country like Sweden the unified market hypothesis implies
that the rate of inflation will be exogeneously determined under a
fixed exchange rate system, because Sweden is too small to have a
noticeable impact on world prices. To check whether this implication
is supported by the data, we postulate that the Swedish rate of

---

[6] Austria, Belgium, Italy, Japan, Norway, Portugal, Sweden, Switzerland, and
U.S.A.

[7] The degrees of freedom were 8,153 and 7,136 respectively.

[8] Atlanta, Baltimore, Boston, Chicago, Cincinnati, Cleveland, Detroit, Los
Angeles, New York, Philadelphia, Pittsburgh, San Francisco, Seattle, St Louis,
and Washington, D.C.

inflation is equal to a constant times the world rate of inflation[9] plus a stochastic error term as in

$$(\dot{P}/P)_{\text{Sweden},t} = c\,(\dot{P}/P)_{\text{World},t} + u_t. \tag{2}$$

We expect to find a value of c close to unity if our hypothesis is true. A regression using quarterly rates of change in the Swedish consumer price index as the dependent variable did give an estimate significantly different from unity at the 5 per cent level (see Table 13.3, row 1). This is likely due to bias towards zero in the estimate as a consequence of measurement errors in the independent variable. In this case we can compute bounds for the estimate of c by reversing the role of the dependent and independent variables (see Table 13.3, row 2). This procedure yielded point estimates of the bounds of $0 \cdot 78$ and $0 \cdot 96$ respectively. Although these are still somewhat low, a two-standard-error confidence region of the bounds will include unity.

Table 13.3 *Relationship Between the Rates of Inflation in Sweden and the Rest of the World*

Dependent variable	Independent variable	Coefficient (standard error)	c	R^2
Sweden	World	$0 \cdot 78$ $(0 \cdot 07)$	$0 \cdot 78$	$0 \cdot 41$
World	Sweden	$1 \cdot 04$ $(0 \cdot 10)$	$0 \cdot 96$	$0 \cdot 10$

Together with the previous evidence these results support the view that Sweden is a small part of an integrated world goods market.

Asset Markets
Asset markets in different countries have often been looked upon as separate entities with only limited interdependence due to various

[9] The definition of the world rate of inflation used here was simply the arithmetic average of the other fifteen countries mentioned above plus Canada. The concept and measurement of the world rate of inflation are investigated in Genberg (1974).

controls and restrictions on international movements of capital. It has been argued that considerable profits could be made from equity portfolio diversification[10] if these restrictions were lifted, and that capital flows between countries respond to *observed* interest rate differentials (or changes in these).[11]

Another view of the international asset markets is that, controls notwithstanding, they approximate a highly integrated market where diversification opportunities are already exploited, and where observed yield differentials are due to exchange-rate-risk, political-risk, and other types of risk, and correspond to equilibrium values.

In the following we shall present evidence consistent with integrated market hypothesis which can be weighed against the evidence for the alternative view.

Equity Market

In two articles[12] Agmon investigated the equity markets in Germany, Japan, U.K., and U.S.A. and concluded after tests carried out on both market indices and individual share prices that his data were consistent with the single-market hypothesis. Furthermore, from the point of view of the U.S. investor, the removal of obstacles to capital flows would not necessarily imply expanded profit opportunities.[13]

Agmon also found that the New York Stock Exchange seemed to determine the prices on the other markets in the sense that the correlation between stock price changes in Frankfurt, London, and Tokyo was small after removal of the common New York effect. Treating prices on the New York Stock Exchange as world market prices we shall here carry out a test of the single-market hypothesis applied to Swedish stock prices. Table 13.4 contains results from regressions of the form

$$R_{i,t} = a_i + b_i R_{\text{U.S.},t} + u_{i,t} \quad i = \text{Sweden, Germany,}$$

and

$$R_{\text{Sweden},t} = a + b R_{\text{U.S.},t} + c R_{\text{Germany},t} + v_t,$$

[10] See, for instance, Grubel (1968).

[11] See Branson (1968), and Branson and Hill (1971).

[12] Agmon (1972), and Agmon (1973).

[13] ibid. Specific country factors were found, but they were not such that international diversification could improve on efficient portfolios based entirely on U.S. stocks.

Table 13.4 *Stock Price Regressions for Sweden and Germany*

Dependent variable	Coefficients[a]			R^2	$D-W$[b]
	a	b	c		
R_{Sweden}	0·0031 (0·0028)	0·37 (0·09)		0·12	1·79
$R_{Germany}$	0·0040 (0·0043)	0·69 (0·13)		0·17	1·65
R_{Sweden}	0·0027 (0·0028)	0·31 (0·09)	0·091 (0·057)	0·14	1·84

[a]Standard errors are given in parentheses.
[b]Durbin–Watson statistic.

where R_t is the monthly rate of change in the relevant stock price index, i.e.

$$R_t = \log(P_t/P_{t-1}),$$
$$P_t = \text{index of stock prices at time } t.[14]$$

Comparing our results with those obtained by Agmon we note that the coefficients as well as the R^2 are of the same order of magnitude. We see also that the German index does not contribute much to the variations in Swedish stock prices after allowing for the U.S. effect, supporting the view of the New York Stock Exchange as the centre of a world equity market.

We can also check whether leads or lags in the U.S. index play a significant role in the explanation of the Swedish index. In a unified and well functioning market all but the current value of the independent variable should have a negligible effect. Table 13.5 presents estimates from the regression

$$R_{Sweden,t} = a + b_{t+i} R_{U.S.,t+i} + \ldots + b_t R_{U.S.,t} + \ldots +$$
$$+ b_{t-i} R_{U.S.,t-i} \qquad i = 1,6.$$

The coefficient estimates and their standard errors clearly support the unified market hypothesis.

[14] Adjusted for dividend payments and capital changes, and converted into \$U.S. by the appropriate spot exchange rate.

Table 13.5 *Lead-Lag Analysis of Swedish Stock Price Changes*

Coefficient	Estimate	Standard error	Estimate	Standard error
a	0·0004	0·003		
b				
$t + 6$	0·129	0·086		
$t + 5$	−0·062	0·089		
$t + 4$	0·185	0·094		
$t + 3$	−0·131	0·093		
$t + 2$	−0·030	0·093		
$t + 1$	0·125	0·094	0·114	0·090
t	0·227	0·093	0·229	0·091
$t - 1$	0·080	0·094	0·088	0·090
$t - 2$	0·063	0·093		
$t - 3$	0·062	0·093		
$t - 4$	0·054	0·093		
$t - 5$	0·075	0·092		
$t - 6$	0·174	0·092		
	$R^2 = 0·19$		$R^2 = 0·09$	
	$D-W = 1·80$		$D-W = 1·79$	

Bond Market

The question of financial market integration as measured by the similarity of interest-rate movements in various countries has recently been studied by several economists. In the course of examining the policy implications of the Euro-dollar market, Scott[15] presented some evidence indicating that short-term interest-rate differentials have tended to decrease since the moves towards currency convertibility in 1958. This is consistent with the view that the development of the Euro-dollar market has increased integration by acting as a link between individual nation's financial markets. Cooper[16] and Argy and Hodjera[17] similarly showed that the variance of national market interest rates at each point in time tended to decrease from 1958 until the middle of the sixties, after which it levelled off or increased slightly. This can be interpreted as a sign of

[15] Scott (1970).
[16] Cooper (1971).
[17] Argy and Hodjera (1973).

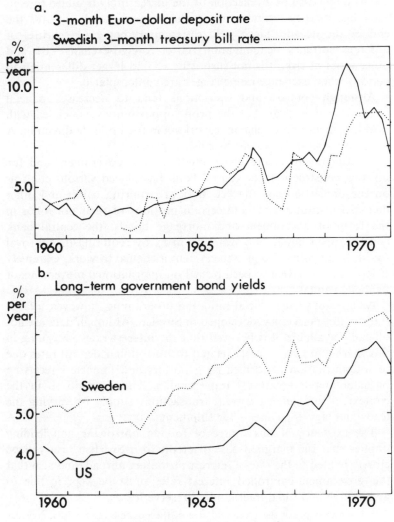

Figure 13.1.   Interest-rate comparisons.

initially increased interdependence subsequent to convertibility halted by the attempts on the part of governments to reverse the trend by imposing restrictions and controls on international capital movements. The increased interest rate divergence after the middle sixties might also be a reflection of the increasingly troubled foreign exchange markets, culminating in the currency crises towards the end of the decade. Since yield differentials between securities of different currency denomination reflect foreign-exchange-risk and other types of risk, it is not surprising to find larger differentials in periods when exchange-rate changes are contemplated.

Although controls and restrictions tend to decrease financial integration it is clear that the profit opportunities associated with avoiding them imply behaviour working in the opposite direction. A good example is the recent Swedish experience.

In attempts to assure cheap credit to the government and for housing construction, the central bank has placed various controls on the domestic bond market. Besides requiring banks and other financial institutions to hold certain portions of their portfolios in the form of government and mortgage bonds, the central bank controls open public borrowing by firms by requiring its approval for all bond issues. To give the system a chance to work, extremely strict controls have also been placed on international movements of financial capital.

As a result of the official rationing programme, however, a large trade credit market has developed in Sweden. Although data are not officially available, it is believed that the interest rates prevailing in this market are very closely related to Euro-dollar deposit rates due to intermediation performed by exporters and importers receiving or extending international trade credits. They can do so in the context of unregulated current transactions simply by varying the leads and lags in payments for shipments.

The existence of this source of foreign borrowing and lending implies that the marginal cost of credit to a Swedish firm will be closely related to the rate of interest prevailing abroad, and also that the government-controlled interest rates must be kept in line to avoid large and rapid international reserve losses.[18]

[18] As an example of the speed and size of the possible reserve loss, consider the following example from Grassman (1971), p. 13 (see also his footnote on the same page): suppose that export and import payments each are of the magnitude 36,000 million Swedish Kronor per year (these are approximately the correct figures for 1970), and suppose they are evenly distributed over each week. Then a two-week lead payment for exports and the same lag for imports implies a reserve loss of 3,000 million kr. This should be compared with the average (for 1970) net international reserve holding of the central bank of approximately 3,300 million kr.

The relatively high degree of correspondence in interest rate movements is apparent in Figures 13.1(a) and (b). Although short-term differences do occur due to the rationed nature of the Swedish market, long-term trends are quite similar. Thus it appears that, as in the goods and equity markets, there are reasons to consider the Swedish security market integrated with the Euro-currency market despite the controls on capital movements.

MONEY SUPPLY, MONEY DEMAND, AND MONETARY POLICY IN SWEDEN

Money Supply

Recent studies of the money supply process in a closed economy have used a framework described concisely by:

$$M^s = m.H, \tag{3}$$

i.e. the money stock is equal to a money multiplier times a monetary base. The multiplier is postulated to summarise the behaviour of the public and the commercial banks with respect to the composition of their assets. This is influenced by wealth and income levels and market rates of return on the one hand, and policy variables of the central bank on the other. The latter include minimum reserve ratios, discount rate policies, and restrictions on interest-rate payments on deposits as well as non-quantifiable policies taking the form of moral suasion, etc.

The monetary base in these studies is assumed to be under the control of the central bank through open market operations. Once we extend the analysis to an open economy on a fixed exchange rate this assumption becomes inappropriate. The rules of a fixed exchange rate system require the central bank to buy or sell domestic base money for foreign exchange at a fixed price. The supply of the domestic monetary base is therefore completely elastic and will be determined by the public sector's demand.

By making use of the central bank's balance sheet identity, the monetary base can be written as the sum of a domestic source component D and a foreign source component R. The foreign source component is made up of the net foreign assets of the central bank, which can thus control directly only the domestic source component through open market operations. In the final section of this chapter we shall present evidence that the central bank in Sweden has only been able to affect the division of the base between R and D except in the immediate short run.

Money Demand

The demand function for money we shall estimate here has a long-run component depending on wealth (permanent income) as a budget constraint for the asset demand and current income as implied by the transactions motive as well as relative price variables such as interest rates and returns on alternative assets. Following Chow[19] we shall also allow for desired departures from the long-run demand in an explicit short-run stock adjustment formulation (eqn 4).

$$\log (M/P)_t^D = \log (M/P)_t^* + \\ + \alpha [\log (M/P)_{t-1} - \log (M/P)_{t-1}^*] + u_t. \tag{4}$$

A value of α of less than unity implies that departures from the optimal long-run position will be made up over time.

The long-run demand will be assumed to take the form:

$$\log (M/P)_t^* = k_0 + k_1 \cdot \log (y_t) + k_2 \cdot \log (i_t) \tag{5}$$

where i represents yields on other assets than money, and y stands for permanent or current income depending on which demand motive is considered.

Results of estimation of the parameters in (4) and (5) using an iterative technique for α are presented in Table 13.6. On the whole the short-run money demand model is in agreement with the data,[20] although the residual serial correlation in the M_2 case might be a sign of left-out variables.

Compared to estimates for other countries, the coefficients of both the permanent and current income variables are somewhat low. This is probably due to the nature of the industrial production index used as a proxy for income in this study (and as a basis for constructing a

[19] Chow (1966).

[20] The coefficients in the long-run function are also in accordance with estimates of a long-run demand function carried out on yearly data. See Genberg (1973), ch. 4.

Table 13.6 Quarterly Short-run Demand for Money Regressions; 1950–II to 1968–IV

Dependent variable	Constant[a]	Price level	Permanent income	Transitory income	Current income	Swedish Gov. bond yield	Yield on common stock	Adjustment coefficient	R^2	D–W[b]	S.E.R.[c]
Nominal M_1	6·80 (1·09)	0·95 (0·17)	0·65 (0·17)	0·15 (0·20)		0·036 (0·025)	−0·0006 (0·0011)	0·924	0·9960	1·64	0·0204
Real M_1	6·90 (1·01)		0·62 (0·12)	0·14 (0·19)		0·036 (0·025)	−0·0006 (0·0011)	0·924	0·9736	1·62	0·0202
Nominal M_1	8·98 (0·16)	1·08 (0·17)			0·44 (0·14)	0·034 (0·026)	−0·0007 (0·0011)	0·933	0·9957	1·61	0·0208
Real M_1	9·25 (0·29)				0·22 (0·18)	0·034 (0·025)	−0·0005 (0·0011)	0·990	0·9725	1·70	0·0205
Nominal M_2	10·15 (1·10)	0·56 (0·13)	0·44 (0·20)	0·33 (0·15)		0·0006 (0·0190)	−0·0007 (0·0008)	0·984	0·9984	0·89	0·0157
Real M_2	11·05 (1·28)		0·20 (0·24)	0·29 (0·16)		0·001 (0·020)	−0·0006 (0·0009)	0·988	0·9928	0·73	0·0165
Nominal M_2	10·82 (0·19)	0·54 (0·13)			0·32 (0·13)	0·0004 (0·0187)	−0·0007 (0·0008)	0·986	0·9985	0·92	0·0153
Real M_2	10·62 (0·20)				0·27 (0·14)	0·001 (0·020)	−0·0006 (0·0008)	0·988	0·9928	0·72	0·0164

[a] Numbers in parentheses are standard errors.   [b] Durbin–Watson statistic.   [c] Standard Error of the Regression.

permanent income series). The greater short-run variance and the higher growth trend of the production index relative to GNP implies such estimates.

The poor performance of the government bond yield is a direct reflection of the controls on bond issues and holdings by the central bank. As suggested on p. 308 above these restrictions make the bond rate an inadequate measure of the opportunity cost of holding money. Due to lack of data, we were unable to test the hypothesis that trade credits are a closer substitute to money. With respect to the yield on common stock, it might be that the current yield is a poor indicator of the anticipated yield as seems to be true for the U.S.[21]

Monetary Policy

Monetary policies in a closed economy are usually assumed to operate either through interest rates or directly on prices and output. In a small economy on a fixed exchange rate, however, we have seen that both the structure of interest rates and the price level will be dominated by foreign influences. In Sweden even the rate of production is dependent on the international business cycle as we can see from Figure 13.2, although government policies undoubtedly can affect both the timing and amplitude of the Swedish fluctuations within narrow limits.

To test whether monetary policy has influenced income to a significant extent, or whether the stock of money is demand determined, a method developed by Sims[22] was applied to Swedish money and income data. The procedure is designed to determine temporal ordering of time series, so the well-known caveats regarding the relationship between temporal precedence and causality must be kept in mind.

Table 13.7 shows the results of regressions relating log-changes in money (M_1) and nominal income with various leads and lags. Assuming that the errors are normally distributed, the F-statistics in the last column indicate that the future values of money in the income regression are marginally non-zero (row 7) and that the future values of income in the money regression are not significantly

---

[21] See Laffer and Zecher (1973), pp. 10 and 11.
[22] Sims (1972).

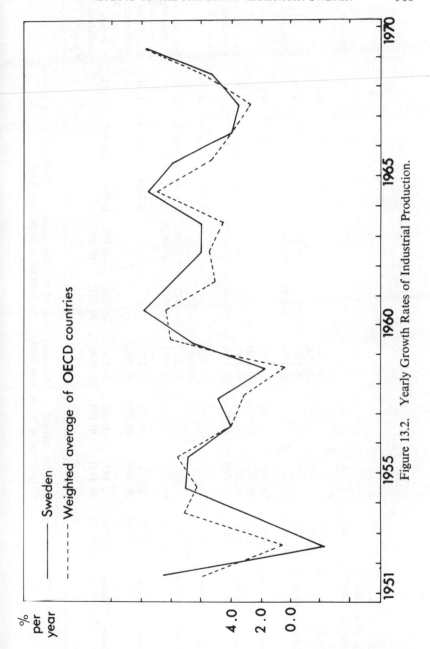

Figure 13.2. Yearly Growth Rates of Industrial Production.

Table 13.7 Money–Income Regressions[a]

Dependent variable	Independent variable	Constant	$t+2$	$t+1$	t	$t-1$	$t-2$	R^2	S.E.R.[b]	D–W[c]	F-statistic
Money	Income	0·0068 (0·0037)			0·471 (0·139)			0·1422	0·0211	2·00	
Money	Income	0·0065 (0·0045)			0·512 (0·132)	−0·367 (0·134)	0·348 (0·129)	0·2770	0·0196	1·89	Two past coefficients; $F_{2,55} = 5·13$[d]
Money	Income	0·0052 (0·0050)	0·326 (0·172)	−0·253 (0·139)	0·500 (0·138)			0·2083	0·0205	1·98	
Money	Income	0·0050 (0·0060)	0·202 (0·170)	−0·130 (0·142)	0·520 (0·136)	−0·322 (0·138)	0·298 (0·138)	0·2977	0·0196	1·90	Two future coefficients; $F_{2,53} = 0·78$
Income	Money	0·0150 (0·0025)			0·302 (0·089)			0·1422	0·0169	1·36	
Income	Money	0·0159 (0·0033)			0·297 (0·091)	−0·042 (0·091)	−0·010 (0·092)	0·1450	0·0171	1·37	Two past coefficients; $F_{2,55} = 0·39$
Income	Money	0·0132 (0·0033)	0·215 (0·100)	−0·076 (0·090)	0·281 (0·088)			0·2084	0·0164	1·21	Two future coefficients; $F_{2,55} = 2·30$[e]
Income	Money	0·0156 (0·0039)	0·297 (0·114)	−0·095 (0·091)	0·271 (0·089)	−0·059 (0·087)	−0·153 (0·102)	0·2374	0·0164	1·24	Two past coefficients; $F_{2,53} = 1·01$

[a] Variables expressed as log-changes. [b] Standard Error of the Regression. [c] Durbin–Watson statistic. [d] Significant at 95 per cent level. [e] Significant at 90 per cent level.

different from zero as a group (row 4). Thus, applying Sims' criterion we conclude that income changes have preceded changes in money in Sweden during the sample period. These findings are consistent with the view that the demand for money has determined the stock in existence, and they do not support the hypothesis that monetary policy has had a systematic effect on the flow of income at least as far as this effect is anything but immediate.[23]

The coefficients of the current and lagged values of the income variable in Table 13.7 are interesting in that the current value alone contributes virtually as much as the sum of all periods taken together. This suggests that the money–income relationship has been con-current on the average throughout the fifties and sixties. It is also a reflection of the fact that the current income variable performed as well as the permanent income series in the demand equations of the previous section.

In an economy with both traded and non-traded goods there might be an impact of monetary policy on the relative price of these classes of goods. In a full-employment theoretical model, an expansionary monetary policy would cause an excess demand for both types of commodities. The demand for traded goods would be met by increased imports or decreased exports but in the non-traded sector the excess demand would have to be eliminated by a price increase. Thus if this effect was powerful enough we should be able to observe a positive relationship between monetary expansion and the relative price of non-traded goods. Figures 13.3(a) and (b) show the behaviour of these variables during the 1960s.[24, 25] It is not possible to discern a relation between them,[26] so this influence of monetary policy does not appear to have been important in Sweden.

---

[23] These results could also be consistent with a potent monetary policy if it was always perfectly anticipated.

[24] The relative price is actually the ratio of a consumer price index to a traded-goods index. This will behave as the theoretically desirable ratio under general conditions. The monetary variable is the relative change in the D/R ratio which will increase as a result of expansionary monetary policy and vice versa.

[25] Figure 13.3(b) shows the price ratio in detrended form in an attempt to allow for different rates of technical progress in the two sectors. Slower technical change in the non-traded goods sector would imply an increasing relative price of non-traded goods over time.

[26] This conclusion was also supported by the regression analysis allowing for lags in the adjustment.

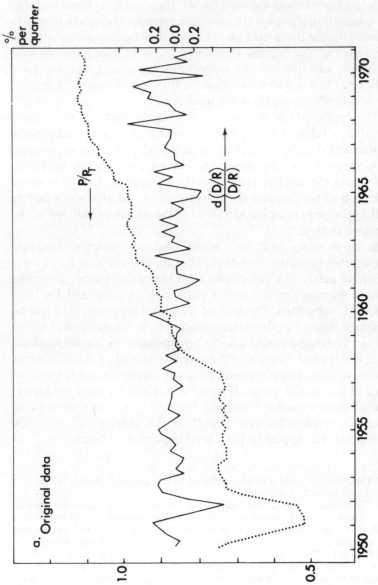

Figure 13.3(a). Monetary policy and the relative price of non-traded goods.

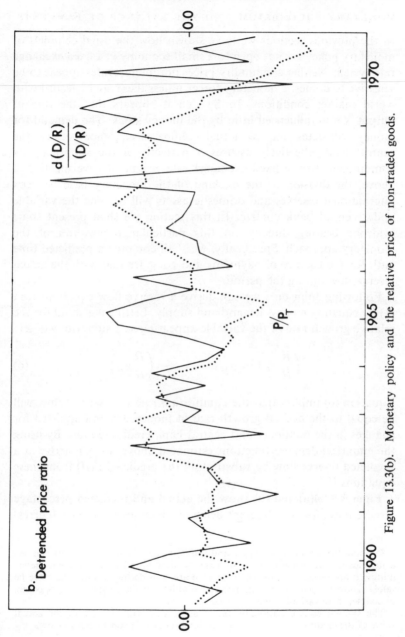

Figure 13.3(b).   Monetary policy and the relative price of non-traded goods.

MONETARY EQUILIBRIUM AND THE BALANCE OF PAYMENTS

In the previous sections we have shown how the usual channels of monetary policy are not open to a small economy in a fixed exchange rate system. Neither commodity prices nor interest rates appear to be sensitive to domestic monetary forces unless these are in accord with world market conditions. In Sweden it appears that the rate of output is also influenced little by the money stock. The demand for money will determine the actual volume in existence because the central bank effectively assures a perfectly elastic supply by its commitment to the fixed exchange rate regime. As we mentioned above, the division of the backing of the monetary base between international reserves and domestic assets will become the variable under central bank control. In this section we shall present some evidence bearing directly on this particular implication of the monetary approach. Specifically, we shall compute a predicted time path for the balance of payments and compare that with the actual reserve flow during the period.

Following Johnson[27] we can derive a reserve flow equation from (1) by equating money demand and supply. Letting a g stand for the relative growth rate of the variable appearing as a subscript we get:

$$\left(\frac{R}{H}g_R\right) = g_M D - g_m - \left(\frac{D}{H}g_D\right) \tag{6}$$

Equation (6) implies that the equilibrium rate of reserve inflow will be equal to the desired growth rate of money demand adjusted for changes in the multiplier and central bank credit creation. By using the empirical demand functions estimated above, we can arrive at a predicted reserve flow by substituting the predicted $\hat{g}_M D$ from these equations.[28]

Figures 13.4(a) and (b) show the actual and predicted percentage reserve flows for two different demand functions for money (corres-

---

[27] See ch. 6.

[28] Using the actual values of g_m and (D/H_D^g) might be subject to criticism. As a justification we argue that in the case of the multiplier, the variables determining it are exogeneous to the system we are considering and can therefore be safely ignored when we test the predictive ability of the model. In forecasting, of course, these variables must be specified in advance.

The simultaneous equation problems associated with the use of the actual value of the credit creation variable will be discussed at some length below.

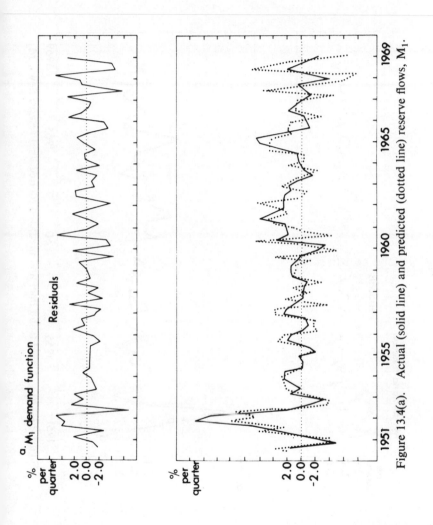

Figure 13.4(a). Actual (solid line) and predicted (dotted line) reserve flows, M_1.

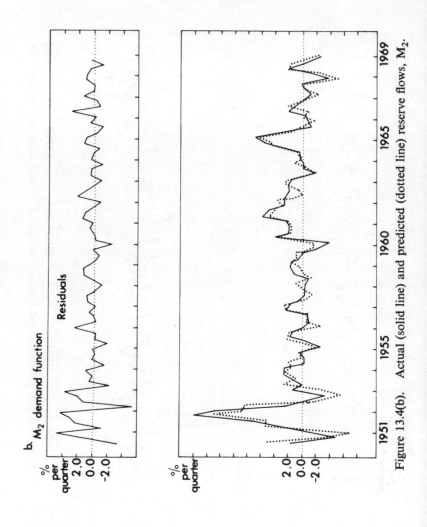

Figure 13.4(b).   Actual (solid line) and predicted (dotted line) reserve flows, M_2.

Table 13.8 *Comparison of Actual and Predicted
Reserve Flows: 1950–III to 1968–IV.*

Definition of money	M_1	M_2
Squared correlation coefficient	0·5012	0·7642
Regr. coeff. of actual on predicted	0·5913	0·8972
Mean absolute error	0·0212	0·0108
Fraction of error due to difference of regr. coeff. from unity	0·3223	0·0401
Fraction of error due to residual variance	0·6715	0·9436

ponding to rows 3 and 7 of Table 13.6 respectively). The obvious
similarity of the series is illustrated quantitatively in Table 13.8
where some summary statistics of the comparison are reported.

The high correlations between the actual and predicted reserve flow
series strongly support the monetary interpretation of balance-of-
payments adjustments. The variance left unexplained in the M_1 case
can be attributed largely to substitution between demand and time
deposits not captured in the empirical demand function,[29] which
could also explain the possible presence of serial correlation in the
residuals from a regression of the actual on the predicted balance of
payments.[30]

The difference of the regression coefficients from unity as indicated
in Table 13.8 could be an indication of a lagged response of reserve
flows to the forces involved in the predicted (desired) series. If an
adjustment equation of the type

$$\left(\frac{R}{H}g_R\right)_t = \left(\frac{R}{H}g_R\right)_{t-1} + \beta\left[\left(\frac{R}{H}g_R\right)_t^D - \left(\frac{R}{H}g_R\right)_{t-1}\right]$$

[29] The different results as between the M_1 and M_2 predictions derive from the
relatively erratic behaviour of the M_1 money multiplier during some periods
in the sixties. This stems from the large changes in the currency-demand deposit
ratio during quarters immediately before and after major changes in indirect
taxes and is witnessed by the importance of the currency ratio as a proximate
determinant of changes in M_1 during the sixties (see Genberg (1973), ch. 3,
table 4, row 3). For M_2 the currency and time deposit ratios work in the opposite
directions with a smaller net effect (ibid., table 4, row 6).

The significance of the currency ratio behaviour in the present context is
that it points to the instability of the M_1 function as specified on page 310 above
relative to the M_2 function.

[30] The Durbin–Watson statistic is 1·63 which is in the uncertain region at
the 95 per cent level. The same regression but with the M_2-based prediction
yielded a Durbin–Watson statistic of 2·06, indicating no significant serial
correlation there.

was relevant, then a lagged relationship between $(R/H)g_R$ and $[(R/H)g_R]^D$ would be appropriate and take the form

$$\left(\frac{R}{H}g_R\right)_t = \beta\left(\frac{R}{H}g_R\right)_t^D + \beta(1-\beta)\left(\frac{R}{H}g_R\right)_{t-1}^D + \beta(1-\beta)^2$$
$$\left(\frac{R}{H}g_R\right)_{t-2}^D + \cdots$$

With our current coefficient estimate of 0.59 for M_1 this would mean a lag pattern of 0.24, 0.10, 0.04, 0.02, 0.01 for the first through fifth lag indicating an average lag of about two months. The M_2 coefficient of 0.90 would similarly imply an average lag of one and a half weeks.

Before too much is made of these calculations, however, we must point out that *if* there is a lag in the adjustment so that desired reserve flows will not be fulfilled, then this should be integrated into the specification and estimation of the money demand functions in which case the 'true' parameters could be found. This problem will be left for future research.

Before we conclude the direct examination of the balance of payments, we must deal with an alternative to the monetary interpretation of our results. Sceptics of the monetary approach argue that the close inverse relationship between reserve flows and domestic credit creation is the result of sterilisation policies of the central bank. An autonomous reserve inflow will, according to this view, cause the central bank to contract domestic credit by the same amount in order to prevent the balance-of-payments surplus from affecting the money supply. This interpretation is implausible for several reasons. Firstly it implies an extraordinary stability of the central bank's behaviour with respect to policy formation. Secondly it implies that the sterilisation is always of a magnitude consistent with the demand for money, since with prices, interest rates and output determined by exogeneous forces, the money market must be equilibrated through either reserve flows or domestic credit creation. It seems far-fetched to assume that this kind of rule is followed by the Swedish central bank. Nevertheless, the possible simultaneous relationship between the two variables suggests that estimation procedures should take it into account. As a suggestive illustration we shall therefore present some results of simultaneous estimation of the system:

$$\left(\frac{R}{H}g_R\right)_t = \alpha_0 + \alpha_1 \left(\frac{D}{H}g_D\right)_t + \alpha_2 g_{m_t} + \alpha_3 (\log P_t - \alpha \log P_{t-1}) +$$

$$+ \alpha_4 (\log y_t - \alpha \log y_{t-1}) + \alpha_7 (\log i_t - \alpha \log i_{t-1}) + \quad (7)$$

$$+ \alpha_8 \log M_{t-1} + U_t$$

$$\left(\frac{D}{H}g_D\right)_t = \beta_0 + \beta_1 \left(\frac{R}{H}g_R\right)_t + \beta_2 g_{\text{Govt. debt outstanding}} + V_t \quad (8)$$

where (7) is the reserve flow equation (6) with the short-run demand for money function (4) of p. 310 substituted for $(g_M D)^D$, and (8) is a government policy reaction function. The latter assumes that open market operations are dictated by the change in international reserves (the sterilisation hypothesis) and the change in government debt outstanding (on the hypothesis that the central bank is a large source of finance for the government).

The two-stage least squares estimates of the parameters given in Table 13.9 indicate first of all that the specification of the central bank reaction function is inadequate in that the government financing variable fails to be significant. This is likely the result of short-run instability of the central bank's policy response due to the existence of many alternative targets. Experiments with yearly data did produce a significantly positive β_2 consistent with the long-run need for deficit financing through the central bank.

As far as the reserve flow equation is concerned, our conclusions still hold, judging from the α_1, α_2, and α_3 estimates which are not significantly different from their *a priori* values of -1 (for the first two) and $+1$. The income- and interest-rate coefficients are estimated with such poor precision that they are not significantly different from the estimates in the demand functions of Table 13.6 above even though the point estimates are contrary to expectations.

In conclusion it does not appear that the sterilisation hypothesis offers a very plausible alternative to our explanation of reserve flows. The monetary approach has passed our tests both as far as its underlying view of the world is concerned and in its implications with respect to the balance of payments.

Table 13.9 *Two-stage Least Squares Estimates of the Parameters in (7) and (8)*

Definition of money	α_0	α_1	α_2	α_3	$\alpha_4{}^a$	$\alpha_5{}^b$	$\alpha_6{}^c$	α_7	α_8	β_0	β_1	β_2
M_1	0·43 (0·26)	−1·31 (1·03)	−0·27 (0·49)	1·12 (0·74)	−0·14 (0·37)	0·02 (0·48)		0·01 (0·03)	−0·04 (0·02)	0·012 (0·004)	−0·57 (0·25)	0·02 (0·06)
M_1	0·39 (0·17)	−1·23 (0·63)	−0·23 (0·30)	1·06 (0·45)			−0·04 (0·25)	0·01 (0·03)	−0·04 (0·02)	0·011 (0·004)	−0·53 (0·27)	0·02 (0·06)
M_2	−0·01 (0·10)	−1·39 (0·28)	−0·87 (0·66)	0·90 (0·33)	−0·58 (0·41)	0·24 (0·47)		0·00 (0·02)	0·01 (0·02)	0·016 (0·003)	−0·94 (0·21)	−0·03 (0·05)
M_2	0·03 (0·05)	−1·11 (0·37)	−0·53 (0·31)	0·81 (0·21)			−0·02 (0·23)	−0·00 (0·02)	−0·00 (0·01)	0·015 (0·003)	−0·88 (0·21)	−0·02 (0·05)

^{a} Permanent income. ^{b} Transitory income. ^{c} Current income.

REFERENCES

Agmon, Tamir, 'Country Risk: The Significance of the Country Factor for Share-Price Movements in the United Kingdom, Germany, and Japan', *The Journal of Business*, 46 (January 1973), 24–32.

Agmon, Tamir, 'The Relation Among Equity Markets: A Study of Share Price Co-movements in the United States, United Kingdom, Germany and Japan', *Journal of Finance*, xxvii (September 1972), 839–55.

Argy, Victor, and Hodjera, Zoran, 'Financial Integration and Interest Rate Linkage in the Industrial Countries', *International Monetary Fund Staff Papers*, xx (March 1973), 1–77.

Branson, William H., *Financial Capital Flows in the U.S. Balance of Payments* (Amsterdam, North-Holland, 1968).

Branson, William H., and Hill, Raymond D., Jr, *Capital Movements in the OECD Area. An Econometric Analysis*. OECD Economic Outlook Occasional Studies (Paris, OECD, December 1971).

Chow, Gregory, 'On the Long-Run and Short-Run Demand for Money', *Journal of Political Economy*, lxxiv (April 1966), 111–31.

Cooper, Richard N., 'Towards an International Capital Market?', *North American and Western European Economic Policies*, Proceedings of a Conference held by the International Economic Association, edited by Charles P. Kindleberger and Andrew Shonfield (New York, St Martin's Press, 1971), 192–208.

Genberg, A. Hans, 'Aspects of the Monetary Approach to Balance of Payments Theory: An Empirical Study of Sweden', unpublished Ph.D. dissertation, University of Chicago (1973).

Genberg, Hans, 'The Concept and Measurement of the World Price Level and Rate of Inflation,' Discussion Paper, GIIS–Ford Foundation International Monetary Research Project (Graduate Institute of International Studies, October 1974).

Grassman, Sven, *Valutareserven och Utrikeshandelns Finansiella Struktur*. Bilaga till betalningsbalansutredningens betänkande. SOU 1971: 32. (Stockholm, Finansdepartementet, 1971).

Grubel, Herbert G., 'Internationally Diversified Portfolios', *American Economic Review*, lviii (December 1968), 1299–1314.

Hultcrantz, Gerhard, 'Prognos och Ekonomisk Verklighet', *Svensk Finanspolitik i Teori och Praktik*, edited by Erik Lundberg *et al.* (Stockholm, Bokforlaget Aldus, 1971), ch. 4.

Johnson, Harry G., 'The Monetary Approach to Balance of Payments Theory,' *Journal of Financial and Quantitative Analysis*, vii (March 1972), 1555–72.

Laffer, Arthur B., and Zecher, J. Richard, 'Some Evidence of the Formation, Efficiency and Accuracy of Anticipations of Nominal Yields', University of Chicago (January 1973), mimeographed.

Organisation for Economic Co-Operation and Development, *Main Economic Indicators, Historical Statistics* (Paris, OECD, 1970).

Scott, Ira O., 'The Euro-dollar Market and Its Public Policy Implications', Economic Policies and Practices, paper no. 12, prepared for the Joint Economic Committee, 91st Congress, 2nd Session. (Washington, U.S. Government Printing Office, 1970).

Sims, Christopher A., 'Money, Income, and Causality', *American Economic Review*, lxii (September 1972), 540–52.

14

International Reserve Flows and Money Market Equilibrium

The Japanese Case[1]

DONNA L. BEAN

INTRODUCTION

The monetary approach to the balance of payments attributes a significant role in the international adjustment process to monetary variables.[2] The model predicts that reserve accumulation is positively related to the rate of growth of domestic income and negatively correlated with the rate of domestic credit expansion. Some of the policy implications which follow from these results contradict the standard Keynesian analysis. The monetary approach implies that the central authorities can exercise some degree of control over the level of international reserves by manipulating the composition of the money supply base through adroit credit creation policies. Alternatively, this framework stresses the role of discretionary monetary policy in sterilising the impacts of the flows in the balance-of-payments accounts.

THE MODEL

The model is derived by applying the basic assumption that the

[1] This chapter is an excerpt from research supported by a National Science Foundation grant when the author was an undergraduate at the University of Chicago. The research was advised by Richard Zecher. The author also benefited greatly from discussions with Jacob Frenkel, Rudiger Dornbusch, and Robert Z. Aliber.
[2] See Johnson (ch. 6) for an elaboration of the monetary approach.

money market is always in equilibrium. The following notation is used in the model:

a = money multiplier,
H = high-powered money,
R = central authorities' international reserves,
D = domestic credit issued to the government or commercial banks which is due to the central bank,
i = interest rate,
P = price level,
y = real income.

The demand for money is described by equation (1), the supply of money by equation (2), and the money market equilibrium condition by equation (3) or equivalently by (4).

$$M^d = P \cdot L(y, i), \tag{1}$$

$$M^s = a(R + D), \tag{2}$$

$$M^d = M^s, \tag{3}$$

$$P \cdot \overset{\cdot}{L}(y, i) = a(R + D). \tag{4}$$

Differentiating equation (4) logarithmically yields:

$$d \log P + n_y \, d \log y + n_i \, d \log i = \\ d \log a + [R/(R + D)] \, d \log R + [D/(R + D)] \, d \log D \tag{5}$$

where n_y and n_i are, respectively, the elasticity of the demand for real cash balances with respect to income and the rate of interest. Solving for $[R/(R + D)] \, d \log R$:

$$[R/(R + D)] \, d \log R = d \log P + n_y \, d \log y + \\ + n_i \, d \log i - d \log a - [D/(R + D)] \, d \log D. \tag{6}$$

Equation (6) is estimated in the following form:

$$[R/(R + D)] \, d \log R = b_1 \, d \log P +$$
$$+ b_2 \, d \log y + b_3 \, d \log i + b_4 \, d \log a + \qquad (6a)$$
$$b_5 \, [\{D/(R + D)\} \, d \log D] + e$$

where e is the stochastic disturbance.

The coefficients for the income and interest-rate variables are the elasticities of the demand for money with respect to these particular parameters. Previous statistical work implies that b_2 should be of the order of magnitude of unity, and b_3 should be a small negative number. Since it is assumed that there is no money illusion the price coefficient should be $+1$. The theory predicts that the elasticity of the dependent variable with respect to the money multiplier and the domestic component of the base is -1.

If we let $r = R/(R + D)$ which implies that $D/R = (1 - r)/r$ then equation (6) can be written as:

$$d \log R = 1/r(d \log P + n_y d \log y +$$
$$+ n_i \, d \log i - d \log a) - [(1 - r)/r] \, d \log D. \qquad (7)$$

Equation (7) is estimated in the following form:

$$d \log R = b_1 d \log P + b_2 d \log y + b_3 d \log i +$$
$$+ b_4 d \log a + b_5 [\{(1 - r)/r\} \, d \log D] + e. \qquad (7a)$$

Estimations for the two forms of the equation are presented.

COMMENTS ON THE OBSERVATION PERIOD

This study examines the Japanese economy for the period 1959–70. The selection of Japan was arbitrary, and it may seem an unlikely candidate for a model applying what is often viewed as a small-country assumption—the price-taking hypothesis (this subject will be discussed further in a subsequent section). The availability of data played some role in the selection of the time interval.[3] By 1956

[3] Quarterly observations for 1957 and 1958 were sampled out as preliminary estimations demonstrated that poorer Durbin–Watson statistics resulted when this period was included.

the recovery of pre-World War II levels of industrial production and productivity were achieved. The pre-war *per capita* income level was attained in 1954. These facts indicate that many of the problems associated with reconstruction after World War II had been eliminated. Inclusion of data subject to the vagaries of post-war occupation and rebuilding seemed undesirable.

The sensational economic growth and radical structural changes which characterise the observation period were linked with growing surpluses in the international accounts. This high growth rate was sustained in part by attractive capital and labour arrangements which stimulated investment. Policies invited depreciation allowances and retained earnings which enabled the authorities to pursue a restrained monetary policy without provoking a severe excess demand for borrowings.

By 1969–70 the prolonged growth period created pressure for appreciation of the exchange rate or a *de facto* parity adjustment through removal of remaining tariff barriers. From 1950–70 the yen was pegged at 360/U.S.$. However, in 1950 the currency was overvalued at this rate, and extensive import controls were used to support this parity. Exchange rate alignment occurred throughout the period by the gradual relaxation of these regulations. These adjustments failed to capture all of the effective appreciation of the yen, and by 1969 the Japanese currency was believed to be greatly undervalued at this exchange rate.

The commercial banking sector is stringently administered by the central bank; in addition, during the 1960s, the corporate business sector had to rely on the banks for external financing due to the under-developed structure of alternative markets. These structural aspects of the banking sector resulted in a cartel of commercial banks in which credit was not regulated solely by means of price competition. Through this medium of the monopoly position of banks in issuing debt instruments, the authorities maintained strict control over the variables affecting money supply.

Two interrelated aggregative financial aspects accompanying this growth are noteworthy.[4] Firstly, the level of reserves was apparently

---

[4] See Michael W. Keran, 'Monetary Policy and the Business Cycle in Postwar Japan', in *Varities of Monetary Experience*, ed. by David Meiselman (Chicago, University of Chicago Press, 1970), and Robert Z. Aliber, 'Japanese Growth and the Equilibrium Foreign Exchange Value of the Yen', (mimeo).

a target variable during part of the decade. During this period, the trade balance fluctuated by more than $1 billion (over half the stock of reserves). Secondly, since fiscal policy was balanced over the long run with only a minor increase in government debt, this phenomenon was apparently achieved through discretionary monetary policies.

Indeed, monetary policy evidenced cyclical tendencies in the 1950s and 1960s and it has been suggested that four declines in productivity during this period were induced by restrictive governmental policy aimed at deterring reserve flows.[5] In sum the authorities were utilising their capacity as domestic credit creators to control reserve flows. The monetary approach to the balance of payments provides the theoretical background which explains why this policy was effective.

THE PRICE VARIABLE

The price-taking assumption refers specifically to price equilibration in the tradeable goods sector and in the long-run steady state. There is no readily available index for Japan for traded goods. A composite of the export and import price indices is especially inadequate in this country's case for two reasons. It is well known that Japan made price concessions in an attempt to increase market share. In addition, the import price index is heavily weighted by raw minerals, unfinished goods, and unprocessed agricultural products. Consumer goods prices are a biased estimator of traded goods because of the high services content. Wholesale prices do not include services but retain non-tradeables such as heavy construction—a sector in which costs have risen rapidly.

Price index movements for Japan during this period are quite diverse. The Japanese consumer price index (CPI) rose twice as fast as the United States CPI from 1953 to 1970. This relative increase cannot be explained by the application of a monopolistic pricing situation to Japan. At the same time, the change in the wholesale price index (WPI) is less than that for the comparable United States index. Meanwhile, the export price index fell in absolute terms from 1957–69.

[5] Keran, op. cit.

One study of several nations concludes that the discrepancy between the CPI and WPI is a function of the rate of growth of output *per capita*; the more rapid the increase in productivity the greater this difference.[6] This greater upward movement in the CPI can be traced to real wage gains which are rapidly translated into price increases in the non-traded goods sector. McKinnon suggests that wholesale price indices, under fixed exchange rates, should be correlated due to international arbitrage, especially if the data are converted into dollar terms. More specifically, he asserts that an appropriate traded-goods index should rise somewhat less than the wholesale price index.[7]

The empirical exception to WPI covariance is Japan; the absolute level of the WPI remained low relative to the rest of the world. McKinnon converts the yen indices into dollar terms using the 360/U.S.$ exchange rate. However, it has been suggested that the yen appreciated and the removal of import barriers and quotas was the mechanism used to implement parity adjustments.

In order to measure the extent of these changes in exchange controls the following method was employed. Data are published on the black market exchange rate. Although there is a premium assessed to buyers for the privilege of being able to obtain dollars which they otherwise could not procure (i.e., the yen is under-valued in relation to the rate which would 'prevail in an unrestricted market), this premium is assumed to be constant throughout the period. Accordingly, the adjusted price indices consist of the raw data multiplied by a black market exchange rate factor.

Summarily, adjustment by a crude measure for conversion of yen into dollars results in a price series which generally supports the price-taking hypothesis. The collinearity between the U.S. WPI and Japanese WPI is more striking when the Japanese prices are adjusted by the changing free market rate; this supports McKinnon's statement concerning international arbitrage.

Having established that the price-taking hypothesis is applicable, it is still necessary to select a price series which represents the measure used by the public to deflate their nominal money balances. Export

---

[6] Ronald I. McKinnon, 'Monetary Theory and Controlled Flexibility in the Foreign Exchanges', Essays in International Finance, no. 84 (Princeton, Princeton University Press, 1971).

[7] ibid, p. 22.

and import price indices do not appear to meet this criterion explictly. McKinnon's analysis supports the notion of using the wholesale price index. However, this index has at times been a target variable of the Japanese policy-makers; this interference makes the index a less appealing price-level proxy. The consumer price index remains; this measure is most frequently utilised in money demand estimations. Both the WPI and CPI are incorporated in the statistical analysis.

Assuming that the free market in yen is not extensive, there is reason to question the appropriateness of using the adjusted indices for the price variable. If it is the case that access to the market is possible on a small scale, then consumers must view this price as the marginal price, for otherwise they would exercise the option of trading in this market in order to capture the rents available. The existence of this market suggests that the free rate represents the shadow price. If it did not, then the opportunities for arbitrage indicate a state of disequilibrium; since all markets are assumed to clear, the price index adjusted by the free market rate must represent the effective price deflator.

RESULTS

The data[8] were seasonally adjusted. Two further pieces of information were generated from these data series—the money multiplier and

[8] Data were primarily obtained from a computer tape of *International Financial Statistics* (IFS). Various issues of the *Economic Statistics Monthly* (ESM) published by the Bank of Japan were also employed. Free market exchange rates are from *Pick's Currency Yearbook*.

Reserves are the foreign assets of the 'monetary authorities' which includes the Bank of Japan, the Foreign Exchange Fund, and Treasury IMF accounts (line 11, IFS). Beginning in 1964 Exchange Fund foreign exchange deposited with domestic commercial banks is not reported in this figure and is subsequently recorded as claims on commercial banks. The 'Monetary Survey' table in the ESM provided an adjustment factor for this phenomenon. It appears that 110 billion yen represents these deposits for the period prior to 1964; this figure was deducted from the data points for 1959–63.

High-powered money is line 14, IFS; those are funds expressly designated as reserves by the monetary authorities. (Note: there is reason to suspect this particular datum due to the close relationship between the central bank and the commercial banks. Alternative definitions which include the combined reserves of these institutions are not included in this analysis.) The domestic backing of the base is the difference between lines 14 and 11; this removes the noise generated by the 'other net' account. No distinction was made between domestic velocity. The multiplier is relatively unstable. Velocity is a reasonably stable function—particularly for the narrow definition of the money stock. This observed stability supports one assumption underlying the model.

The results of the estimations are presented in Tables 14.1 and 14.2 for both forms of the equation. In general, form 1 is statistically more significant, yielding higher R^2s, better Durbin–Watson statistics, and larger t-statistics.

All of the estimated coefficients have the predicted sign. The income elasticity is consistently smaller than unity.[9] The use of the Japanese discount rate results in a larger interest rate elasticity than when the United States treasury bill rate is used, but the difference is not statistically significant. The money multiplier is not appreciably different from the predicted value of unity.[10] Estimates of the elasticity of the domestic component of the base are smaller than the expected magnitude.[11]

---

credit issued to the government or the commercial banks. Essentially, the balance sheet of the central bank was collapsed to two accounts so that the identity, $H = R + D$, is operable.

Money is defined in a broad sense to include currency, savings deposits, and time deposits (lines 34 and 35, IFS). Different accounting practice was adopted in 1964; yen balances of non-residents (previously included in demand and time deposits) were transferred to the category foreign liabilities. This had a substantial effect on the third item included in the money stock. Unfortunately, it is not possible to isolate the size of these deposits. As the model is expressed in percentage changes, this difficulty was circumvented by sampling out the quarter in which the transformation occurs.

Income is represented by the Gross National Product. This figure is a quarterly level not projected to an equivalent annual flow.

The only series of interest rates obtainable from the tape is the discount rate. As this rate was comparatively stable, and is a discretionary policy variable, it is a less than optimal indicator of the movements in the prices of financial assets. Using the perfect capital market assumption, the U.S. treasury bill rate (line 60b, IFS) was also employed for the cost of capital variable. The last variable, commodity prices, are lines 63 and 64, IFS.

[9] A permanent income series should produce a larger magnitude. When the regression was run for semi-annual data, the income elasticity rose to approximately $0 \cdot 70$.

[10] Using the narrow definition of money does not significantly alter the level of statistical significance. The only noteworthy change is that the coefficient of the money multiplier falls, but this is the expected result.

[11] As mentioned in footnote 8, high-powered money may be more appropriately measured by a definition which includes a portion of the deposits of the commercial banking system. If it is true that increases in foreign reserves were hidden in the

Looking at Table 14.1, it is clear that the confidence levels of the coefficients are greater when the U.S. treasury bill rate is used (see columns 1 and 2, 5 and 6). In order to isolate the impact of alternative price indices the results using the treasury bill rate will be compared.

Over all, the consumer price index performs better than the wholesale price index. For the latter index serial correlation (as indicated by the Durbin–Watson statistic) may result from the authorities' policy of controlling wholesale prices during certain sub-periods.

Adjusting the price index by the free market rate has two effects. Firstly, the coefficient of the consumer price index more closely approximates unity (see Table 14.1, columns 1 and 5). In addition the statistical reliability of the WPI estimates improve (see Table 14.1, columns 3 and 7).

CONCLUDING REMARKS

The empirical analysis of Japan presented in this study strongly supports the theses of the monetary approach and suggests that it is a useful framework for analysing these phenomena.[12] Moreover, it is obvious that statistical estimations are sensitive to the definitions of the variables which are employed. The nominal balances and income deflator are more appropriately specified by adjusting for the exchange rate since money demand can be satisfied in either the domestic or the foreign sector.

The theory implies that through discretionary credit-creation policies the authorities can minimise the impact of reserve flows on the economy. Alternatively, given a particular rate of growth of money demand, the authorities can peg reserves by manipulating the domestic component of the base. From 1964–6 international reserves stabilised around $2 billion. Demand deposits did not reach their

---

commercial banks' accounts, then the elasticity of reserve flows with respect to domestic credit expansion should increase if the estimation was run for this alternative measure of high-powered money.

[12] Criticism of this formulation might be centred on the assumption that the money market clears instantaneously. However, it should be noted that this model is geared to long-run analysis and acknowledges the transitory periods of stock adjustment. Regressions involving yearly data may yield estimates of the coefficients which more precisely reflect the postulated magnitudes.

Table 14.1 Form 1, Equation (6a)

$$(R/(R+D))d \log R = b_1 d \log P + b_2 d \log y + b_3 d \log i + b_4 d \log a + b_5[\{D/(R+D)\}d \log D] + e$$

Quarterly: 1959–70 Price Index and Interest Rate Variable[a]

Column	1 CPI TB	2 CPI Disc. rate	3 WPI TB	4 WPI Disc. rate	5 ACPI TB	6 ACPI Disc. rate	7 AWPI TB	8 AWPI Disc. rate
Price	1·31 (6·34)[b]	1·19 (5·38)	1·36 (2·67)	1·12 (2·37)	1·06 (6·83)	0·90 (5·60)	1·12 (4·70)	0·84 (3·85)
Income	0·56 (6·73)	0·52 (6·36)	0·58 (6·17)	0·52 (5·67)	0·62 (7·44)	0·55 (6·68)	0·63 (7·10)	0·55 (6·36)
Interest rate	−0·05 (−1·55)	−0·11 (−1·22)	−0·06 (−1·76)	−0·21 (−2·20)	−0·07 (−2·14)	−0·14 (−1·49)	−0·07 (−2·21)	−0·19 (−2·02)
Money Multiplier	−0·84 (−5·42)	−0·82 (−5·29)	−0·71 (−4·16)	−0·72 (−4·33)	−0·86 (−5·37)	−0·81 (−5·04)	−0·78 (−4·68)	−0·76 (−4·54)
Domestic Component of the Base	−0·72 (−9·20)	−0·67 (−8·32)	−0·65 (−7·63)	−0·59 (−7·07)	−0·69 (−8·83)	−0·63 (−7·82)	−0·64 (−7·86)	−0·58 (−7·05)
R^2	0·65	0·65	0·56	0·58	0·64	0·62	0·59	0·58
S.E.[c]	0·021	0·021	0·024	0·023	0·021	0·022	0·023	0·023
D.W.[d]	2·03	1·99	1·48	1·58	1·86	1·82	1·54	1·63

[a] The price indices are for consumer or wholesale prices. An 'A' preceding the index abbreviation indicates those series adjusted by the exchange rate. The United States treasury bill rate is series 'TB' and 'Disc. rate' represents the Japanese discount rate.
[b] t-statistic.
[c] Standard error of the regression.
[d] Durbin–Watson statistic.

Table 14.2 Form 2, Equation (7a)

$$(d \log R = b_1 d \log P + b_2 d \log y + b_3 d \log i + b_4 \log a + b_5[((1-r)/r)d \log D] + e$$

Quarterly: 1959–70 Price Index and Interest Rate Variable[a]

Column	1 CPI TB	2 CPI Disc. rate	3 WPI TB	4 WPI Disc. rate	5 ACPI TB	6 ACPI Disc. rate	7 AWPI TB	8 AWPI Disc. rate
Price	0·99 (5·40)[b]	0·89 (4·87)	1·11 (2·57)	0·98 (2·45)	0·81 (5·47)	0·74 (4·95)	0·84 (3·74)	0·71 (3·48)
Income	0·39 (4·84)	0·37 (4·71)	0·39 (4·44)	0·37 (4·31)	0·46 (5·59)	0·42 (5·29)	0·47 (5·13)	0·42 (4·94)
Interest Rate	−0·04 (−1·42)	−0·13 (−1·70)	−0·04 (−1·61)	−0·19 (−2·37)	−0·05 (−1·83)	−0·15 (−2·00)	−0·05 (−1·83)	−0·19 (−2·36)
Money Multiplier	−0·80 (−4·71)	−0·82 (−4·88)	−0·67 (−3·69)	−0·74 (−4·10)	−0·86 (−4·87)	−0·87 (−4·96)	−0·77 (−4·17)	−0·81 (−4·45)
Domestic Component of the Base	−0·55 (−6·54)	−0·52 (−6·20)	−0·49 (−5·40)	−0·45 (−5·23)	−0·57 (−6·50)	−0·52 (−6·08)	−0·53 (−5·72)	−0·48 (−5·46)
R^2	0·47	0·48	0·35	0·39	0·45	0·46	0·37	0·40
S.E.[c]	0·058	0·057	0·064	0·062	0·058	0·058	0·063	0·061
D.W.[d]	1·84	1·96	1·33	1·58	1·71	1·93	1·39	1·69

[a] The price indices are for consumer or wholesale prices. An 'A' preceding the index abbreviation indicates those series adjusted by the exchange rate. The United States treasury bill rate is series 'TB' and 'Disc. rate' represents the Japanese discount rate.
[b] t-statistic.
[c] Standard error of the regression.
[d] Durbin–Watson statistic.

fourth-quarter 1963 level until 1966; because of the disparity in the data series (see footnote 8), it is impossible to determine the extent of measurement bias and actual reduction in the rate of growth of money demand. However, it is clear that the central bank did control the composition of its assets by varying the rate of growth of domestic credit so that international reserves were not depleted.

15

The Balance of Payments as a
Monetary Phenomenon

Empirical Evidence, Spain 1955–71

MANUEL GUITIAN[1]

1 INTRODUCTION

This chapter provides an empirical study of the Spanish economy during the period 1955–71. Major emphasis is placed on the economy's external developments in an attempt to test the theoretical proposition that the balance of payments is a monetary phenomenon. This proposition derives from what Johnson and Mundell have called a new approach to the theory of the balance of payments and of the adjustment process.[2]

The empirical analysis will investigate the relationship between the balance of payments and the rate of domestic credit expansion. Further, an attempt will be made to ascertain the importance of the latter relative to variables like the exchange rate, domestic prices and gross national product, in determining balance-of-payments outcomes. It should be noted at the outset that exchange rate changes during the period under study were once-and-for-all phenomena. They can temporarily improve the balance of payments but cannot on their own sustain the improvement unless complemented by appropriate domestic monetary policies.[3] These policies are reflected in the rate of domestic credit expansion and may reinforce or

[1] The views expressed in the chapter are the author's and not necessarily those of the International Monetary Fund.

[2] See 'The Balance of Payments' in Mundell [6]; Mundell [7]; Johnson [4], [5].

[3] For a complete theoretical exposition of these points see Mundell [6], [7]; Johnson [4], [5]; and Guitian [2].

dampen the effects of changes in the exchange rate. As we shall see below, both instances are evidenced in the 1959 and 1967 Spanish devaluations.

The plan of the chapter is as follows: Section 2 provides a brief background of developments in the Spanish economy during the period of analysis. Section 3 contains the empirical tests for different concepts of the balance of payments and of domestic credit. Finally, section 4 sets out the main conclusions.

2 THE PERIOD OF ANALYSIS

The period 1955-71 has been chosen mainly on the basis of the availability of homogeneous data. The choice, however, appears quite justified as the Spanish economy underwent considerable changes during this period. If the relationships estimated hold reasonably well in the presence of structural changes, the implication may be drawn that they represent the true state of the world.[4] Prior to 1959, inflationary domestic (monetary and fiscal) policies had led to the introduction of all sorts of trade restrictions and to the adoption of multiple exchange rates.[5] The lack of effectiveness of these measures became evident as the external imbalances persisted during the second half of the 1950s (see Table 15.1). These balance-of-payments deficits reflected mostly large public sector budget deficits financed by recourse to the banking system.

Given the critical external position of the economy,[6] in 1959 the authorities introduced a stabilisation plan. The plan was submitted as a Government Memorandum to the International Monetary Fund and to the OECD. Both organisations, as well as the United States and OECD member countries which were creditors of Spain, provided financial support for the implementation of the stabilisation policies.

The stabilisation program undertaken by the Spanish authorities

---

[4] This *a priori* implication is based on the belief that other things not being equal tends to be a disturbing factor for *ceteris paribus* hypotheses.

[5] See Tamames [8] for a complete and detailed description of the whole period. A clear and concise description of Spain's monetary policy and instruments during the last twenty years can be found in Browne [1].

[6] The stock of international reserves which amounted to $225 million in 1955 (about one-third of that year's import payments) was down to about $70 million by 1958 (or 8 per cent of imports).

was comprehensive and affected practically all sectors of the economy. The most important measures adopted were fiscal and monetary. They included limits on the total expenditures of the public sector, increased taxes, the elimination of public sector's recourse to central bank financing and ceilings on the extension of bank credit to the private sector. Furthermore, the issuance of automatically re-discountable Government paper was discontinued and attempts were made to introduce flexibility in the structure of interest rates. On the external side, the existing multiple exchange rates were eliminated and a new single official exchange rate of ptas 60 per U.S.$1 was established. All these measures were accompanied by a general liberalisation of most international (trade and capital) transactions and by a reduction in internal price controls and in governmental intervention.[7]

The global impact of the stabilisation plan began to show in 1960. The rate of growth of aggregate demand was reduced relative to earlier years and real output did not rise. Along with this came a reduction in the rate of inflation and large balance-of-payments surpluses. The money stock soon started to increase rapidly and by 1965, after a few years of austerity, domestic credit proceeded to expand at quite high rates (see Table 15.2). As a consequence, aggregate demand pressures rose substantially. The pressures were met by output increases (made possible by using unemployed resources), by domestic price rises and growing trade deficits. The over-all balance of payments, however, registered surpluses until 1964 due to sizeable transfers from abroad, increasing tourism proceeds and net capital inflows. Thus, the first half of the 1960s can be described as a period of rapid growth, price increases and consistent external surpluses.

During the second part of the decade, on the other hand, the real rate of growth slowed down while the price increases, started in 1962 and continued in 1963–64, gathered force. This led the authorities to adopt some measures to bring inflation under control.[8] On the

---

[7] One of the effects of the 1959 measures was to increase the openness of the economy. The ratio of the country's expenditure on foreign goods and services to total expenditure on goods and services rose from 8 per cent in 1955 to close to 20 per cent in 1970.

[8] The measures, though, were non-monetary: tariff reductions, food imports and new lists of liberalised merchandise imports. They probably helped to reduce domestic price rises, but at the cost of a large increase in the trade deficit.

Table 15.1 *Spain: Balance of Payments (In millions of U.S. dollars)*

	1955	1956	1957	1958	1959	1960	1961	1962	1963	1964	1965	1966	1967	1968	1969	1970	1971
Current account	−69	−182	−107	−142	−28	393	221	50	−186	33	−486	−564	−456	−242	−394	78	855
Trade balance	−230	−338	−276	−287	−235	57	−279	−638	−1,013	−1,070	−1,759	−1,992	−1,781	−1,575	−1,871	−1,874	−1,600
Net services	66	93	102	71	134	246	337	467	569	782	913	1,009	875	886	945	1,293	1,688
Net transfers	95	63	67	74	73	90	163	221	258	321	360	419	450	448	532	659	767
Long-term capital account	30	46	12	14	98	126	212	121	219	255	309	344	536	581	506	669	499
Short-term capital and errors and omissions	47	70	51	86	—	−59	−94	35	72	39	−46	−32	−215	−268	−342	66	−97
SDRs	—	—	—	—	—	—	—	—	—	—	—	—	—	—	—	42	42
Over-all balance	8	−66	−44	−42	70	460	339	206	105	327	−131	−188	−136	71	−230	855	1,299

Sources. Ministry of Commerce and Bank of Spain.

external side, the balance of payments turned into a deficit in 1965. It persisted in 1966–7. Contrary to their early policy of nonsterilisation, the authorities did not allow these deficits to have their contractionary impact on domestic liquidity and large offsetting bank credits were extended. Given this situation, the authorities, at the end of 1965, introduced some tax increases and took steps to limit the increase in public sector's expenditure. On the monetary side, the Bank of Spain's rate of discount was marginally raised and a 17 per cent limit was set on the commercial bank's credit expansion.

In 1966, some economic indicators pointed at a downturn in economic activity: employment declined, private investment and new orders began to slow down or fall. Public and private consumption nevertheless continued to rise rapidly. The Government once again engaged in partial *ad hoc* measures to stabilise the economy.[9] Despite all of these measures, prices continued to rise (though at a lower rate than before) and the balance of payments recorded another deficit. Again, the deficit was 'oversterilised' and the central bank's credit expansion was more than three times the size of the deficit.

During the first ten months of 1967, the same approach of partial policy measures was followed. Finally the Government, following the British pound devaluation, depreciated the currency by 16·7 per cent. The country's basic balance registered a small surplus, but not because of the devaluation. It rather reflected the reduction in imports caused by the decline in domestic activity, the increase in exports due to the recovery of neighbouring countries from the 1966 recession and a large long-term net capital inflow. The over-all balance showed a deficit resulting from a large short-term capital outflow. As in the two previous years, the deficit was sterilised.

At the time of the devaluation, a package of complementary measures was introduced: higher official interest rates, salary freezes, price controls and administrative reforms to help cure fiscal imbalances. To minimise the impact of the devaluation on the domestic price level, some tariff reductions were granted, especially on food imports. During 1968, indicators such as industrial produc-

---

[9] Measures at times conflicting with one another: for example, further increases in the Bank of Spain discount rate along with increases in the amount of rediscounts that the banks were allowed to perform. This is a curious example of an attempt to control both price and quantity.

Table 15.2 *Spain: Changes in Money and Domestic Credit (in billions of Spanish pesetas)*

	C	M_1	M_2	D_1	D_2
1955	4·1	15·1	28·5	8·2	5·0
1956	8·9	22·0	35·2	15·9	15·0
1957	10·9	23·6	35·7	13·5	7·5
1958	10·0	22·3	37·0	12·2	12·6
1959	2·8	10·8	22·5	−8·4	−9·5
1960	6·0	0·9	50·3	−14·7	−19·1
1961	10·3	26·8	65·8	7·9	−13·1
1962	15·8	42·0	102·8	7·8	0·5
1963	16·9	46·2	98·0	5·6	3·6
1964	22·4	59·2	136·7	3·7	−2·3
1965	24·0	54·6	134·2	30·3	29·7
1966	23·0	51·4	130·1	34·6	35·6
1967	24·4	65·0	160·7	29·0	31·8
1968	18·8	66·3	225·8	23·5	13·2
1969	27·7	89·5	268·3	50·7	34·5
1970	21·4	41·2	255·8	−27·6	−26·4
1971	35·3	175·1	467·7	−42·7	−53·1

C: Note and currency issue,
M_1: Currency in circulation plus demand deposits,
M_2: M_1 plus time and saving deposits,
D_1: Bank of Spain's domestic credit expansion,
D_2: Banking system's net domestic credit expansion.
Source. Bank of Spain: Statistical Bulletin.

tion and employment indices pointed at a recovery in economic activity, domestic credit expansion was somewhat reduced and the basic balance showed a large surplus. The improvement in the over-all balance, however, was considerably smaller because of heavy short-term capital outflows. The combination of smaller domestic credit expansion and the devaluation probably account for 1968's balance-of-payments surplus. Whichever favourable effects the devaluation could still have had in 1969 were more than offset by the large expansion in domestic credit during the year. As a consequence, the balance of payments recorded a deficit larger than those of the pre-devaluation years.

This general picture drastically changes in 1970–71. The change appears to have been brought about mainly by the adoption of appropriate domestic credit policies. The Bank of Spain's credit was severely curtailed during both years and as a consequence the country's stock of international reserves, which were under $1 billion in 1969, tripled to $3 billion by the end of 1971. Recent data for the first half of 1972 indicate further reserve accumulation in excess of $500 million.

3 THE MONETARY CHARACTER OF BALANCE-OF-PAYMENTS PROBLEMS: AN EMPIRICAL TEST

The tests undertaken in this section are intended to determine two simple sets of relationships. Firstly, the effects of domestic credit expansion on the balance on current account and on the over-all balance of payments. Secondly, the connection between these two external accounts and the following variables: gross domestic product, domestic and foreign prices and the rate of domestic credit expansion. The nature of the tests indicates that the analysis has been conducted in terms of the flow market for money (hoarding). This approach is theoretically legitimate given the interdependence of the flow markets in the economy imposed by Walras' Law. The balance on current account is explicitly considered because if we assume no capital movements, any analysis made from the standpoint of the flow market for money is equivalent to an analysis made in terms of the market for goods and services. In this case, the relevant balance-of-payments concept is the balance on current account. If instead we allow for capital movements the analysis based on equilibrium in the flow money market only ensures equilibrium in the market for commodities *and* security flows.[10] The relevant concept of the balance of payments is the over-all balance as no distinction is drawn among securities by maturity term.

The relationships estimated for the first test were of the general form:

$$B_{CA} = F_{1j}[\Delta D_j]; j = 1, 2, \ldots, 10, \tag{1}$$

$$\Delta B_{CA} = F_{2j}[\Delta^2 D_j]; j = 1, 2, \ldots, 10. \tag{2}$$

[10] For a more complete elaboration, see Guitian [3].

$$B = F_{3j}[\Delta D_j]; \; j = 1, 2, \ldots, 10, \tag{3}$$

$$\Delta B = F_{4j}[\Delta^2 D_j]; \; j = 1, 2, \ldots, 10, \tag{4}$$

where: B_{CA} and B stand for the balance on current account and the over-all balance of payments, respectively, and the ΔD_js are different concepts of domestic credit expansion. Ten such definitions were considered.[11] The first four definitions correspond to central bank variables and the other six to consolidated banking system variables. They were derived from their respective balance sheets as follows:

A. Central Bank Credit Variables

ΔD_1 is net credit to the public sector, banking institutions and the private sector. This corresponds to the central bank's currency issue minus net foreign and other miscellaneous assets.

ΔD_2 is equal to ΔD_1 plus net miscellaneous assets. Thus, it is equivalent to currency issue minus net international reserves.

ΔD_3 is gross credit to the three sectors mentioned above. It corresponds to high-powered money minus net foreign and other miscellaneous assets.

ΔD_4 is equal to ΔD_3 plus net miscellaneous assets.

B. Banking System Credit Variables

ΔD_5 is credit to the public and private sectors, equivalent to narrow money (M_1) minus net foreign and other miscellaneous assets.

ΔD_6 is equal to ΔD_5 plus net miscellaneous assets.

ΔD_7 is gross credit to the private and public sectors. It corresponds to wide money (M_2) minus net foreign and other miscellaneous assets.

ΔD_8 is equal to ΔD_7 plus net miscellaneous assets.

ΔD_9 is net credit to both sectors, i.e. currency in circulation minus net foreign and other miscellaneous assets.

ΔD_{10} is equal to ΔD_9 plus net miscellaneous assets.

The results were similar for the four sets of relationships: both balance-of-payments concepts were accurately explained by six out of the ten domestic credit variables (see Tables 15.3 and 15.4). The

[11] For a theoretical treatment of this definitional issue, see Guitian [2].

regressions of the actual values all show R^2 (corrected for degrees of freedom) ranging from 0·556 to 0·932 for the balance of payments and from 0·65 to 0·898 for the current account. Furthermore, the t ratios of the slope coefficients are consistently significant at the 0·001 level. An equivalent over-all picture is obtained from the regressions of first differences.

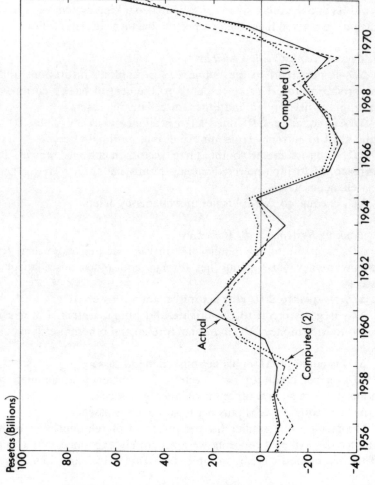

Figure 15.1.   Spain: Current Account Balance

These initial results strongly point at the monetary character of balance-of-payments disequilibria. They also indicate a significant relationship between the balance of payments (and the current account) and two major concepts of domestic credit: the rate of expansion of central bank's domestic credit (however defined) and the rate of expansion of net banking system's credit.

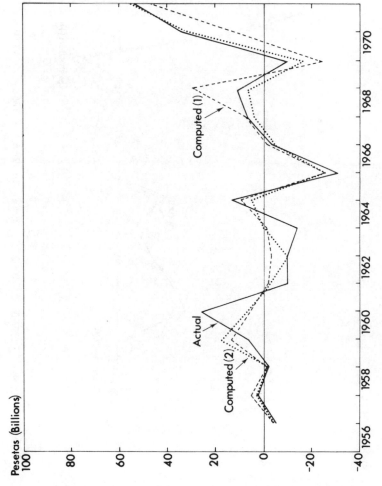

Figure 15.2. Spain: Changes in Current Account Balance

The second set of estimates were of the general form:

$$B_{CA} = H_{1j}[Y, p, ep_f, \Delta D_j]; j = 1, 2, \ldots, 10, \qquad (5)$$

$$B = H_{2j}[Y, p, ep_f, \Delta D_j]; j = 1, 2, \ldots, 10, \qquad (6)$$

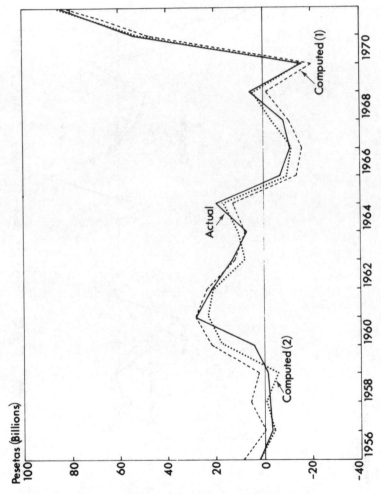

Figure 15.3. Spain: Balance of Payments

where: Y is gross domestic product, p is Spain's cost of living index[12] and ep_f, an index of foreign prices. The latter was approximated by taking a weighted average (with import shares as weights) of the export prices of ten major European countries and of the United States, the major trading partners of Spain. The index was converted to Spanish pesetas using the exchange rate.[13] Thus, the foreign price index will fully reflect the changes in the exchange rate. These relationships were also estimated in first differences.

As far as the domestic credit variables are concerned, the results are similar to those of the previous sets of regressions. The best fits are provided by the central bank's credit expansion (ΔD_i, $i = 1, \ldots, 4$) and by the banking system's net credit expansion (ΔD_9, ΔD_{10}). The contribution of the other variables is more difficult to assess. The t values of their respective coefficients are consistently not significant (see Tables 15.5 and 15.6).

If these results are correct, it may be inferred that the safest way to cope with external imbalances is to control the rate of central bank credit expansion or the rate of net credit expansion by the banking system. Such control must be consistent with the balance-of-payments constraint. If domestic credit (thus defined) expands at a larger (smaller) rate than that at which the economy wants to hoard cash balances, an external deficit (surplus) will tend to appear.

Here we have the case of an economy where two devaluations were undertaken in less than ten years. One of them was followed by surpluses in the balance of payments. The second one had a much more limited impact or none whatsoever (see Figures 15.1 to 15.4). The strong improvement in 1970-1 is probably not due to the 1967 devaluation. Rather it has been caused, as we have seen in the previous section, by the introduction of restrictive domestic credit policies.

From the point of view of the demand for money, the results indirectly emphasise variables like high-powered money, currency issue and other narrow money definitions. This follows from the strong correlation between the domestic credit variables corresponding to such concepts and the balance of payments.

12 This is a relatively poor proxy for the domestic price index. It was used for lack of better alternatives.

13 For the period 1955-8, when Spain followed a multiple exchange rate system, the free market exchange rate was used to convert the foreign price index to Spanish currency.

Table 15.3 Spain: the Current Account and Domestic Credit Expansion

Equation	Constant	ΔD_1	ΔD_2	ΔD_3	ΔD_4	ΔD_9	ΔD_{10}	$\bar{R}^{2a}$	D–W
				A. Levels					
1	−2·114	−0·6893 (10·033)[b]						0·862	2·050
2	−1·817		−0·727 (8·089)[b]					0·801	2·457
3	3·009			−0·8762 (8·145)[b]				0·803	2·775
4	3·041				−0·8529 (5·540)[b]			0·650	2·514
5	−0·0281					−0·754 (8·152)[b]		0·804	1·673
6	−0·3879						−0·9125 (11·910)[b]	0·898	2·891
				B. Differences					
7	0·4155	−0·622 (5·273)[b]						0·641	2·606
8	1·585		−0·5273 (3·592)[b]					0·442	2·064
9	2·079			−0·5842 (3·443)[b]				0·420	2·110
10	3·131				−0·4069 (2·183)			0·201	1·580
11	1·461					−0·5399 (5·944)[b]		0·696	1·923
12	1·133						−0·7723 (5·291)[b]	0·643	2·505

Note. The numbers in parentheses are *t* values.   [a] Adjusted for degrees of freedom.   [b] Coefficient significant at the 0·005 level.

Table 15.4 Spain: Balance of Payments and Domestic Credit Expansion

Equation	Constant	ΔD_1	ΔD_2	ΔD_3	ΔD_4	ΔD_9	ΔD_{10}	$\bar{R}^{2a}$	D–W
				A. Levels					
1	13·28	-0.8356 $(14.896)^b$						0·932	0·926
2	13·69		-0.9002 $(12.583)^b$					0·908	1·029
3	19·15			-1.019 $(7.960)^b$				0·796	0·551
4	19·39				-1.017 $(5.916)^b$			0·680	0·826
5	14·94					-0.7451 $(4.584)^b$		0·556	1·286
6	15·10						-1.036 $(9.370)^b$	0·844	0·529
				B. Differences					
7	0·7898	-0.8274 $(12.730)^b$						0·915	3·225
8	1·847		-0.8131 $(10.744)^b$					0·844	2·545
9	2·57			-0.9133 $(9.969)^b$				0·868	2·626
10	3·913				-0.7882 $(6.402)^b$			0·727	1·613
11	3·331					-0.4673 $(3.181)^b$		0·378	2·339
12	1·791						-1.015 $(11.223)^b$	0·893	2·915

Note. The numbers in parentheses are *t* values. [a] Adjusted for degrees of freedom. [b] Coefficient significant at the 0·005 level.

Table 15.5 *Spain: the Current Account, GDP, Prices and Credit Expansion*

Equation	Constant	GDP	Domestic Price	Foreign Price	ΔD_1	ΔD_2	ΔD_3	ΔD_4	ΔD_9	$\bar{R}^{2a}$	D–W
A. Levels											
1	14·34	−0·1709 (1·664)	−0·4682 (0·943)	0·1972 (0·663)	−0·827 (7·228)[b]					0·891	3·07
2	15·61	−0·1166 (0·785)	−0·4475 (0·623)	0·1453 (0·328)		−0·8215 (4·449)[b]				0·775	2·92
3	22·60	[c]	−1·087 (2·822)	0·4949 (1·933)			−0·5683 (5·166)[b]			0·920	2·592
4	27·27	−0·09286 (3·545)	−1·189 (2·936)	0·4834 (1·736)				−0·5533 (5·166)[b]		0·908	2·34
5	11·31	0·2308 (2·593)	−0·6042 (1·178)	0·3046 (0·904)					−0·6011 (5·578)[b]	0·852	2·714
B. Differences											
6	−10·46	−0·3148 (2·508)	0·2456 (0·376)	0·5738 (0·911)	−0·7428 (5·856)[b]					0·711	2·226
7	−14·86	−0·3178 (1·843)	0·2179 (0·249)	0·7129 (0·852)		−0·6663 (3·847)[b]				0·486	1·639
8	−1·246	−0·1105 (2·345)	−0·2403 (0·443)	0·3423 (0·720)			−0·5199 (4·740)[b]			0·795	3·022
9	−2·312	−0·1297 (2·801)	−0·2149 (0·408)	0·3423 (0·743)				−0·496 (4·954)[b]		0·807	2·98
10	2·153	0·1047 (0·847)	−0·09839 (0·135)	0·5284 (0·743)					−0·567 (4·929)[b]	0·626	2·172

Note. The numbers in parentheses are *t* values. [a] Adjusted for degrees of freedom. [b] Coefficient significant at the 0·001 level. [c] Not significantly different from zero.

Table 15.6 *Spain: Balance of Payments, GDP, Prices and Credit Expansion*

Equation	Constant	GDP	Domestic Price	Foreign Price	ΔD_1	ΔD_2	ΔD_3	ΔD_4	ΔD_9	ΔD_{10}	$\bar{R}^{2a}$	D–W
						A. Levels						
1	5·493	−0·08186 (1·199)	c	c	−0·863 (11·351)[b]						0·965	2·525
2	9·282	−0·08354 (1·045)	0·156 (0·404)	0·2147 (0·903)		−0·9576 (9·648)[b]					0·952	2·357
3	17·88	c	0·4039 (1·393)	c			−0·8793 (11·678)[b]				0·967	3·039
4	25·11	c	−0·5068 (1·851)	c				−0·8809 (12·163)[b]			0·969	3·144
5	0·9916	0·3978 (3·517)	−0·5093 (0·782)	0·3707 (0·865)					−0·487 (3·683)[b]		0·825	2·79
6	6·878	c	0·5182 (1·747)	−0·4944 (2·385)						−1·509 (11·714)[b]	0·971	2·455
						B. Differences						
7	3·348	c	0·3286 (0·725)	−0·2951 (0·675)	−0·8618 (9·750)[b]						0·891	3·006
8	−2·057	−0·07067 (0·707)	0·4209 (0·830)	−0·2043 (0·422)		−0·8689 (8·660)[b]					0·865	2·419
9	0·6348	c	c	−0·06429 (0·148)			−0·8991 (9·002)[b]				0·867	3·164
10	−1·253	−0·05587 (1·366)	c	−0·05662 (0·139)				−0·8526 (9·644)[b]			0·882	3·064
11	9·411	0·3689 (2·081)	−0·3774 (0·359)	−0·5744 (0·560)					−0·5110 (3·083)		0·393	2·814
12	3·29	c	0·6756 (1·578)	−0·8228 (2·210)						−1·085 (10·891)[b]	0·908	3·132

Note. The numbers in parentheses are t values.   [a] Adjusted for degrees of freedom.   [b] Significant at the 0·001 level.
[c] Not significantly different from zero.

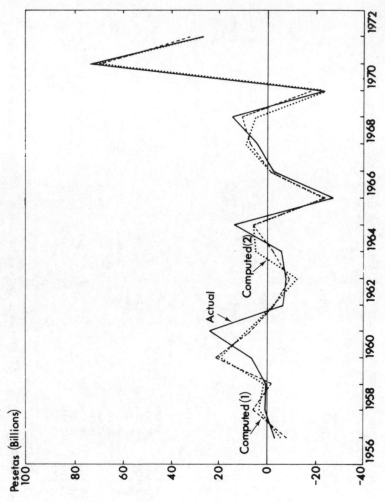

Figure 15.4.   Spain: Change in the Balance of Payments

4 SUMMARY AND CONCLUSION

This chapter has described two simple empirical tests to investigate
the relationship of the balance of payments to the rate of domestic

credit expansion and to the exchange rate. The latter was considered indirectly by incorporating it into an index of foreign prices. Given that the two Spanish devaluations had different effects on the balance of payments, other explanatory factors must be taken into account. The tests appear to establish domestic credit expansion as the major determinant of the evolution of the balance of payments. The behaviour of domestic credit after the 1959 devaluation is remarkably different from its behaviour after the 1967 devaluation. While credit policies in the early 1960s complemented the change in the exchange rate, those following the 1967 depreciation tended instead to offset them.

The experience of the Spanish economy during this period supports the view that exchange rate changes are not effective unless accompanied by appropriate credit policies. Furthermore, there is no sustainable trade-off between devaluation and restrictive credit policies. The real trade-off is between the devaluation and the degree of restrictiveness of internal policies. The results of the tests also point out the importance of central bank credit variables in the determination of the balance of payments. This finding, if accurate, is of relevance from the policy point of view because the monetary authorities can clearly control the rate of central bank credit expansion. Their control over this variable may enable the monetary authorities, for any given demand for money, to attain their desired stock of international reserves.

REFERENCES

[1] Browne, C., 'The Evolution of Monetary Instruments and Policy in Spain', International Monetary Fund Departmental Memoranda, DM/73/38 (May 1973).
[2] Guitian, M., 'Devaluation, Monetary Policy and the Balance of Payments', unpublished Ph.D. dissertation, University of Chicago (1973).
[3] Guitian, M., 'Credit Versus Money as an Instrument of Control', *IMF Staff Papers*, xx, no. 3 (November 1973).
[4] Johnson, H. G., 'The Monetary Approach to Balance of Payments Theory', Ch. 6 of this book.
[5] Johnson, H. G., *Inflation and the Monetarist Controversy* (Amsterdam, North-Holland, 1972).
[6] Mundell, R. A., *International Economics* (New York, Macmillan, 1968).
[7] Mundell, R. A., *Monetary Theory* (Pacific Palisades, Goodyear, 1971).
[8] Tamames, R., *Estructura Economica de Espana*, 5th edn (Madrid, Guadiana de Publicaciones, 1970).

DATA SOURCES

Bank of Spain:
Statistical Bulletin
Annual Reports

International Monetary Fund:
International Financial Statistics
Direction of Trade
Balance of Payments Yearbook

Ministry of Commerce of Spain:
The Spanish Balance of Payments
Informacion Comercial Espanola

V. APPLICATION TO ECONOMIC HISTORY

16

How the Gold Standard Worked, 1880–1913[1]

DONALD N. McCLOSKEY AND J. RICHARD ZECHER

1 THE MONETARY THEORY AND ITS IMPLICATIONS FOR THE GOLD STANDARD

Each intellectual generation since the mercantilists has revised or refined the understanding of how the balance of payments is kept in equilibrium under a system of fixed exchange rates, and all these understandings find a place in the historical literature on the gold standard of the late nineteenth century. It is difficult, therefore, to locate the orthodox view on how the gold standard worked, for it is many views. If one can find historical and economic writings describing the gold standard (and other systems of fixed exchange rates) in the manner of Hume, as a price–specie–flow mechanism, involving changes in the level of prices, one can also find writings describing it in the manner of Marshall, involving changes in the interest rate, or of Taussig, involving changes in the relative price of exportables and importables, or of Ohlin, involving changes in income. The theoretical jumble is made still more confusing by a

[1] An earlier and longer version of this essay (available on request) was presented to the Workshop in Economic History at the University of Chicago and to the Cliometrics Conference at the University of Wisconsin. We wish to thank the participants in these meetings for their comments. The friendly scepticism of Moses Abramovitz, C. K. Harley, Hugh Rockoff, Jeffrey Williamson, and our colleagues at the University of Chicago, among them Stanley Fischer, Robert J. Gordon, A. C. Harberger, Harry G. Johnson, Arthur Laffer, and H. Gregg Lewis, contributed to a sharpening of the argument.

number of factual anomalies uncovered lately.[2] Among other difficulties with the orthodox views, it has been found that the gold standard, even in its heyday, was a standard involving the major currencies as well as gold itself, and that few, if any, central banks followed the putative 'rules of the game'.

This essay reinterprets the gold standard by applying the monetary theory of the balance of payments to the experience of the two most important countries on it, America and Britain. Before explaining, testing, and using the theory in detail, it will be useful to indicate a few of the ways in which accepting it will change the interpretation of the gold standard of the late nineteenth century. The most direct implication is that central bankers did not have control over the variables over which they and their historians have believed they had control. The theory assumes that interest rates and prices are determined on world markets, and therefore that the central bank of a small country has little influence over them and the central bank of a large country has influence over them only by way of its influence over the world as a whole.

A case in point is the Bank of England. It is often asserted, as Keynes put it, that 'During the latter half of the nineteenth century the influence of London on credit conditions throughout the world was so predominant that the Bank of England could almost have claimed to be the conductor of the international orchestra. By modifying the terms on which she was prepared to lend, aided by her own readiness to vary the volume of her gold reserves and the unreadiness of other central banks to vary the volume of theirs, she could to a large extent determine the credit conditions prevailing elsewhere.'[3] When this musical metaphor is examined in the light of the monetary theory it loses much of its charm. If it is supposed, as in the monetary theory, that the world's economy was unified by arbitrage, and if it is supposed further that the level of prices in the world market was determined, other things equal, by the amount of money existing in the world, it follows that the Bank's potential

[2] Many of these have been published in the Princeton Studies in International Finance. For example, Arthur I. Bloomfield, *Short-term Capital Movements under the Pre-1914 Gold Standard* (1963); the work cited below; and Peter H. Lindert, *Key Currencies and Gold, 1900–1913* (1969). Bloomfield's *Monetary Policy under the International Gold Standard* (New York, Federal Reserve Bank of New York, 1959) is seminal to this literature.

[3] J. M. Keynes, *Treatise on Money* (London, Macmillan, 1930), vol. II, 306–7.

influence on prices (and perhaps through prices on interest rates) depended simply on its power to accumulate or disburse gold and other reserves available to support the world's supply of money. By raising the interest rate (the bank rate) at which it would lend to brokers of commercial bills, the Bank could induce the brokers or whoever else in the British capital market was caught short of funds to seek loans abroad, bringing gold into the country and eventually into the vaults of the Bank. If it merely issued bank-notes to pay for the gold the reserves available to support the supply of money would be unchanged, for Bank of England notes were used both at home and abroad as reserves. Only by decreasing the securities and increasing the gold it held—an automatic result when it discouraged brokers from selling more bills to the Bank and allowed the bills it already held to come to maturity—could the Bank exert a net effect on the world's reserves. In other words, a rise in the bank rate was effective only to the extent that it was accompanied by an open market operation, that is, by a shift in the assets of the Bank of England out of securities and into gold. The amounts of these two assets held by the Bank, then, provide extreme limits on the influence of the Bank on the world's money supply. Had the Bank in 1913 sold off all the securities held in its banking department it would have decreased world reserves by only 0.6 per cent; had it sold off all the gold in its issue department, it would have increased world reserves by only 0.5 per cent.[4] Apparently the Bank was no more than the second violinist, not to say the triangle player, in the world's orchestra. The result hinges on the assumption of the monetary theory that the world's economy was unified, much as each nation's economy is assumed to be in any theory of the gold standard. If the assumption is correct the historical inference is that the Bank of England had no more independent influence over the prices and interest rates it faced than, say, the First National Bank of Chicago has over the prices and interest rates it faces, and for the same reason.

A related inference from the monetary theory is that the United Kingdom, the United States, and other countries on the gold standard had little influence over their money supplies. Since money,

[4] World official reserves at the end of 1913 of $7,100 million (16 per cent of which was foreign exchange, a good part of it sterling) are estimated by Lindert, op. cit., 10–12.

like other commodities, could be imported and exported, the supply of money in a country could adjust to its demand and the demand would depend on the country's income and on prices and interest rates determined in the world market. The creation of money in a little country would have little influence on these determinants of demand and in consequence little influence over the amount actually supplied. How 'little' America and Britain were depends on how large they were relative to the world market, and in a world of full employment and well-functioning markets the relevant magnitude is simply the share of the nation's supply of money in the world's supply. One must depend on an assumption that the money owned by citizens of a country was in rough proportion to its income, for the historical study of the world's money supply is still in its infancy.[5] In 1913 America and Britain together earned about 40 per cent of the world's income, America alone 27 per cent.[6] A rise in the

---

[5] In 1964 Robert Triffin undertook to act as midwife, but as he concedes, the infant is still in poor health (see his *The Evolution of the International Monetary System: Historical Reappraisal and Future Perspectives*, Princeton Studies in International Finance, no. 12 [Princeton, Department of Economics, 1964] appendix I).

[6] Needless to say, these are crude estimates: to continue the metaphor above, the historical study of world income is barely into its adolescence. The estimate of $362 billion for 1913 world income in 1955 prices begins with Alfred Maizels's compilation of figures on gross *domestic* product at factor cost for twenty-one countries, given in his *Industrial Growth and World Trade* (Cambridge, Cambridge University Press, 1965), appendix E, p. 531. Czech and Hungarian income was estimated from Austrian income (post-1919 boundaries) on the basis of Colin Clark's ratios among the three (in *The Conditions of Economic Progress*, 2nd edn [London, Macmillan, 1951] p. 155). Russian income was estimated by extrapolating Simon Kuznets' estimate for 1958 back to 1913 on the basis of his figure for the decennial rate of growth, 1913–58 (in *Modern Economic Growth* [New Haven, Yale University Press, 1966] 65 and 360), yielding a figure of $207 *per capita* in 1958 prices, which appears to be a reasonable order of magnitude. The Russian *per capita* figure was then applied to the population of Bulgaria, Greece, Poland, Romania, and Spain, completing the coverage of Europe (boundary changes during the decade of war, 1910 to 1920, were especially important for these countries, except Spain; estimates of the relevant populations are given in R. R. Palmer, *Atlas of World History* [Chicago, Rand McNally, 1957] p. 193). Maizels gives estimates of national income for Canada, Australia, New Zealand, South Africa, Argentina, and Japan in 1913. Income per head in 1955 dollars was taken to be $50 in Africa except South Africa, $100 in Latin America except Argentina, $50 in India, and $60 in Asia except India and Japan, all on the basis of Maizels' estimates for 1929 and an assumption of little growth. Population figures for these groups of countries around 1910 were taken from D. V. Glass and E. Grebenik, 'World Population, 1800–1950', in H. J. Habakkuk and M. Postan, *Cambridge Economic History of*

American money supply of 10 per cent, then, would raise the world's money supply on the order of 2·7 per cent; the comparable British figure is half the American. Clearly, in the jargon of international economics, America and Britain were not literally 'small countries'. Yet 2·7 per cent is far from the 10 per cent implied by the usual model, that of a closed monetary system, and the British figure is far enough from it to make it unnecessary for most purposes in dealing with the British experience to look closely into the world-wide impact of British policy.

Finally, the monetary theory implies that it matters little whether or not central banks under the gold standard played conscientiously the 'rules of the game', that is, the rule that a deficit in the balance of payments should be accompanied by domestic policies to deflate the economy. The theory argues that neither gold flows nor domestic deflation have effects on prevailing prices, interest rates, and incomes. The inconsequentiality of the rules of the game may perhaps explain why they were ignored by most central bankers in the period of the gold standard, in deed if not in words, with no dire effects on the stability of the system.

2 EMPIRICAL ANOMALIES IN THE LITERATURE ON THE GOLD STANDARD

If the orthodox theories of the gold standard are incorrect, it should be possible to observe signs of strain in the literature when they are applied to the experience of the late nineteenth century. This is the case. Indeed, in the midst of their difficulties in applying the theories earlier observers have anticipated most of the elements of the alternative theory proposed here.

On the broadest level it has always been puzzling that the gold standard in its prime worked so smoothly. After all, the mechanism described by Hume, in which an initial divergence in price levels was to be corrected by flows of gold inducing a return to parity, might be expected to work fairly slowly, requiring alterations in the money supply and, more important, in expectations concerning the level and rate of change of prices which would have been difficult to

---

Europe, Vol. VI, part 1 (Cambridge, Cambridge University Press, 1965) p. 58, with adjustments for the countries included in Maizels' estimates, from his population figures (op. cit., p. 540).

achieve. The actual flows of gold in the late nineteenth century, furthermore, appear to be too small to play the large role assigned to them.[7] Of course, one should ask, 'Too small relative to what?' Gold was a substantial part of the monetary base, and one could rescue the argument by positing, as Milton Friedman and Anna Schwartz have done in their classic study of American monetary history, a close causal connection between the monetary base ('high-powered money' in their terminology) on the one hand and money and the price level on the other. This is an attractive argument for the United Kingdom, as might be expected for a country with nearly 100 per cent gold reserves against its currency and with no gold mines. For the United States, however, it is considerably less attractive. Only half of the variations in the American stock of high-powered money from 1880 to 1913 can be explained directly by gold flows, and other national monies with a less mechanical connection to external flows of gold than the British, such as the French and German, could be expected to have a similar record.[8] Most observers, perhaps anticipating these results, have emphasised the function of gold flows as a mere signal to central bankers to contract or expand their economies. If central bankers did play the rules of the game, reacting to a small outflow of gold by reducing the monetary base still further, a small flow of gold could, of course, have large effects, at any rate if one believes the orthodox theories. To repeat, however, central bankers often did not play the rules: the Bank of France and the National Bank of Belgium, for example, kept their discount rates low regardless of gold flows.[9] An alternative

[7] Scepticism on this point has long been widespread. Consider, for example, J. W. Angell, *The Theory of International Prices* (Cambridge, Harvard University Press, 1926), p. 400: 'It is perfectly obvious that neither the magnitudes nor the directions of the international flows of gold were adequate to explain those close and comparatively rapid adjustments of payments-disequilibria, and of price relationships, which were witnessed before the war.'

[8] The American and British record is examined later in Table 16.2 below. Bruce Brittain of the Research Department, First National City Bank of New York, is currently engaged in examining the French experience in the light of the monetary theory.

[9] P. Barrett Whale, 'The Working of the Pre-War Gold Standard', *Economica*, N.S., 4: 18–32, February 1937; reprinted in T. S. Ashton and R. S. Sayers, eds., *Papers in English Monetary History* (Oxford University Press, 1953), to which subsequent reference is made, p. 153. Compare R. H. I. Palgrave, ed., *Dictionary of Political Economy* (London, Macmillan, 1901), article on Banks, France: 'The Bank of France endeavours to keep an even rate of

indicator of the extent to which central bankers played the rules is the extent to which the relationship between inflows of gold and increases in domestic credit (that is, increases in the portion of the money supply determined by factors other than the inflow of gold) was positive. Once again, the indications are that in the late nineteenth century the monetary authorities, in this case American and British, cheated: the correlation between gold flows and annual changes in domestic credit was $-0 \cdot 07$ in the United States and $-0 \cdot 74$ in the United Kingdom.[10]

Yet the gold standard, it is said, worked quickly and well. The exchange rate between sterling and dollars, among many other rates, remained virtually unchanged from January 1879, when the United States put itself back on gold, to August 1914, when the war put the United Kingdom effectively off it. Nobody ran out of gold. And over this third of a century the restrictions on flows of gold, commodities, immigrants, and capital that were in the eighteenth century and have become again in the twentieth such popular instruments of government policy either were not used (for gold, immigrants, and capital) or were used for purposes other than correcting deficits in the balance of payments (for commodities). In view of its strange efficacy central bankers may be forgiven for looking back on the gold standard of the late nineteenth century with the pious awe usually reserved for religious mysteries.

The mystery of the smooth working of the gold standard fades if the central postulate of the monetary theory, the unity of commodity and capital markets, is an adequate characterisation of the world's economy in the late nineteenth century. If the postulate is accepted, it implies that the wrenching adjustments of prices, interest rates, and incomes that the orthodox theory in its many forms holds necessary for re-establishing equilibrium in the balance of payments were in fact not necessary. The world's economy determined the prices and interest rates prevailing in each nation's economy and it was the flow of gold itself that re-established equilibrium in the money market by satisfying the demand for money that prompted the flow in the first place.

---

discount. Thus for about five years, between 1883 and 1888, its rate of discount remained at 3%, while there were no fewer than 36 changes varying from 2% to 5% at the Bank of England during the same time.'

[10] The sources for this calculation are given in Table 16.2 below.

Whether the postulate of unified markets is acceptable or not is an empirical matter to be examined below. What is relevant here is that writers on the history of the gold standard, even as they have passed by its implications, have accepted it in part. The postulate is most easily defended (in fact, nearly universally accepted) for goods that enter international trade. Hume himself emphasised that the prices of such goods could differ only by transport or tariff costs, and Jacob Viner, in his survey in 1937 of the development of the theory of the gold standard, quoting Hume to this effect, was emphatic that all important subsequent writers agreed.[11] Frank Taussig certainly did. He wrote in 1906: 'Those commodities that enter into international trade have a common price the world over. The extraordinary cheapening of transportation during the last half-century, the perfected organisation of markets and exchanges, contribute to make this assumption a safe one for all the great staples.'[12] Taussig, like many others before and since, went on to emphasise that non-traded goods existed, arguing that the gold standard re-established equilibrium in a nation's balance of payments by altering the price of non-traded relative to traded goods. It is worth remarking here that it is not enough to reject the postulate of unified markets that non-traded goods merely exist: as will be argued in detail below, there must be low substitutability between traded and non-traded goods in both consumption and production. In any case, later writers have made larger concessions to the force of arbitrage in commodity markets. In his massive study of the interwar gold standard published in 1940, W. A. Brown, for example, asserted that 'the international influence of the London or Liverpool price of many important commodities was a factor tending to prevent substantial divergence in the movements of *general* prices of countries adhering to the international gold standard'.[13] And in 1964, Robert Triffin, in an important piece of iconoclasm on the gold standard, was still more explicit:

[11] Jacob Viner, *Studies in the Theory of International Trade* (1937; reprinted New York, A. M. Kelley, 1965), pp. 314–18.
[12] Frank Taussig, 'Wages and Prices in Relation to International Trade', *Quarterly Journal of Economics*, 20: 497–522, August 1906, p. 499.
[13] William A. Brown, *The International Gold Standard Reinterpreted, 1914–1934* (New York, National Bureau of Economic Research, 1940), p. 775, italics added.

'Under these conditions, national price and wage levels remained closely linked together internationally, even in the face of divergent rates of monetary and credit expansion, as import and export competition constituted a powerful brake on the emergence of any large disparity between internal and external price and cost levels. Inflationary pressures could not be contained within the domestic market, but spilled out *directly* to a considerable extent, into balance-of-payments deficits rather than into uncontrolled rises of internal prices, costs, and wage levels.'[14]

A flow of gold is by no means a necessary part of this process of arbitrage. In fact, the mere *threat* of arbitrage may be sufficient to bring a nation's prices and interest rates into line with the world's, without flows of anything. The usual justification for seizing on the flow of gold as the central mechanism of adjustment in prices and interest rates among countries on the gold standard is that gold is cheap to ship: slight variations in the exchange rate between two currencies caused by disturbances in the balance of payments and correctable by changes in prices and interest rates will cause gold to flow if the two currencies are both attached to gold at fixed rates. As Marshall put it in the early 1920s, when the exchange rate between French and Belgian money is favourable to France, 'really it is favourable to those who bring goods to France from Belgium and it is unfavourable to all who send goods in the opposite direction. *One* of the goods, which may be sent, is gold.'[15] Marshall was choosing his words carefully, as he usually did, for he realised that other commodities could and did serve this function as well. Gold, being cheap to transport, was always close to the price at which it would be exported (if foreign means of payments were especially desired by, say, Englishmen) or imported (if English means of payment were especially desired by foreigners); but a large number of commodities or securities would also at any one time be

[14] Robert Triffin, *The Evolution of the International Monetary System*, Princeton Studies in International Finance, no. 12 (Princeton, Department of Economics, 1964), p. 10 (his italics). P. B. Whale's article of 1937, cited above, is a startlingly complete anticipation of this and other elements in the monetary theory.

[15] Alfred Marshall, *Money, Credit and Commerce* (London, Macmillan, 1923), p. 145 (italics added). Compare p. 228, where he argues that a duty placed on some of a country's imports will increase duty-free imports and that 'Gold and silver will *generally find a place* among these' (italics added).

at their export or import price if arbitrage, allowing for transport costs and tariffs, were effective. At the end of the same chapter, in a section entitled, in Marshall's descriptive manner, 'So long as national currencies are effectively based on gold, the wholesale price of each commodity tends to equality everywhere', he agrees, speaking by analogy with the gold points of the 'leadpoint' and the 'Egyptian bond-point' without drawing explicitly the inference that gold does not in that case play the central role in forcing parallel movements of prices and interest rates in different nations assigned to it in the orthodox theories.[16] The firm belief of the classical and neo-classical economists in the unity of world markets under modern conditions did not fit well with their views on the gold standard.

The behaviour of prices in the late nineteenth century has suggested to some observers that the view that it was gold flows that were transmitting price changes from one country to another is indeed flawed. Over a short period, perhaps a year or so, the simple price–specie–flow mechanism predicts an inverse correlation in the price levels of two countries interacting with each other on the gold standard. A monetary expansion in Britain, the story goes, would raise the British price level, making British exports less competitive. This would produce a deficit in Britain's payments, equivalent to an outflow of gold. The outflow of gold would reduce the supply of money in Britain and raise it elsewhere, driving prices in Britain down and prices in, say, America up. Yet, as Triffin has noted and as we shall demonstrate presently, even over a period as brief as a single year, what is impressive is 'the overall parallelism—rather than divergence—of price movements, expressed in the same unit of measurement, between the various trading countries maintaining a minimum degree of freedom of trade and exchange in their inter-national transactions'.[17]

Over a longer period of time, of course, the parallelism is consistent with the theory of price–specie–flow. In fact, one is free to assume that the lags in its mechanism are shorter than a year, attributing the close correlations among national price levels within the same

16 Marshall, op. cit., pp. 152–4.
17 Triffin, op. cit., p. 4. He used export unit values. One could object that for many of the eleven countries he examined over the period 1870–1960 export unit values could be similar (namely, world wholesale prices for manufactures) without a corresponding similarity in the prices of domestic goods. Section 3 below overcomes this objection.

year to a speedy flow of gold and a speedy price change resulting from the flow rather than to direct and rapid arbitrage. One is not free, however, to assume that there were no lags at all; in the price–specie–flow theory inflows of gold must precede increases in prices by at least the number of months necessary for the money supply to adjust to the new gold and for the increased amount of money to have its inflationary effect. The American inflation following the resumption of specie payments in January 1879 is a good example. After examining the annual statistics on gold flows and price levels for the period, Friedman and Schwartz concluded that 'It would be hard to find a much neater example in history of the classical gold-standard mechanism in operation.'[18] Gold flowed in during 1879, 1880, and 1881 and American prices rose each year. Yet the monthly statistics on American gold flows and price changes tell a very different story. Changes in the Warren and Pearson whole-sale price index during 1879–81 run closely parallel month by month with gold flows, rising prices corresponding to net inflows of gold. There is no tendency for prices to lag behind a gold flow and some tendency for them to lead it, suggesting not only that the episode is an especially poor example of the price–specie–flow theory in operation, but also that it might well be a reasonably good one of the monetary theory.[19]

The strain of interpreting the gold standard of the late nineteenth century in terms of the available theories shows most clearly in the relations uncovered in empirical work between gold flows and income. After World War I economists put increasing emphasis on variations in income induced by deficits or surpluses in the balance of payments as the critical element in re-establishing equilibrium.

---

[18] Milton Friedman and Anna J. Schwartz, *A Monetary History of the United States, 1867–1960* (Princeton, Princeton University Press, 1963), p. 99.

[19] The price index is given in George F. Warren and Frank Pearson, *Prices* (New York, Wiley, 1933, pp. 11–13). The statistics on gold flows (silver flows do not disturb the pattern) are from the U.S. Commerce Department, Census Bureau, *Monthly Summary of Foreign Commerce*, for January 1879 through December 1882. In 1882 the association between gold and prices reported in the text breaks down: prices rose in the first half of 1882 yet gold flowed out. This change, however, is consistent with the monetary theory, for in early 1882, according to the dating of the National Bureau of Economic Research, the business expansion that had begun in early 1879 came to an end. As the next few paragraphs in the text will emphasise, a fall in income reduces the demand for money and, other things equal, releases money for export.

As the matter was put in one historical survey of the gold standard, 'What is important to note . . . is that the adjustment attributed to price changes and gold flows in the nineteenth century was swift and smooth, not because of the power of price changes to effect adjustment, but because income changes were always acting in the same direction to reinforce the price change.'[20] Yet the negative correlation between income and gold inflows over the course of the business cycle predicted by such assertions did not hold, at any rate not during the late nineteenth century in the United Kingdom and the United States, and this uncomfortable fact has long been known. To a first approximation (the succeeding approximations will be presented in Section 4 below), the monetary theory predicts the opposite correlation, which is the correlation in fact observed: as incomes rise in a country the demand for money of its citizens will rise as well, and the demand can be satisfied, if it is not satisfied by the domestic monetary authorities, by an importation of gold, that is to say, by a surplus—not a deficit—in the balance of payments.[21]

[20] W. M. Scammel, 'The Working of the Gold Standard', *Yorkshire Bulletin of Economic and Social Research*, 17: 32–45, May 1965.

[21] The incorrect predictions of the orthodox theory on this point arise in part from a confusion between the balance of *trade* and the balance of *payments*. The working model is that the balance of payments is equal to the balance of trade plus a random error term (the balance on capital account). See, for example, Viner, *Studies*, cited above, and J. E. Meade, *The Balance of Payments* (London, Oxford University Press, 1951) p. 80. George Macesich used just such a model to explain the behaviour of the American economy in an early period of the gold standard ('Sources of Monetary Disturbances in the United States, 1834–1845', *Journal of Economic History* 20: 407–34, September 1960). He asserted (p. 414) that 'The heavy and varied capital flows thus had implications for the required behavior of exchange rates, specie flows, money supply, relative prices and the balance of trade.' The exogeneity and randomness of the capital account in the American experience during the nineteenth century was asserted still more explicitly by J. Ernest Tanner and Vittorio Bonomo, in a criticism of the book by Williamson cited below (Tanner and Bonomo, 'Gold, Capital Flows and Long Swings in American Business Activity', *Journal of Political Economy* 76: 44–52, Jan./Feb. 1968). Williamson, however, in an attack on Macesich's argument (J. G. Williamson, 'International Trade and United States Economic Development, 1827–1843', *Journal of Economic History* 21: 372–83, September 1961) made the decisive point (p. 377): 'concomitant with real growth, there is a tendency to generate excess demands for real money balances, reflected, under a gold standard system, by an increasing inflow of gold. The solution is a general equilibrium one. . . . demands for money (gold), goods and securities must be solved simultaneously in a general equilibrium context'. This is a clear anticipation of the foundations of the monetary theory.

A. P. Andrew observed as early as 1907 that this was the case for the United States in the late nineteenth century, and W. E. Beach in 1935 and Alec Ford in 1962 that it was the case for the United Kingdom as well.[22] In a book on the American balance of payments during the nineteenth century published in 1964, and in a set of related articles, Jeffrey Williamson went further, arguing explicitly that a rise in income in the United States, when not accompanied by a rise in the internal supply of money (as it was, for example, during the period of intensive exploitation of the Californian gold discoveries), produced an excess demand for real money balances and, therefore, a surplus in the balance of payments.[23] And an article by P. B. Whale in 1937 is a still earlier anticipation of this point in the monetary theory. Citing Andrew and Beach, he wrote:

'[T]he suggestion is that in a regime of fixed exchange rates the monetary requirements of a particular country may be altered by changes in prices or trade activity independent of any prior change in the supply of money. . . . evidence of concomitant [domestic] movements of gold into and out of circulation [concomitant, that is, with evidence of inward and outward movements of gold

[22] A. P. Andrew, 'The Treasury and the Banks under Secretary Shaw', *Quarterly Journal of Economics*, 21: 519–68, August 1907. W. E. Beach, *British International Gold Movements and Banking Policy, 1881–1913* (Cambridge, Harvard University Press, 1935; see especially Charts xvii, xviii, and xix, and p. 77: 'In general gold imports became important during the latter stages of the periods of business expansion, and at the same time the volume of currency in the hands of the public was expanding. In recession the flows were reversed'). A. G. Ford, *The Gold Standard 1880–1914, Britain and Argentina* (Oxford, Clarendon Press, 1962); see especially p. 36: 'international gold movements, instead of being the determinants of the supply of money in Britain in this period, were probably determined by domestic monetary needs to some extent'.

[23] J. G. Williamson, *American Growth and the Balance of Payments* (Chapel Hill: University of North Carolina Press, 1964), especially Chapter V; Williamson, 'Real Growth, Monetary Disturbances and the Transfer Process: the United States, 1879–1900', *Southern Economic Journal*, 29: 167–80, January 1963; and his article cited in the footnote above. It is testimony to the staying power of the tradition that Williamson is attacking that most of his work concerns the influences on the commodity and capital account separately. As was noted above, this procedure is otiose if it is indeed the balance of payments that is at issue. Williamson himself makes this point, in the chapter of his book (V) that presents the germ of the monetary theory: 'in previous chapters we have exaggerated the independence of the movements in net capital flows and the trade balance. . . . the main point seems to be that gold flows cannot be treated simply as residuals' from the trade and capital accounts together (pp. 163–4).

internationally, which was correlated positively with the business cycle] confirms the view that it was the monetary requirements determined by a given price level which provided the underlying cause of the international gold movements.'[24]

At another point he refers approvingly to a contemporary German writer who treated 'gold flows somewhat similarly as a result of an excess of money balances at the equilibrium level of incomes', that is to say, in precisely the manner of the monetary theory.[25] Evidently, it would be grossly unfair to earlier work on the gold standard of the nineteenth century to claim that the elements drawn together in this essay are novel with us. They are all in the earlier work, however uncomfortably they fit with the successive versions of the orthodox theory.

3 DID INTERNATIONAL MARKETS WORK WELL?

If arbitrage—or, more precisely, a close correlation among national price levels brought about by the ordinary working of markets—can be shown to characterise the international economy of the late nineteenth century many of the conclusions of the monetary theory will follow directly and the rest will gain in plausibility. In the monetary theory, the international market short-circuits the effects of domestic policy on American prices, and the expansion of the domestic supply of money spills directly into a deficit in the balance of payments.

It is essential, therefore, to examine the evidence for this short-circuiting. As a criterion of its effectiveness, we use the size of the contemporaneous correlations among changes in the prices of the same commodities in different countries. We have chosen a sample of the voluminous information on prices for examination here.[26] The statistical power of the tests is not as high as one might wish, for even if two nations shared no markets they could none the less exhibit common movements in prices if they shared similar

[24] Whale, op. cit., pp. 158–9.
[25] Whale, op. cit., p. 156. He was referring to K. F. Maier, *Goldwanderungen: ein Beitrag zur Theorie des Geldes* [*Migration of Gold: A Contribution to the Theory of Money*], 1935.
[26] The sample is described in the appendix of the longer paper, available from the authors on request.

experiences of climate, technological change, income growth, or any of the other determinants of prices. In the long run, indeed, the other theories of the balance of payments imply some degree of correlation among national prices. For this reason we have resisted the temptation to improve the correlations by elaborate experimentation with lags and have concentrated on contemporaneous correlations, that is, on correlations among prices in the same year. If international markets worked as sluggishly as the other theories assume, there would be little reason to expect contemporaneous correlations to be high.

The simplest way to think about arbitrage is in terms of a single market. Given fixed exchange rates and the vigorous pursuit of profit through arbitrage, the correlation between price changes for a homogeneous commodity in two countries, say America and Britain, separated by transportation costs and tariffs, would be zero within the limits of the export and import points and unity at those points. A regression of British on American prices would test simultaneously for the lowness of the commodity's cost of transportation, including tariffs, relative to its price and the vigour with which prices were arbitraged. The good would not actually have to be traded between the two countries for the correlation to be high: the mere threat of arbitrage, or a common source of supply or demand, would be sufficient for goods with low transport costs. For goods actually flowing in trade in a uniform direction over the period 1880 to 1913, such as wheat from America to Britain, one would expect the correlation to be perfect and the slope of the corresponding regression to be unity, no matter what the cost of transport or the level of tariffs, so long as these did not change. They both did change, of course, as exemplified by the failure of the German price of wheat to fall as far as the British or American during the 1880s, as the Germans imposed protective duties on wheat imports.[27] None the less, the average correlation among the changes in American, British, and German prices of wheat is high, about $0 \cdot 78$. A regression of the annual change in British prices on the change in American prices (Britain had no tariffs on wheat, but the cost of ocean transport was falling sharply in the period) yields the following result (all the variables here and elsewhere in this section

[27] From 1880–2 to 1889–91 the ratio of the Berlin to the British price of wheat increased 30 per cent and remained at the higher ratio thereafter.

are measured as annual absolute changes; the figures below the coefficients in parentheses are standard errors; the levels of the variables have been converted to an index in which the average levels are equal to one):[28]

$$BWT = 0\cdot0076 + 0\cdot646\ AWT \qquad R^2 = 0\cdot58$$
$$(0\cdot0012)\quad(0\cdot102) \qquad\qquad D.-W. = 2\cdot02$$

One would expect errors in the independent variable to affect this and the later regressions, biasing the slope towards zero (there were changes in the source of the American wheat price, for example, and after 1890 it is a New York price alone). The value of $0\cdot646$ would be a lower bound on the true slope and the value implied by a regression of the American on the British price $(1\cdot124)$ an upper bound. The two bounds bracket reasonably closely the value to be expected theoretically, namely, $1\cdot0$, and the constants in both regressions (which represent the trend in the dependent price over time) are insignificantly different from zero. Not surprisingly, in short, wheat appears to have had a unified world market in the late nineteenth century; *a fortiori*, so did gold, silver, copper, diamonds, racehorses, and fine art.

This conclusion can be reinforced from another direction. For wheat the reinforcement is unnecessary, for few would doubt the international character of the wheat market, but it is useful to develop here the line of argument. Because of transport costs, information costs, and other impediments to a perfect correlation among changes in national prices, any use of the notion of a perfectly unified market must be an approximation, within one country as well as between two countries. For purposes of explaining the balance of payments economists have been willing to accept the approximation that within each country there is one price for each product, setting aside as a second-order matter the indisputable lack of perfect correlation between price changes in California and Massachusetts or between price changes in Cornwall and Midlothian. It is reasonable, therefore, to use the level of the contemporaneous correlation between the prices of a good in different regions within a country as a standard against which to judge the unity of the

---

[28] This and all subsequent regressions were subjected to the Cochrane–Orcutt iterative technique, removing in all cases understatement of the standard errors of the coefficients resulting from any auto-correlation of the residuals.

market for that good between different countries. If the correlations between the prices of wheat in America, Britain, and Germany were no lower than those between the prices of wheat in, say, different parts of Germany, there would be no grounds for distinguishing between the degree of unity in the national German market and in the international market for wheat. This was in fact the case. The average correlation between changes in the prices of wheat in pairs of German cities (Berlin, Breslau, Frankfurt, Konigsberg, Leipzig, Lindau, and Mannheim) from 1881 to 1912 was $0 \cdot 85$, quite close to the average correlation for the three countries over the same period of $0 \cdot 78$.

One could proceed in this fashion through all individual prices, but a shorter route to the same objective is to examine correlations across countries between pairs of aggregate price indexes. Contrary to the intuition embodied in this thought, however, there is no guarantee, at any rate none that we have been able to discover, that the correlation of the indexes is an unbiased estimator of the average degree of correlation among the individual prices or, for that matter, that it is biased in any particular direction.[29] In other words, barriers to trade could be high or low in each individual market without the aggregate correlation necessarily registering these truths. None the less, putting these doubts to one side, we will trust henceforth to the intuition.

The pioneers of the method of index numbers, Laspeyres, Jevons,

[29] We have received a good deal of enlightenment on this point from H. Gregg Lewis of the University of Chicago and Hugh Rockoff of Rutgers University. The issue is as follows. Suppose, to simplify at the outset, that one chooses the same set of weights $(w_1, w_2, \ldots, w_N)$ to form the two indexes of prices (I_A and I_B) in the two countries (A and B). What is the relationship between the weighted average of the individual correlations,

$$w_1(\text{corr } P_1^A, P_1^B) + w_2(\text{corr } P_2^A, P_2^B) + \ldots + w_N(\text{corr } P_N^A, P_N^B),$$

and the correlation of the weighted averages, corr (I_A, I_B) (where $I_A = w_1 P_1^A + w_2 P_2^A + \ldots + w_N P_N^A$)? For the case of two prices we have written out both correlations in terms of the relevant covariances (expressing the prices in standardised form, thereby eliminating variances of the individual prices and making the corresponding covariances identical to correlation coefficients), with no very illuminating results. If no restrictions are placed on the covariances we can generate counter-examples to the proposition that the two are equal. But we suspect that we are neglecting true restrictions among the covariances (one set implying values for another set) and, further, that the case of large N would give more useful results.

and others writing in the middle of the nineteenth century, produced indexes of wholesale prices—believable indexes of retail prices began to be produced only in the 1890s and implicit GNP deflators, of course, much later—and in consequence wholesale price indexes dominated empirical work on the balance of payments in the formative years of the theory. The contemporaneous correlation between annual changes in British and American wholesale prices 1880–1913 is $0 \cdot 66$, high enough in view of the differences in weights in the indexes and in view of the low correlation of annual changes implied by the lags operating in the orthodox theories to lend support to the postulate of a unified world market.

It is at this point, however, that supporters of the orthodox theory begin to quarrel with the argument, as did Taussig with those bold enough to suggest that world markets in more than merely traded goods were integrated in the late nineteenth century, or as did the many doubters of the theory of purchasing power parity with those who used wholesale prices to indicate the appropriate rates of exchange after World War I. The standard objection has been that wholesale price indexes are biased samples from the distribution of correlations because they consist largely of easily traded goods, ignoring non-traded services and under-representing non-traded goods. A large lower tail of the distribution, it is said, is left off, leading to a false impression that national price levels are closely correlated.

A point that must be made at once, however, is that traded goods, in the sense of goods actually traded and goods identical to those actually traded, were not a small proportion of national income. Historians and economists have usually thought of the openness of economies in terms of the ratio of actual exports or imports to national income, and have inferred that the United States, with a ratio of exports to national income of about $0 \cdot 07$ in the late nineteenth century, was relatively isolated from the influence of international prices and that the United Kingdom, with a ratio of $0 \cdot 28$, was relatively open to it. Yet in both countries consumption of tradeable goods, defined as all goods that figured in the import and export lists, was on the order of half of national income.[30] If

[30] For the calculation for the U.K. in 1913, see D. N. McCloskey, *Markets Abroad and British Economic Growth, 1820–1913*, ch. 1 (MS available on request) p. 18.

any substantial part of the national consumption or production of wheat, coal, or cloth entered international markets in which the country in question was a small supplier or demander, the prices of these items at home would be determined exogenously by prices abroad. Wholesale indexes, if they do indeed consist chiefly of traded goods, are not so unrepresentative of all of national income as might be supposed.

But what of the other, non-tradeable half of national income? Surely, as James Angell wrote in 1926, 'for non-traded articles there is of course no direct equalisation [of price] at all'.[31] The operative word in this assertion is 'direct', for without it the assertion is incorrect. The price of a good in one country is constrained not only by the direct limits of transport costs to and from world markets but by the indirect constraints arising from the good's substitutability for other goods in consumption or production. This was clear to Bertil Ohlin, who asked, 'To what extent are interregional discrepancies in home market prices kept within narrow limits not only through the potential trade in these goods that would come into existence if interregional price differences exceeded the costs of transfer, but also through the actual trade in *other* goods?'[32] It is

---

[31] J. W. Angell, *The Theory of International Prices* (Cambridge, Harvard University Press, 1926) p. 381. Later Angell conceded in part the point made below, although he believed (p. 392) that 'it cannot be adequate to explain the comparatively quick adjustments [of domestic to international prices] that actually take place'.

[32] Bertil Ohlin, *Interregional and International Trade*, rev. edn. (Cambridge: Harvard University Press, 1967) p. 104. His italics, question mark added; first edn., 1933. Contrast Jacob Viner's *Canada's Balance of International Indebtedness 1900–1913* (Cambridge, Harvard University Press, 1924) p. 210: 'The prices of services and what may be termed "domestic commodities", commodities which are too perishable or too bulky to enter regularly and substantially into foreign trade, are wholly or largely independent of *direct* relationship with foreign prices. World price-factors influence them only through their influence on the prices of international commodities, with which the prices of domestic commodities, as part of a common price-system, must retain a somewhat flexible relationship' (his italics). Although this is an improvement on the earlier formulation by Cairnes (quoted by Viner on the next page) that 'with regard to these, there is nothing to prevent the widest divergence in their gold prices', it falls short of a full analysis of what is meant by 'direct' and 'somewhat flexible', an analysis provided by Ohlin. In long-run equilibrium the distinction between direct and indirect is beside the point and the relationship of domestic to international prices is not even somewhat flexible. Viner's work incidentally, is one of a series of books on the balance of payments published in the Harvard Economic Studies in the 1920s and 1930s under the influence, direct or indirect,

not surprising to find Ohlin asking such a question, for the analytical issue is identical to the one that gave birth to that errant child of the Heckscher–Ohlin theory, factor–price equalisation. The price of the milk used as much as the wage of the labour used is affected by the international price of butter and cheese. A rise in the price of a traded good will cause substitutions in production and consumption that will raise the prices of non-traded goods. To put the point more extremely than is necessary for present purposes, in a general equilibrium of prices the fixing of any one price by trade determines all the rest. The adjustment to the real equilibrium of relative prices, which must be achieved eventually, can be slow or quick. The monetary theory assumes that it is quick.

If it were in fact slow, one would expect the contemporaneous correlation between prices for countries on the gold standard to fall sharply as more comprehensive price indexes, embodying non-traded goods, are compared. This is not the case. The correlation between the annual changes in the GNP deflators 1880–1912 for America and Britain is $0 \cdot 60$, to be compared with the correlation for wholesale prices alone of $0 \cdot 66$. The regressions of the annual changes of American on British deflators and British on American were (standard errors in parentheses; levels of the price variables converted to indexes with their averages as the base):

$AP = 0 \cdot 0002 + 0 \cdot 961 \ BP$ $R^2 = 0 \cdot 35, \ D.-W. = 1 \cdot 98$
$(0 \cdot 0050) \ (0 \cdot 266)$ Standard error of the regression as a percentage of the average level of the American price $= 2 \cdot 5\%$

$BP = 0 \cdot 0017 + 0 \cdot 33 \ AP$ $R^2 = 0 \cdot 34, \ D.-W. = 1 \cdot 92$
$(0 \cdot 0028) \ (0 \cdot 089)$ Standard error of the regression as a percentage of the average level of the British price $= 1 \cdot 4\%$

---

of Taussig: J. H. Williams, *Argentine International Trade under Inconvertible Paper Money: 1880–1900* (1920); Viner (1924); Angell (1926); Ohlin (1933); Harry D. White, *The French International Accounts, 1880–1913* (1933); and Beach (1935). Students of the history of economic thought will find it significant that of these Ohlin, who acknowledges explicitly his debt to the Stockholm School (among them Cassel, Heckscher, and Wicksell, all of whom emphasised the intimate relationship between domestic and international prices), broke most sharply with Taussig on this issue.

The correlations of the German GNP deflator with the American (0·40) and the British (0·45) are considerably lower, but this may be simply a reflection of the inevitable frailties of Walther Hoffman's pioneering effort to produce such a deflator, or, perhaps, a reflection of the sharp rises in German tariffs. More countries have retail price indexes (generally with weights from working-class budgets) than have reliable GNP deflators, and these statistics tell a story that is equally encouraging for the postulate of arbitrage. The correlation matrix of annual changes in retail prices for the United States, the United Kingdom, Germany, France, and Sweden is shown in Table 16.1. The British–American correlation (0·57) is again not markedly below the correlation of the wholesale indexes, despite the importance of such non-traded goods as housing in the retail indexes.[33]

Table 16.1 *Simple Correlations between Annual Changes in Retail Prices, 1880–1912*

	U.S.A.	U.K.	Germany	France	Sweden
U.S.A.	1·00	0·57	0·28	0·24	0·38
U.K.		1·00	0·53	0·42	0·57
Germany			1·00	0·45	0·62
France				1·00	0·32
Sweden					1·00

The correlation of American with British retail prices is probably not attributable to the trade in food offsetting a lower correlation between non-traded goods, for the simple correlation between American and British food prices in the years for which it is available (1894–1913) is lower, 0·49 compared with 0·57. Against this encouraging finding, however, must be put a less encouraging one. The average correlation between the changes in food prices in five regions of the United States (North Atlantic, South Atlantic, North

[33] The notion of an 'Atlantic Economy', incidentally, receives support from these figures: the average correlation of French with other retail price indexes, a crude measure of the appropriateness of including a country in the Atlantic economy, is 0·36, while the same statistic for the United States is 0·37; on this reading, it would be as appropriate to exclude France from the economy of Western Europe as to exclude the United States.

Central, South Central, and the West) for 1891–1913 is very high, 0·87, contrasted with the British–American correlation of only 0·49. If food prices were as well arbitraged between as inside countries the British–American correlation would have to be much higher than it is. Still, even with perfect unity in the market for each item of food, one would not expect countries with substantially different budget shares to exhibit close correlations in the aggregate indexes. The lower correlation between Britain and the United States than between regions of the United States, then, may well reflect international differences of tastes and income rather than lower arbitrage.

If one proceeds in this fashion further in the direction of less traded goods the results continue to be mixed, although on balance giving support to the postulate of unity in world markets. The most obvious non-traded good is labour. The correlation between changes in wages of British and American coal-miners 1891–1913 is 0·42 but the correlation between those of British and American farm labourers is only 0·26. Both are lower than the correlations between changes in the wages of the two employments in each country, 0·65 in Britain and 0·53 in America. The correlation between the annual changes in Paul Douglas' index of hourly earnings of union men in American building and the changes in A. L. Bowley's index of wages in British building from 1891 to 1901 is negligible, only 0·10. On the other hand, the average correlation among bricklayers' hourly wages in four cities (Boston, Cincinnati, Cleveland, and Philadelphia) selected from the mass of data for 1890–1903 in the 19th Annual Report of the U.S. Commissioner of Labor is only 0·14. The correlations for changes in wages between countries are low, in other words, but there is reason to believe that they are nearly as low within a geographically large country like the United States as well.

The same is true for an unambiguously non-traded commodity, common brick. That it is non-traded, that is a poor substitute for traded goods, and that it enters into the production of non-traded commodities is evident from the negligible correlation between changes in its average price in Britain and America. Yet from 1894, when the statistics first become available, to 1913, the average correlation between prices of common brick at the plant in seven scattered states of the United States (California, Georgia, Illinois,

New York, Ohio, Pennsylvania, and Texas) was only $0\cdot11$, and even between three states in the same region (New York, Ohio, and Pennsylvania) it was only $0\cdot13$. This degree of correlation may be taken as an indicator of the correlation between regions of the United States attributable to a common experience of general inflation, technological change, and growth of income rather than to the unity of markets. It is small. In any case, common brick is a good at the lower end of the distribution of goods by their correlations, and there is little evidence of greater integration of markets within than between countries.

All these tests can be much expanded and improved, and we plan to do so in later work.[34] What has been established here is that there is a reasonable case, if not at this stage an overwhelming one, for the postulate of integrated commodity markets between the British and American economies in the late nineteenth century, vindicating the monetary theory. There appears to be little reason to treat these

[34] We have passed by, for example, the issue of how unified were the markets for assets. The correlation between the annual changes in the British and American long-term interest rates 1882 to 1913 used in the model fitted below was $0\cdot36$, and could no doubt be improved by a closer attention to gathering homogeneous data than we have thought necessary for now. Michael Edelstein, for example, reports in his 'The Determinants of U.K. Investment Abroad: The U.S. Case' (unpublished MS, p. 10n) a correlation coefficient of $0\cdot77$ between annual changes in the levels of yields on first-class American railway bonds offered in London and in New York from 1871 to 1913, a period including years before the refixing of the sterling–dollar exchange rate in 1879. The discount rates of central banks may be taken as a rough measure of the short-term interest rate. The recent revisionist literature on the gold standard has emphasised the close correlations between these rates in different countries. Triffin (op. cit., p. 9), for example, quotes Bloomfield, approvingly, to the effect that 'the annual averages of the discount rates of twelve [European] central banks reveal the . . . interesting fact that, in their larger movements at least, the discount rates of virtually all the banks tended to rise and fall together' (A. I. Bloomfield, *Monetary Policy under the International Gold Standard*, as cited, p. 35). Bloomfield and Triffin attribute the parallelism to a corresponding parallelism in the business cycles of the nations involved, but the finding can also be interpreted as evidence of direct or indirect arbitrage in the international capital market. Lance E. Davis' finding that the internal American capital market was poorly arbitraged in this period, suggests that for America at least arbitrage was little better within than between countries (Davis' work is summarised in his contribution to R. W. Fogel and S. L. Engerman, *The Reinterpretation of American Economic History* [New York, Harper and Row, 1971], 'Capital Mobility and American Economic Growth', pp. 285–300). The widely-believed assertion that domestic British industry was starved of funds in favour of British investment in Argentine railways and Indian government bonds can be given a similar interpretation.

two countries on the gold standard differently in their monetary transactions from any two regions within each country.

4 MONEY, GOLD, AND THE BALANCE OF PAYMENTS

If international arbitrage of prices and interest rates was thorough-going and if the growth of real income in a country was exogenous to its supply of money, then the country's demand for money can be estimated by relatively straightforward econometric techniques. The balance of payments—identified here with flows of gold—predicted by the monetary theory can then be estimated as the difference between the growth in the country's total predicted demand for money and the growth in its actual domestic supply. If, further, the actual flow of gold closely approximates the flow implied by the estimated change in the demand for money minus the actual change in the domestic supply of money, the monetary theory of the gold standard warrants serious consideration. In fact, to a remarkable degree the monetary theory for the United States and the United Kingdom from 1880 to 1913 passes this final test.

In Table 16.2 are presented the average movements of the British and American variables to be explained (the movements, that is, in money supplies and in that part of the money supply attributable to international flows of gold) and the average movements of the variables with which the monetary theory would explain them (the movements in prices, interest rates, and incomes affecting the demand for money and the movements in that part of the money supply attributable to domestic forces). The average percentage change in the money supply was decomposed in a merely arithmetical way (described in the footnote to the table) into a part reflecting how the money supply would have behaved if all gold flows into or out of the country had been allowed to affect it (by way of the multiple effects of reserves on the money supply) and a residual reflecting all other influences. Arithmetically speaking, the causes of changes in British and American money supplies differed sharply; virtually all the change in Britain was attributable to international flows of gold while virtually all the change in America was attributable to other, domestic sources of new money. Economically speaking, the differences are less sharp. Although over these three decades on average the rate of change of the money supply was far larger in

Table 16.2 *Average Annual Rates of Change 1882–1913 of American and British Money Supplies (Domestic and International), Incomes, Prices, and Interest Rates. (percentages; standard errors in parentheses)*

	United Kingdom	United States
1 Money supply attributable to gold flows	2·22 (2·41)	−0·09 (2·89)
2 Money supply attributable to other influences	0·12 (2·51)	5·77 (4·56)
3 Total money supply	2·35 (1·78)	5·68 (5·21)
4 Real income	1·84 (2·33)	3·69 (5·35)
5 Implicit price deflator	0·24 (1·75)	0·23 (3·09)
6 Long-term interest rates (absolute change in basis points)	2·9 (2·0)	−2·3 (15·0)

Sources:
Line 1. The rate of change of the money supply attributable to gold flows was calculated as:

$$100\left[\log\left(M_{t-1} + \frac{M_t}{H_t}R_t\right) - \log M_{t-1}\right]$$

where M is the total money supply, H is 'high-powered money' (M_t/H_t, therefore, is the so-called 'money multiplier') and R is the annual net flow of gold. The figures on money supply and high-powered money for the United Kingdom were taken from D. K. Sheppard, 'Asset Preferences and the Money Supply in the United Kingdom 1880–1962', University of Birmingham Discussion Papers, Ser. A, No. 111 (November 1969), p. 16; and for the United States from Friedman and Schwartz, op. cit., pp. 704–7. The figures on gold flows for the United Kingdom were compiled from Beach, op. cit., p. 46f. These are for England alone, excluding Scotland and Ireland, but there is little doubt that they cover the great bulk of flows into and out of the United Kingdom. Gold flows for the United States are given in U.S. Bureau of the Census, *Historical Statistics of the United States* (Washington, D.C.: 1960), series U6.
Line 2 = Line 3 − Line 1.
Line 3. Source as in Line 1.
Line 4. U.S. real gross national product is from Simon Kuznets' worksheets, reported in R. E. Lipsey, *Price and Quantity Trends in the Foreign Trade of the United States* (New York: National Bureau of Economic Research, 1963), p. 423; for years before 1889, the Kuznets figure Lipsey used was inferred from Lipsey's ratio of GNP to farm income and his estimate of farm income (pp. 423–4). U.K. real gross *domestic* product is from C. H. Feinstein, *National Income, Expenditure and Output of the United Kingdom, 1855–1965* (Cambridge: Cambridge University Press, 1971), Appendix Table 6, col. 4.

Line 5. For the U.S. the figure is from Lipsey, as in Line 4. For the U.K. the figure is from Feinstein, Appendix Table 61, col. 7.

Line 6. The U.S. interest rate is Macauley's unadjusted index number of yields of American railway bonds (*Historical Statistics of the U.S.*, as cited, series X332). The U.K. rate is the yield of consolidated government bonds (consols) in Mitchell, *Abstract of British Historical Statistics* (Cambridge, Cambridge University Press, 1962), p. 455.

America than in Britain, the difference is adequately explained in terms of the monetary theory by the faster growth of American income, given the similarity (in accord with the findings of the last section) in the behaviour of prices and given the relative fall in American interest rates.

So much is apparent from the arithmetic of the British and American experience. To go further one needs a behavioural model explaining the annual balance of payments in terms of the monetary theory. The model is simplicity itself. It begins with a demand function for money, the only behavioural function in the model, asserting that the annual rate of change in the demand for money balances depends on the rates of change of the price level and of real income and on the absolute change in interest rates (asterisks signify rates of change):

$$M_d^* = P^* + f(y^*, \Delta i).$$

And it ends with a domestic money supply function (literally, an identity using the observed money multiplier, as explained in the footnote to Table 16.2) and the statement that the money not supplied domestically was supplied through the balance of payments. It is evident that the monetary theory is simply a comparative statics theory of money's supply and demand, in which the balance of payments satisfies demands for money not satisfied by domestic sources.

By virtue of the unity of world markets and the assumed exogeneity of the growth of real income to the supply of money (which is itself a consequence of market unity and the availability of an elastic supply of money abroad), there is no simultaneous equation bias in estimating the demand for money by ordinary least squares. It is convenient to estimate the demand in real terms. The result for the United States 1884–1913 of regressing the rate of change of real balances on the rate of change in real income and the absolute change in the interest rate is (t-statistics in parentheses):

$$(M/P)^* = 0 \cdot 030 + 0 \cdot 61 \quad y^* - 0 \cdot 10 \; \Delta i \qquad R^2 = 0 \cdot 59$$
$$(4 \cdot 5) \qquad (4 \cdot 9) \qquad (2 \cdot 6) \qquad\qquad D.-W. = 2 \cdot 02$$

And for the United Kingdom:[35]

$$(M/P)^* = 0 \cdot 014 + 0 \cdot 32 \; y^* - 0 \cdot 005 \; i \qquad R^2 = 0 \cdot 27$$
$$(2 \cdot 4) \qquad (2 \cdot 2) \qquad (-1 \cdot 2) \qquad D.-W. = 1 \cdot 89$$

These appear to be reasonable demand equations, although the income elasticity in the equation for the United Kingdom is low, perhaps an artefact of errors in the series for income, which, given the low variability of British income, would reduce the fitted regression coefficient. Another explanation might be the substantial ownership of British money by foreigners, which would reduce the relevance of movements in British income to the 'British' money supply. Still, both demand equations accord reasonably well with other work on the demand for money.

The acid test of the model, of course, is its performance in predicting the balance of payments as a residual from the predicted demand for money and the actual domestically determined supply. Its performance is startlingly good. The good fit of the American demand equation offsets the relative unimportance of gold flows to the American supply, while the relative importance of gold flows to the British supply offsets the poor fit of the British demand equation. Figures 16.1 and 16.2 exhibit the results, comparing the actual effect of gold flows on the American and British money supplies with the predicted effect. The actual effect is calculated annually by applying the observed ratio of money to reserves (including gold) to the actual flow of gold, the predicted effect by subtracting the domestic sources of money from the demand for money predicted by the regressions. In other words, the predicted effect is the excess demand for money predicted by the regressions in conjunction with the actual changes

---

[35] The evidence is described in the footnote to Table 16.2. The interest rate on three-month bankers' bills (Mitchell, *Abstract of British Historical Statistics* (Cambridge University Press, 1962), p. 460) performed better than the consol rate, and was used here.

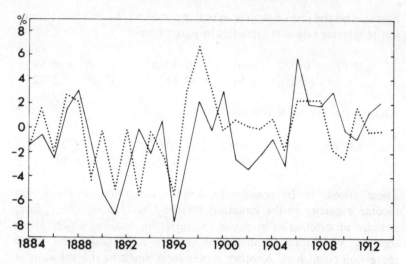

Graph 1. Predicted (——) and Actual (- - -) Effects of Gold
Flows on the U.S. Money Stock, Annual Rates of Change,
1884–1913.

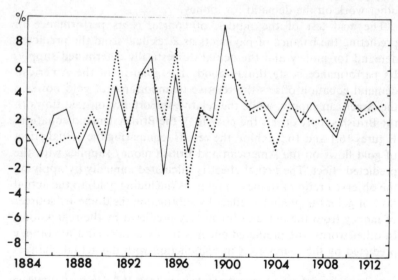

Graph 2. Predicted (——) and Actual (- - -) Effects of Gold
Flows on the U.K. Money Stock, Annual Rates of Change,
1884–1913.

in the money supply due to domestic sources. One could just as well make the comparison of predicted with actual flows of gold, translating the predicted excess demand for money in each country into an equivalent demand for gold imports. The result would be the same, namely, a close correspondence between the predictions of the theory and the observed behaviour of the British and American stock of money and balance of payments.

No doubt the tests could be refined and more evidence could be examined. We believe, however, that we have established at least a prima facie case for viewing the world of the nineteenth-century gold standard as a world of unified markets, in which flows of gold represented the routine satisfaction of demands for money. We do not claim to have rejected decisively the view of the gold standard that depends on poor arbitrage between national markets or the view that predicts an inverse rather than a positive correlation between gold inflows and income or any of the other variants of the orthodox theories. Indeed, it is perfectly possible that these variants are partly true, perhaps true in the very short run, or under special circumstances, such as mass unemployment—the monetary theory is, in the sense described earlier, an equilibrium theory, which could be consistent with any number of theories about how the British and American economies behaved out of equilibrium. But a balance-of-payments surplus or deficit is not in itself, as has often been assumed, evidence that the economy in question is in fact out of equilibrium. The monetary theory's central message is that a growing, open economy, buffeted by external variations in prices and interest rates, will have a varying demand for money, which would only fortuitously be supplied exactly from domestic sources. A country's balance of payments, in other words, could be positive or negative over the course of a year even if all asset and commodity markets in the country were continuously in equilibrium, for the flow of money into the country during the year could exactly meet the year's change in the demand for money. The source of the simplicity of the monetary theory of the gold standard is clear: the monetary theory is an equilibrium model, whereas the alternative theories are to a greater or lesser extent dynamic, disequilibrium models. We believe (as must be evident by now) that the simpler model yields a persuasive interpretation of how the gold standard worked, 1880–1913.

AUTHOR INDEX